PRAISE FOR *IMAGINABLE*

"Reading this book is like sitting down with a creative, optimistic friend—and getting up as a new version of yourself. Jane McGonigal has long been a visionary. Now she teaches the rest of us how to be one too." **—Daniel H. Pink,**
New York Times bestselling author of
When and *To Sell Is Human*

"Jane McGonigal is unusually adept at anticipating events that most of us can't even fathom. In this eye-opening, actionable book, she teaches you how to widen your peripheral vision, extend your imagination further into the future, and conceive of the inconceivable." **—Adam Grant,**
#1 *New York Times* bestselling author of
Think Again and host of the TED podcast *WorkLife*

"Futurist and game designer McGonigal delivers an illuminating look at how imagining the future can help to change one's own life while making a difference in the world. Expertly blending practical advice and big-picture thinking, this is a stimulating guide to preparing for the future. Readers will be inspired to put their imaginations to use." **—Publishers Weekly**

"*Imaginable* is a delightful and actionable antidote to apocalypse: an invitation to play with the future as if it were limited by nothing but our own imaginative capacity. An inspiring read." **—Douglas Rushkoff,**
author of *Present Shock* and *Team Human*

"A fascinating book about how the future does not have to be an undiscovered country. McGonigal, a future forecaster, game designer, and bestselling author of *Reality Is Broken* and *SuperBetter*, firmly believes that it is possible to consider the possibilities of the future in a systematic, disciplined way, and her narrative draws on a large body of personal experience, research studies, and knowledge gleaned from her work as a game designer. . . . A wealth of interesting ideas combined with practical guidance for new thinking." **—Kirkus Reviews**

"*Imaginable* is more than a book, it's a mindset upgrade. It teaches you to think more creatively and optimistically about what's next. You'll be excited about the future rather than fearful of it. Your brain will be on fire with new possibilities. And you'll never call anything 'unimaginable' or 'unthinkable' again." **—Peter H. Diamandis, MD,**
New York Times bestselling author of
The Future Is Faster Than You Think

"With *Imaginable*, Jane McGonigal has pulled off a rare and essential feat: she's written a book filled with inspiring ideas about how the future might play out that also provides immediate, practical tools to help you think more creatively about how you can change that future yourself." —**Steven Johnson**,
New York Times bestselling author of
Where Good Ideas Come From and *Farsighted*

"*Imaginable* is one of those rare and thrilling books that actually changes you. It translates scientific insights into psychological breakthroughs, giving you a new set of tools to feel more hopeful, more creative, more awake to your dreams for the future. It empowers you with what McGonigal calls a sense of 'urgent optimism.' It will help you transcend the present moment to realize your full potential and make a future that's better for all." —**Scott Barry Kaufman**,
psychologist and author of *Transcend:
The New Science of Self-Actualization* and *Wired to Create*

"A unique and insightful look at how games and simulations can not only teach us about the past but give us a window into our future. Jane McGonigal's work provides us with a whole new set of tools to make important decisions better, faster, and more transparently." —**Sid Meier**,
creator of *Civilization*

"In challenging times, it can be tempting to put our heads in the sand. In *Imaginable*, futurist Jane McGonigal offers us her outstretched hand. McGonigal plows years of research and simulation into an actionable guide that proves that we are vastly more capable of building desirable solutions than we realize. Fueled by her conversational tone of 'urgent optimism,' McGonigal's questions and challenges are a galvanizing, must-read road map to a sustainable, desired future for all who can imagine." —**Julie Lythcott-Haims**,
New York Times bestselling author of *How to Raise an Adult*

"In *Imaginable*, Jane McGonigal teaches us to bring soul-stirring imagination to our daily lives. As she persuasively demonstrates, imagination training is more than just a skill set: it's a creativity boost, a mindset shift, and an emotional uplift all rolled up in one. The life-changing techniques you'll learn in this science-packed book will help you choose your future and feel more in control of what happens next." —**Nir Eyal**,
author of *Hooked* and *Indistractable*

"Everyone should be imagining the future as a basic survival skill. . . . [T]he only book I know of that will teach you the proven techniques that futurists use to forecast the future. . . . Do yourself a favor: Read this book." —**Kevin Kelly**,
New York Times bestselling author of
The Inevitable and senior maverick for *Wired*

IMAGINABLE

How to Create a Hopeful Future—
in Your Own Life,
Your Community, the World

Jane McGonigal

*Spiegel
and Grau*

Spiegel & Grau, New York
www.spiegelandgrau.com

Jacket design by Strick&Williams
Interior design by Susan Turner

Library of Congress Cataloging-in-Publication Data Available Upon Request

ISBN 978-1-954118-33-1 (TP)
ISBN 978-1-954118-10-2 (eBook)

Printed in the United States of America

First Paperback Edition
10 9 8 7 6 5 4 3 2 1

For Kelly McGonigal, who lives six minutes in the future

IMAGINABLE

CONTENTS

GAMES, SCENARIOS, AND SIMULATIONS

~~~

Looking for a future to play with?

~~~~~~~~

Welcome to the Age of Unimaginable Events and Unthinkable Change

THE STATE OF THE PLANET IS ONE OF COLLECTIVE SHOCK.

In the years 2020 and 2021 alone, there were over 2.5 million English-language news stories with the word "unimaginable" in them.

There were over three million news stories with the word "unthinkable."[1]

We've all lived through these stories together.

Stories about the previously unimaginable impacts of a pandemic: health care systems collapsing, hundreds of millions of "nonessential" jobs vanishing overnight, the average life expectancy dropping by years on the global scale.

Stories about the previously unthinkable changes we made to survive the pandemic: border lockdowns, stay-at-home orders, school closures, mask mandates, remote work, remote everything.

Stories about unprecedented weather events and their toll on our towns and bodies: record-breaking heat, flooding, extreme storms, relentless wildfires, toxic air pollution.

Stories about strange things we'd never seen before: An apartment building eroded by climate change collapsing in the middle of the night. A mob storming the US Capitol in an attempt to overturn the results of a presidential election. A shockingly effective misinformation campaign that convinced 20 percent of Americans the government was injecting microchips into vaccines, leading them to reject a free, lifesaving intervention.

In 2022, Russia's invasion of Ukraine gave us yet another global shock. Now, we told stories about the inconceivable scale of a new refugee crisis, including the fastest large-scale displacement of children since World War II. We faced threats that geopolitical experts would have described only weeks earlier as unthinkable, as Russia asserted its right to use nuclear weapons. We lived through the consequences of what economists described as the biggest market shock in decades, as governments enacted historically extreme economic sanctions against Russia.

The ubiquity of the words "unthinkable" and "unimaginable" in our stories tells us something important about our global condition. We feel blindsided by reality. We find ourselves struggling to make sense of events that shattered our assumptions and challenged our beliefs.

And it's not just that we didn't see this coming. There is grief baked into these words. We use the word "unimaginable" as another way of saying "heartbreaking"—as in unimaginable pain, or unimaginable loss, that defies even our best efforts at empathy. We use the word "unthinkable" to mean "unjust," "cruel," or "unacceptable"—as in an unthinkable failure to act, an unthinkable lack of concern for others. These two words that we use so frequently these days speak not just to shock but to trauma.

How do we make plans for the future in an age of seemingly endless shocks? How can we feel at peace or secure today, when we are constantly bracing ourselves for the next "unimaginable" event or "unthinkable" change? How do we feel hope for our future, when it seems impossible to predict what the world will be like next week, let alone next year?

But perhaps we need to start with more fundamental questions. Were the most shocking events of the recent past really unimaginable before they happened? Should their consequences really have been unthinkable to us before we lived through them?

Let me tell you a story.

IN EARLY JANUARY 2020, WHEN the pandemic was first appearing on people's radar, I started getting a lot of interesting emails and text messages that all said something like this: "Jane, didn't you run a simulation of a respiratory pandemic? What do you make of what's going on right now? What should we be doing?" These messages were coming not just from my friends and family but from top executives at the biggest Silicon Valley tech companies, from government agencies, from international foundations. And they were right: yes, I had run a pandemic simulation.

I'm a game designer, and I specialize in creating simulations that help people imagine the biggest global challenges we might face in the future. In 2008, I was the lead designer for a six-week future-forecasting simulation called Superstruct. The simulation was run by the Ten-Year Forecast group at the Institute for the Future in Palo Alto, California. Our goal was to map out the full range of economic, political, social, and emotional ripple effects of global threats like pandemics. We set the game eleven years in the future, in the fall of 2019. During this game, nearly ten thousand people worldwide simulated living through five different threats, including a global outbreak of a fictional virus called ReDS, short for respiratory distress syndrome.

There were no mathematical computations involved in our simulation. Instead, we simply asked people to predict how they personally would feel and what they would do in their own lives during this kind of rapidly spreading outbreak. How would they change their daily habits? What social interactions would they avoid? Would they—could they—work from home? Would they choose to self-quarantine—and if so, when, why, and for how long? During a government-mandated quarantine, what problems might they experience? What kinds of support and resources would they need? How would they try to help others? Our simulation was low on algorithms but high on social and emotional intelligence. Our participants told thousands of stories about what they, personally, would do during a respiratory pandemic, which we collected and analyzed online.

When the novel coronavirus first came to global attention in early 2020, I thought the most important findings to share with the world from our massive multiplayer simulation would be the predictions that people had made. For example, one of my main research questions had been: Under what circumstances would people resist voluntary quarantine and social distancing? Our data showed the most likely superspreading risks would be religious services, followed by weddings and funerals. People were likely to continue participating in these activities no matter what the perceived risks. And we saw clearly that if they were young and single, people still wanted to go out to nightclubs and parties, even if these gatherings were illegal.

Based on our findings, early in February 2020, I held an "Ask a Futurist" public webinar with my colleague at the Institute for the Future, Vanessa Mason. We gave our best urgent advice for the newly unfolding pandemic that barely had a name yet. For example: "Data suggests that if you lead a religious congregation or community of any kind, you need to plan now to create a space for virtual religious worship." And: "If you're planning a wedding, professional conference or networking event, or party, you should proactively cancel it now, because people will risk their health to attend these affairs even during a pandemic." The headlines that followed in the months after clearly proved these insights from our simulation to be both useful and actionable. During the real pandemic, people did what our players predicted they would do during our simulation: they held large weddings despite rules against it, went to nightclubs despite the urgent messaging to stay at home, participated in in-person religious services despite testing positive for COVID-19, attended funerals despite having symptoms and being told to self-isolate. And these scenarios all turned into common, real-world superspreading events.[2]

In the February 2020 webinar and in my advice to people who contacted me, I also shared our data on how uncomfortable many people felt about wearing masks. During the Superstruct game, we asked people to actually go out into their everyday lives and practice wearing masks in different social environments. We wanted people to get used to this habit, so it might be easier to adopt again in a real pandemic. But based on what players self-reported, we knew how high the social barriers might be to overcome mask resistance and to make the behavior feel "normal." Of course, we saw this problem play out on a much larger scale during the real COVID-19 pandemic later, especially in the United States.

And we talked about how big a problem we anticipated it would be for working moms if schools closed during the pandemic, because moms in our game talked about the impossibility of juggling their jobs with the need to homeschool, if it came to that. Now, we see that, as a result of COVID-19, millions of moms had to voluntarily leave the workforce to care for children when schools closed down.[3]

One more bit of research we reported in the webinar was how hard it would be for people to follow public health guidelines, and to stay home or self-isolate, if they weren't given significant economic support. We talked about the need to proactively provide cash payments, and today, when we consider the global COVID-19 response, we see clearly that in places where governments provided recurring cash payments or paycheck protection, people did follow the guidelines more strictly, and the spread of the virus was better contained.[4]

I'm proud of how accurate our forecasts turned out to be. But now, looking back at how slow society was to react to the growing threat and how stuck so many of our leaders were in old ways of thinking and doing, I no longer believe that the most important work of a large-scale social simulation like Superstruct is to accurately predict what people will do. Instead, the most important work of a future simulation is to prepare our minds and stretch our collective imagination, so we are more flexible, adaptable, agile, and resilient when the "unthinkable" happens.

And based on Superstruct, we have evidence that future simulations can have this positive effect. In January 2020, I started receiving emails and Facebook messages from people who had participated in the pandemic simulation. They wrote things like, "I'm not freaking out, I already worked through the panic and anxiety when we imagined it ten years ago." They said, "Mask up!" and "Time to start social distancing!" and "I'm starting to prepare for this now," weeks before it hit mainstream consciousness outside of China that we needed to start making serious changes to our habits and plans. Simulation participants kept telling me, in their own ways, that pre-feeling the future helped them pre-process the anxiety, the overwhelming uncertainty, and the sense of helplessness, so they could move more rapidly to adapt and act resiliently when the future actually arrived.

The simulation participants' early 2020 messages remind me now of what we would later see play out during the COVID-19 pandemic in Hong Kong, Taiwan, and Singapore. Experts have noted that in places that suffered major outbreaks of the first severe acute respiratory syndrome (SARS) in 2003, governments and businesses spent less time debating whether to take strong measures to prevent the spread of the novel virus. They acted faster, because they knew firsthand how bad things could get. And citizens in countries that had lived through the deadly 2003 SARS outbreak adopted public health measures like masking and social distancing faster, and more willingly, than their Western counterparts.[5] All of this led to significantly more containment of the virus. A similar phenomenon occurred in West Africa, where local experience with the 2014 Ebola outbreak led countries to adopt much stronger measures than seen in Europe or the Americas, and faster. There was also higher compliance with mask wearing. This fast response due to previous pandemic experience has been cited as the primary reason that most African countries fared much better than their Western counterparts during the first two waves of the pandemic, despite having far fewer resources.[6]

What I see in my simulation participants' reactions to COVID-19 is something almost like the fortitude of having lived through a real pandemic. Their minds were prepared to act faster and adapt faster. Less shock, more resilience. And it wasn't just because more than a decade ago they'd imagined themselves living through a pandemic. The simulation had kick-started a habit, for many, of paying closer attention to real-world pandemic news. As one participant wrote me, "I've been following what's happening in Wuhan closely, you could say I've had my radar up for pandemic news since Superstruct. It just always stuck in my mind to keep paying attention." I've observed this fascinating and common "side effect" of participating in a future simulation countless times. A deep immersion into a possible future creates lasting mental habits, especially when it comes to watching the real world for evidence that the simulated possibility is becoming more likely.

Now, it's one thing to get lucky and run a single accurate simulation. But if I'm going to convince you to read the rest of this book and make futures thinking a regular part of your life, I'd better tell you another story.

In 2010, I led another large-scale future simulation game, this time for the World Bank. It was called EVOKE, and it was set a decade in the future, in the year 2020. This time, nearly twenty thousand players showed up to predict what actions they could take to help others during a complex outbreak of possible future global crises, including a pandemic and extreme weather from climate change happening at the same time. EVOKE ran for ten weeks, and each week a new compounding crisis was added to the mix.

Players were immersed in a future world that was dealing with a global respiratory pandemic called the Pearl River flu that had started in China . . . *and* an outbreak of social media–driven misinformation and conspiracy theories about the pandemic . . . *and* historic wildfires up and down the West Coast of the United States due to climate change . . . *and* a shocking collapse of the power grid due to aging in-frastructure and extreme weather. The misinformation and conspiracy theories, spread in our story by a group we called "Citizen X," com-plicated the efforts of individuals to understand what was really hap-pening and what they needed to do to stay safe. Meanwhile, the wildfires and power outages forced many to leave their homes at a time when staying safe from the pandemic meant staying at home.

The storylines that we wrote a decade in advance turned out to be pretty much exactly what we saw in the headlines of the real 2020 and early 2021. First the global spread of COVID-19 in early 2020, followed by the historic West Coast wildfires of the summer of 2020 that burned for months and required millions of people to evacuate their homes and relocate. Then, the rise of the QAnon conspiracy move-ment on social media, which created an "infodemic" of misinforma-tion that COVID-19 was a hoax and vaccines would implant a microchip in your arm. Later, the "unthinkable" power grid failure in Texas that left three million people without electricity or water, blamed on "unimaginable" extreme cold weather that the aging infrastructure was unable to withstand. You would be hard-pressed to find a predic-tion in the EVOKE simulation that didn't turn out correctly, most of them in the very same year we forecast they might happen.

Which explains why, in the middle of the real year of 2020, I got a call from Robert Hawkins, a senior World Bank executive, who led the educational outreach and technology strategy on the EVOKE project. He said, "Look at how many specific forecasts from EVOKE are happening now! It's uncanny. How did you get so much right?"

And that's a question I'm going to answer by way of this book.

In **Part I: Unstick Your Mind**, I'm going to teach you some mental habits that professional futurists practice, and some social games that we play, to keep our minds open to "unthinkable" and "unimaginable" possibilities. You can use these habits and games to train *your* brain to think like a futurist.

When you think like a futurist, you think more creatively. You're not stuck in old patterns or limited by what has been true in the past. And more than getting you ready for the future, these futures-thinking habits and games can make you feel better today. Research studies have shown them to increase hope and motivation for the future and reduce symptoms of depression and anxiety. So if like many millions of others, you have some emotional healing to do after the pandemic and other shocks of the recent past, I believe these techniques will help. Think of them as a kind of post-traumatic growth for our post-pandemic planet.

Because I want you to have confidence in these techniques, I'll share with you the science behind how futures thinking strengthens key pathways in the brain to build realistic hope, creativity, and a more resilient response to stress. And while I can't offer you an fMRI scan to show you how *your* brain is activated by futures thinking, I can teach you the same scoring methods that researchers use in scientific studies to document the benefits of futures thinking. You'll be able to measure your own progress so that you can be confident your personal growth is real.

In **Part II: Think the Unthinkable**, I'm going to show you how to use the same techniques that we used at the Institute for the Future to develop our highly accurate Superstruct and EVOKE forecasts—so you can start to see what's coming too. These techniques will help you spot any kind of change faster—so you can act faster, adapt faster, and not be blindsided by surprising events.

Finally, in **Part III: Imagine the Unimaginable**, we will play a brand-new game together so you can get firsthand experience of the power of a social simulation. I will lead you through three different future scenarios set in the year 2033. You'll be immersed in a world in which things we take for granted today change virtually overnight, and new social movements, technologies, and policies transform every aspect of our lives in surprising and profound ways. You will be able to participate in the simulations just by reading this book and keeping a journal for ten days about your mental time travel to the year 2033. How would you, personally, react to these scenarios? What would you think, feel, and do? How would you help? If you wish to share some of your future stories with others, and see what others are imagining, there will be a place online for you to do that as well.

These simulations will truly put to the test all of the skills and habits you've learned in the first two parts of *Imaginable*. I assure you the scenarios you encounter will sound as "far out" and inconceivable to you today as the Superstruct and EVOKE scenarios seemed to our simulation participants in 2008 and 2010. But by the time you reach this part of the book, you *will* be ready to imagine them.

Then it's your turn to make the future. I'll explain my design process and give you all the information you need to create and run your own social simulation, about any future topic you want.

Along the way, I will be giving you many forecasts for the next decade of unthinkable change, covering everything from the future of learning and the future of work to the future of food and the future of money; from the future of social media and the future of health care to the future of climate action and government—all so you have a better idea of the risks, opportunities, and dilemmas ahead.

These ten-year forecasts will help you become more resilient to future shocks. They will help you lean into the fact that there is no "going back to normal." They will also give you some ideas about how you might take advantage of this historic period of disruption and reinvention to change your own life, your community, or the world for the better. The next decade is likely to be the most significant opportunity most of us have in our lifetimes to really transform the way society works—and we all have a part to play in creating that positive long-term change.

THERE ARE MANY OTHER BOOKS about how to think about the future. What makes this book different? Well, I'm a professional futurist and I'm a game designer. It's not a common combination of career paths—as far as I know, I'm the only one in the world. But it's a career combination that makes a lot of sense. As both a game designer and a futurist, I see my job as transporting people to imaginary worlds, to worlds that don't exist—either because they're virtual or because they're future worlds that haven't happened yet and may never happen. My goal is to make sure that when people *leave* these imagined worlds, they feel more creative, more optimistic, and more confident in their own ability to transform those worlds, to take actions and make decisions that change the shape of that reality.

It's easy to feel powerful and creative when we play games. Every move we make, every action we take—whether in a card game, sport, board game, or video game—clearly impacts the state of the game. But when we think about the future, it's harder for most people to feel the same kind of agency. We aren't as confident that we personally can take actions or make decisions that truly help determine what happens next, especially when it comes to the bigger futures that we all share: society's future, the planet's future.

So I've tried to bring these two approaches to creating imaginary worlds—designing games and writing future forecasts—closer together. I've spent the past fifteen years as the director of game research and development at the Institute for the Future. The Institute for the Future is the world's oldest future-forecasting organization, founded in 1968, and it pioneered many of the methods that are standard practice for professional futurists today. At the institute, my job is to invent games that teach players futures-thinking habits and skills, the same kind used by researchers at the institute. I specialize in creating large-scale social simulations of the future with thousands of participants, the kind you've already read about. These simulations do more than stretch individuals' imaginations. They build actionable collective intelligence, by revealing otherwise hard-to-predict phenomena and ripple effects. As we say at the institute, "It's better to be surprised by a simulation than blindsided by reality." In fact, one way we measure the success of a simulation is by how surprising the results of the game are to experts in the field.

Over the past fifteen years at the institute, I've developed custom future forecasts, trainings, and simulations for plenty of experts and leaders—including clients at Google, IBM, Cisco, Intel, Disney, GSK, the Rockefeller Foundation, the US Department of Defense, the National Academy of Sciences, and the World Economic Forum. But my favorite kind of work is bringing futures thinking directly to the public, whether through simulations or teaching. I love watching people move from feeling anxious and insecure about the future to feeling confident, hopeful, and energized. It's why I created the How to Think Like a Futurist workshop for Stanford University's Continuing Studies program, where it has been one of the most popular classes for the past five years—in fact, students fly in from all over the world just to take the course. It's why I created a Futures Thinking certification program with the Institute for the Future on the online learning platform Coursera, where my classes currently have over thirty thousand students. And it's why, when we launched the Coursera program—the first free, public training in futures thinking offered at scale—I coined the phrase "Foresight is a human right."

It's my mission to give as many people as possible the skills not just to change the outcome of a game but to change the outcome of our future.

I'M EXCITED TO GO ON this journey with you. Before we begin, let me share one more thing—it's my favorite maxim of professional futures thinking:

> In dealing with the future . . . it is more important to be imaginative and insightful than to be one hundred percent "right."[7]

This bit of wisdom comes from Alvin Toffler, author of the 1970 book *Future Shock*, which kicked off professional futures thinking as we know it today. Toffler proposed the idea that society occasionally experiences a period of profound and sustained change previously so unthinkable that the people who live through it suffer a kind of "future shock." We're disoriented. Our strategies for being happy, healthy, and successful no longer work. Old assumptions no longer hold up. And it's incredibly difficult to wrap our minds around what exactly is happening, and why. It feels like a collective trauma, the psychological equivalent of being struck by a freight train. The turbulent period of the late 1960s, when Toffler wrote this seminal text, was a time of future shock for many. The 2020s, now, even more so.

It might seem that getting ahead of the next shock by making the most accurate predictions we can about the future is our ticket out of this trauma. And yes, seeing what's coming so it doesn't blindside us *is* helpful. But there's a deeper truth to futures thinking that goes beyond just trying to be right.

Being "right" means making your best prediction and then waiting for whatever you think is most likely today to actually happen. But what if the most "likely" future isn't one you want? What if it's a catastrophe? What if it's unjust? Would you rather be correct, or would you like to prove yourself wrong—and change what's most probable today into something better?

Yes, we want to think about the future in ways that are highly plausible and likely, so our forecasts are helpful. But if we're lucky, correctly anticipating future risks and challenges will help us start solving problems creatively *today*. We can use our new foresight not just to prepare for the future but to imagine new opportunities for ourselves right now, to be innovators and change something in our lives for the better today.

Let me give you two examples, from my own experience.

I always participate in the social simulations that I run, so that I can contribute my own personal insights and get the same benefits as other participants. During the Superstruct simulation back in 2008, I was trying to figure out what I would do during a pandemic to help others. How could I use my unique skills and experience to make a difference?

I tried to think of a new way a game designer could uniquely help during a pandemic. It occurred to me that the negative stereotype of gamers as people who like to stay home alone in their basements playing video games would actually be a positive behavior during a pandemic. After all, what would public health experts be telling everyone to do if a deadly virus were spreading? "Stay home, alone!"

So I started describing a hypothetical game project that I imagined future me creating, a kind of virtual dance club where you could meet up online and dance in front of your webcam with others, to make it easier to stay home *and* stay socially connected. I added this idea to the simulation database, which other players could search to find ideas they wanted to build on. I was soon contacted by a researcher at the Centers for Disease Control (CDC), who was also participating in Superstruct, and who was intrigued by my dance game idea. She told me that in real pandemics, outbreaks are often linked to dance clubs. She suggested that epidemiologists could work with game developers during a real pandemic, to promote stay-at-home games when community spread of the virus is high. As Superstruct continued, we brainstormed how public health officials and game developers might collaborate in the future and about how doctors might prescribe games to patients to keep them home. It was a fascinating conversation, but I had no idea at the time that it would inspire me to embark on a life-changing project within a year's time.

Nine months after the simulation ended, I hit my head and suffered a concussion that turned my life upside down. My symptoms, including brain fog, excruciating headaches, vertigo, and memory problems, wouldn't go away, no matter how much I rested. I developed panic attacks, severe depression, and even suicidal thoughts that lasted for months. At my lowest point, I decided to try to make a game to help myself heal. I used everything I knew about how games could increase motivation, optimism, attention, creativity, and collaboration to design some quests and challenges that might jump-start my brain back to a more hopeful and capable state. It worked. This game, called *SuperBetter*, became the subject of a TED talk with over seven million views, a best-selling book of the same title, and an app that has helped more than a million people tackle their own health challenges. But the only reason I had the confidence to tell anyone about this deeply personal game I made for myself, let alone make an app for others to try, was the previous experience I'd had sharing ideas with that CDC researcher. Her enthusiasm about my vision of a collaboration between health professionals and game developers, and her willingness to entertain this strange idea that a doctor might prescribe a video game, planted a seed. That seed helped me imagine that I might be taken seriously, that it was worth giving it a try.

The simulation gave me a sneak preview of the kind of real-world contribution I could make—not just in a pandemic, as it turned out, but in health crises more generally. And so when the opportunity arose, I was ready to take it. This is the gift that I want futures thinking to give to you: a chance to think more creatively and confidently *right now* about the things you could make, the solutions you could invent, the communities you could help.

I had another, bigger "aha" moment while immersing myself in an imagined future pandemic, and this one was even more personal. The first thing we asked Superstruct participants to do was to create a future profile on our social network. The profile asked ordinary questions—how old are you, where do you live, whom do you live with, what's your occupation, what communities are you a part of? The challenge was to answer these questions for your *future* self, ten years ahead. As I filled out my future profile, I wrote something that surprised me. I wrote that I lived with my husband, Kiyash—whom I was already married to, in the present—and my seven-year-old daughter, Pepper. I could see her so vividly in my mind—a spunky, playful girl who was at the center of our adventures in the year 2019.

But at this point in 2008, when we ran the simulation, my husband and I did not have any children. We had been married for three years and weren't in any rush to start a family. I had never pinned my hopes on becoming a mom, and we certainly hadn't made any plans to try to get pregnant. Still, this imagined daughter in the simulation, she felt very real to me. She felt important to the life I wanted to lead. I could see her so clearly in my imagination, this person who didn't yet exist but who felt key to the rest of the life I wanted to lead. Just by filling out this simple profile, I discovered something I truly hadn't known about myself. To my surprise, I really did want to be a mom.

It turned out to be very important that I came to this realization when I did. It would take many years and fertility treatments and extraordinary help from others for my husband and me to start our family. Seven years after I imagined a possible daughter, I finally became a mom to twin daughters, and it's the best thing that ever happened to me. And I don't know if we would have been able to make our family in this way if we hadn't had so much runway—so much time to make the hoped-for future real.

Clearly, neither of these personal insights prevented the COVID-19 pandemic from happening. They didn't even prevent me from catching the coronavirus—although, like a good futurist, I "got there early" and came down with it in early 2020 before anyone suspected the virus had arrived in the United States. But comparing my experience with others', I am certain I felt less anxiety than most during our long pandemic, because I felt prepared. And without a doubt, what I imagined during the Superstruct simulation changed my life and my future for the better. It gave me foresight about what I really wanted. And it gave me confidence to try to help others in a way that I'd never imagined I was capable of.

When we think about how the future might be different, we better understand how we might become different too.

That's why this book is called *Imaginable*. Yes, I want you to be able to imagine the "unthinkable" risks we need to prepare for and the "unimaginable" pain we want to avoid—so we can, in fact, prevent them or at least mitigate their harms. But I also want you to be able to imagine doing something new and exciting for the next ten years of your life, and beyond. I want you to be able to imagine yourself rising to the historic occasion of our post-pandemic, climate-crisis moment and being of service to others in a way that brings more meaning to the suffering we've all just been through. I want you to be able to imagine yourself doing and creating amazing things that would have been "unthinkable" and "unimaginable" before you had the futures-thinking tools to inspire you.

The reality is, there will always be future forces beyond our individual control. This book is not about your becoming a superhero who saves the world from the brink of disaster. Futures thinking isn't a superpower, and you don't have to fix everything or save everyone. But futures thinking *is* an incredibly useful, practical tool to prepare your mind to adapt faster to new challenges, build hope and resilience, reduce anxiety and depression, and inspire you to take actions today that set yourself up for future happiness and success.

If we all stretch our collective imagination together, we *will* pick ourselves back up from the shock of the early 2020s faster. But not because we'll be "right" about what's next. We'll heal and recover faster because we won't be sitting around waiting for the next decade to happen to us. We'll be making the decade together.

At the start of the global COVID-19 outbreak, author and activist Arundhati Roy wrote: "Historically, pandemics have forced humans to break with the past and imagine their world anew. This one is no different. It is a portal, a gateway between one world and the next."[8] I hope this book can serve as a portal for you: from our current world that needs to heal from a long pandemic, extreme social divisions, and the growing climate crisis, to a world where you find real new reasons to hope and feel ready for anything—even things that seem impossible to imagine today.

BEFORE WE START YOUR IMAGINATION training, I want to ask you three questions that will give you a baseline sense of your "future mindset":

Question #1: When you think about the next ten years, do you think things will mostly *stay the same and go on as normal?* Or do you expect that most of us will dramatically rethink and reinvent how we do things? Rate your outlook on a scale of 1 to 10. 1 is almost everything stays the same, 10 is almost everything will be dramatically different.

Question #2: When you think about how the world and your life will change over the next ten years, are you *mostly worried or mostly optimistic?* Rate your outlook on a scale of 1 to 10. 1 is extremely worried, 10 is extremely optimistic.

Question #3: *How much control or influence* do you feel *you* personally have in determining how the world and your life change over the next ten years? Rate your outlook on a scale of 1 to 10. 1 is almost no control or influence, 10 is almost complete control or influence.

These three questions give you a good idea of the kind of imagination training we're going to do in this book. In fact, each of the three parts of the book is specifically designed to increase your score on one of these questions by at least +1.

First, we're going to focus on the opportunity for rethinking and reinventing. Why rethinking and reinventing? Well, it's easy to prepare for futures that are similar to today. It's the dramatically different stuff that catches us off guard. So it's important to spend time getting ready for the futures that will feel stranger and less familiar. Focusing on rethinking and reinventing also puts us in a better position to help decide *how* the future will be different. Having lived through the COVID-19 pandemic, each of us will know for the rest of our lives that almost anything can change virtually overnight—for worse or for better. We know that it is absolutely possible to make radical changes to how we live, work, learn, and care for each other—and to make those changes fast. This gives us a collective power of imagination unprecedented in human history. We need to use this moment strategically and creatively.

Second, I want to help you create a more balanced mindset between hopes and worries for the future. At the Institute for the Future, we call this using your *positive imagination* and your *shadow imagination.*

Positive imagination asks the question: What's something good that could happen? It builds confidence that the future will be better.

Shadow imagination asks the question: What's something bad that could happen? It builds readiness to face future challenges.

Whatever your instinctive feelings are about the future right now, you will benefit from cultivating at least a little bit of the flip-side feeling. So I'll teach you imagination techniques that help you see *both* sides of the future: the risks that it makes sense to worry about, and the opportunities that are cause for optimism.

Just know that wherever you are right now in your outlook on the future is fine. Whether super-worried, super-optimistic, or somewhere in between, be ready to stretch your imagination in the opposite direction, so you can hold both hopes and worries in mind at the same time.

As you develop your positive and shadow imagination, you might be surprised to find that seeing risks more clearly and defining your worries more concretely can actually help you feel more hopeful. As you get better at anticipating global challenges, you'll feel more optimistic overall. There is a good reason for this paradox: you're increasing your awareness not just of what might go wrong but also of the bold plans and innovative solutions that are already being envisioned and implemented. And deep down, you know that you're putting yourself in a stronger position to help yourself and others by seriously imagining a future crisis instead of denying that it could ever happen.

Finally, we'll focus on building your confidence in how much influence you have to help determine how the future turns out. This book is about more than just anticipating the future. It's about acting to create the future you want: happier, healthier, safer, more just, more sustainable, more beautiful, more equitable. So I'll show you future-forecasting techniques that you can use to discover what contributions only *you* can make toward a better future, and how you can start making them today. And then I'll help you learn how to communicate your ideas for future change so that others are more likely to pay attention to them and feel inspired to act with you. If anything can increase your ability to influence how the future turns out, it's this: planting seeds of imagination in the minds of tens or hundreds or thousands of other people who can help you make whatever changes you're imagining.

If you add all three of these mini-mindsets up—focusing on the opportunity to rethink and reinvent, using both positive and shadow imagination, and looking for actionable ways to increase your ability to shape the future—you get what I believe will be the biggest takeaway you'll have from training your imagination. It's what I call *urgent optimism*.

Urgent optimism is a balanced feeling. It's recognizing that, yes, there are great challenges and risks ahead, while also staying realistically hopeful that you have something to contribute to how we solve those challenges and face those risks. Urgent optimism means you're not staying awake all night worrying about what might happen. Instead, you're leaping out of bed in the morning with a fire in your pants to do something about it. Urgent optimism is knowing that you have agency and the ability to use your unique talents, skills, and life experiences to create the world you want to live in.

Make a note of your score for the three questions above. (Write your numbers in the margins or send yourself an email you can search for later.) You'll see these questions again as we move through each of the three phases of your imagination training. At the end of the book, I'll ask you to answer them one more time, so you can compare your scores and see for yourself just how much your skills have grown and your thinking has changed. My biggest hope for you is that reading this book will increase your overall urgent optimism score by at least +1, if not +2, +3, or more. Actually, it's not just a hope—it's an expectation, based on my own teaching experiences and the results of scientific research. When I teach How to Think Like a Futurist in the Continuing Studies program at Stanford University, I ask these same questions at the start and end of the class—and the scores consistently go up. I've also been able to ask nearly fifty thousand Futures Thinking learners from around the world these same questions on Coursera. And I can report that learners who complete their online training with the Institute for the Future really do anticipate more dramatic change, feel more optimistic, and have a stronger sense of agency over how their future turns out.

Perhaps even more convincingly, World Bank researchers ran a randomized controlled study of EVOKE with three hundred college students, using a new future scenario set in the year 2026. In the study, half the students (the control group) took conventional coursework in social innovation and global challenges. The other half participated, for college credit, in a sixteen-week EVOKE social simulation, imagining what they could do to help during a future crisis involving human trafficking and people displaced from their homes by war. Compared with the students who completed conventional coursework, the EVOKE players became more optimistic that global challenges could be solved. And at the end of the simulation, they expressed more confidence that they could use their own voices and actions to bring about a better and more peaceful future.[9]

The EVOKE players also measurably improved a specific set of imagination skills, which were tested at the start and end of the sixteen-week game and evaluated by peers throughout the study. Compared with the control group, they showed a statistically significant increase in their ability to "view familiar things in a different light," "produce original and novel ideas through the willingness to take risks and try something different," "dream of creative ways to resolve a conflict or problem," and "initiate forward-looking solutions." Sounds good, right? Who wouldn't want to get better at these things? Most importantly, their skill growth and newfound agency to influence the future were similar across genders, ethnicities, ages, and academic fields of study. This suggests that futures-thinking training and participation in social simulations can empower people from diverse backgrounds to become optimistic agents of change. And that includes you!

Turn the page, and let's take our first trip to the future together.

PART I

~~~~~~

UNSTICK YOUR MIND

To be hopeful means to be uncertain about the future, to be tender toward possibilities, to be dedicated to change all the way down to the bottom of your heart.

—REBECCA SOLNIT, historian and activist

The only way to make sense out of change is to plunge into it, move with it, and join the dance.

—ALAN WATTS, philosopher

Growth is painful. Change is painful. But nothing is as painful as staying stuck where you don't belong.

—MANDY HALE, author

When you think about the next ten years, do you think things will mostly <u>stay the same and go on as normal</u>?

Or do you expect that most of us will dramatically <u>rethink and reinvent how we do things</u>?

. . . .

Rate your outlook on a scale of 1 to 10.

1 is almost everything stays the same, 10 is almost everything will be dramatically different.

1

~~~~~~~~

Take a Ten-Year Trip

You are not crazy. You are just ready to change.

—Nnedi Okorafor, author

You may be familiar with the saying "The future starts now." As catchy as this phrase may be, it is fundamentally not true. The future doesn't start now, or tomorrow, or next month—at least not if you want to get the most out of mental time travel. It takes much longer than that for the full benefits of the future to kick in. But when *exactly* the future starts depends on who you are and what your life circumstances are like. Let me tell you about a simple game I invented. If you play along, you'll get a pretty good idea of when the future starts for you.

Every time I teach a futures-thinking class or workshop, I begin with a quick game of When Does the Future Start? I ask everyone: "If the future is a time when many or most things in your life will be different than they are today, how long from now does that future start?" I ask them to write down their answer in days, weeks, months, or years.

This isn't a trick question, and there's no single correct answer. In fact, usually there are dozens of different answers, all of them valid: a year from now, five years from now, ten years from now, twenty years from now. (If you want to play along, go ahead and think of *your* answer to this question now.) I ask everyone to hold up their answers for others to see and then organize themselves in a line—or, more specifically, a timeline. The person who answered with the shortest amount of time goes first in line. The person who answered with the longest amount of time goes last. Everyone else orders themselves from shortest to longest in between.

At this point, it becomes obvious that there is a wide variety of responses. So I ask people at the very front and end of the line to explain their responses, along with a few in between. Their answers are often deeply personal. "Six months from today," a woman in my Continuing Studies class at Stanford once said. She shared that her husband had recently and suddenly passed away. For her, everything had changed literally overnight. She was feeling a lot of uncertainty about whether she could expect anything to be reliably the same for long. In my experience, this is quite common: the person who answers the question "When does the future start?" with the shortest amount of time is someone who recently experienced a significant loss or shock.

On the other hand: "Three months," a young man in a workshop I ran for high school students once said, for quite the opposite reason. He was graduating from high school in three months. That turning point felt like the start of something completely new. Studies show that this is also quite common: We become more open to the possibility of change as we get closer to achieving a long-term goal.[1] We anticipate the end of one journey and look ahead to a new one beginning.

"Five hundred twenty-one days from today," another student of mine once answered, quite specifically. It turned out that she had done some quick math. In 521 days, exactly, she would be turning thirty years old. Milestone birthdays, too, often cause us to anticipate big change, not just in our own lives but in the world around us.[2] Thinking the whole world will change when we do may be a bit of egocentric thinking! Still, it's useful to have a number of regularly scheduled moments in our lives when we can lean into dramatic change.

When else does the future start? "On Tuesday, November 3, 2020," someone replied in the year 2017. "The date of the next United States presidential election," he helpfully explained, clearly hoping the next election would yield different results. Not everyone has such a precise tipping point for the future in mind. But many people do think about dramatic change as a kind of regularly scheduled process, so that hope for something new and different is always on the horizon. Think: political elections, or drafts for sports fans, or even the new Pantone color of the year, as a very artistic student of mine once suggested.

Then again, just as often as not, people will say that they have no good reason for what they wrote. "The future starts in ten years," someone might say, "just because it feels so far away." And that's profoundly true. *The future is whatever time feels far enough away for things to really change.* It is a completely subjective truth. The future starts whenever *you* feel ready for dramatic change: big change, scary change, prayed-for change, crazy change.

That's why I love to play When Does the Future Start? A person's answer tells me something important about their state of mind. A shorter answer—less than five years—means they are either very sensitive to change, or open to it, or smack in the middle of change happening right now. An unusually long answer—like forty, fifty, or even one hundred years—suggests a number of things: Someone might feel stuck and frustrated with the pace of change in society or their life so that they can't realistically imagine dramatic change anytime soon, perhaps not even in their lifetime. Or they might be a very patient person with a lot of grit and determination, planning for a very long road ahead. Or perhaps they see no need for major change and are happy for things to stay the same for as long as possible. It takes some discussion to find out which situation is relevant, but in my experience a conversation that begins with "When does the future start?" is one worth having.

. . .

THAT SAID, WITH ALL THIS fascinating variation, ten years is far and away the most common answer to the question "When does the future start?" In the responses I've collected from more than ten thousand students, almost everyone agrees: Ten years is enough time for society and my own life to become dramatically different.

What makes ten years such a magic number for the mind?

Most of us have internalized the power of ten years to create change through a combination of our own lived experience and social convention. We think about our own lives as a series of ten-year-long periods: our twenties, our thirties, our forties, and so on. We use these milestone birthdays to reflect on what we want our next decade of life to be like. And we talk about decades as units of time in which society changes: think about how different the 1920s were from the 1910s, the 1960s from the 1950s, or how different the 2020s have already been from the 2010s. Anyone who has lived through more than one decade, or studied history, already has a clear mental model of just how much can change in ten years.

If you look at recent history, ten years really does seem almost like a magic number. You can find myriad examples of new ideas and actions creating a previously unimaginable social reality over the time span of a decade, give or take a few months. This is particularly true when it comes to social movements achieving historic victories, and new technologies achieving global impact. To consider just a few examples, it took, give or take a few months:

- ten years for the civil rights movement against racial segregation in the United States to go from its first boycott of segregated bus seating to the successful passage of the federal Civil Rights Act (1955–1964)
- ten years for the first international economic sanctions against South Africa's segregationist apartheid system to lead to a new

constitution that enfranchised Black South Africans and other racial groups (1985–1996)

- ten years for same-sex marriage to go from being considered controversial when it was legalized by a country for the first time (the Netherlands) to being supported in global surveys by a majority of people in a majority of countries (2001–2010)
- ten years for marijuana to go from being legalized for all uses in one US state, Colorado, to being decriminalized in forty-four out of fifty states (2012–2021)

And it took:

- ten years from when just sixteen million people, mostly scientists and other academic researchers, were using the internet—they thought it would be used mostly to share scientific data—to when a billion people were using it (1991–2001)
- ten years from the first iPhone release until a majority of people on the planet had smartphones, creating a new era of always-on communication (2007–2017)
- ten years for Facebook to go from one user to one billion daily users, on its way to becoming the first product used by more than one in three humans on the planet (2004–2015)
- ten years for Bitcoin to go from being a hypothetical idea discussed in a scientific article to having a nearly US\$1 trillion market capitalization, larger than the three biggest US banks combined (2008–2019)
- ten years from Airbnb's and Uber's foundings for a full 36 percent of US workers to be engaged in some form of "gig work" (2008–2018)
- ten years for Zoom to go from its first user testing session to becoming a critical lifeline for humanity during the COVID-19 pandemic, as the de facto tool for learning, work meetings, and staying in touch with friends and family (2011–2020)

In other words: things that are small experiments today in ten years can become ubiquitous and world-changing. And social change that seems improbable or unimaginable—well, in ten years that can change too.

Of course, not all goals for change can be achieved in a decade—many social movements take much longer. And progress doesn't just stop after ten years. The purpose of looking ten years ahead isn't to see that everything will happen on that timeline—but there is ample evidence that almost anything *could* happen on that timeline. And for that reason, ten years helps unstick our minds. Ten years helps us consider possibilities we would otherwise dismiss. Ten years even relaxes us a bit as we try to imagine preparing for dramatic disruptions or for a radical rethinking of what's normal—because ten years gives us time to get ready. And it's for this reason that whenever I send people on mental time trips to the future, I almost always send them ten years ahead. Futurists want people to go somewhere they believe anything can be different—even things that seem impossible to change today.

WHEN WE THINK ON A ten-year timeline, it's not just that we are more likely to believe that dramatic change can happen in the world. We become more optimistic and hopeful about what *we* can change through our own efforts. This has to do with a psychological phenomenon known as *time spaciousness*. It's the relaxing and empowering feeling that we have enough time to do what really matters—to consider our options, make a plan, and act more confidently to create the future we want. It is almost impossible to create a sense of time spaciousness when we're thinking in a matter of days or weeks. But when thinking ahead ten years . . . ah, it's so much time! On a ten-year timeline, we don't feel rushed. We have plenty of opportunity to develop new skills, collect resources, recruit allies, learn from our mistakes, bounce back from setbacks, and do whatever else we need to do to get the best possible outcome. This feeling of abundance makes us less risk-averse and therefore more creative. We have all the time we need to play with ideas, try new things, and experiment until we figure out what works.

Interestingly, brains respond to abundant *space* in the same way as they do to abundant time. Studies have found that we also think more creatively and set higher, "maximal," goals for ourselves when we're in rooms with higher ceilings or outside in a wide-open environment.[3] With maximal goals, we focus on the upper boundary: What is the highest and best possible outcome we can imagine? So I like to think of a ten-year timeline as a kind of cathedral or Grand Canyon for the mind. It lifts the ceiling on our imagination.

When we feel *time-poor*, on the other hand, it's like being stuck in a tiny, depressing room with no windows. We shrink ourselves and imagine less. We adopt "minimal" goals, which means we try to do just enough to avoid a bad outcome. As one team of expert psychologists put it: "A maximal goal reflects the most that one could wish for, whereas a minimal goal reflects bare necessities or the least one could comfortably tolerate."[4]

Do you have a sense of whether you're waking up each day focused on maximal or minimal goals? Whether you're feeling time-rich or time-poor? Setting goals for yourself (or your family, or your community, or your organization) on too short a timeline usually creates the feeling of being time-rushed. So does being too busy, but that's not something you can always control. So rather than drastically reduce what's on your schedule, it's much easier to control how far out in the future you're imagining when you think about changes you'd like to achieve.

You may not be used to goal setting on a ten-year timeline. We usually think about making personal change year by year, most commonly by making resolutions at the start of the New Year. But a one-year resolution won't help you think maximally, and you won't feel a sense of time spaciousness if you're trying to achieve a big goal in just one year. So next New Year's Day, why not try a new tradition? Make a *ten-year resolution*. What could you (or your family, or your community, or your organization) accomplish if you had ten years to do it? What would the long-term impact of a new habit be if you practiced it for ten years? Let your mind play with some bigger possibilities. Now this idea may not sound appealing to you at first. When it comes to making resolutions, you don't want to be different in ten years; you want to be different as soon as possible! So go ahead and keep making short-term resolutions. *And* try to stretch your imagination a decade further too, while you're at it.

If you want to get a taste of time spaciousness right now, here's a trick you can try: pick a tiny task like finishing this book—and give yourself ten years to do it. You might think that having all this time will make you more likely to procrastinate, and you'll never actually get around to reading it. But procrastination, paradoxically, is more likely to happen when you feel time-poor.[5] When you feel like you have less time to get things done, you do less. And when you feel you have ample time, you do more. Studies show this is true completely independent of how much "free" or unscheduled time a person has. What matters is whether your brain perceives an abundance of time. So give it a try. Give yourself luxurious ten-year deadlines. You might be surprised at how much faster and more happily you do things you'd otherwise put off when you feel time-rich, and therefore more in control of your timeline.

I want you to try this, for real: go ahead and put a deadline to finish this book, or some other small goal, on your personal calendar, for ten years from today. Google's and Apple's calendar apps will let you schedule things ten years in the future. In fact, you can use these apps to schedule something one hundred years in the future, if you'd like to imagine something that might happen one hundred years from today. I highly recommend it as a thought experiment!

While you've got your mental or digital calendar open, let's try a mental time trip. Imagine it's ten years from today, and you wake up incredibly excited about . . . something. You've got a special event on the calendar. What is it?

To help you imagine this future more clearly, skip ahead in your digital calendar to ten years from today. Now, fill in the blank space.

What do you have planned, ten years from today? Who are you doing it with? What will you be wearing? What supplies will you need? Why is this activity important or exciting for you? And how do you feel now that the day is here? Try to answer all these questions and imagine the day ahead as vividly as you can. Be sure to think about how you and your life circumstances might be different from today, and how those differences might change what you want or are able to do.

As with any mental time trip to far in the future, it may take a few moments for your brain to start filling in the blanks. Sometimes it helps to plant the seed of imagination in your mind now and come back to it later. Just keep the calendar open and keep playing with possibilities. My challenge for you is to put something exciting—maybe even something life-changing—on your real-world calendar for ten years from today. You'll have a whole decade to decide if you want to actually make it happen.

For inspiration, let me tell you about a community that has truly embraced the ten-year timeline as a tool for dramatic change. In Germany's Osing farming region, they do something remarkable every ten years. Each year that ends in a four (for example, 2024), the community gathers to conduct the "Osingverlosung," a lottery in which all 213 local lots of farmland are randomly redistributed.

If you live in Osing, whatever property you owned and managed for the past ten years is now given over to someone else for the next decade. And you get to start over with a new lot. Fishing, hunting, and fruit-picking rights are raffled off as well. This ten-year lottery tradition started centuries ago and has continued on the local calendar uninterrupted. Today, the handover is celebrated with music, a feast, and festival activities.

Can *you* imagine committing to this kind of dramatic change every decade? Can you imagine having to trade some of your personal assets with a neighbor every ten years—perhaps your collection of books, or your wardrobe, or your home? What would it feel like to give what you

own back to the community every ten years and start over with someone else's lot? Can you picture yourself joyfully celebrating this random redistribution, as the Osing residents do, instead of fearing or
resenting it? It's difficult, isn't it? But it's not a fantasy; there are people
who do go along with it, voluntarily, happily. So why is such a lottery
unimaginable for most people?

To find out, make a list of all the barriers and obstacles you can
think of. What *are* the reasons such a lottery would never work where
you live? Why would people refuse to participate? And then consider:
How willing are you to suspend your certainty about those obstacles?
Is there anything on that list you think *could* change or be overcome?
Can you think of any urgent crisis, or social movement, or technological breakthrough, or shift in popular beliefs that could make this unimaginable thing imaginable?

That's the kind of imagination stretching we're doing together in
this book. The Osing lottery, but in your own town, is just the first of
many "impossible" futures we're going to consider.

To be fair, there are people who will tell you they need much longer
than a decade to create and prepare for dramatic change. When I play
When Does the Future Start? I sometimes notice another large cluster
of answers, in the twenty-to-thirty-year range. This group, it turns out,
tends to have a very specific mental model of how things change. They
think about the world in terms of *generational change*, in which most
changes are a result of young people growing up and doing things
differently than previous generations.

This is a reasonable way to think about change, but it has at least
three drawbacks. First, it's an awfully long time to wait if you are urgently hoping for change. Second, it puts all the agency in the hands
of one demographic: the most recently grown-up generation. What if
you're not a part of that group? Third, it gets harder for your imagination to fill in the blanks of the future when you have less and less
information about what it might be like—at thirty years out, you're

more likely to be making random guesses than helpful predictions. When I train people with this generational view of change, I don't try to talk them out of their mental model—but I do encourage them to practice futures thinking on the ten-year timeline, in order to help them start their own future faster.

Unfortunately, imagining ten years out is not a habit that most people come by easily. A few years ago, as part of my research at the Institute for the Future, I conducted the first major survey of futures thinking in the United States.[6] In it, 2,818 people reflected on how frequently they imagine what they might personally do at different timescales of the future: a month, a year, three years, and so on, all the way up to thirty years into the future. (Respondents were eighteen or older, and the survey has a margin of error of ±2 percentage points.) I expected that most people would think about the far future less than I, as a professional futurist, do. But I was surprised by just *how much* less they did. Thirty-seven percent of people said they never imagine the world or their lives ten years into the future. Another 15 percent said they think about it at most once a year. Add those groups up and you've got a majority of people who are completely missing out on the power of the ten-year timeline in their own lives.

Closer futures are imagined more often by most people: 56 percent of people say they imagine something they might do a year from now every day or almost every day. So it's not that futures thinking doesn't come naturally to us. It's just that most of us don't push the timeline far enough.

LET ME TRY TO CONVINCE you with one more scientific finding that *you* should be thinking ten years into the future pretty much every single day.

When you take a mental time trip ten years into the future, your brain starts to think with a different point of view. This isn't a metaphor—it's a literal fact. Scientists describe this as switching your imagination from *first-person* to *third-person* perspective.

In first-person perspective, you imagine the world from your own point of view, from inside your own body. This is how you normally move through life, experiencing yourself as the center of reality. In third-person perspective, you imagine yourself from an outside point of view, almost like an out-of-body experience. You're floating above or apart from the action, not stuck inside it. When you're thinking in first person, you're totally immersed in your own thoughts and feelings. When you're thinking in third person, you escape your own ego and get a more objective and expansive perspective.

Virtually everyone thinks in first person when they imagine their recent past, present, or near future. Likewise, almost everyone switches to third person when they think about their far past or far future, usually defined in the scientific literature as ten years in either direction from today. This shift in mental perspective is why you can often look back at emotionally charged moments in your life, after enough time has passed, and see things from a more detached, clearer point of view. Your brain is literally processing them from a more insightful vantage point. Likewise, this is why taking a mental time trip ten years to the future can help you feel "unstuck" emotionally. You momentarily get a break from your normal mode of thinking and feeling and get to float above it all, like a satellite looking down from space.

Psychology researchers have devised a clever way of demonstrating this perspective-switching phenomenon. In studies, they use something called "the letter-tracing task." And you can try this task with a partner to create your own "aha" moment about what's happening in your brain. Here's an example of how the letter-tracing task works:

In one study, participants were asked to close their eyes and imagine themselves walking along a beach either *tomorrow* or *in ten years' time*. After twenty seconds had gone by, but while still imagining the beach walk, participants were instructed to draw the letter *C* just in front of their forehead (without touching the skin), using the index finger on their dominant hand. They were told that this action should be performed as quickly and thoughtlessly as possible.

The researchers reported a fascinating pattern in their observations. Almost everyone who imagined walking on the beach *tomorrow* traced the letter *C* so that it appeared correctly from their own point of view, but backward to the researcher sitting across from them. But 70 percent of the participants who imagined walking on the beach *ten years in the future* traced the *C* the opposite way, so that it appeared correctly to the researcher and backward to themselves. In other words, people thinking about the present were still looking at the world with a first-person perspective, from inside their own heads. But people thinking about the far future zoomed out into a third-person perspective. They adopted a more empathetic perspective, as evidenced by their drawing the *C* for someone else's point of view. It really is as if, when they took the ten-year trip, they were looking at the scene from outside their own body.[7]

You can try this experiment with a friend, if you like, and experience the phenomenon for yourself. Just keep in mind: You need to be sitting or standing across from your partner in the same physical space for the effect to work (you can't do it over the phone). And it won't work for everyone; somewhere around 20 to 30 percent of people will always trace the letter the same way, even if they've switched between actor and observer mode. Still, the letter-tracing task is strong confirmation that zooming out in time really does help us zoom out from ourselves. If we can get some distance from the present moment, we can get some distance in our perspective too.

As the letter-tracing task suggests, a major benefit of switching from first person to third person is that it's a huge empathy booster. In scientific language, we "reduce our egocentric biases" and become "less ego-identified"—which means we get out of our own heads and can start to see things the way someone else might. We're better able to consider that others might have different wants, needs, values, or ideas than we do.[8]

We also become more open-minded—and this is particularly important when it comes to thinking about how the future might be different, or how we ourselves might change. Studies show that when we zoom out in time and perspective, we become much more likely to take in new information that runs counter to our existing beliefs.[9] This is a kind of mental superpower.

Most of the time, when we're exposed to information that challenges our beliefs, we shut it out. Our brains have various defense mechanisms, including paying less attention to "disconfirming data" and forgetting it faster if we notice it at all. If you've ever told someone, "I don't want to hear it," when they're trying to convince you of something, you know exactly what I'm talking about! Your brain really does not want to hear it—it actively filters out and rejects information that causes it discomfort, or "cognitive dissonance."

There are good reasons for these defense mechanisms, according to cognitive scientists. Our brains don't want to waste energy reassessing our mental models every time we get new information. We need to save that energy for all the other important thinking, planning, and problem solving we have to do. And we'd never take any action at all if we didn't have some degree of confidence in our ability to understand the world around us. In fact, if we don't have relatively stable beliefs, we are likely to experience significant psychological distress: we may feel we have a weaker self-identity, or that we are simply unable to understand the world around us. This can lead to anxiety and even despair. So, of course, our brains want to avoid going into a tailspin every time we encounter a piece of information that might require us to rethink what we know. But if we always shut out challenging information, we'll never learn or grow. And we certainly won't adapt quickly to disruptions or surprising events.[10]

When we get a little distance from our own point of view, we're less likely to get stuck in old ways of thinking that no longer serve us. When we take a mental time trip to ten years in the future, we are choosing to open our minds at least temporarily and see what we discover. It's like opening a window to get fresh air—a ten-year timeline opens our mind to get fresh ideas. This openness to surprising or uncomfortable information is a gift. It helps us overcome blind spots and imagine what others refuse to think about.

• • •

A LITTLE OVER TEN YEARS ago, I was invited to the corporate headquar-
ters of a major automotive manufacturer to give a talk to their innovation team about how video game technology might be incorporated
into future cars. During a tour of a research facility, I got into a heated
discussion with a few senior executives about whether self-driving, or
autonomous, cars would ever take off as a popular alternative to
people-driven cars.

"Absolutely not," one of them said.

"We're not even looking at that as a serious possibility," another said.

I asked why they were so confident in their opinion.

"Cars are the ultimate expression of individual freedom," one re-
sponded. "When you get in your car, you decide where to go, you're
in control. People are never going to be willing to give up that sense of
freedom and control by letting the car drive them."

Another executive talked about the psychological power and cultural importance of the driver's license. "There's a reason why getting
your first driver's license is such an important rite of passage," he said.
"It marks the moment when a young person finally feels in control of
their own life. That's just not going to change."

I asked if they thought that the possibility of reducing motor vehicle fatalities would be a stronger motivator than being in charge of
your life. What if self-driving cars were ultimately safer than people-
driven cars? What if we could eliminate some of the nearly 1.5 million
car-related fatalities that happen globally each year? No, they all
agreed. Safety gains would never trump a sense of individual freedom
and control. I shared a few other reasons I thought autonomous cars
would become commonplace, but I didn't get any traction. The executives were locked in to their assumption.

As their guest, I didn't want to get into an argument with them, so
I said, "I hope we have a chance to talk about this again in ten years."
And then as soon as I had a moment to myself, I pulled out the tiny
notebook I always carry with me, and I wrote up everything I could

remember about the conversation. I wanted to capture the conversation because I was fascinated by the certainty they expressed in rejecting this possible future. I didn't take their opinions to be an official company position—and I later learned that there were already people within the company advocating for taking self-driving cars more seriously. But our conversation stood out to me as a clear example of how an idea can get labeled "unthinkable," and how, once the idea is labeled, it is hard to get people to change their minds about it, even in a team tasked with innovation.

Before I started training as a futurist, I was probably just as stubborn about my own views of the world. But at the Institute for the Future, I quickly discovered how important it would be never to let my mind get stuck on a certain point of view. In meetings, my new colleagues would often repeat a particular mantra, which I learned was coined by a former president of the institute. Whenever they got into a heated conversation, they would stop, take a breath, and say: "Strong opinions, lightly held." And then they would take a closer look at their assumptions.

It took me a while to figure out exactly what this mantra meant. On one hand, it's important to have strong points of view, especially when we're trying to stretch our imaginations. If we want to prepare for unthinkable events and create previously unimaginable change, then, by definition, we have to be willing to propose extremely provocative and challenging ideas. But on the other hand, just because we can imagine that something can *possibly* be true in the future doesn't mean we have to believe it *will* be true with absolute certainty. We need to be open to letting our assumptions and beliefs go when they no longer serve us, especially if we get new information that makes us rethink our original position.

"Strong opinions, lightly held"—I really do love this mantra. It's an expression of humility and willingness to learn. It reminds us that no matter what we think we know for sure, the future can still surprise us. So I use this mantra whenever I feel myself getting overinvested in a particular outcome—not just about the future but in any disagreement

I'm having. (Yes, I even use it to press pause on arguments with my husband!) It's a reminder to myself, and a promise to whomever I'm in a conversation with, that I will keep a flexible, open mind.

I've learned a lot about futures thinking since that conversation with the innovation team more than ten years ago. What would I do differently if I had known then what I know now? I'd definitely invite them to take a quick mental time trip with me, so they could imagine their very first time riding in a completely autonomous vehicle.

"Imagine it as vividly and realistically as you can," I'd say to them. "What color is the car? Where are you going? How comfortable is the seat? Is anyone with you?" I'd give them a moment to pre-feel this future, and then I'd ask, "In one word, how would you describe the emotion you're feeling during this first ride?" I'm confident that it would open their minds, especially if they had a chance to share their mental time travel trip reports with each other.

I've since had thousands of students take on this exact imagination challenge as a mental warm-up for class. (Although in recent years, as self-driving technology has actually entered the marketplace, I've had to revise it slightly: "If you've already had this experience of riding in a completely autonomous vehicle, what was the main emotion you felt?") I invite everyone to share their one-word emotional reaction on a giant whiteboard at the front of the classroom or, if we're learning online, in chat. This is my favorite part, as everyone takes in the inev-itably wide range of feelings. People predict they would feel excited, nervous, awed, terrified, curious, nauseated, grateful, thrilled, con-fused, vigilant, asleep, free. The words they share run the full gamut of positive and negative emotions, with no consensus whatsoever.

With this kind of insight into other people's imagined futures, it becomes much harder to hold any strong opinion about self-driving cars too tightly. This is especially true if we try to understand—or better yet, have a conversation about—why exactly someone else might feel nervous about the ride while we would feel excited, why someone else might feel free during the ride while we might feel nau-seated, why some people want this future and others don't.

In other words, imagining the future is most mind-opening when we do it with others. We can notice how differently others feel about the same possible future. We can take in the details of their imagination so we have material to work with in our own mind. When we take ten-year trips to the future together, it's much easier to keep adapting and evolving our own beliefs.

Speaking of which . . . twelve years later, that automotive company I visited is now manufacturing self-driving cars. They definitely got their minds unstuck about that idea! Still, regardless of whether this particular technology becomes ubiquitous, it's likely that they (and we too) will need to do even more rethinking in the next ten years as even bigger changes loom on the horizon. The future, even more now, is resisting our strongly held assumptions about the importance of cars to modern life. Here's another clue to plant in your mind about how the future might be different:

During the 2020 pandemic, cities around the world experimented with closing large areas of streets to cars. The roadways were opened up for pedestrians, bicycles, and outdoor dining, so people could spend more time socializing and staying active, while still staying a safe distance from each other. These experiments proved extremely popular, and they will likely have lasting impacts on people's ideas about cars. When the international market research and data analytics firm You-Gov conducted a survey in twenty-one cities across France, Germany, Italy, Spain, the UK, and Belgium, for example, it found that 78 percent of people wanted to keep the restrictions on cars put in place during the pandemic as a way to lower air pollution and limit the role of cars in urban life.

Meanwhile, young people are increasingly opting not to get a driver's license. In the United States today, 40 percent of eighteen-year-olds have opted not to get their license yet. The top reasons they gave in a survey by the University of Michigan Transportation Research Institute: "too busy or not enough time to get a driver's license" (37 percent); "owning and maintaining a vehicle is too expensive" (32 percent); "able to get transportation from others" (31 percent); "prefer to bike or walk" (22 percent); "prefer to use public transportation" (17 percent); "concerned about how driving impacts the environment" (9 percent).[11] And in a separate survey by the AAA Foundation for Traffic Safety, nearly half of teens who chose not to get a license said that driving was a risky activity that made them feel anxious.[12] What do I take from this data? Freedom clearly has a wider range of meaning to young people today when it comes to cars—not just personal mobility or control over a machine but also freedom from debt, freedom from feeling guilty about the environmental impacts, freedom from anxiety about risky activities.

To me, these clues alongside the advance of self-driving technology suggest we are probably past the "peak-driving" moment in history for humans, at least for our lifetimes. This will increasingly change where we live, whom we live near, how we work, how we learn, how we shop, what kind of infrastructure we need, and how young people gain independence and mark rites of passage. There are so many things we can start to rethink and reinvent if we allow ourselves to consider this change.

As you imagine your life and the world ten years from now, it might be worth occasionally constructing a scene with dramatically fewer cars and less human driving. What would be different in this future? Could you live where you live today? What would change in your community? The next time you take a ten-year trip, see what creative ideas for personal or social change a post-car world inspires for you. This is just one of many large-scale societal changes we'll be imagining together in this book.

THERE IS ONE IMPORTANT CAVEAT to all this ten-year thinking. For some people, and with good reason, a ten-year timeline is too long. In my national survey of futures thinking, I found that the very oldest respondents, individuals in their eighties or nineties, were the least likely to think that far ahead in time. Their most often cited reason: "I don't expect to be here in ten years." Even for professional futurists, it's necessary to acknowledge that advanced age, illness, or dangerous conditions can make imagining a ten-year future feel pointless or distressing. If your life circumstances make ten years into the future feel like a bridge too far, I encourage you to imagine a future that still feels further out than you would ordinarily think about. Let the future start wherever you feel that slightly uncomfortable reaching and stretching and opening in your mind, wherever you believe dramatic change is possible.

IMAGINATION TRAINING

RULE #1: Take a Ten-Year Trip.

When you think about the future, focus your imagination ten years out. A ten-year timeline will lift the ceiling on your imagination and give you that magical feeling of "time spaciousness." It will help you open your mind, take in new information, reduce your blind spots, increase your empathy, set more optimistic goals, and see a much bigger picture. If your mind feels stuck or rushed, give yourself a ten-year deadline, make a ten-year resolution, create an event on your calendar for ten years from now, or talk to others about how the world might be different ten years from now. It will change how you think and feel today.

~~~~~

Learn to Time Travel

It's a poor sort of memory that only works backwards.

—Lewis Carroll, author

For the next thirty seconds, I want you to imagine yourself waking up tomorrow morning. Try to picture it in your mind or describe it to yourself as clearly as possible.

These questions might help you make your imagined scene clearer: What room or space are you in? What wakes you up—is it an alarm, the sunlight, someone nudging you or calling you? Is it light out, or still dark? Is there anyone with you? Which side of the bed are you on? (If you're in a bed—or are you somewhere else?) What are you wearing? What kind of mood are you in? And what's the very first thing you do, now that you're awake? Keep imagining your tomorrow morning until you have a clear answer to all of these questions.

Good job. This quick mental time trip you just took is an example of a *highly imaginable* future. It was likely quite easy for you to envision, with plenty of vivid details.

What makes it so imaginable? Well, there's not too much room for uncertainty between now and tomorrow morning. You probably have a good idea where you'll be waking up. Your physical environment isn't likely to be completely different by tomorrow. Your habits and life circumstances aren't likely to dramatically change overnight. In other words, you can reasonably expect tomorrow morning to be at least somewhat similar to most mornings you've experienced recently. That doesn't mean you can predict it with certainty. But you have all the information you need to simulate in your mind, clearly, at least one likely possibility.

Now let's try something a little more challenging. For the next thirty seconds, I want you to imagine yourself waking up *one year from today*.

Again, try to envision this future moment as clearly as possible. Feel free to change as many or as few details as you want from the first scene you imagined.

One year from today, are you waking up somewhere different? Or is there something different about your bed, or your room? Is someone different with you? Are *you* physically changed in some way?

Would you like to imagine waking up in a completely different mood than you expect to wake up in tomorrow? What might put you in this new mood?

Do you have a different morning habit a year from now, something you do as soon as you wake up that you don't do today? What might that new habit be?

Keep imagining your morning one year from now until you have answers to all of these questions—even the ones that seem harder to predict. Did this exercise stretch your imagination a bit more? Notice how easily and automatically ideas came to you, or how hard you had to work to come up with details. Notice how inclined you were to describe a moment similar to today, or how freely you started to invent change. Notice whether your body and brain felt relaxed or active with effort. Take a quick inventory of your reactions, and then let's try one more act of imagination.

This time, I want you to imagine yourself waking up *ten years from today*.

Take as long as you need to come up with a vivid and plausible image—of yourself, of the space that you're in, and who might be with you.

Where are you ten years from today? What's around you? What do you see, hear, smell, and feel? What's the first thing on your mind when you wake up? What do you have planned for the day? How are you physically different in this future?

Try not to make this future scene a total fantasy. Stay grounded in what you feel is genuinely realistic and possible for you.

If you're having any difficulty with this challenge, one trick you might try is to write down a description of what you imagine instead of trying to hold all the details in your mind. For some people, it's easier to think about the future with words rather than with mental images.

Keep thinking about this moment ten years from now, until you've filled in as many details as possible.

What did you see in your far future? Did you expect things to be more or less the same? Or did you fill your future with alternatives to how things are today? There's no right or wrong answer. Just notice.

Did you picture a morning you'd like to wake up to? Or did you find yourself exploring possibilities that might be painful to encounter? Both are helpful forms of imagination—your positive and shadow side. Just notice which direction you went to first.

Most importantly, did you feel a difference in your brain and body as you stretched your imagination ten years into the future? For most people, the sensation of this activity is like reaching for something that isn't quite there.

Some people feel it mentally, some physically, and others both. You may have noticed that your eyes started moving almost involuntarily, as if looking around for clues. This is quite common when we try to imagine the future; it helps us "see" what isn't there yet. Or perhaps you noticed your fingers rubbing together, or your hands moving around and touching things, unconsciously, as if feeling for information. Touch is the first way we learn about the world, and in times of uncertainty we often revert to "feeling" our way.[1] Even if you didn't have any physical reaction, you probably felt the mental effort. Your brain works significantly harder the further you stretch your imagination into the future. And ten years is a particularly tricky challenge compared with one year, or two years, or five.

Why is that? To begin with, you've never been ten years older than you are right now. Your brain hasn't been there before, so it doesn't know what to expect. And there's so much opportunity for things to change in ten years—your body, your relationships, your life circumstances, your physical environment. Your brain intuitively grasps this uncertainty, this unknowability. It doesn't have the necessary data to simulate, perfectly, what might happen. So instead of projecting confidently one possibility into the future, your brain opens up *a blank space* for you to consider multiple possibilities. At this point, you have to start making intentional choices about what you *want* to imagine in your future. You have to fill in the blanks.

Filling in the blanks takes considerable mental effort. But it's precisely because of that stretch, that strain, that this kind of imagination is so powerful. Instead of simply remembering what it already knows, your brain has to invent a new possibility. It draws on past experiences, current hopes and fears, and your intuitions about what might change in the years ahead to bring something into the world that doesn't exist yet. You may have actually felt this "mental stretching" happening while you tried to imagine waking up ten years from today, your brain forging new neurological pathways, making a brand-new memory of something you haven't even lived through yet.

After you've made this new memory, something amazing happens: what was previously unimaginable to your brain is now *imaginable*. The next time you try to think about this possible future, a vivid mental image or detailed description will spring immediately to mind. You can use this new "memory of the future" to plan and prepare for the future much more effectively. You can revisit this memory whenever you want and examine how it makes you feel. Does it spark positive or negative emotions? These pre-feelings can help you figure out: Should you change what you're doing today to make this possible future more or less likely? And because you invented this memory, you can change it when-ever you want. You can alter the details as your hopes or fears change, or as you get more information about what your future might be like.

Scientists call this form of imagination *episodic future thinking*, or EFT. It's the mental ability to transport yourself forward in time and pre-experience a future event. EFT is often described as a kind of "mental time travel" because your brain is working to help you see and feel the future as clearly and vividly as if you were already there. But EFT isn't just thinking about the future; it's simulating the future in your mind. It's the difference between knowing that it's probably going to rain tomorrow—a kind of "fact" or abstract thought about the future—and *vividly imagining yourself in the rain*, trying to pre-feel the rain on your skin, and using everything you know about what tomorrow might be like to make the scenario more detailed and realistic. EFT might entail picturing where exactly you'll be when it starts to rain, what you might be wearing, who might be with you, whether you're likely to be annoyed by the rain or delighted by it, whether you'll rush to get somewhere dry or stroll leisurely through it, and so on.

Another way to understand EFT is to think of it as replaying in your mind an episode of a documentary or reality television series starring you, only the episode you're watching is set in the future. This analogy captures the often highly visual and narrative qualities of EFT: you see possible events of the future unfolding in your mind's eye as if they had already been captured on video.* More importantly, it

---

* For many people, imagination is a highly visual process—but this may not apply to everyone. You may not be a visual thinker, or you may be unable to conjure up mental images at all—that is, you may be part of the estimated 2 percent of the population that has the neurological condition aphantasia, or an inability to see with the "mind's eye." If so, you may find it helpful to work primarily with words and other sense memories instead of mental visualizations to complete the challenges and thought experiments in this book. Research shows that aphantasia does not impair creativity or foresight, so you can expect to benefit from imagination training as much as someone using his or her "mind's eye." Likewise, if you are visually impaired, and especially if you have been blind from birth, your imagination has a different quality than sighted people's, drawing more on shapes, textures, sounds, smells, etc. Studies suggest that in all other ways, however, mental simulation operates similarly for sighted and visually impaired individuals. So you can expect the techniques and research in this book to apply to you.

underscores the fact that EFT should be plausible, grounded in reality. EFT is *not* a daydream in which you fantasize about living a completely different life or waking up in a world where all your problems are magically solved. It is a way of connecting who you are today with what you might really feel and do in the future. This future might very well be better than today, but it will also undoubtedly come with challenges. So EFT isn't an escape from reality. It's a way of *playing with reality*, to discover risks and opportunities you might not previously have considered.

Because EFT allows us to pre-feel different possible futures, it's a powerful decision-making, planning, and motivational tool. It helps us decide: Is this a world I want to wake up in? What do I need to be ready for it? Should I try to change what I'm doing today to make this future more or less likely? It's also an incredibly demanding cognitive task. It's hard work for your brain to conjure up something that doesn't exist yet but *plausibly could*.

According to fMRI studies, which reveal patterns of brain activity, EFT involves heightened activity and increased connectivity between eleven distinct brain regions.[2] Compare this to remembering a past event or daydreaming about what someone else might be doing in the present. These forms of imagination activate just six of the same eleven regions of the brain as EFT; you need five additional regions firing to go on a mental time trip to your future.

Why does EFT require so much more mental effort than casual daydreaming or remembering? During EFT, you're not only trying to simulate in your mind something that isn't right in front of you; you're also actively trying to *make sense of it*.

There are three major kinds of sense making that happen when you time travel, mentally, to your future.

First, your brain has to do what cognitive scientists call *scene construction*—mentally building the world of the future. Where are you, what do you see, what's going on, and who else is there? Think of this as building the stage set, cast, and props for a theatrical play. Before you can imagine what you're going to do, feel, and say in this future, you have to know where it takes place, who's with you, and what objects surround you.

Scene construction also means establishing basic facts of the world, or what scientists call the *semantics*. Have you ever watched a movie trailer that began with a voice-over: "In a world where . . ." "In a land where . . ." "In a time when . . ."? Well, the same kind of voice-over moment happens in your brain at the start of EFT. The voice might say, "In a world that's pretty much the same as today," if you're not trying to stretch your imagination very far. But as you start to use EFT to imagine change in your own life and society, your scene construction might start with more surprising descriptions: "In a world where college is free," or "In a land where cars are banned," or "In a time when my kids are fully grown and out of the house," or "In a time when my kids are fully grown and back *in* the house." Playing with the semantics, or rules, of the future is one of the most important and creative tasks of EFT. The more freely you play with possibilities, the more challenges you'll be prepared for and the more opportunities you'll discover.

This scene-construction work is all hypothetical, of course. The future hasn't happened yet, so you can fill your mental stage with anything, and you can make any rules you want. So where, exactly, do these possibilities come from? How does your brain decide what to imagine?

During EFT, your brain goes on a kind of scavenger hunt for realistic details and plausible ideas. To do this, it activates the hippocampus, the seat of memory and learning, and starts digging through all of your memories, plus any other facts and ideas you've stored away. Depending on what kind of future you're trying to imagine—a hopeful one or a nerve-racking one, a familiar one or a strange one—the hippocampus identifies the most relevant stuff, and then retrieves and recombines it into a new scene. This means that *whatever you see in your future will always come from information your brain has already perceived and processed.* Anyone can imagine a future that looks more or less like today. But ideally, as you get better at imagining the unimaginable, you'll construct your scenes with an eye for change—incorporating not just obvious ideas and things that have been important in your past but also surprising ideas and things that could be important in your future.

That's why the single most important element of imagination training you'll do in this book is to start filling your brain with what I call "clues to the future," concrete examples of new and strange ideas that might shape how the future turns out. Looking for clues to the future means finding and examining evidence of changes that are already starting to happen today. When you have a hippocampus full of clues, your brain will have better data to draw on, and the scenes you construct will be way more interesting. This book is full of clues.

So YOUR HIPPOCAMPUS IS FIRED up, making up the rules for the future and setting the stage. What happens next during EFT?

After scene construction, your brain starts to do a kind of work that cognitive scientists call *opportunity detection*. In opportunity detection, you look for ways to fulfill your needs and achieve your goals. For example: If you predict you might be hungry when you wake up ten years from now, what will future you eat? If you imagine yourself lonely when you wake up, who will future you try to connect with? Opportunity detection is like an actor showing up for rehearsal and asking, "What's my motivation?" In other words: What do I want in this scene?

To figure out your motivation, your brain fires up the ventromedial prefrontal cortex (vmPFC), a region that's heavily used whenever you set goals and track your progress toward them. Like the hippocampus, which can draw on any memories or facts it wants, the vmPFC can suggest any goals you've ever had or previously considered. That's lots of raw material available. So how does the vmPFC decide which motivation to suggest?

One of the most interesting things about episodic future thinking is that the kinds of motivations that pop into your mind first are likely to be closely linked to your deepest values and most essential needs—especially when you think further into the future.[3] During EFT, your brain is freed from having to think about the practical details and duties of the present. Today, you may have a to-do list with a bunch of stuff on it that you'd rather not do, or that won't matter much in the long run. But when you consider your to-do list for ten years from today, you're starting with a clean slate. There aren't already twenty items on it, so you can imagine yourself doing whatever you *really* want. This is quite a lot of fun for your vmPFC. Now it can start generating goals that are entirely self-directed, based on whatever you've decided matters most. Maybe that's always learning something new, or helping others, or pushing yourself to do brave things, or taking care of your family, or being creative and putting new ideas or art into the world.

Whatever your future goals are, you still have to figure out the best way for future you to achieve them. At this point, one of the vmPFC's biggest helpers kicks in: the putamen, which is also part of the motivation and reward system. The putamen helps keep track of which specific actions and behaviors typically lead to positive results. It's the part of your brain that knows things like, "I feel better when I get some fresh air"; "I make my mom happy when I text her back right away"; "If I'm having a bad day, cooking helps"; "If I try to run a half marathon again without any training, I'm going to really regret it"; or "If I don't stand up for myself in the moment, I'll beat myself up about it later." The putamen is like a reality check on your future imagination. It helps you think more critically and strategically about whether the actions you envision yourself taking will in fact help you get what you want.

Since the putamen is trained on real experiences you've already had, whatever future actions it suggests will be heavily influenced by strategies that have worked for you in the past. That's why part of your imagination training in this book will be to try out new behaviors that might prove useful in the future. I call these *micro-actions*. They require you to take no more than five minutes to do something today that you've never done before. When you experiment with these kinds of tiny new actions, you expand what your putamen considers useful and realistic behavior. This will give you more ideas to work with as you try to imagine yourself being clever, helpful, brave, caring, creative, or whatever else you most want to be in your future.

Finally, as your brain works to transport you to the future, feelings will kick in. The insula and amygdala, both emotion centers in the brain, fire up to give you a preview, or pre-feeling, of how you might feel in the imagined scene: excited, disappointed, hopeful, afraid, proud, jealous, joyful, sad, curious, bored, embarrassed, relieved, loved, lonely, awed, confused, stressed out, or free. Positive or negative, these emotions give you important information. They help you decide: Is this a future I want to wake up in? Should I take actions today to make this future more or less likely?

Crucially, these aren't simulated feelings. They are real feelings. Studies show that the emotions you experience during EFT can be just as psychologically powerful as emotions experienced in the present.[4] This is one reason why many of us prefer to imagine best-case-scenario futures, and why we avoid imagining the futures that scare us—from climate change to economic bubbles bursting, what the next pandemic might be like or the possibility of life without a loved one. It's natural to feel this way. But there are real benefits to intentionally and carefully imagining futures that scare you. That's why the imagination training you'll do in this book will help you master techniques for acknowledging and transforming the negative emotions that come up as you do the important work of getting ready for anything—even the things you'd rather not think about, let alone actually experience, someday.

FROM SCENE CONSTRUCTION TO OPPORTUNITY detection to pre-feeling your emotions—now you know why it feels like you're really stretching your mind when you try to fill in the blanks of the future. From the hippocampus to the ventromedial prefrontal cortex, the putamen to the insula and amygdala, not to mention all the other supporting regions that get called into play—eleven different regions of your brain really are reaching out to each other to cooperate and create new neurological pathways. It's a complex process, but you can boil it down to something much simpler. Episodic future thinking, or taking a mental time trip to the future, means asking yourself four questions:

1. Where exactly am I, in my future—who else is here, and what's around me?
2. What's true in this version of reality that isn't true today?
3. What do I *really* want in this future moment, and how will I get it?
4. How do I feel, now that I'm here?

You might be wondering at this point how we know so much about episodic future thinking and the brain. In the past twenty years, there have been over five thousand peer-reviewed scientific studies published on the topic.[5] Why do scientists study it? For four reasons, mainly.

First, EFT is strongly linked with mental well-being.[6] People who engage in EFT are more likely to feel optimistic, motivated, and in control of their future. They are less likely to feel anxious or depressed. Researchers believe this is because *when you practice EFT, you learn to control your imagination.*

Scientists who study EFT have found that people who suffer from depression tend to imagine their future with only the vaguest of details. For them, a positive future is hard to imagine because their brain leaves too many of the mental blanks unfilled. For this reason, they can't vividly anticipate pleasure. They don't feel motivated by possible positive events. And they can't convincingly envision their future as being different from today. Their imagination gets stuck and leaves them, almost literally, with nothing to look forward to.

Individuals with anxiety tend to have the opposite problem. Their brain gets stuck thinking about possible negative future events in extremely vivid detail. They simulate, mentally, in highly convincing ways all the futures that scare them—no blank left unfilled. But they skip the step in EFT where their brain focuses on their deepest values and motivations and then strategizes how to get what they want and need.

EFT gives both groups more control over what they see in their mind's eye. Studies show that people with depression can use EFT to train their imagination to construct highly detailed scenes instead of vague ones, and choose to fill them with positive possibilities that really feel plausible. This significantly reduces symptoms of depression. Meanwhile, people with anxiety can train their imagination to always remember their positive motivations—the deepest values that drive them to move forward, bravely, even when there is risk of a negative outcome. And they can use EFT to make it easier to remember all the effective actions they already know how to take to help control how the future turns out. This significantly reduces symptoms of anxiety.[7]

Scientists also study EFT because a decline in EFT skills can be caused by a variety of health challenges that impact cognitive health, including aging-related dementia, post-traumatic stress disorder, concussion, and brain fog induced by chronic pain or chronic illness. A decline in EFT skills can cause people to have difficulty planning, preparing, and motivating themselves effectively for the future. This can lead to problems with everyday activities, like knowing what to bring with you when you leave home because you'll need it later, or actually buying a ticket for an event you plan to attend. And in extreme cases, especially with traumatic brain injury, an inability to vividly imagine the future can lead to suicidal ideation—because the brain literally can't imagine any future, let alone a positive one.

The growing evidence on how EFT relates to psychological well-being and cognitive health has led researchers to experiment with training techniques to improve EFT skills, to significant success. Many of the futures-thinking games and habits you're going to learn throughout this book are inspired by the same techniques used with clinical patients to improve their mental health and restore their cognitive abilities.

A third reason many researchers are interested in EFT is that it seems to be a highly effective tool for behavior change. Research shows that people who learn how to more vividly and plausibly imagine their own personal futures are more likely to make healthy eating choices, keep up new exercise or meditation habits, save money for long-term goals, complete their education, vote in elections, buy more sustainable and environmentally friendly products, break the cycle of addiction, and stick with any kind of long-term resolution to change.[8] What all these behaviors have in common is that they require us to make an effort or choice today that will have a *delayed benefit*. We have to be able to envision a long-term payoff, even if it's far in the future. That's where EFT comes in. If we spend more time imagining our future, it gets easier to make this kind of long-term investment. And we get a motivation boost from pre-feeling our future positive emotions.

What's particularly fascinating about the research literature on EFT is that *you don't have to imagine the future consequences of a particular behavior today* to feel more motivated to do that behavior. In other words, you don't have to specifically imagine yourself being fit, or graduating, or living in a beautiful, stable climate in the far future to become more likely to exercise, study hard, or buy sustainably today. Imagining literally *anything* you might experience in the far future, as vividly and realistically as you can, increases your motivation and likelihood of doing *anything* that has a longer-term benefit today. It's a completely generalizable benefit. So as you immerse yourself in a range of possible futures throughout this book, know that you're not just getting ready for that particular future. You're also priming yourself to do things today that will likely make you happier and healthier in whatever future you wind up in.

The fourth and final reason we know so much about what happens in the brain during EFT is that it's linked with creativity, something many people want to get better at.[9] In studies, when individuals complete an EFT challenge—challenges very much like the one you completed at the start of this chapter, such as, "Imagine yourself meeting a friend for breakfast a year from today," or "Imagine yourself taking a walk ten years from today"—they subsequently perform significantly better on various tests of creativity. The further out the future imagined, the stronger the effect: in studies, thinking about a year from today increased creative performance more than thinking about to-morrow, and looking ten years out increased it even more.

The relationship between EFT and creativity is so strong that even when researchers aren't studying EFT, they often use an EFT challenge to get study participants into a more creative mindset. It's a go-to trick for scientists who want to study creativity itself. So whatever your starting point in terms of EFT skill or creativity, when you practice and get better at EFT, you can expect to increase your general creativity as well.

OFTEN, WHEN I TEACH OR speak about EFT and its connections to mental health, cognitive ability, behavior change, and creativity, a parent or educator will ask me, "Should we be teaching this in schools?" or "Is this something I should be practicing with my kids? How young can you start doing this kind of training?" The simple answer is yes, I believe we should teach EFT in schools, and students can start quite young. The research shows that children typically develop all of the basic cognitive abilities necessary for EFT by the time they are just four or five years old.[10] Teens can certainly handle the imagination-training challenges in this book. If you're interested in working with younger kids to develop their future imagination, studies suggest that simply asking them the question, "What's something you're looking forward to doing (tomorrow, this weekend, on your birthday, next summer)?" can build EFT skills—especially if you then prompt them to draw a picture of this "future memory" or write a story about it, or even if you just ask follow-up questions that encourage them to share more specific and vivid details about the future event they're imagining.[11]

And while my own work has focused on engaging the public with large-scale simulations of potential future events, my colleagues at the Institute for the Future have also worked on much more targeted interventions, including EFT collaborations with aid workers providing psychological support for Syrian refugees; social workers helping formerly incarcerated people reduce their risk of being arrested for a new crime; and peace workers trying to end civil war in places like Sudan. What they have found is that episodic future thinking can be a powerful tool for hope, even in contexts where change is hard to imagine and futures are not guaranteed.

EPISODIC FUTURE THINKING IS THE central activity of preparing for "unthinkable" events and planning for "unimaginable" change—so I want you to get very good at it. Now that you know what EFT is, the rest of this book is organized to help you improve your EFT skills as you explore what future risks you want to be ready for and what positive changes you want to make in society and in your own life.

Would you like to know how good you are right now at episodic future thinking? Scientists have developed a number of tools to measure individual skill and ability at EFT. I've included an adapted version of these tools at the end of this chapter, and I encourage you to try them out. You can use these tools to track your progress and skill growth as you train your imagination. Whatever your score is the first time you measure your EFT skills, I am confident it will increase with each chapter of this book.

I WANT YOU TO TRY one more time travel experiment with me. Imagination works both ways in time. So let's take a ten-year trip in the opposite direction.

Let's go to the past and visit *ten-years-ago* you.

To imagine dramatic change in the future, it can help to remind yourself just how much has already changed in your life. When you're ready, I want you to picture in your mind's eye a day more or less ten years ago today.

Where would you have been on a typical day? What would you have been doing? Can you picture what you might have been wearing? Who were you with? What were you excited about ten years ago?

What were you worried about? What life goal were you working toward, or what life problem were you trying to solve?

It might not be easy to recall all these details at first. Keep working at it. Like episodic future thinking, *episodic memory* also requires you to stretch your imagination—if only because you're retrieving memories and reactivating thought patterns you haven't used in a while.

As you construct this ten-years-ago scene in your imagination, pay close attention to what was true about your life then that is no longer true today. How has your life changed in the past decade? Is there anything that's true about your life today that would have surprised past you? See if you can identify at least two or three surprising changes from ten years ago to today.

At the Institute for the Future, we call this technique "looking back to look forward." It's another excellent strategy for unsticking your mind. As the historian and activist Rebecca Solnit has written, "When you don't know how much things have changed, you don't see that they are changing or that they can change." When you need to look far ahead, try looking back at how far you've come.

IMAGINATION TRAINING

RULE #2: Learn to Time Travel.

Simulate in your mind what you might experience, feel, and do in the future as vividly and realistically as you can. This mental time travel, or episodic future thinking, stretches your imagination and helps you prepare for change by creating new memories of possible futures.

You can stretch your imagination further by asking yourself these questions:

Where exactly am I, in my future—who else is here, and what's around me? (*Build the scene.*)

What's true in this version of reality that isn't true today? (*Make the rules.*)

What do I *really* want in this future moment, and how will I get it? (*Detect opportunity.*)

How do I feel, now that I'm here? (*Pre-feel the future.*)

When you practice mental time travel, pay special attention to anything that could possibly, plausibly be different from today.

Score Your Mental Time Travel Ability

Each time you take a mental time trip to the future, you can score the power of your imagination using the following inventories. (An *inventory* is a scientifically validated questionnaire used to measure thoughts and feelings.) These inventories measure four different qualities of your imagination: how vivid and detailed it is, how absorbing and immersive it is, how emotionally provocative it is, and how flexible and creative it is. A higher score represents a stronger skill and ability at episodic future thinking.[12]

Even if you don't wind up using these inventories very often, try them out at least once or twice. It will increase your intuition about what it means to be "good" at mental time travel. And it will help you develop an internal sense of when you're stretching your imagination far enough, and when you might want to stretch further.

Tool #1: *How vivid and detailed is your imagination?*

Rate your response to the following questions on a scale of 1 to 7.

Overall, how vivid was the future scene you imagined?
(1 = it was very vague, 7 = it was extremely vivid.)

How clearly did you picture the imagined location or physical environment?
(1 = it was very vague, 7 = it was extremely clear in my mind.)

How clearly did you picture your physical self—and any possible changes to your body or what you look like—in this future?
(1 = it was very vague, 7 = it was extremely clear in my mind.)

How clearly did you picture other people and objects in the scene?
(1 = it was very vague, 7 = it was extremely clear in my mind.)

How many other sensory details, like sounds, smells, or physical sensations, did you imagine?
(1 = I imagined almost no details, 7 = I imagined many details.)

A higher score indicates a higher skill at episodic future thinking.

Tool #2: *How absorbing and immersive is your imagination?*

Rate your response to the following questions on a scale of 1 to 7.

How much do you agree with the following statement? "When I imagined the future scene, I had a feeling of pre-experiencing the event."
(1 = I don't agree at all, 7 = I totally agree.)

How much do you agree with the following statement? "I was completely absorbed in the scene I imagined. It was a very immersive experience."
(1 = I don't agree at all, 7 = I totally agree.)

A higher score indicates a higher skill at episodic future thinking.

Tool #3: *How emotionally provocative is your imagination?*

Rate your response to the following question on a scale of 1 to 7.

How strong an emotional reaction today did you have in the present as you imagined this future scene? The emotions might be positive (excitement, hope, pride, joy, curiosity, relief, contentment, love, awe, etc.) or negative (anxiety, sadness, embarrassment, jealousy, disappointment, fear, loneliness, etc.) or a combination of both. In other words, how much did you "pre-feel," in your mind and body today, the feelings you might have in this future?
(1 = I had almost no emotional reaction, 7 = I had an extremely powerful emotional reaction.)

A higher score indicates a higher skill at episodic future thinking.

Tool #4: *How flexible and creative is your imagination?*

Rate your response to the following questions on a scale of 1 to 7.

Reimagine the same future scene, but this time try to change as many details as possible while still keeping it plausible and realistic. For example, instead of waking up at 8:00 a.m., now imagine you're waking up at 5:00 a.m. Why would this be true, and how does it change the rest of the scene and story? The best way to use this measure is to *write down* a description of the future scene you've already imagined and *count the number* of details included. You can then try to change each and every detail to see how complete a reimagination you are able to achieve. How different would you say this new, reimagined scene is from the one you previously imagined?
(1 = the new scene is almost exactly the same, 7 = the new scene is almost entirely different.)

How realistic and plausible would you say this new, reimagined scene is? In other words, how believable is it to you that it could really happen?

(1 = it is extremely unbelievable, 7 = it is extremely believable.)

A higher score indicates a higher skill at episodic future thinking.

~~~~~~~~~~

Play with Future Scenarios

There are best-case scenarios, and there are worst-case scenarios.
But neither of them ever happens in the real world. What
happens in the real world is always a sideways-case scenario.

—BRUCE STERLING, science fiction writer

TEN YEARS INTO THE FUTURE IS A LONG WAY TO GO WITHOUT A GUIDE.
So for your next mental time trip, I'm going to send you off with a
resource you can use to find your way around an unfamiliar future—
something professional futurists call a *future scenario*.

A future scenario is a detailed description of a particular future
you might wake up in, a future in which at least one thing is dramatically different from today.

When you first encounter a future scenario, you'll find out: What,
exactly, has changed? How do things work now? What's the new
normal?

Your goal is to imagine waking up in this strange new world and
to envision it as vividly and realistically as you can, using your episodic

future thinking skills. When you imagine *yourself* in this future scenario, where exactly do you see yourself—and who else is with you? What do you really want to do in this future? How does it make you feel?

After you've stretched your imagination to answer these questions, you'll be asked to make a choice: "Now that you're in this future, what decision would you make if . . . ?" This decision point, or moment of choice, will be different for each scenario. It will give you the chance to consider how you might personally respond to the unique challenges and opportunities of this possible future.

Every social simulation I run starts with a future scenario. It helps everyone imagine the same possible future at the same time. And learning how to play with scenarios is your next imagination-training challenge. You can think about scenarios this way: before you take a trip, it helps to know where you're going. A future scenario gives you a *specific destination* for your imagination.

WHEN PLAYING WITH A FUTURE scenario, keep in mind two important rules:

Rule #1: Suspend your disbelief. No matter how strange the scenario seems to you, accept that this future is possible and works as described. Don't get into a mental argument with yourself about why it would never happen or how it could never work. Just go with it. You might think the changes described in a scenario are unlikely. Or you might flat-out hate the idea and want to skip right away to arguing why it could never happen. You can feel that way *and* you can still stretch your mind to imagine what you would do in the scenario anyway. In order to train your brain to think the unthinkable, you have to actively put possibilities in your brain *that your brain will naturally resist.* You don't want something to be unimaginable simply because you refuse to imagine it. Be willing to think hard about ideas you would normally dismiss as impossible, impractical, or even dangerous. In fact, if a scenario makes you feel a bit uncomfortable, that's a good sign that it's working.

Rule #2: See the future scenario from your unique point of view. If you wake up in this new world someday, you will still be you. A scenario isn't an exercise in fiction; it's an opportunity for personal exploration. Assume that in the future, you will have many if not all of the same values, personality traits, talents, strengths, and weaknesses that you have today. Be honest with yourself about how you might react and what you might feel. Positive emotions, negative emotions, helpful actions, selfish actions—everything is fair game and worth considering. No matter how different the new normal sounds, stay authentic and realistic to yourself.

Now that you know how scenarios work, let's start playing. It's time for a trip ten years into the future. It's not just any day we're leaping ahead to—it's a new national holiday called Thank You Day. When you get there, you'll discover you have a very important decision to make.

Future Scenario #1: Thank You Day

February 2, ten years from now

You wake up and it's February 2. You know what that means: it's Thank You Day. Every year on this holiday, you receive $2,000 from the government. You get to keep half. You have twenty-four hours to give away the other half.

You can't give the money to just anyone. This is a holiday meant to honor essential and frontline workers. There's a national registry of eligible recipients for your thank-you dollars. It includes health and care workers, teachers, public librarians, park employees, city bus drivers, and farmworkers. Everyone on the registry is someone who works in service of others, and whose salary doesn't reflect the full value of what they contribute to society.

On February 2, you get to honor someone on the registry who made a positive difference in your life—whether it was your favorite high school teacher, a nurse who cared for your premature baby in the NICU, or a maintenance worker at your neighborhood park. Or you can thank someone you've never met. The Thank You Day database will match you with someone based on your request—for example, a fruit picker who works at a farm that provides produce to your local grocery store. Each year, the registry is updated to reflect additional workers who were uniquely called upon to serve—whether firefighters during a historic wildfire season or grocery workers during a pandemic.

Thank You Day was created as a new kind of economic stimulus aimed to improve social well-being as much as economic security. The first $1,000 is universally paid to every citizen at least sixteen years of age. The second $1,000 gives participants the opportunity to do a powerful act of good for someone else, with the goal of creating stronger social ties in the community. You can make your gift anonymously, but most people celebrate Thank You Day by writing a gratitude letter or making a video for the person they are sending their thank-you dollars to. Many of the letters and videos are shared publicly online, and the most emotional go viral on social media.

Another goal of Thank You Day is to make lower-paid, essential jobs more financially attractive without mandating by law a significantly higher minimum wage for frontline workers. Although the rewards of Thank You Day are unpredictable, many people find themselves benefitting from an annual windfall.

If you prefer not to participate, you can say "No thank you," and the $2,000 assigned to you (and any other gifts you might receive) will be returned to the government.

~~~~~~

MOMENT OF CHOICE: Imagine waking up on Thank You Day ten years from now. Are you going to say "Thank you" or "No thank you"? If you do choose to participate, whom will you send your thank-you dollars to today, and why?

Welcome back to the present. Now that you've made your decision, let's keep playing with this possible future. Here are some additional questions to consider. Just let your mind wander through the possibilities:

- What was your first reaction to the idea of a Thank You Day? Do you love it? Hate it? Why?
- If you had to sum up your future emotions on Thank You Day in one word, what would it be?
- What kind of worker or volunteer would you advocate to add to the registry? Whom else would you want to thank in this future?
- Does this economic policy feel fair to you, or unfair? What would you change to make it more fair?
- Would having this system in place make you consider a change in your work life or career path? Do you think it would potentially change other people's career choices?
- How do you predict a national Thank You Day might change your relationships to others—particularly the people you thank or are thanked by?
- Did your mind jump to how people might try to game this system or exploit it? What might people do to corrupt the original intention of this holiday? Would these loopholes invalidate the idea for you, or would you tolerate them?
- Who might feel bad on Thank You Day, or choose to opt out? Can you think of a way to make this system work for them?
- What else might you do with friends or family on Thank You Day? What personal rituals or traditions would you add?

One of my favorite things about playing with future scenarios is that other people often have reactions that surprise me.

"I would feel proud in this future," one young woman told me about Thank You Day, "because it would be the first time in my life I could give that kind of help to someone else."

"I would feel at peace in this future," another person said, "because I could give back to people who have helped me in ways that I sometimes feel guilty about, like I don't deserve it."

"I'm sure there would be a lot of debate about who should be eligible for thank-you money," an activist friend of mine predicted. "So I would want to be an advocate for groups who might be overlooked. And I would feel excited to do that work."

I also heard from people who might be eligible for thank-you dollars in this future scenario:

"I'd feel left out if no one thanked me. I'd worry about being forgotten on Thank You Day."

"I'd feel too embarrassed to take advantage of it. I don't want to have to ask people to pick me instead of someone else on Thank You Day. It feels like begging."

"I would feel nervous. It would be easier if we could count on a higher regular salary instead of waiting to see how much we get thanked. But I can also think of so many people I'd want to thank, and that makes me happy. I love and hate this idea at the same time."

Having a love-hate relationship with a future scenario is a good thing. It means you're using both your positive and shadow imagination. You're asking: What's something good that could happen in this scenario? And: What's something bad that could happen in this scenario? You're considering it from more than one angle. And the more people you talk to about a scenario, the more angles you'll see. One friend I shared the scenario with wrote me back:

"My first thought was I'd want to throw a thank-you shower, like a surprise party where everyone gives their thank-you dollars to the same person, so we could really change their life. And then later it occurred to me, why not throw someone a thank-you shower for real? Not to shower them with $1,000 checks, that's not gonna happen, but to shower them with gratitude letters. Now I'm thinking I actually want to try this!"

"I would feel busy in this future," an entrepreneurial friend predicted. "Because I'd be setting up a new business called GoThankMe

.com. It would work just like GoFundMe, but it would help people tell their thank-you stories and put a spotlight on eligible workers. We would take a small percentage of the thank-you dollars as a service fee. Two hundred million adults, sending $1,000 each, we take 3 percent, that's potentially half a billion dollars a year revenue."

And another friend wrote me: "What this scenario is really making me think about is why we don't pay people more fairly. I'm sure if I woke up on Thank You Day, I would be excited to thank someone and curious to find out who all my friends and family thanked. But right now, my mind is spinning to figure out how else we could fix the problem of people who take care of us getting paid so little."

Any time you play with a future scenario, I encourage you to invite someone else along. So if there's someone you might like to share the "Thank You Day" scenario with, please do! Have a conversation about it and game out some possibilities together. When you go on a mental time trip with someone else, it helps to see the world through their eyes. It can teach you something about what matters most to them. And however they react, it gives your brain more ideas, more data, to imagine the future from a different point of view. If you really want to stretch your imagination, go ahead and post this scenario on social media. See how your entire network reacts! This is my favorite way to collect data about the future.

COULD SOMETHING LIKE "THANK YOU DAY" really happen? *Should* something like "Thank You Day" really happen? Every scenario in this book will be based on changes that are already starting to take place today. So let's start with what makes the "Thank You Day" scenario plausible.

Governments are increasingly experimenting with frequent cash payments as a form of economic stimulus. If you're an American, you may have experienced this yourself as a recipient of pandemic relief stimulus checks or child cash stimulus payments. Or you may have heard about the growing number of pilot programs for universal basic income (UBI), in which local residents receive an unconditional cash stipend to support their basic needs, often in the range of US$500–$1,000 a month. These programs are happening right now in places from rural South Korea to the suburbs of Rio de Janeiro to Stockton, California. And in 2021, Evanston, Illinois, became the first city in the United States to pay cash reparations to Black residents, who historically faced housing discrimination and were therefore unable to benefit financially from an appreciation in home values. Whether it's just-in-time relief checks, UBI, or cash reparations, there's a greater openness to previously unthinkable economic policies right now that could lead to any number of surprising new kinds of stimuli—such as the one in the "Thank You Day" scenario, which is paid for by the government but gifted by individuals.

There's also growing frustration with the disparity between what we call "essential work" and how we pay our essential workers. The people doing the most important jobs, the kinds of jobs that could not be shut down during the COVID-19 pandemic, are by no means being compensated with the highest salaries. We could imagine a more traditional approach to addressing this problem; for example, a state or the federal government might decide to make all income up to a certain amount tax-free for the most underpaid essential workers. Or we might see local, state, or federal minimum wages set significantly higher for frontline workers. (And frankly, these might be better solutions than the scenario you just considered.) But Thank You Day is an interesting if radical possibility for another reason. Filling in some of the income gap with cash paid by the government but gifted by individuals might help address another underlying condition in society: our fragile social trust and political division.

Eighty percent of Americans, according to the Pew Research Center, believe there is a fundamental incompatibility between their own core values and what many other Americans value—a difference usually defined by political party lines.[1] This polarization, fueled by partisan journalism, social media, and deeply rooted cultural divides, means that many of us have started viewing more people with suspicion or anger and approaching fewer people with a sense of common identity and compassion. Could a national day of gratitude and universal cash transfers help heal some of these divisions?

You could think of Thank You Day as a kind of reconciliation process, intended to remind people, regardless of our political views, of our common values and the benefits we all receive from essential and frontline workers. It might not actually lead to significant social healing, but what we're exploring here are reasons *why this policy might be created in the first place*, why it might be true in the future. And what's true today is that policy think tanks of both the conservative and progressive varieties have started advocating for experimental approaches to decreasing polarization.[2] So perhaps an idea like Thank You Day would be given a chance, as part of some future Great American Reconciliation plan.

Finally, consider this: a common reason given in surveys by people who oppose universal cash payments by the government is "money might go to people who don't really need or deserve it." In one large Reuters poll of Americans, for example, 52 percent of respondents said the government isn't doing enough to help the economically insecure— but among that same group who support *more* government aid, 40 percent said that most people who already receive cash aid don't deserve it.[3] This ambivalence is driven by a number of factors, ranging from a lack of awareness of the full range of reasons someone might experience economic insecurity to racist views that ethnic minority groups are less deserving than white people. For me as a futurist, knowing that nearly half of all people who support government cash aid would prefer to be able to pick and choose who "deserves" it— well, that's part of what makes me imagine that a scenario like "Thank You Day" is plausible and would be popular. At the same time, it makes me wonder what kinds of harmful biases and prejudices might be baked into and exacerbated by a system like Thank You Day.

So is this scenario a future we would actually want? I think it's fair to say there are potential upsides that make it exciting to imagine, and downsides that make it worrisome to imagine. Fortunately, we don't have to debate its merits with the urgency we would bring to a policy idea that's currently on the table. This, too, is a benefit of taking ten-year trips to the future. We can have strong opinions, but lightly held and open to reconsideration—because we're not being asked to make an important and binding decision today.

At the same time, taking this holiday seriously enough to imagine what it would feel like to celebrate it, even for a just a few moments, plants a creative seed. That seed might grow into real, actionable ideas—for example, about how to express our individual gratitude in new ways. Or it might point our attention to a problem in the present that deserves more of our collective creativity, like economic insecurity among our most essential workers. We don't have to wait a decade to take advantage of the insights a ten-year scenario affords.

"THANK YOU DAY" IS NOT a prediction of what the future will be like, or an argument for what the future *should* be like. It's an exploration of what the future *could* be like, based on things that are already true today. This is a key difference that we'll return to, again and again, in this book. Future scenarios should be plausible, but they don't have to be probable or even desirable to spark creative thinking and important conversations today.

Now that you've played with your first future scenario, let me tell you a little bit more about why scenarios are such an effective tool for strengthening your imagination.

Most people find it much easier to vividly imagine a future with the essential facts already filled in. A scenario does just that. When you play with a scenario, your brain doesn't have to do the "semantics" part of scene construction, where your hippocampus tries to answer the question, What's true in this future that isn't true today? This is often where people get stuck on mental time trips—they don't know how to begin to imagine a *specific* future. The scenario does this work for you. It lays out the basic description of a new reality, so you get to skip straight to the part where you make it personal and think about what *you* would do and feel in this future.

The decision point, or moment of choice, at the end of a scenario helps fill in another key mental blank of episodic future thinking: opportunity detection, in which you look for opportunities to take actions that are aligned with your deepest values and help you achieve your most important goals. A scenario's decision point defines the *first* opportunity for action for you. It helps make sure you don't find yourself at a loss for ideas. Instead, you get to jump right into making a move.

Not all professional futurists include a decision point in their scenarios. I do it because of something I learned in the video game industry. Professional game developers will tell you that if you want someone to stick with a game, you have to give them an opportunity to be successful in the first few minutes. A player who wanders around a new game without a clear sense of purpose is not going to have as much fun as someone with a goal. And a player with no idea what actions they can take in the game is not going to stick around very long. The same thing is true, I've found, for thinking about the future.

If we are given a clear purpose within the first minute of imagining the future—*here is a choice you have to make right now*—we feel more engaged. And we get to experience a quick moment of agency when we realize, "This is a decision I would feel good about making," or "Yes, this is an action I really could see myself taking." This moment of agency changes our relationship to a possible future. The future starts to feel a little more familiar, like a place where we could find our way, discover something new, help others, and achieve our goals. In other words, the future starts to feel more like a good game.

That's why, when I create new scenarios, I playtest them just as I would playtest a new game. I run the scenario by as many people as possible to make sure it makes sense and draws them in. I ask people: Is this fun to think about? Is it obvious what the first challenge or obstacle or choice in this future is? Were you able to come up with a strategy you feel good about?

I also watch to see if people make lots of different choices and come up with lots of different strategies. A diversity in possible moves and strategy is essential in any game; if every player plays the same way, the game gets boring fast. (Think: tic-tac-toe.) The same goes for future scenarios. The more divergent the reactions, the more we can learn from each other about what the future could or should be like.

When I playtest a scenario, I also wait to see if someone has a surprising reaction, one that catches me off guard. In gaming, this is called "unintentional emergence"—when the players do something truly unexpected, like the *Minecraft* players who started re-creating ancient cities and building working roller coasters, guitars, and even quantum computers inside the virtual world. As a game designer, you look forward to these moments, because they mean you're helping people express and increase their creativity. So when I collect reactions to future scenarios, I look out for surprises and then I keep adjusting the details of the scenario, the same way I would fine-tune the rules of a game, until I reliably see that spark of deep attention and creativity that tells me the future scenario is guiding people to a future worth imagining.

Speaking of fine-tuning: there's one more thing I want you to keep in mind as you play with the scenarios in this book. If there is something about the way the future world is described that you would like to change to make it more plausible or desirable, feel free to change it. For example, if some detail in the "Thank You Day" scenario made you think the policy would fail or lead to unintended harms, just rewrite it to make that future possibility better. Scenarios, like the future, are never "stuck"; rewriting a future scenario is a rehearsal for changing reality itself.

READY FOR ANOTHER TEN-YEAR TRIP? Let's play with another future scenario together.

Future Scenario #2:
"Have You Checked the Asteroid Forecast?"

A Monday morning, ten years from today

You wake up to breaking news: the United Nations Office for Outer Space Affairs has released its latest asteroid forecast. The news isn't great. The likelihood of a catastrophic event has increased to 5 percent. Last month, it was only 1 percent.

The impact date is still the same: May 1, three years from now. There is plenty of time to get ready . . . if there's anything you really need to get ready for. There's still a 95 percent chance nothing bad will happen.

Here's what the scientists *are* sure about: Multiple space agencies have detected an asteroid approaching Earth. The exact size of the asteroid isn't known. It could be as small as fifty meters or as large as one kilometer. The good news: At worst that's only one-tenth the size of the asteroid that killed off the dinosaurs sixty-six million years ago. Humanity will survive this impact.

The bad news: it's still big enough to wipe out an entire city, at the low end of the size estimate, and at the high end, a whole country.

No one knows for sure where the asteroid will hit, if it hits. But based on current orbits, scientists have identified a potential "ring of impact" around the planet. Depending on where Earth is in its rotation when the asteroid hits, any city or country located on the ring is vulnerable.

The place where *you* live is on the ring of impact.

Scientists and governments are working together to create a plan to deflect the asteroid, using lasers, spacecraft, and potentially a nuclear bomb. Will the plan work? It's never been tried before. Some experts sound confident, but many others are urging communities located on the ring of impact to start planning for mass evacuation and relocation should the probability of impact increase.

You can't help but wonder: How seriously are you supposed to take this forecast? Is mass evacuation and relocation of an entire city, let alone an entire country, even possible in less than three years? What if people don't start evacuating until months, or weeks, or days before impact? What resources will people need to leave? What if people are unwilling to leave? Should *you* be getting ready to leave? Where will you go? These are the thoughts spinning in your mind as you absorb the latest asteroid forecast and get ready for your day.

Imagine yourself waking up to this news ten years from now. Visualize the scene as clearly as you can. Where are you waking up, and whom are you with? How do you get the news? Is it a notification on your phone or a trending story on social media, a livestream video or a link from a family member? In one word, how do you feel? Remember: the more specific details you fill in, the more effective your mental time trip to the future will be.

When you have the scene clearly in your mind, it's time for you to make your first decision in this future.

~~~~~~~

MOMENT OF CHOICE: After hearing the news, whom do you want to talk to about what this asteroid forecast means for you? Will you hold a family meeting? Or call a company meeting? Is there a trusted friend or spiritual advisor whose opinion you would seek out? Will you organize a neighborhood or campus meetup? What thoughts would you share? What options would you discuss?

Welcome back to the present. Now that you've made your choice, let's keep playing with this possible future. Here are some additional questions to consider. Just let your mind wander through the possibilities:

- If this really happened, would you think about the asteroid forecast often, or would you try to block it from your mind and get on with normal life?

- Do you think a forecast like this would cause widespread panic, or would most people shrug it off?
- Would you personally make an effort to learn more about the science of asteroid detection and prevention, or would you leave it to the experts?
- What kinds of actions could you imagine yourself or other people taking in the coming weeks and months after hearing this news?
- How high do you think the probability of the forecast would have to get for most people to take action to prepare for impact? Fifty percent? Eighty percent? One hundred percent?
- Are there any risks to telling the public about a future asteroid impact?
- What do you think might be one positive result of a forecast like this? Can you imagine it leading to something good—either in your own life, or in society?

I encourage you to give these questions a good think or to have a quick discussion with someone else about this scenario before you read on.

COULD A SCENARIO LIKE "HAVE You Checked the Asteroid Forecast?" really happen? Definitely.

The United Nations Office for Outer Space Affairs really exists, and together with the European Space Agency and the International Academy of Astronautics, they host an event every two years called the Planetary Defense Conference. (I was lucky enough to attend in 2021.) Experts from around the world gather to discuss the threat to Earth posed by asteroids and comets, and to consider what actions could be taken to deflect a threatening object. Participants debate how best to share information and research about potential threats with the public. Most exciting to me, the conference includes a weeklong social simulation, using a scenario similar to the one you just imagined. The attendees work together to analyze evolving data about a fictional asteroid and debate various recommendations for how the planet should respond.

Everything you just read in the scenario above is based on how these space agencies already track, study, analyze, and publicly provide forecasts of asteroid threats. You can check out NASA's current one-hundred-year asteroid forecast for yourself if you like; as of this writing, they are tracking twenty-one near-Earth objects that could potentially collide with our planet.[4] Fortunately, according to NASA, the probability of an asteroid capable of destroying a city striking Earth is extremely low: just 0.1 percent every year. If one does hit Earth, there's a 70 percent chance it will land in the ocean and a 25 percent chance it will land over a relatively unpopulated area, leaving just a 5 percent chance an actual city would be impacted. The asteroid forecasts you hear in your lifetime will almost certainly not be quite as dramatic as the one you just imagined. But given how disruptive and life-altering it would be if NASA really *did* sound the alarm, wouldn't you like to have spent at least a little time pre-feeling your anxiety and pre-thinking your strategy? It's good for imagination training, at any rate.

There's another future scenario lurking underneath this one that *is* much more likely to happen—in fact, it's almost inevitable, according to most climate scientists. It's the possibility that many cities and nations will need to relocate their entire populations over the next fifty years, because of the growing climate crisis. If you change "asteroid" to "rising sea levels," "year-round wildfires," or "extreme heat incompatible with human life," you can increase the probability of this scenario from one in twenty thousand to closer to one in two. Yet even with this much higher degree of scientific certainty, humanity is not acting very quickly to plan for a safe, peaceful, and equitable mass migration. This is a topic we'll return to later in this book, because there is an urgent need for creative thinking around how to handle large-scale climate relocation. The United Nations currently estimates that between 150 million people and 1 billion people will be faced with the question of whether to stay in their homes and continue trying to defend their land from climate threats or become climate migrants.[5] Low-lying cities like Miami, New Orleans, Copenhagen, and Shanghai could disappear as sea levels rise. Large portions of northern Africa, the Middle East, northern South America, South Asia, and parts of Australia would be so hot as to be "incompatible with human life," according to a 2020 study prepared by an international research team of archaeologists, ecologists, and climate scientists. We all should start to pre-feel and pre-experience a mass migration event in our own communities, so we can start to prepare for an event exponentially bigger than the migration and refugee crises we are already experiencing today.

YOU MAY HAVE NOTICED THAT the asteroid scenario sounds more like the premise for a Hollywood blockbuster than a long-term climate forecast. This is intentional, and another benefit of playing with scenarios. To convince our brains to do the hard work of imagining hard-to-imagine futures, we have to move out of a state of boredom, distraction, or indifference and into a mindset of high interest, curiosity, and attention. The asteroid scenario, while far less probable than a mass climate migration, is a much more vivid kind of crisis to imagine. There's a giant fiery object hurtling through space! And an asteroid moves so much faster—over forty thousand miles per hour!—than the comparatively plodding pace of the sea level rising one-eighth of an inch per year. It is more exciting (if also potentially horrifying) for most people to think about, compared to the "mundane" climate crisis that so many people have already learned to ignore. The asteroid just sounds like something we should be tackling more urgently.

Many of the scenarios that you'll play with in this book will be significantly more dramatic-sounding than the actual futures you might need to prepare for. This is by design. When we face more extreme circumstances, we are more creative in our responses and more

willing to consider doing things differently. The drama helps boost the
brain's willingness to play. But using an asteroid scenario as a stand-in
for thinking about a climate crisis isn't just about upping the drama. It
also creates psychological distance from the real topic of climate
change, which many people are either completely checked out of (because they don't think it's a serious risk) or emotionally exhausted by
(because they feel powerless to stop it). Most people aren't mentally
stuck when it comes to the subject of asteroids, if for no other reason
than that they haven't really thought about planetary defense deeply
enough to have a strong fixed opinion on it yet. They haven't been
lectured or lobbied about asteroids enough yet to feel any "asteroid
fatigue" the way we do with climate change. An asteroid crisis feels
fantastic enough and far enough removed from reality for us to be able
to safely imagine it without getting anxious or overwhelmed, and to
not be so stuck in our preexisting assumptions.

The point isn't to trick people into thinking about something
they'd rather not think about—although if that's the only way you can
get them to do it when it comes to a truly urgent global challenge, I
say it's fair play. When I use the asteroid scenario in class, I explain to
students *before* we play with it that it's designed to help us think through
our response to the climate crisis. They know they're getting psychological distance, and they *still* benefit from the game.

Scenarios can be about futures we never expect to actually live
through, and still be incredibly useful. But for me, the asteroid scenario already hits home. My family is having the climate migration
conversation right now.

We live in an area of California that's high-risk for wildfires. Each
year, we find ourselves living through longer and longer periods of
wildfire trauma. For two to three months, that means near-constant
evacuation warnings. It means living with all our valuables and keep-
sakes in a box by the front door so we can take it with us if we have to
flee quickly. It means preemptive power outages that reduce fire risk
(good) but leave us without internet or electricity for days at a time

(bad). It's air quality that's so dangerous, so full of toxic smoke and pollution, that we have to put duct tape over every window and vent, and we can't spend even a minute outside without harming our health.

It feels, frankly, unlivable. But the rest of the year, we love our home and our community and nearby family; so for now, it *also* feels unimaginable to consider leaving.

We are trying to imagine it. We are making space in our minds to consider the very real possibility that our home, and our town, will become uninhabitable because of extreme fire risk—and not just for our family but for the entire community. Some futurists have gone so far as to suggest that Californians with the means to do so will become a kind of migratory species, relocating to another part of the world for a couple of months every year to avoid the annual nightmare.

I've tried to envision an annual migration. So far we haven't come up with any ideas that feel realistic for our family, and we're not sure we could convince our extended family to migrate with us. We'll keep imagining. Perhaps with remote work and remote school, we could make it work. In the meantime, we are advocating for things that will make it possible to stay here in the wildlife-urban interface, like increasing road access in and out of town so more people can safely evacuate if need be. We vote for political candidates who want to adopt and fund aggressive fire-mitigation strategies, such as controlled burns that create a buffer zone between high-risk land and people's homes. We donate to places like the Stanford Woods Institute for the Environment, which is working on technologies that give us hope for the future—like a sprayable gel made from natural materials that acts like an annual wildfire vaccine for high-risk vegetation.

We do these things because the more vividly we imagine the worst-case scenario, the more motivated we feel to try to prevent it. At the same time, if we do one day have to leave—if we *all* have to leave—our family will be better mentally prepared to make that difficult decision for having imagined it now, and be better able to help others who have to make the same choice.

. . .

THE COVID-19 PANDEMIC UNFOLDED MORE like an asteroid scenario
than like climate change. It motivated social sacrifice and global scientific coordination faster than any previous event in human history. The
novelty of the crisis and the fact that it could surge anywhere on the
planet next created a sense of urgency, a willingness to try radical
collective action. We didn't have time (at least not in those first few
weeks and months) to normalize the potential harm or suffering. Instead, humanity reacted to the emergency it was.

But there are other preventable global threats that kill far more
people each year than the coronavirus did, and we more or less ignore
them. Air pollution from burning coal, gasoline, and diesel kills an
estimated 8.7 million people every year, four times as many as
COVID-19 did in 2020, accounting for nearly one in five deaths
worldwide.[6] Meanwhile, 1.5 million people die from drinking contaminated water each year, and 1.5 million people are killed in roadway
accidents.[7] Where's the coordinated, urgent global response? These
threats have been unfolding for decades, and many of us have normal-
ized their impacts. We barely even try to imagine a world in which
pollution and motor vehicles don't kill millions of people annually. It
doesn't help that 92 percent of pollution-related deaths happen in
low- and middle-income countries, or that the crash death rate is three
times higher in low-income countries.[8] Richer countries feel they've
escaped the "ring of impact" of these ongoing crises. Maybe if we
could unstick our minds and see these crises with the urgency and
unity of a pandemic, we might find that so many seemingly unsolvable
problems are in fact solvable, and fast.

Can you imagine what we could accomplish if humans—governments, scientists, schools, workplaces—tackled a different global challenge each year with the urgency, creativity, unity, and willingness to
sacrifice of our COVID-19 response? Let's at least *try* to imagine it.

In this book, you'll have the chance to play with twelve more future scenarios, some of which are designed to create a bit more of that

"asteroid urgency" or COVID-19 unity for crises many of us seem to have stopped worrying about. I hope they inspire you to rethink just how quickly and dramatically we could make a better world for all in the coming decade.

IMAGINATION TRAINING

RULE #3: Play with Scenarios.

Take a mental time trip to a specific future where at least one thing is dramatically different from today. When you play with a scenario, suspend your disbelief and stay realistic and authentic to yourself. Embrace the drama of an extreme scenario to increase your creativity and open-mindedness. Find a sideways approach to imagining the futures you'd rather not think about. Invite others to play with scenarios with you, so you can expand your imagination and feel the future from others' points of view.

4

Be Ridiculous, at First

Every now and then one's mind is stretched by a new idea or
sensation, and never shrinks back to its former dimensions.
—OLIVER WENDELL HOLMES SR., poet and physician

WHERE DO IDEAS FOR FUTURE SCENARIOS COME FROM?

If *you* wanted to describe a world that doesn't exist yet, how would you start?

It's one thing to be able to imagine a scenario that a professional futurist comes up with. It's another creative challenge entirely to invent your own "unthinkable" futures. I want to unlock this creative process for you. It starts with something known to futurists as Dator's law.*

---

* Dator's law is named for Jim Dator, one of the founders and leading figures in futures thinking, best known for creating the first PhD program in future studies in the world, within the department of political science of the University of Hawai'i at Manoa. After forty years of teaching future studies and doing future research, he formalized his "laws of the future" in a 2007 self-published essay, "What Futures Studies Is, and Is Not" (http://www.futures.hawaii.edu/publications/futures-studies /WhatFSis1995.pdf).

Dator's law is so fundamental to futures thinking that if you visit the Institute for the Future in Palo Alto, California, you will find it painted right on our front windows:

"Any useful statement about the future should at first seem ridiculous."

Stay with that for a minute. *Any useful statement about the future should at first seem ridiculous.* What, exactly, does that mean?

Well, it's easy to prepare for futures that are similar to today, futures that "make sense," that seem normal and reasonable. It's the weird stuff that catches us off guard. It's the possibilities that make us say, "That's ridiculous, that could never happen," or "I can't even imagine it"—those are the possibilities we have to spend time taking seriously. Because those are the futures that will be most shocking, disruptive, and challenging if they come to pass.

Imagine if, in late 2019, you had been asked to consider the following ideas: In the near future, virtually all nations will shut and lock down their borders. One billion children will stop going to school and do all of their learning at home. Four hundred million jobs will be deemed nonessential and disappear virtually overnight. It will be against the law to hug your grandmother. (Where I live in California, that was true, thanks to social distancing rules, for most of 2020.) In 2019, wouldn't these ideas have seemed ridiculous, at first? But a few months later, they were our reality. If you'd had even just a few extra months to imagine how a pandemic lockdown might affect you before it actually started, how might you have practiced or prepared? Who would you have been better able to help?

We need to prepare our collective imagination for exactly these kinds of "unimaginable" possibilities—so if they do happen, we're not frozen with anxiety or stuck in our old ways. The good news is, all it requires is that we become willing to *take in information that challenges our assumptions about what can and cannot change.* And this is precisely what Dator's law encourages us to do.

It may seem like a paradox, but it is precisely *because* a future scenario seems ridiculous that it can be so useful. Any scenario that you instinctively dismiss as impossible or outrageous reveals a potential blind spot in your imagination. Now, I'm not saying you should spend all your time getting ready for wild possibilities that may or may not have any real probability of happening. What makes for a useful future scenario is that it seems surprising or improbable or unfathomable *at first*. It's *ridiculous, at first*, but the more you think about it, the more plausible it seems. This is the crucial second half of Dator's law. A useful future scenario is like a tip-off you can use to investigate further. You discover that if you look in the news and around your own community, you can find evidence for the scenario in changes that are already starting to happen today, changes that for most people would be easy to underestimate or overlook.

Coming up with ridiculous, at first, ideas about the future means having your eyes fully open, so you can collect evidence of new and surprising possibilities. It means having an ear to the ground, so you notice the rumbles of change faster and can warn others about what's coming. To do this, you also have to somehow find a way to trick your brain into noticing things it would ordinarily overlook. But how do you build these skills?

At the Institute for the Future, I've designed and tested numerous ways to help people get better at coming up with ridiculous, at first, ideas. The two most effective training methods, it turns out, are both brainstorming games that work best when you play them with others. Learning how to play these games, so you can generate your own ridiculous, at first, ideas, is the first step to developing your own future scenarios. When you get the hang of the rules, you can invite others to brainstorm the future with you.

In this chapter, we'll play Stump the Futurist.

I'll be the futurist. You try to stump me.

Your goal is to make a list of things that cannot change, will not change, in the next decade. What do you think is true about how the world works today that you believe will *definitely* still be true at least a decade from now? For example: In ten years . . . governments will still require citizens to pay taxes. In ten years . . . cars will still have wheels. In ten years . . . dogs will still be the most popular pets. In ten years . . . most people on earth will still own and use mobile phones. Before you read on, take a moment to write down at least one unchangeable fact. (I encourage you to write it down somewhere because we're going to try to prove you wrong later!)

I give my students this exact same challenge on the first day of my How to Think Like a Futurist class. "Go ahead," I say, "what is one thing you are nearly 100 percent confident will be pretty much exactly the same ten years from today?" The two answers I hear most often from my students are, "It takes a man and a woman to make a baby," and "Humans will always need oxygen to breathe." Fair enough!

Whatever they come up with, I take their assertions back to my colleagues at the institute, and together we try to prove them wrong. We look for clues that those seemingly unchangeable truths might already in fact be changing. And what do you know, just a few weeks after the very first time I played Stump the Futurist, this headline popped up: "Exclusive: World's First Baby Born with New '3 Parent' Technique."[1] A news story from England described an experimental fertility treatment called "pronuclear transfer," which combines the genetic material of *two women* and one man to make one baby. It's being used today primarily to help parents avoid passing on genetic diseases, and it's legal in only a few countries. But babies are already being born using this method, which means that the most basic fact of human reproduction—that it combines the genetic material of just two people—can already be different.

As a futurist, I can't help but start to consider the implications of this clue. The "three-parent" fertility treatment is very rare today. But can we imagine a future where the *default preference* for making a baby is to do it as a trio instead of a duo? No, I don't think this is a likely scenario. But I really enjoy how it opens my mind. I like trying to empathize with why a future family might want to make a baby as a threesome. What *would* a world with a "traditional three-parent household" be like? How might work and caretaking and parenting roles evolve if everyone did it in threes? There's already tremendous diversity in family structure, from single-parent households to unmarried co-parenting to blended families. Changing the *reproductive* structure to a three-parent one, where many babies have two biological mothers and one biological father, would add a new possibility to the mix.

If you feel your brain fervently resisting this possibility of three-parent babies—if you hate it, if you find it ridiculous, or if you have moral or ethical concerns burning you up as you imagine it— great! You have found a scenario that will help you practice taking in information that makes you uncomfortable. This is a crucial imagination-training skill.

The second time I tried playing Stump the Futurist with a class, another clue appeared: Cambridge University researchers are figuring out how to create babies with genetic material from two same-sex parents, announced a news story.[2] This truly was news to me at the time. Although no baby has been born this way yet, scientists seem optimistic that within a decade, their method of using stem cells and gene editing could allow *just* two men, or *just* two women, to make an embryo—no opposite-sex genetic material required. It would be a real game changer for LGBTQ couples who want to start a family.

By the third time I played Stump the Futurist, this had happened: Scientists in China had successfully created healthy mice babies with same-sex parents, also using stem cells and gene editing.[3] The babies had two female genetic parents; no male mice contributed any genetic material to the offspring whatsoever. This "unchangeable" future was moving even faster than I expected.

By the most recent time I played Stump the Futurist, even more had changed: now scientists were talking about creating life from scratch, using artificial wombs, no eggs, no sperm, no traditional genetic parent required at all![4] Then in early 2021, researchers at the Weizmann Institute of Science in Israel revealed that they had been able to remove embryos from the uteruses of mice at five days of gestation, about a quarter of the way through a full mouse gestation period, and then grow them for six more days in artificial wombs.[5] (For ethical reasons, the scientists stopped halfway short of incubating the embryos to full-term.) Their achievement raises profound questions about whether, when, and why humans might decide to explore a shorter natural gestation period for their babies followed by a longer artificial one.

The artificial womb concept is alarming to many people who view it as a violation of the natural order of life. If this describes your own reaction, you may be reassured by the public position of most researchers working on this technology: it's being developed only to help extremely premature babies and not as a wide-scale alternative to traditional pregnancy. But as we've seen so many times in human history, a technology often gets used in ways its creators did not intend or anticipate. And although vastly fewer in number, some researchers are openly discussing the potential benefits of liberating women from the physical, psychological, and economic toll of a nine-month pregnancy.[6]

For those willing to take this ridiculous, at first, idea seriously, it opens up an important conversation about whether many or any women would want the option to gestate a baby externally—and if so, why. It also gives us the chance, before the technology works in humans, to predict possible harms that would come along with any benefits. For example: Would mothers deemed "high-risk" because of a history of drug use or alcohol abuse be forced against their will to gestate externally, to protect the baby? Would women considering abortion be required to allow the state to gestate their embryo to full-term, before putting the baby up for adoption? Far better to start discussing these potential consequences now, while there's still at least a decade to influence policy and regulation.

As we collected these clues to the future of human reproduction, my students and I became more and more curious about the motivations for this kind of research. Why might humans want to be able to create life from scratch, without eggs and sperm? What perceived needs or desires have convinced scientists to develop these technologies? We discovered that many researchers are predicting a significant decline in human fertility in the coming decades.

Reproductive epidemiologists have found that over the past fifty years, the total sperm count of men worldwide has dropped by more than 50 percent, and the DNA carried by sperm is increasingly damaged. Miscarriage rates for women have also increased every year for the past two decades.[7] Why? Hormone-disrupting chemicals in plastics, electronics, food packaging, and other everyday objects have altered the natural levels of testosterone and estrogen in our bodies. Exposure to air pollution of all kinds, from industrial emissions to wildfire smoke, is also linked to fertility decline.[8] Men in particular seem affected. If these trends continue, a decade or more from now, artificial reproductive technologies may become not just a curiosity but a necessity.

The ridiculous, at first, idea that you won't need a man *or* a woman to make a baby in the future does turn out, I think, to be a useful one. It draws our attention to trends that are harming human health—trends we could do something about now, for example, by banning hormone-altering chemicals, or at least eliminating them from our own bodies and homes, and taking steps to lower toxic air pollution. It points us to alternatives to conventional parenting and family structures, which might be helpful to explore for social, psychological, and economic benefits, even aside from fertility methods. It gives us a chance to tackle ethical concerns about new technologies before they are widespread and harder to control. And like all useful ideas about the future, it may bring clarity to decisions we have to make today.

At the end of each class I teach, I ask students to share with me their biggest "aha" moment. Teresa, who works for the government in Brazil, took my online class in 2021, and the clues we discovered to the future of fertility made a deep impression on her. I asked for permission to share Teresa's "aha" moment for this book:

> I come from a very religious family. When I had my third miscarriage, I was told it was God's plan for me. I didn't see it that way.

My husband and I wanted to try IVF. But IVF is not acceptable in our church. So we have been unsure and torn about what to do.

I took the Futures Thinking class for work, and maybe that was part of God's plan. It helped me imagine living in a future where it's normal to get help having babies. I imagined that it was ten years from today, and I had chosen to not use IVF when I had the chance. As a result, we never had children. Future me felt very angry that I had been talked out of doing something I wanted to do.

I realized I don't want to wake up and look around and see, wow, now it's possible to do all of these crazy extreme things to make a baby, and I didn't even try IVF. I could really feel how much I would regret it. And I just felt certain that the future would not judge us for doing this, that in the future it will be better understood and acceptable. So we are going forward, we are going to try to start our family with IVF. I don't need to wait for the future to give me permission, I am giving myself permission now.

You may not be thinking about having a baby in the future, let alone a three-parent baby, a "from scratch" baby, or an externally gestated baby. But paying attention to these kinds of clues is important. This mental habit, of always challenging what you believe could or could not be different, and actively looking for evidence that literally anything can change—even something that has been true for all of evolutionary history—gives you a powerful foundation for spotting any kind of change faster, so you can adapt faster and prepare to help others more effectively.

There's one more important rule to Stump the Futurist. When I play with my students, we discuss all the evidence I've collected, and then I ask them to vote on whether I've convinced them: Could this "unchangeable" fact be different in the next decade, or not? I make it a point of pride that I am very rarely stumped with a truly unchangeable fact. I can open most students' minds to the possibility of pretty much anything becoming different in the next ten years. And this is a skill *you're* going to develop too.

So let's try it again. What else can't be different in the next decade? Here's one that almost really did stump me when a student suggested it: "The sun rises in the east and sets in the west every day." Yes, it is very hard to imagine such a fact changing! But I did what all good futurists do when we have no idea what a particular future might be like: I started Googling "the future of sunsets." I was looking for recent news stories, scientific papers, and experts on social media who had anything to say on the topic.

I quickly discovered evidence that for some humans, sunsets really could be different in the future. Some people may soon live in a world with sunrises and sunsets that *don't* happen every day—at least, not by our standard definition of a "day" on Earth. Anyone living on Mars would have to wait longer than a day (at least, an Earth day) for a sunrise or sunset, because a day on Mars is slightly longer than a day on Earth. I excitedly brought back to my class videos and photographs of the sun rising and setting on Mars, captured by NASA's Mars-exploring robot. *Ta-da!* Proof that the future of sunsets could be different.

But wait, they said. Who, exactly, is going to be watching the sun rise differently on Mars in the next decade? Is this a ridiculous, at first, idea—or just a ridiculous one?

We dug deeper. It turns out there are plenty of space entrepreneurs trying to develop the technology to help humans settle on Mars as soon as possible. Elon Musk and his SpaceX company is the best known, but there are at least thirteen other companies working with NASA to make Mars settlement more feasible—including Lockheed Martin, which is developing autonomous robots to grow and harvest plants so people could feed themselves in space.[9] Meanwhile, the United States, China, Japan, Russia, India, and the United Arab Emirates all have unmanned research programs underway aimed at the red planet, with an eye toward sending humans in the 2030s. Musk meanwhile predicted in 2019: "It's possible to make a self-sustaining city on Mars by 2050, if we start in 5 years."[10] And the UAE says it wants to build a massive Martian city of six hundred thousand inhabitants by the year 2117. That's a lot longer than ten years away. But if the first manned missions to Mars start in the 2030s, then at least *someone* will potentially be living in the future of sunsets relatively soon.[11]

And Mars is definitely a place where everything can be different—not just sunsets. To survive on the red planet, we would have to reinvent society: how we eat, how we organize, how we vote, how we live. Musk and Amazon founder Jeff Bezos have both publicly stated that they are excited to rethink things like governance and laws on Mars, using the newly settled planet as a chance to experiment and redesign civilization. I can't come up with a better reason for more of us, not just the space entrepreneurs, to start thinking seriously about life on Mars. After all, who do we want reimagining and reinventing civilization for future generations? Should it be a few men lucky enough to be able to afford to take Mars settlement seriously, or should it be all of us?

I personally don't intend to be a Mars settler, and I'm not sure how happy I would be if my kids decided to volunteer as space settlers. (Honestly, I'm already preparing for that conversation thirty years from now and trying to imagine myself being a supportive parent!) However, I *would* like to think that I could help shape the next version of society with my ideas, that I could be one of the ancestors who helped imagine a more equitable future. I'm not going to sit it out just because my two feet won't ever touch the red soil. It may seem preposterous to worry about equality, safety, and opportunity on another planet generations from now, when there are so many injustices happening today, affecting far more people, right here on Earth. But who is to say that the ideas we come up with for Mars won't inspire us to try things a new way today? At the Institute for the Future, we have a lab set up specifically to study the future of governance. And we have certainly found that it's easier for people to think creatively about change when they can zoom out from the "unchangeable" realities of the current system to imagine, instead, creating a new constitution for a fictional future country, or for another planet.[12]

Last year, just to inform myself on the topic, I attended a four-day online conference on the topic of "The Institutions of Extraterrestrial Liberty." Astrophysicists, economists, and political scientists gathered to debate what ways of organizing would best preserve our freedoms and help advance human rights in space. The conference was free and open to the public, if not particularly well advertised. If you're not regularly looking for clues to the future, you might not realize how many opportunities there are like this just to show up and participate in mind-blowing conversations. This is my favorite side effect of looking for evidence that anything can be different in the next decade: I discover communities of change I can learn from and get involved with today.

Who else might come up with new ideas for life on Mars? Well, in China, a company called C-Space has opened up a simulated Mars colony in the Gobi Desert, one of the most Mars-like places on Earth. Visitors to the educational facility have a chance to immerse themselves in the environment and try to solve problems they might face on Mars, like food supply and power generation.[13] It fascinates me that we now have the first generation of young people who can realistically expect to have the opportunity to live on another planet. What are the social and psychological impacts of believing there is life for them beyond Earth?

Even if we never get to Mars, the effort itself may change what it means to be human. Researchers are already working on ways to edit our genes so that humans are "fit for Mars." On the top of their wish list are genes that eliminate body odor (which is very important for long-term confinement in small spaceships!), protect cells from the harms of radiation, and help people survive on radically less food and lower oxygen levels.[14] As scientists try to genetically engineer these Mars-ready humans, can you imagine the disruption to our economy and way of life on Earth if some of us no longer needed regular food or oxygen? I mean, besides going to Mars, what would *you* do if you didn't need to eat every day or could go for extended periods of time without breathing oxygen? Which is all to say, the future is a place where everything can be different. Even how often the sun rises, even whether humans need continuous oxygen to breathe.

IDEAS ABOUT THE FUTURE CAN be useful because they help us prepare for a challenge before it happens; or because they give us time to try to prevent a crisis; or because they open our minds and inspire us to make changes in our lives and communities today. Another way ideas—especially ridiculous, at first, ones—can be useful is that they spark creativity and innovation. They help us think of things we've never thought before—that *no* one has thought before. And that's perhaps the biggest reason I like talking about the future of Mars. I've seen it spark a lot of creativity in people who otherwise feel stuck in their studies, their careers, or their art practices.

Kaja Antlej is a great example. She's a young professor of engineering and industrial design at Deakin University in Australia. Her specialty is using new technologies, like virtual reality and 3D food printing, to create interactive experiences for museum visitors. After playing with Mars ideas in our class, she realized these skills could be applied to inventing the future of space travel and settlement. "Today, I build interactive experiences for museums, but I see myself building them for space as my next career move," she updated me recently. "I'm interested in how platforms for curiosity and creativity can support the emotional, mental, and identity needs of the astronauts and space travelers on long-duration missions." What a novel idea! I'd never imagined it myself—to start designing media, games, and communications to address the specific social and psychological needs of people undergoing the extreme isolation and physical limitations of space travel. It makes me wonder how similar ideas might be applied to improve the mental health and emotional well-being of others who are limited in movement or confined in space, whether it's people with chronic illness who tend to spend more time at home and in their bedrooms, or people in assisted-living facilities, or individuals who have been incarcerated. Kaja could be inventing an entirely new field of design and art practice. This is how you become a pioneer. And it's something I've seen again and again: it's so much easier to come up with new innovations, to imagine new products and services and businesses and art forms, when you play with ridiculous, at first, ideas— because far fewer people are thinking about and getting ready for these "unthinkable" futures. You get to the ideas first.

Kaja didn't just think about this possibility; she acted on it. "Already I have attended a few virtual space conferences and completed International Space University's intensive five-week Southern Hemisphere Space Studies Program," she told me. And she's bringing her students along on her creative journey. "Now I give space-design projects to my students—right now they are designing a space station hotel and habitats on the moon and Mars."

I love hearing how just a quick mental time trip can create a whole new pathway for learning and innovation. You never know when a clue to how the future could be different will turn into a clue to how *your* future could be different.

ARE YOU READY TO CHALLENGE your imagination again? Let's spend a little more time with one of these ridiculous, at first, ideas.

Imagine that ten years from now, humanity will undergo a truly dramatic fertility crisis that will require us to consider previously unthinkable technological interventions. There's no shortage of dystopian fiction to help us imagine such a crisis. From Margaret Atwood's *The Handmaid's Tale* to Aldous Huxley's *Brave New World* to the blockbuster movie *Children of Men*, we've thoroughly envisioned the most nightmarish outcomes to a mass fertility crisis: enslaving young women, genetically engineering a society of identical "perfect" people, creating violent police states. What there *does* seem to be a shortage of are efforts to realistically imagine what a thoughtful, ethical global response to an urgent fertility crisis might look like.

I want to take seriously the alarm being sounded by leading reproductive epidemiologists, including Shanna Swan, a professor of environmental medicine and public health at the Icahn School of Medicine at Mount Sinai in New York City, who has written:

> The current state of reproductive affairs can't continue much longer without threatening human survival. . . . Some people are in denial about the reality and gravity of the issue, and others shrug it off, saying the earth is overpopulated. . . . In some ways, the sperm-count decline is akin to where global warming was forty years ago—reported upon but denied or ignored. . . . [N]ow, the climate crisis has been accepted—at least, by most people—as a real threat. My hope is that the same will happen with the reproductive turmoil that's upon us. Increasingly, scientists are in agreement on the threat; now, we need the public to take this issue seriously.[15]

The first step to taking a future threat seriously is to imagine it seriously.

If we really had to solve this problem, and not just tell dystopian stories about it, what actions could we plausibly take? What technological solutions might we be willing to try? What social interventions would we become willing to accept?

Maybe we'll never need to find out. There is ongoing, vigorous debate in the scientific community about the long-term implications of decreasing sperm counts and sperm quality, and whether it constitutes a genuine crisis. Some researchers argue that it won't be a problem if most men wind up with a "low" sperm count in the tens of millions, because it doesn't take that much sperm to make a baby.[16] Others suggest that for all we know, the sperm count fifty-plus years ago, when scientists first started tracking it, was abnormally *high*;

maybe it's just now falling back to levels that were normal hundreds or thousands of years ago.[17] How much mental energy should we put into imagining a hypothetical global fertility crisis today if the risks might turn out to be overblown?

Professional futurists have a term for scenarios that have a low probability of happening but that would have a huge impact on society if they actually occurred. They're called *high-impact, low-probability* events, or HILP events for short. And yes, most futurists will tell you that, by definition, it's important to imagine seriously HILP events—like an asteroid hitting Earth—because it's precisely their low probability that makes people dismiss them and so disastrously underprepare for them. Consider that, prior to 2020, one of the standard examples of an HILP event given in strategic foresight glossaries and textbooks was this: pandemic.[18]

THE SCENARIO BELOW IS NOT a prediction of what will happen. It's not a recommendation of what should happen. It's an opening to a collective imagining of a high-impact, low-probability event: If the current infertility crisis became as global and severe as the COVID-19 pandemic, what radical options might we be willing to consider?

Future Scenario #3:
The Global Emergency Sperm Drive

Ten years from today

It's finally happening. After months of scientists calling for urgent action, the Global Emergency Sperm Drive starts today.

Men all over the world under the age of sixty are being encouraged to donate their genetic material. Not to make babies today—but potentially to make babies thirty, forty, fifty, or even one hundred years from now.

This turn of events is a bit of a shock. Yes, sperm count has been decreasing worldwide for decades. But hormone-disrupting chemicals have been banned in most countries for years now. Scientists predicted that the decline in fertility would soon reverse itself. Yet sperm count and quality are continuing to decline, and miscarriages are still on the rise. The birthrate is down at least 30 percent in almost every country.

So reproductive epidemiologists have sounded the alarm: Humanity must urgently collect and freeze as much sperm as possible as a hedge against the worst-case scenario. Without an emergency sperm bank, they say, we could wind up with a rapidly aging population on a mostly childless planet.

More than fifty million men have registered to donate to the Global Emergency Sperm Drive so far, according to Facebook, which is assisting with donor turnout. But scientists say at least 250 million men will need to donate to guarantee enough high-quality sperm to protect future generations.

Today has the feeling of an important election day. Workers are being given paid time off to encourage participation in the sperm drive. People are volunteering to give others rides to donation centers. And famous athletes, actors, musicians, and other celebrities have started sharing selfies with "I Donated" and "Future Dad" stickers to increase community turnout. Organizers have pledged to work to ensure an equitable turnout and sufficient genetic variation. "It's essential that the full genetic diversity of humanity is collected," says the community-outreach messaging. But there are growing concerns about underrepresentation from various racial groups who may face structural barriers to donating, and who owing to historical discrimination and mistreatment may be less likely to trust the government and medical community.

Scientists are doing their best to build trust in the sperm-preservation effort. They've stated that the reserve sperm will not be used unless the global population-replacement rate falls under 0.5 children born per woman of childbearing age. At that rate, the global population would fall from nearly 9 billion to 1.5 billion in just a few generations' time. Still, conspiracy theories are running rampant on social media. "FAKE EMERGENCY" is trending and "What Is This Genetic Material

Really Going to Be Used For?" videos are going viral. Even among people who accept the validity of the crisis, the fine print on the donor consent form is raising eyebrows. It requires donors to grant "perpetual, irrevocable rights to the Global Emergency Sperm Bank to use or replicate your genetic material for the purpose of creating new life anywhere worldwide, without limitation, forever." All of this makes you wonder: Is this the last generation of biological dads?

Imagine yourself living through this strange moment in human history. The first-ever Global Emergency Sperm Drive is now underway. How would *you* respond to the crisis? And where would you turn for trusted information and advice?

~~~~~~~~

MOMENT OF CHOICE: If you are biologically able to donate sperm: Do you donate your genetic material to the Global Emergency Sperm Bank? Why or why not?

If you are not biologically able to donate sperm: What do you say to close male friends and family who ask for your advice? Do you encourage them or discourage them from donating? Why?

If you're unsure, what information, or whose input, would you need to help you make your decision?

Welcome back to the present. Now that you've made your choice, let's keep playing with this possible future. Here are some additional questions to consider. Let your mind wander through the possibilities:

- How would a fertility crisis ten years from now affect you or your loved ones?
- What would it take for *you* to trust a group like this with your genetic material (sperm, eggs, DNA, or otherwise)? What assurances would you need about how the material might be used?

- What moral and ethical concerns would you have in this future? Can you think of a way to address them?
- If the emergency sperm were needed fifty years in the future, how should it be distributed? Would women get to choose donors, the way they do today? How much information would they get about donors? Who should be making these rules—governments, scientists, doctors, an independent ethics board, a global vote?
- If several generations of men became unable to contribute their own sperm to make babies, do you think family life would change significantly? What would partnering and parenting look like in a future with biological moms but no biological dads?
- On a scale of 1 to 10, how comfortable are you thinking about this scenario? (1 is extremely uncomfortable, 10 is extremely comfortable.)

Could this scenario really happen? In fact, scientists are already working to prevent long-term biodiversity loss on our planet by creating underground safehouses to preserve genetic material for the future. The Frozen Ark, founded in 2004 and named as a nod to the biblical Noah's ark, is a UK-based charity that works with zoologists and conservationists worldwide to collect and preserve the DNA of animal species at risk of extinction, of which there are currently more than thirty-five thousand.[19] This practice is known as *endangered animal biobanking*.

In 2021, biobanking took a leap forward with the creation of Nature's SAFE (an acronym for Save Animals from Extinction), a dedicated facility in Shropshire, England, for storing ovarian and testicular tissue from endangered animals. Scientists at Nature's SAFE have made it clear that the point of this biobanking isn't simply to preserve a complete genetic history of species. Their intention is to one day thaw this material and use it to establish pregnancies, making it possible for the reproduction of endangered or extinct species to resume.

It's not just animals that are being biobanked. The Millennium Seed Bank, also based in the UK and founded in 2000, has preserved over 2.4 billion seeds from around the world for the future. The seeds are stored in subzero temperatures, in underground vaults that are flood-, bomb-, and radiation-proof. They have successfully biobanked more than 10 percent of all the world's plant species so far, including twelve that have gone globally extinct since the seed bank collected them. If humans ever need to repopulate the planet's wildlife, perhaps after an extreme climate disaster, the seed bank will be able to provide the genetic material. Meanwhile, in 2021, the nonprofit organization Great Barrier Reef Legacy revealed design plans for the Living Coral Biobank, a coral ark that will contain all eight hundred known hard coral species. Oceans could potentially be repopulated too.[20]

So far, biobanking as a hedge against extinction is just for animals and plants. Will human biodiversity be similarly protected? Even if society never has to grapple with an infertility crisis on such an extreme scale as the "Global Emergency Sperm Drive" scenario, it seems wise to at least get some practice thinking about safe and equitable biobanking. We don't want our collective imagination to come up empty if and when, as absurd as this scenario may sound today, we need to take coordinated global action to ensure we have the human genetic material we need to get to the next century.

I can't say for sure what challenges we might face as a result of human biobanking, crisis-inspired or otherwise. But I am confident we will be better off in the future if we warm up our imaginations to the possibilities today. By being willing to consider just how strange things might get, we reduce the risk of being shocked by our future, and we increase our ability to shape it.

In early 2021, a participant in the 2008 Superstruct pandemic simulation reached out to me with a particularly striking email: "Things that came up during the pandemic this past year felt more like familiar old memories instead of new experiences," he wrote. "I felt weirdly less traumatized by things other people were freaking out about."

This makes sense: vividly imagining a possible future creates memories of things we haven't actually lived through yet, so the pandemic felt familiar to him. And research suggests that "future memories" have a real psychological benefit if and when a traumatic future we imagined actually happens. It's not just that we're less surprised by what happens. We also get a significant boost of self-confidence from having been "right" about the future. And this confidence makes us more likely to take action and help others.

Here's why: the fact that we *saw the future coming* before it happened creates a specific response in the brain. The very first emotion we feel isn't shock but recognition. We recognize this strange new world because we've spent time there, in our imagination, before. Recognition communicates to us: *You know this. You've got this.* It's a powerful antidote to feelings of helplessness and fear. Our foreknowledge of what happened causes us to feel less overwhelmed, more in control, and better able to help.

Angus Fletcher, a neuroscientist who studies the effects of storytelling on the brain, has described it this way: "That position of foreknowledge stimulates a powerful sensation of cosmic irony in the 'perspective-taking network' of our brain's prefrontal cortex, giving us a godlike experience of looking down on [events]." This may remind you of the benefits of zooming out to a ten-year timeline to adopt a third-person perspective. Foreknowledge causes the same exact mindset shift, only this time it's triggered by a feeling of *I've seen this all before.* "This God's-Eye vantage reduces activity in our brain's deep emotion zones, acting as a neural shock absorber against the traumatic events before us," Fletcher writes. He adds, "This neural feeling is deeply therapeutic. . . . [It shifts] our tragic feeling of helplessness into a psychological sensation of help*ful*ness."

Fletcher is interested in how novels, plays, and movies can give readers and audiences that same beneficial feeling of foreknowledge. He recommends Greek tragedies, which often start by warning the audience of all the terrible things that will happen by the end of the play, as most reliably stimulating that feeling. And he points to research on the performance of Greek tragedies for combat veterans as part of their treatment for post-traumatic stress disorder (PTSD); studies show that the veterans self-report a decrease in feelings of anxiety and help-lessness when they also experience a feeling of foreknowledge in re-sponse to the story. "So, even though we're no more able than Oedipus to stop the inevitable, [it] strengthens our capacity to manage when the inevitable arrives," Fletcher writes, in reference to one of the most famous Greek tragedies that begins with a prophecy of future trauma.[21]

The same is true for playing with shocking scenarios, whether you came up with the future scenario yourself or just were smart enough to be willing to take it seriously. Willful imagination acts as a kind of *pre-exposure therapy* for difficult futures, similar to exposure therapy treatments for anxiety and PTSD. Such treatments desensitize the brain's shock and fear response through repeated imagining and re-membering of the emotionally triggering event. So too can simulating a difficult future in your mind serve as a kind of vaccine against future shock.

James Araci, a senior science and innovation officer at the British High Commission in New Zealand, recently told me an amazing story. James took my online class Simulation Skills, part of the Futures Thinking program, in 2019. One of the main assignments was a brief replay of the Superstruct simulation. Learners were asked to submit their answer to this question: "Imagine the world is dealing with a dangerous respiratory pandemic, with no vaccine or cure. How do you use your unique skills and personal strengths to help?" This means, oddly enough, that nearly seven thousand of my students, including James, were actively making plans to help others during a COVID-19-like scenario in the very weeks and months before the first COVID-19 case was detected.

"Playing the game and thinking about a pandemic pre-COVID actually prepared me to use my skills in dealing with the COVID pan-demic itself," James wrote me when I reached out to some of the

Simulations Skills students to see if they had turned their foresight into action. He described how he was ready to jump into action when the real pandemic started, volunteering to project-manage his employer's COVID-19 emergency response. He worked with the Ministry of Business, Innovation, and Employment to launch an innovation accelerator fund to support New Zealand businesses that had ideas to fight COVID-19. And he helped deliver rapid training to support New Zealand organizations pivoting to remote work and remote collaboration, so they could move into full lockdown without laying off or furloughing any staff during what was one of the most stringent lockdowns anywhere in the world.

"I had been through the queasiness and uncertainty caused by thinking about pandemics already, so when COVID-19 started emerging, I had already thought about what skills I might have to help. It really did help me move fast," James said. "I saw people in states of shock over the last eighteen months. But for me, the future simulations were a bit like martial arts training—you're practicing skills and techniques in a safe environment so that you can be quicker and more effective whilst remaining calm." The work James helped lead was a finalist for the Most Adaptive/Courageous Project of the Year Award from the Project Management Institute New Zealand, a prestigious award in his field. Adaptive and courageous—I can't think of a better way to sum up the benefits of being willing to be ridiculous, at first, when imagining and planning for the future.

As you keep playing with scenarios in this book, you'll find yourself open to more ridiculous, at first, ideas, and better equipped with a wider range of foreknowledge that can act as a neural shock absorber and confidence builder. Just as simulating a pandemic changed many participants' reactions to the real pandemic, having a memory of this weird Global Emergency Sperm Drive future in your brain will affect how *you* react to an urgent worldwide fertility crisis—if it ever comes to that. You'll be less surprised, the problem will feel more familiar, and you'll be more likely to look for ways to help. And if we never live through such a crisis, you've still improved your ability to take in new information about challenges to human reproduction. Who knows what new clues you'll discover about this future, now that your brain is trained to pay attention?

TAKING IN INFORMATION THAT MAKES you uncomfortable isn't something you do once. You keep it up, like a habit. And the more clues to change that you find, the more open and less shockable your mind becomes.

In a couple of chapters we'll revisit this Stump the Futurist brainstorming game. But the next time we play, *you're* going to be the futurist. I'm going to give you a chance to challenge your own assumptions, by finding evidence that whatever unchangeable fact *you* named just a few pages ago is already starting to change.

One final word on Dator's law: different people find different future ideas and scenarios ridiculous. There are no *objectively* ridiculous ideas about the future. An idea can only seem ridiculous to you if it challenges your deeply held assumptions about how things are, how they need to be, and how they always will be.

We all bring our own set of assumptions to how we view the world. The more ridiculous an idea about the future seems to you, the more potentially useful it is to you—because it suggests the kind of change that will be hardest for you, personally, to see coming. By playing Stump the Futurist, you're developing your own sense of what *you* instinctively dismiss as impossible—so you can commit yourself to taking a closer look at the evidence for potential changes to the world as you know it.

IMAGINATION TRAINING

RULE #4: Be Ridiculous, at First.

Be playful as you brainstorm ways that anything could be different in the future. Entertain any possibility, no matter how absurd it seems at first. Keep in mind that future possibilities that seem unthinkable or impossible today are the ones that will be hardest to adapt to, so we need more time to prepare.

To build this skill, play Stump the Futurist: Make a list of things that you believe cannot, will not change in the next decade. Then look for evidence that these far-fetched possibilities could really happen, or may in fact already be happening today. This game will improve your ability to take in information that challenges your assumptions and will stretch your mind to new dimensions.

5

~~~

Turn the World Upside Down

I'm always trying to turn things upside down and see if they look any better.

—TIBOR KALMAN, graphic designer

NOW THAT YOUR MIND IS WARMED UP AND OPEN TO RIDICULOUS, AT FIRST, possibilities, I can teach you my other favorite brainstorming game for inspiring future scenarios. It's called One Hundred Ways Anything Can Be Different in the Future. Here's how it works: First, you pick a topic, like work, or food, or learning. Then you list one hundred things that are true about it today. The simpler or more obvious the fact, the better. Next, you rewrite each fact, one by one, so that *ten years from now the opposite is true*—no matter how ridiculous, at first, the new ideas sound. Finally, you look for clues, or evidence of change already happening today, that these ideas are plausible and realistic.

It sounds simple, but it's incredibly mind-opening. Let's do a quick demonstration of the game with one of my favorite topics: shoes. What ridiculous, at first, ideas can we imagine for the future of shoes?

Now that we have a topic, let's start listing facts about shoes!

- **FACT:** Shoes aren't free. People have to buy them.
- **FACT:** Most people own more than one pair of shoes, different types for different occasions.
- **FACT:** People take their shoes off when they go to sleep at night; they don't sleep with their shoes on.

So that's three facts, only ninety-seven more to go!

You'll notice that these facts about shoes are *generally true*, for most people, in many parts of the world. The facts you come up with don't have to be 100 percent true for all people, everywhere, all the time. They can even just apply to your school, your company, or your family.

We won't do all one hundred facts about shoes right now—you get the idea. And by the way, it's quite difficult to come up with one hundred facts about anything by yourself. I have a spreadsheet of facts about shoes, and I only came up with about twenty before I had to ask other people for help! That's why this game is best played in a group— more people, more facts. If you still can't get all the way to one hundred facts, that's fine. One hundred is a stretch goal, a reminder to push your thinking as far as you can.

Now comes the fun part. We take our facts and flip them upside down. Think of this as creating our own "upside-down world," where everything we know is suddenly different. Here are upside-down versions of our first three shoe facts:

1. Ten years from now, shoes are free.
2. Ten years from now, most people own only one pair.
3. Ten years from now, many people sleep with their shoes on.

The important thing during this part of the game is not to worry about making sense. Even if the "flipped" version of a fact seems impossible or unthinkable, go for it. That's the whole point—to generate as many ridiculous, at first, ideas as we can. So we flip every fact until we have a list of up to one hundred alternatives to how things are today.

Now, the challenging part. We have to pick some of our "flipped" facts and try to make sense of them. How does this new reality work, exactly? And why did this change happen? *Why* are shoes free now? *Why* are people sleeping with their shoes on? During this part of the game, we try to turn what might be simply a "ridiculous idea" into a ridiculous, *at first*, idea, one that makes more sense the longer you think about it. And the best way to do this is the same way we play Stump the Futurist. We have to find real trends or disruptions that are already underway, that could potentially, plausibly, lead to the strange new future we've defined.

So why would shoes be free in the future? Well, looking around today, we might notice that there is already a trend toward discounts and giveaways of services and products in return for customer-provided data that companies can monetize or make use of—think of platforms like Facebook, or how Fitbit provided free fitness trackers to citizens in Singapore for use in their public health program.[1] And there are plenty of shoes being developed with sensors that can track location, physical activity, weight, gait, and social proximity, or even whom you are standing near or walking by. So perhaps in the future, governments or health insurance companies that want this kind of data would give away "smart shoes" for free? This seems like a plausible future to me, especially in a post-pandemic age when we're considering lots of new surveillance technology to control and prevent future outbreaks.

But why in the future would most people own only one pair of shoes? Well, maybe over the next ten years, we will see a huge downward shift in consumption, possibly due to economic reality (are we heading into a global post-pandemic economic depression?) or maybe as part of global climate action. In 2019, we saw a significant trend in Sweden called *flygskam*, or "flight shaming," where people get shamed out of taking unnecessary air travel because of the heavy carbon and climate impact. Maybe in the next decade, this will move beyond the carbon impact of travel to the carbon impact of consumer goods? I am definitely going to be shoe shamed if in the future it becomes a signal of climate commitment to own only one pair of shoes!

And ten years from now, why might people sleep with their shoes on? Well, I actually lived through one signal of change that could inspire an explanation. During the wildfire outbreaks in California this year, I was advised by an evacuation and rescue expert at the American Red Cross either to sleep with my shoes right by my bed or to wear them while I sleep because people panic and lose precious time looking for shoes when they have to escape a quickly spreading fire. For those of us in the western United States, and no doubt also in Australia in recent years, the wildfires have been traumatic. So maybe in some parts of the world where extreme weather and climate risk continue to escalate, some of us live with a climate-related post-traumatic stress disorder? And just in case—as a symptom of our climate PTSD—we sleep with our shoes on? It's a small detail of one possible future, but it opens up important conversations about the long-term collective emotional and psychological consequences of crises we're experiencing today.

Free shoes, shoe shaming, post-traumatic shoe sleeping . . . any of these ridiculous, at first, ideas could inspire a mental time trip. In one word, how would you feel in that future? What are the risks? What are the opportunities? What actions could you take to make this world better? This is the final challenge of One Hundred Ways Anything Can Be Different in the Future. Spend some time seriously imagining one or more of the most provocative possibilities. Use your episodic future thinking skills. Immerse yourself in the upside-down world that you've just invented. For example:

Imagine you just received a pair of free smart shoes that reports key health data to your doctor, city, employer, school, or health care provider. In one word, how do you feel? Do you wear the shoes?

Imagine you have just been called out for wearing multiple pairs of shoes in one week. You have just been publicly shoe shamed for having too many pairs of shoes. How do you feel? How do you react?

Imagine that you have just been advised by an emergency alert notification to sleep with your shoes on for the next seven days in case you need to evacuate during a weather or wildfire event. How do you feel? Do you do it? If so, which pair of shoes do you sleep in?

This kind of a quick, postgame EFT challenge can help you make more sense of the upside-down ideas you come up with. And it's an excellent opportunity to keep training your imagination. Fill the blanks of these future ideas with as many personal details as you can. Each time you take a trip to an upside-down future, you're strengthening the neurological pathways that make it possible for you to think effectively about things you've never directly experienced.

AFTER THE 2020 PANDEMIC SHUTDOWNS began, I started getting an unusually high number of requests to lead groups in One Hundred Ways Anything Can Be Different in the Future. I ran One Hundred Ways games on the future of libraries, the future of fashion, the future of public gardens, the future of video games, the future of higher education, the future of manufacturing, and the future of professional sports. So many companies and organizations, it seemed, wanted to throw out their assumptions and get some fresh thinking on how they could accomplish their goals.

I had a fascinating conversation with the artistic director of a major ballet company, who asked me to help brainstorm how live ballet performance might change during and after the COVID-19 lockdowns. We did a quick version of the One Hundred Ways game to come up with some testable ideas and soon found ourselves thinking beyond the short-term constraints of a pandemic. One of the facts we flipped was: "Professional ballet dancers have a short career compared with other professions, usually retiring from performance between the ages of thirty-five and forty." Here's how we rewrote it, so that the opposite might be true: "In the future, professional ballet dancers perform into their seventies, eighties, and even nineties." We talked about what that might mean for the future of choreography.

What kinds of dance movements can aging bodies perform? We explored what it could mean for the art form. What new kinds of stories would you tell in ballet if you were featuring older dancers? We tried to make sense of this flipped fact. What change might lead to having much older dancers on stage? One possible explanation really captured my imagination. We talked about the possibility that famous ballet roles, or characters, could age alongside dancers, through sequels and serial storytelling, similar to long-running television shows or movie franchises. Just as Carrie Fisher, for example, played Princess Leia in *Star Wars* movies over a span of forty years, her fictional character aging alongside the actress, what if a ballet dancer could dance the role of Aurora in *Sleeping Beauty* or the Sugar Plum Fairy in *The Nutcracker* throughout her entire career? What new stories could be told about older versions of these female characters, who have never before been allowed to age on stage? I don't know if the ballet company will pursue this idea further, but I'm excited that the idea now exists in the world for someone to pick up and run with.

I also helped prepare a team of researchers at the Institute for the Future to lead a One Hundred Ways game with an organization called One Fair Wage, which seeks to improve the economics of restaurant and other service industries. One Fair Wage was particularly curious about what upside-down ideas might help end the practice of paying workers a subminimum wage. Subminimum wages are a kind of legal loophole; they allow employers to pay workers less than minimum wage, with the expectation that workers will make up the difference in customer-paid tips. This practice currently results in one out of six restaurant workers living below the poverty line, according to the Economic Policy Institute.[2]

One Fair Wage saw the pandemic period of upheaval as an opportunity for restaurant owners to think more radically about their business models. After all, restaurants were already switching to takeout and delivery, creating new outdoor dining experiences, and otherwise rethinking what restaurants can be. Could the next assumption to be overturned be that restaurants can be profitable only if they're built on cheap labor?

One Fair Wage invited a number of restaurant owners to participate in a One Hundred Ways workshop, and the results were published in a report called *Roadmap to Reimagine Restaurants*.[3] By
challenging facts like "Restaurants are physical places where people
come to eat" and "Customers pay for their meals," they proposed a
number of new, more equitable business models for the future, including my favorite: "In the future, restaurants will enjoy a more predictable, sustainable revenue stream by accepting grants and government
contracts to provide meals for free to the hungry." Instead of customers paying for their own meals, a third party would cover all costs.
Restaurants could enter into long-term contracts with relief organizations and government agencies, using their kitchens for a few hours or
days a week to make and deliver free or low-cost meals for people in
need. Day-to-day revenue is unpredictable for most restaurants, with
little financial cushion to pay workers more. But long-term grants and
contracts would give owners a new steady revenue model. And if customers aren't paying for their own meals, tips no longer come into
play. One Fair Wage called this idea "High Road Kitchens." The program has already been adopted in over one hundred restaurants across
the United States; the restaurants must commit to paying their workers full wages in order to receive the new grants and contracts.

I'VE COME TO REALIZE THAT there is no global issue too serious or too
urgent to benefit from playing with ridiculous, at first, ideas. I recently
came across an article in the *Bulletin of the Atomic Scientists* called "Transforming Our Nuclear Future with Ridiculous Ideas."[4] The author,
Emma Belcher, suggests that after seventy years of failed attempts, the
global effort for nuclear disarmament requires radical reimagining.
She cites Dator's law and argues that the field needs to challenge its
two biggest assumptions with ridiculous, at first, ideas. It's assumed
that nuclear disarmament will be a slow, protracted, and incremental
process that takes decades to achieve. But what if nuclear disarmament could happen fast—as fast as global COVID-19 lockdowns?

Second, it's assumed that the power to decide whether and when we rid the world of nuclear bombs lies in the hands of the nine nation-states that currently possess them: the US, the UK, Russia, China, and so on. But what if some other powerful agent—working outside normal diplomatic channels, unrelated to these national governments—found a way to force the issue?

It *is* possible to imagine such a surprising scenario, if you're willing to find a way to make sense of these kinds of flipped facts. An arms control alliance called N Square commissioned Institute for the Future fellow Jamais Cascio to do just that. Together, they created five scenarios describing surprising and unthinkable nuclear security outcomes. They published these ridiculous, at first, ideas in a fictional September 2045 issue of the *Journal of Nuclear Security Innovation*.[5] The one I find most mind-blowing is a scenario in which private companies decide they've had enough of governments failing to act, and so they band together to lead a rapid nuclear disarmament effort.

Here's exactly what the scenario envisions: a decade or so from now, a few leading technology companies have figured out how to engineer solutions to the most dangerous global challenges, like global warming and uncontrollable pandemics. Their technological solutions become the ultimate form of geopolitical leverage—because every government on earth desperately needs them. So the companies decide to make nation-states a deal they can't afford to refuse: any country that wants access to their humanity-saving technology must first completely dismantle its nuclear arsenal. Want this geoengineering solution that safely reverses the local effects of climate change? First get rid of your bombs. Want a vaccine for this deadly, uncontrollable virus? Disarm, and we'll sell it to you.

This scenario was created in 2015. It certainly was hard to imagine back then that there might be a crisis so urgent, and a privately developed technology so miraculous, that together they could work as leverage against nuclear-weapon-state actors. But now that we have lived through the COVID-19 pandemic, the idea seems *slightly* less ridiculous. What if the makers of the breakthrough RNA vaccines had

all agreed that they would sell the vaccines only to nuclear-free countries? Would that have been significant enough leverage to convince
countries to disarm? What if the pandemic were deadlier and harder
to control? Might it work then? It sounds absurd. Ridiculous! Truly
mad! But what *will* it take to end the madness of nuclear proliferation
if not something completely unexpected?

Upon revisiting this scenario, I discovered that the 2021 United
States budget includes $100 billion for six hundred new nuclear mis-
siles. I found out that the US government will spend an estimated $1.7
trillion just to maintain its nuclear infrastructure over the next
twenty-five years.[6] And I learned that political scientists expect India
and Pakistan, both nuclear-weapon states, to undergo such severe climate crises this century that the region may become much more un-
stable and at risk of nuclear war. When I think about what that money
could accomplish, and further consider the growing risk of geopolitical instability due to climate change and the psychological toll of living
under a constant risk of nuclear annihilation, I too am filled with the
desire to come up with ridiculous, at first, ideas.

ARE YOU READY TO PLAY? Let's talk practical details. I've run the One
Hundred Ways games pretty much anywhere you can have a brainstorming conversation—in classrooms, at conferences, in Zoom meetings, on Slack channels, in Google spreadsheets, in Facebook groups,
even by posting facts on sticky notes in a dorm hallway and giving
residents a month to flip them all. You can gather a bunch of people
and play a quick version of the game in an hour. Or you can create a
space for the game to play out, online or in a real physical environment, over the course of a few days, weeks, or longer. Let people add
facts and flip futures whenever they want, and you can all meet up
again later on to make sense of the flipped facts together. At the end
of this chapter, you'll find my favorite discussion questions for analyzing the results of a One Hundred Ways game.

Now that you know how the game works, you can play One Hundred Ways Anything Can Be Different in the Future with teams at work, school, conferences, clubs—or even at home with your family.

One of my online students, Jeremy from Saint Louis, wrote me in early January 2020 to tell me about why he played the One Hundred Ways game with his fifteen-year-old daughter, and how it helped them make an important family decision. Here's what he said:

> My daughter is cautious, anxious, artsy, and imaginative and has been having a hard time in high school. Her school recently started a program where you can be a full-time online student. You're still enrolled in the school, you could go to dances and pep rallies if you want—but all of your coursework is online. She was trying to decide whether or not she wanted to take this route, but overall felt really low autonomy and intuitively felt the future of school wasn't looking very good. I had her write down one hundred things that are true about school today. Then she chose three of these facts and flipped them, and then combined those three to tell a new story about what she would actually want from school if she had more power. It was a great way to shake her out of having no agency in making her decisions, and it greatly reduced her anxiety. It helped her realize she does have a choice in these matters, and that many of her assumptions about school aren't necessarily true. She decided to do the online school option! And, she also was able to anticipate inbound changes, like finding new ways to create meaningful social interactions because she will be more isolated.

What I love about Jeremy's story is that it demonstrates two of the biggest benefits of the One Hundred Ways game—the quick win *and* the longer-term payoff. It immediately improved Jeremy's daughter's mood, moving her from anxiety to feeling more in control of her future. That's the quick win. But more surprisingly, Jeremy's entire family was amazed to find themselves incredibly well prepared for the COVID-19 school and work shutdowns that hit the world a few months later, having preimagined ways to stay socially connected while physically distant. Sometimes it takes ten years for the ridiculous, at first, future to arrive—and sometimes it takes only ten weeks.

IF YOU WANT TO FLIP some facts about your own life, here's a quick challenge you can try. Make a list of at least five things that are true about your life today. Then rewrite them so that the opposite is now true, or offer a strange new alternative. Whatever alternative pops into your mind first, go for it. For example, on my own list, I wrote, "I'm an American citizen," "I have two daughters," "I'm a writer," "I sleep at night," and "I hate flying," and then I flipped those facts so they became, "I'm a British citizen," "I have three daughters," "I manage a doughnut shop," "I sleep during the day," and "I love flying."

Whatever you come up with, pick one flipped fact and take a quick mental time trip to the future to see how vividly and realistically you can imagine the change being true. What might lead to this change? (This is important—don't skip this part. Try to come up with a convincing explanation, no matter how absurd the change sounds at first!) How does it feel? What actions would you take in this upside-down future that you can't take today? Why do you think this particular alternative popped into your mind?

The point of this mini-game is not to come up with an actual plan to dramatically change your life. It's simply another way to train your imagination to be more flexible. And it may help you get a fresh perspective on what assumptions about your own life you might be willing to let go of. You might decide that every alternative you came up with has virtually zero probability of happening. Or you might feel liberated to become upside-down you, today.

Whatever you imagine, just by taking these alternative possibilities about your life seriously enough to simulate them in your mind, you're improving your ability to take in new ideas. You're getting better at examining ridiculous, at first, ideas for plausibility and potential benefits. And you may find, as I do, that taking a few minutes to freely imagine waking up in a completely different life gives you a subtle, but noticeable, sensation of freedom and creativity today.

TIME TO TAKE ANOTHER TEN-YEAR trip into the future! This next scenario is inspired by a round of One Hundred Ways Anything Can Be Different in the Future that a student of mine, a medical doctor and professor, played with her medical students. They decided to take one true fact about the medical profession today—"Doctors prescribe medications"—and flip it upside down to reimagine their profession in as many different ways as they could. In the future, what could doctors prescribe beyond drugs?

Prescriptions are a powerful lever for change, in two ways. First, they make change more affordable: a health care provider or insurer will typically cover some or all of the costs of whatever's prescribed. Second, they make change more likely: studies show that patients are more likely to comply with a doctor's advice for behavior change, like exercising or meditating, if it's written as a formal prescription.[7]

So what else besides drugs could doctors prescribe in the future? Here are some of the ideas medical students came up with, along with some clues I found to support them.

Ten years from now, doctors prescribe hugs. It didn't take me long to come up with a clue to this future. Remember the social media post that went viral in 2021 when a doctor wrote a prescription to a newly COVID-19-vaccinated grandmother: "You are allowed to hug your granddaughter"? Imagine that, as part of a mental health plan, we could all receive travel stipends to hug a faraway friend or family member at least once a year.

Ten years from now, doctors prescribe games. In 2020, after seven years of clinical trials, the US Food and Drug Administration approved the first prescription video game, *EndeavorRx*, for children between the ages of eight and twelve who struggle with ADHD. Researchers found that a dose of twenty-five minutes of play, five days a week, improved attention skills and cognitive control after four weeks. Imagine if ten years from now, you could choose from hundreds of officially "good for you" prescription video games at your doctor's visit.[8]

Ten years from now, doctors prescribe puppies. Research shows that kids who grow up with a dog in the home have lower rates of asthma, allergies, and diabetes. Dogs expose kids to a wider range of bacteria and gut microbes, which stimulate a healthier immune system and metabolism for life. This is an enormous benefit! But dog ownership is expensive, and not every family can afford it. Could a future prescription plan cover the full costs of dog food and vet care during the first few years of a child's life?[9]

Ten years from now, doctors prescribe shoes. Doctors already prescribe exercise, with support from global health initiatives like Exercise Is Medicine. But research funded by the National Institutes of Health found that a common but overlooked barrier to physical activity is not having the right clothing or footwear.[10] So perhaps in the future, any doctor who prescribes exercise also gives you a prescription for new walking or running shoes? (Aha! Another way shoes could be free in the future!)

Free hugs, games, puppies, shoes as part of a health care approach that supports social, emotional, mental, *and* physical health—okay, it's definitely a little ridiculous. But it does make you wonder if health care systems could (or should) one day soon evolve into a more dynamic infrastructure to support our whole well-being.

Let's imagine that idea a little more seriously. This next scenario is about future prescriptions, and it's a bit different from other ones you've played with so far. It's a *location-specific* scenario. When you bring a scenario to a specific environment, the details of the real world help you fill in the gaps of your imagination and envision that future much more vividly. Think of it as a kind of augmented reality for your brain, no fancy glasses or screens required. By imagining one way the future could be different *in the same kind of physical environment as where the scenario takes place*, you'll be able to imagine and project the future right onto the real world around you.

Future Scenario #4: Medicine Bag

At a grocery store, roadside fruit stand, or farmers' market, ten years from today

It's your first shopping trip out with your new "medicine bag." You can't wait to fill it. The medicine bag is a reusable tote bag with a unique barcode printed on the fabric that links the bag to your health care profile. Once a week, you can fill the bag with whatever fresh produce you want, for free. Any fruit, any vegetable—at the grocery store, at a farmers' market, at a corner or roadside fruit stand—you want it, you got it.

You could have chosen to get a community-supported agriculture (CSA) box delivered weekly, but you picked the bag instead. You liked the idea of going on your own version of a "supermarket sweep" up and down the produce aisle, grabbing as much as you want without having to worry about or even check the price. Your medicine bag is part of your health insurer's new program to get primary care doctors to prescribe fresh fruits and vegetables to as many people as possible. The program was originally created for higher-risk individuals, like patients with heart disease and diabetes, but the benefits were so dramatic in terms of improved health outcomes and lower health care costs that it was eventually expanded to everyone. Everyone in a household gets their own bag—kids too.

Imagine you're in this future. It's a world where healthy food is free—at least a bagful a person, every week. To help you imagine this future more vividly, I want you to file this scenario away in your brain until the next time you are somewhere surrounded by actual fresh produce—at a grocery store, or a farmers' market, or a fruit stand. As you take in your real-world surroundings, play back this scenario in your mind. Let this upside-down future where doctors prescribe free fruits and vegetables act as a mental augmented-reality filter that

changes how you experience your present-day environment. Don't just
think about it; try to feel it.

When you're someplace where you can blend this future scenario
with the real world, go ahead and make your first decision in this future:

~~~~~~~~~

MOMENT OF CHOICE: Look around and imagine it's all free to
you. What do you fill your bag with? And in one word, how do
you feel in this future?

Could this future really happen? I'd say it's extremely high-probability.
The National Produce Prescription Collaborative and the Food Is
Medicine Coalition are two associations working to make it happen in
the United States right now. These groups, made up of public health
scientists, doctors, and produce growers, argue that the best way to
prevent chronic disease and improve public health is to make it easier
for people to enjoy high-quality, fresh produce. They are part of a
growing movement, with support from research groups like the Center
for Health Law and Policy Innovation of Harvard Law School and
funders like the Rockefeller Foundation, which aims to "mainstream"
the idea of produce prescription programs.

The National Produce Prescription Collaborative defines a produce prescription program as "a medical treatment or preventative
service for patients who are eligible due to a diet-related health risk or
condition, food insecurity or other documented challenges in access to
nutritious foods, and are referred by a health care provider or health
insurance plan. These prescriptions are fulfilled through food retail
and enable patients to access healthy produce with no added fats, sugars, or salt, at low or no cost to the patient."[11] Hundreds of thousands
of Americans already have access to such a program, right now. One
example is the nonprofit Wholesome Wave's fruit and vegetable prescription (FVRx) program. The FVRx program deposits funds of an
average of one hundred US dollars per month in low-income households' shopping accounts to cover fresh produce purchases. Cancer

patients also get prescriptions through FVRx. Fruits and vegetables, studies show, replenish the body's micronutrients and antioxidants that make chemotherapy more effective. The FVRx program prescribed 1.8 million free servings of fruits and vegetables in 2020. These kinds of programs are being encouraged in the US, in part, by the inclusion of $25 million in the 2018 Farm Bill to provide funding support for produce prescription pilot projects through 2023. And the National Institutes of Health recently released a ten-year strategic plan, looking ahead to the year 2030, which includes a specific focus on food as medicine—yet another clue that a scenario like "Medicine Bag" is plausible.

Do these programs really work? Early evidence says yes. One recent study found that based on the current impacts of existing programs, a fruit and vegetable prescription program that reached one in three Americans would prevent 1.93 million strokes and heart attacks and 350,000 deaths, *and* save $40 billion in health care costs, over an eighteen-year period. It would take only five years, researchers estimated, for the program to save more money than it would cost to run.[12] In other words, it is going to be a lot more expensive *not* to do a program like this at scale than to do it.

If this scenario captures your imagination, you may want to consider what the ripple effects of a wide-scale free fruit and vegetable program might be. If overall demand for fresh produce increased, how would farms adapt? What new businesses for filling people's "medicine bags" might start to pop up, beyond traditional groceries, farmers markets, and fruit stands? And if more and more kitchens were full of fresh produce, what else might change about how we cook and eat? Can you think of any downsides or risks to a prescription food program? A scenario isn't a final destination for your imagination. It's a starting point. As one thing changes, many more new opportunities follow.

If it becomes thinkable in the future to prescribe produce to everyone, what else beyond drugs might officially become "medicine" in the future? Maybe the thought of all-you-can-eat fruits and veggies doesn't excite you. What *would* you want to fill a future medicine bag with? Today, coalitions called Food Is Medicine and Exercise Is Medicine promote those respective ideas. What can you imagine as another future "is medicine" movement?

"Medicine Bag" is a reminder that future scenarios don't have to be about a crisis or extreme disruption to be useful. Sometimes, it just feels good to spend time in a world where things can be better, where we have more opportunities and power to help ourselves and others than we do today. Bring your own flipped facts with you as you move through the world and you'll start to see and feel alternative future possibilities wherever you go.

One Hundred Ways Anything Can Be Different in the Future—Discussion Questions

After you've flipped some facts and come up with some ridiculous, at first, ideas, take some time to analyze what you've imagined. Here are some questions to consider and discuss as a group:

- Which fact about today do you think is most important to challenge going forward? What assumption are you ready to leave behind?
- What reasons for change were most compelling, or came up most frequently, as you looked for clues to explain the upside-down futures?
- Which of the possible upside-down futures would you most want to wake up in? Why?
- Ten years from now, what actions would you be proud to have taken today to make this future *more* likely?
- Which of the possible upside-down futures would you most want to avoid? Why?
- Ten years from now, what actions would you be proud to have taken today to make this future *less* likely?

IMAGINATION TRAINING

RULE #5: Turn the World Upside Down.

If your imagination feels stuck in the present, then rewrite the facts of today. Make a list of up to one hundred things that are true today, and then flip them upside down so that the opposite is now true. Offer a "ridiculous, at first," future alternative for each and every example.

Spend time mentally immersed in these "upside-down worlds." Make sense of them. Why did this change happen? How does this new reality work? Keep looking for clues—in the news, on social media, and in your own life and community—that make these flipped facts seem more plausible and realistic. Turning the world upside down can help you get clarity about what you want to make different, in society and in your own life.

PART II

THINK THE UNTHINKABLE

Whatever hasn't happened will happen, and no one will be safe from it.

—J. B. S. HALDANE, evolutionary biologist

A group of caterpillars or nymphs might not see flight in their future, but it's inevitable. It's destiny.

—ADRIENNE MAREE BROWN, social justice activist

When you think about how the world and your life will change over the next ten years, are you <u>mostly worried or mostly optimistic</u>?

. . . .

Rate your outlook on a scale of 1 to 10.

1 is extremely worried, 10 is extremely optimistic.

6

Look for Clues

I have a habit of letting my imagination run away from me.
It always comes back though . . . drenched with possibilities.

—VALAIDA FULLWOOD, philanthropist

A SCULPTOR WORKS WITH CLAY, A WRITER WITH WORDS, A COMPUTER programmer with code, a composer with musical notes, a chef with ingredients, a fashion designer with fabric. Every form of creativity has its own raw material.

For futurists, the raw material is clues. We collect, combine, and build future scenarios out of *clues to how the future might be different.*

To find future clues, you need to develop a new way of looking at the world around you, a way to spot weird stuff that others overlook. You have to be constantly honing in on things you haven't previously encountered, things that make you say, "Huh, that's strange," and "Hmmm . . . I wonder why that's happening," and "Wow, this is weird, and I want to understand it better."

I call this way of looking at the world *strangesight*. Instead of being drawn to people, information, and ideas that fit with your expectations, you become increasingly drawn to things that challenge your assumptions, that feel unusual or surprising in a way that can be unsettling or hard to understand at first.

Strangesight is a precursor to foresight. Before you can get better at predicting what might happen or what might be needed in the future, you have to fill your brain with clues. And there is one kind of clue, in particular, that futurists are trained to detect and work with: *signals of change.*

A signal of change is a concrete example of how the world could one day be different. It might be a tiny change happening in just one town, or just one school, or just one company, or just one person's life. But it's real. It's not a hypothetical possibility. It is happening right now, and it proves that a specific kind of change is possible. As the science fiction author William Gibson famously stated, "The future is already here. It's just not evenly distributed." A signal of change draws your attention to where the ideas, technologies, and habits of the future are being actively experimented with, tested, seeded, and invented, today.

You can find signals of change in the news and on social media, in scientific journals and in TEDx talks, in podcast interviews and at protests. They pop up wherever new ideas are shared and wherever surprising events are documented. You can even find one right now, just by typing "future of [anything]" into your favorite search engine. (Go ahead, give it a try. Pick something fun, like a hobby, sport, or favorite food. I just searched for "future of cake" and my mind is blown. There is actually a plan for how to make a "galactic" cake out of "edible gel cubes" to celebrate the birth of the first baby on Mars, using a recipe transmitted from Earth to a 3D food printer.)[1] Keep in mind, as you look for clues, that signals aren't general trends like "artificial intelligence" or "the decline of religious affiliation among young people." They are vivid, detailed, specific examples of innovation, change, or invention—like "Mindar," a six-foot-tall, aluminum, androgynous robotic priest that preaches Buddhist sermons inside a four-hundred-year-old temple in Japan, to get younger people interested in religious teachings.[2] Now that's a signal, of both the future of artificial intelligence and the future of religion.

You know you've found a signal if you can tell a story about it—a who, what, when, where, and why. And in my experience, the most powerful and mind-opening signals are the ones you encounter in your own community and life. Let me tell you a story about a signal of change I encountered five years ago in a local park—and why it's still influencing how I think, and what I do, today.

I was starting an early morning hike with my husband at Point Pinole Regional Shoreline, which runs along an eastern part of San Francisco Bay, when I noticed a sign by the front entrance that read No Drone Zone, with an illustration of a small unmanned aerial vehicle inside the official "don't do it" symbol, a red circle-backslash.

"That's new, isn't it?" I asked my husband. He agreed—we definitely hadn't seen this sign before. "Huh," I said. "Are there so many people using drones now that there needs to be an official policy?"

To my futurist mind, this sign bolted to a tree marked a potential turning point. It signaled a change from a world where drones are a novelty that only a small number of technologically savvy people use, to a world where drones are suddenly commonplace enough to require signage at my local park. It triggered my strangesight and made me curious. Were drones the new normal? Should I be preparing myself for a world full of them—maybe as many drones as there are cars or mobile phones today?

My husband and I started interpreting the signal of change as we walked. "Why do you think the park banned drones?" I asked. We brainstormed possible motivations.

Drones can make an annoying buzzing sound. Maybe the ban was designed to prevent noise pollution. Or maybe it was meant to prevent visual pollution—if you're in a park, you want to be able to look up and see blue skies, not a bunch of machines flying all around. Or could it be for privacy reasons? Many drones have cameras on them.

Who knows who could be watching when one flies overhead? I'd heard rumors that some US cities were starting to explore using drones for remote policing. Maybe the No Drone Zone sign was actually a ban on police use of drones. A sign like that could be a promise rather than a prohibition: *Welcome to a surveillance-free space! The local community has prohibited drone policing here.*

The more we talked about it, the more questions I had: How would a drone ban be enforced? Who would monitor the airspace and track down a remote drone operator when someone could be piloting it from more than six miles away? If I see a drone, am I supposed to tell someone? Whom do I report it to? And by the way, is the public being given a chance to discuss and help shape these drone rules and regulations?

The philosopher Sam Keen has said, "To be on a quest is nothing more or less than to become an asker of questions."[3] Investigating a signal of change *is* like being on a quest. The purpose of the quest is not to predict what the future will be; it's to ask question after question after question about what the future *could* be.

A signal can be "weak"—you can find only one example of it. Or it can be "strong"—the more you look, the more examples of change you find. I wanted to see if I could find more examples of this signal of change, so later that day, I did an image search online for "no drone zone." I found out that similar No Drone Zone signs were appearing all over the world. This wasn't a weak signal of change; it was a strong one.

Many of the images I found were from China, so I asked a friend who lives there what she knew about them. I discovered that something was happening there that was even weirder than what I'd experienced in the US: tiny "selfie drones" were starting to become popular. A selfie drone, I learned, is like having your own personal aerial photographer. It lifts off from your fingertips, spins 360 degrees, and captures dramatic panoramic photographs from above, starring you, before returning to your hand. Apparently so many people were using selfie drones at popular tourist spots in China that the sky was getting annoyingly full of them, and the authorities banned them. Or at least, that's the reason for the ban that was given publicly. Some people wondered, quietly, if it was really a government effort to limit and control who can see from the skies.

Now I knew I had found a strong signal of change. But what, exactly, was changing? People were using technology in a new way. And these new behaviors were creating new potential harms, like visual and noise pollution, and new risks, like privacy infringement, and new powers, like documenting reality with aerial video. In response, officials were creating new rules and regulations. All of these changes suggested to me that we were approaching a tipping point—but it was still unclear in what direction we were tipping.

This much *was* clear: we were entering a period of uncertainty and unease about when to accept, and when to limit, drones in public spaces. It's precisely this uncertainty and unease that makes the earliest stages of change so interesting.

When there's uncertainty, there's still a chance to have a say in what happens next.

When there's unease, there's an opportunity to figure out what we're afraid of—and to decide whether we want to heed that discomfort or overcome it.

Since that day at the park, I've become a user of drone technology myself, so I can gain firsthand knowledge and work through my own discomfort. I'm still following the clues to better understand where this technology is going, and how it might change our lives.

This is the magic of strangesight: you develop a highly effective radar for finding new evidence—so that without your even consciously looking for them, the clues just keep jumping out at you. For example, during the pandemic, I was struck by the power of drone cameras to change the way we see the world. Drone footage of eerily empty city streets during lockdown became a window to a world we were no longer permitted to explore. It gave us a kind of vicarious escape; it was freeing, but it was also shocking. It was one thing to stay at home and know, intellectually, that others were staying home too. It was a different kind of "aha" moment to really see, from a bird's-eye view, the world seemingly emptied out entirely.

But what gives ordinary people new visual power gives authorities new power too. Another signal of change: during the pandemic, drones became more prominent as tools of surveillance. From the US to Spain to China to Morocco, public health and police departments used drones to enforce stay-at-home orders, to disperse groups not obeying distancing rules, and to remind people to wear masks. Some drones were even equipped with biometric capabilities, to detect fever, coughing, and other COVID-19 symptoms from a distance. These experiments didn't lead to a permanent drone surveillance infrastructure in any of these cities. But a seed was planted, and it may yet grow. Having tried drone law enforcement once, authorities will find it easier to try again, and at larger scales. We will have to weigh the potential benefits of creating widespread access to this new form of visual power against the potential harms of a creeping encroachment of drones into our everyday, private lives.

I found myself holding this tension in my mind on April 20, 2021, the day that Minnesota police officer Derek Chauvin was found guilty of the murder of an unarmed Black man, George Floyd. This crime, which catalyzed a year of global protests as part of the growing Black Lives Matter movement, was documented on video by then seventeen-year-old Darnella Frazier. Her courage to press record and bear witness changed history, leading to the first moment of meaningful accountability for systemic racist violence in US law enforcement. And her access to a technology of visual power was essential to this historic moment. Could a moment like this have happened if cameras on mobile phones had been banned, early in their adoption, because of potential privacy risks? The day of the guilty verdict, a researcher I know recalled a moment from decades earlier. "In early 2007, I was at a conference where the idea of a smartphone with a camera was met with strong objection by many," he wrote on social media. "Boy, was that ever wrong, yet again proved today."

Putting camera phones in billions of hands made it possible for citizens to record the truth and hold people in power accountable—for injustice, for atrocities, for violations of human rights. Drones can capture footage that mobile phones can't, in places where individuals might be unable to record safely with a camera in hand—in conflict zones, in protester clashes with police, during acts of genocide and natural disasters. If drone cameras become as ubiquitous and democratized as mobile phone cameras, imagine how many future Darnella Fraziers there could be, bravely bearing witness and making it impossible for the world to look away.

We may soon decide to resist the rise of "no drone zones" if we want to protect our collective right to access aerial views. As much as I may wish to avoid surveillance, and as much as I'd like to keep enjoying the natural beauty of quiet, clear skies, a future in which this visual power belongs only to the police, the government, and the military is not a world I want to wake up in.

A CHANCE ENCOUNTER WITH A signal of change can help you cultivate your curiosity about important new technologies, ideas, and social movements. And it can inspire you to try doing something different yourself, right now. So where did all the drone clues lead me and my husband after we first spotted that No Drone Zone sign five years ago?

I started donating regularly to Witness, an organization that helps people use video and technology to document injustice and protect human rights—because I can vividly imagine a future where citizens use aerial footage to create positive change in their own communities. My husband, a writer and filmmaker, started incorporating drone footage into his own videos. He tells me he can produce more feelings of awe, wonder, and humility through his work now, "because it's so easy with a drone to show how small human beings are in the grand sweep of everything." Together, we decided to get a camera drone for our kids, for a few reasons: so they grow up feeling confident in using the technology, so they can spend more time adopting a zoomed-out perspective, and so they can develop opinions about the future of drones that are informed by their own real-life experiences.

Finally, I added "drone infrastructure" and "drone surveillance" to the ethical technology trainings that I help run for the Institute for the Future—so that participants in our trainings, from city mayors to Silicon Valley executives, can be in conversation with each other about the long-term risks and benefits of transforming our skies. One important insight that has come out of these conversations is the need for a trauma-informed approach to developing urban drone infrastructure. Many millions of people worldwide live with PTSD symptoms either from having lived under the terrorizing threat of military drone strikes or from having participated in violent military drone strikes themselves. Creating a world full of drones can't be done, *shouldn't* be done, without acknowledging the extreme harm that they have caused as a weapon of war.

When *you* find a signal of change that really sparks your passion, roll up your sleeves and get involved. As the philosopher Alan Watts wrote, "The only way to make sense out of change is to plunge into it, move with it, and join the dance."[4] You're less likely to be shocked by the future, or to feel left out of it, if you jump in to be a part of the changes that are already underway. You may decide you want to slow down those changes or reverse them; or you may want to help accelerate them. Or you may just enjoy the confidence-building feeling of having seen it coming, of having recognized and participated in the future while it was still being made.

SIGNALS OF CHANGE ARE RAW material for futurists. But how do we transmute that raw material into a story about a possible future? Here's the fastest way to turn a signal into a scenario: describe a world in which the signal of change is no longer strange. It's now widespread and totally normal. Share that description with others. Ask them what *they* would do, and how they would feel, in this new reality.

Let's try it together, with a few more clues and questions about drones.

HAVE YOU SEEN A DRONE constellation in the sky yet? If not, you will. In Seoul, mid-pandemic, more than three hundred illuminated drones flew in a synchronized display, creating temporary light constellations that were visible from miles away. The drones formed images reminding people to wear masks and spelled out slogans that promoted the government's pandemic economic recovery policies. In Philadelphia and London, drone constellations sent messages of thanks to frontline and health care workers. And in 2021, in Shanghai, 1,500 drones created a massive illuminated QR code in the sky; onlookers could snap a photo of the code, which opened a website for a popular video game—perhaps the world's first example of drone constellation advertising.

Looking at these three clues, I can't help but wonder: Will there be hate speech, harassment, and conspiracy theories via "sky media" in the future, the way they exist on social media today? Do we need to start preparing now for free speech arguments about what can and cannot be written in the stars? Is there any good that can come out of this new medium for expression?

Now, let's transmute these clues and questions into a quick thought experiment. Here's the scenario:

Imagine that ten years from now, you're a member of a "constellation collective." Along with fifty thousand other people, you pay a monthly fee to share in the costs of maintaining and flying a fleet of illuminating drones. Once a month, you get thirty seconds of "airtime" to spell out any message or create any image you want in your local sky.

Today, it's your turn. What do you do with your airtime? What message or image are you putting in the sky? What time do you schedule it for, and where will it appear? In one word, how do you feel when the drones create your constellation, just as you designed it? (If you'd like to make your imagination even more vivid, try making a quick sketch of it.)

LET'S DO IT AGAIN—MORE CLUES, more questions, and one more scenario.

Have you received a drone delivery yet? If not, you'll be able to soon. Companies like Altitude Angel in the United Kingdom, Zipline in Ghana, and Wingcopter in Japan have started building drone network infrastructures to allow faster deliveries of medical supplies, like blood, medications, and vaccines, in both cities and remote rural areas. Less urgent drone deliveries may also become commonplace in many parts of the world, starting with the United States. Drone divisions created by Amazon, Google, and United Parcel Service have all received permission from the Federal Aviation Administration to start testing drone delivery services. How will it work? One idea for urban drone infrastructure that has been patented already involves floating warehouses that hover over a city or neighborhood to quickly dispatch and restock the delivery drones.[5]

I'm trying to imagine how I might feel in the future with a giant Amazon warehouse hovering over my neighborhood. Is there *any* limit to what we'll give up in the name of convenience? Forget No Drone Zone signs. Who do I talk to about putting up a No Floating Warehouse Zone sign? When I think about this possible future, I already feel nostalgic for quiet, clear skies that I haven't even lost yet. I find myself spending more time now looking up at the empty sky and savoring it.

Now, the scenario, combining these new clues with some of the other drone signals we've discussed. Imagine that ten years from now, free drone delivery is commonplace for anything you might order online. Not only is it cheaper and faster, it's more sustainable: it turns out that drone delivery cuts greenhouse gas emissions significantly compared with conventional delivery by truck. It's no surprise that it caught on. But other kinds of drones are common now, too, including police surveillance, activist-led human rights–monitoring, and data-collecting drones operated by technology companies like Facebook and Google.

It's not entirely clear what kinds of data the tech companies are collecting. Google says it's monitoring environmental data, like coastal erosion and deforestation, among "other projects." Facebook reportedly has facial recognition algorithms optimized for drones that can successfully identify someone on the ground from more than half a mile away. (This technology was already being developed and tested by the US military in 2021.)

Now imagine that you're in this future, and you hear the familiar buzzing sound of a drone approaching. Where are you? What do you do? What's the first feeling you have in response to hearing a drone?

After you've imagined your own reaction, try this scenario out with others. The range of "first feelings" I've encountered, from excitement to relief to curiosity to exhaustion to solidarity to anger to fear, have helped me see this future from many different points of view—including this response, which took the scenario one step further: "I won't even hear the drone because ten years from now, soundproofing in homes and noise-canceling headphones will be something we use to deal with the new noise pollution." Point taken!

MANY OF MY STUDENTS TELL me that looking for signals of change is the most enduring habit they've picked up from my classes—they describe this habit as "fun," "exciting," and "inspiring." When I conducted a survey this year of Institute for the Future alumni to ask if their futures-thinking training had any lasting impacts, signals came up quite a lot:

"I'm looking at the world differently, constantly scanning for signals and thinking in new ways. It feels as if I've been given a secret key that unlocks doors and opportunities."

"The signals are everywhere when you really look, and it's something that you can't unsee once you see them."

"Learning how to find signals of change was, for me, like releasing the cork on a champagne bottle. It has revitalized my enthusiasm and passion for making a difference. I'm bubbling over with new ideas."

You can collect signals about anything, but picking a topic that has personal significance can make the practice even more meaningful. Raul, for example, is a father of two young daughters. He lives in Dublin, Ireland, and recently started collecting signals about the future of neurodiversity. Neurodiversity is the wide variation in the human brain regarding sociability, learning, attention, mood, and other mental functions; it includes autism spectrum disorders as part of this normal range, rather than as a pathology or disability. It's an important topic for Raul, because both of his daughters are autistic. "I always felt like if I wanted the world to be ready for when my daughters were adults, I needed to start now. They are five and seven at the moment," he told me in an email. "I figured out that if I envision how I want things to be ten years from now, I can be a lot more focused in how I try to make the world better for them."

Many people with autism are extremely sensitive to what they hear, see, smell, taste, or touch. Something that other people might not even notice, or might be able to ignore, like a bright light, a clothing tag rubbing against their skin, or an appliance's humming noise, can lead to extreme discomfort, difficulty concentrating, and emotional meltdowns. So Raul looks for signals of "sensory accommodation."

"There are places now where there are quiet or dark rooms to help with sensory overload, mostly airports, but also IKEA," Raul wrote. "Other places have sensory-friendly hours, such as supermarkets or cinemas. My vision is that everywhere should be like that. If I find and share these early signals, maybe I can inspire more people to make the same kind of accommodation."

He also studies signals of change in the LGBTQ community, which he thinks might provide the autism community with clues about how to increase its own visibility and self-acceptance. "I want young people to feel known, accepted, with it not being an issue to disclose autism. Hopefully by the time my daughters are older, we can move from having World Autism Awareness Day to something that's more celebratory, a Neurodiverse Pride Day or Pride Month instead."

Raul told me that he doesn't just collect signals of change; he tries to be one. "I believe there will be a time when, if a neurodiverse kid has a meltdown in a supermarket, people will not look at you like you are a terrible parent, because they'll know what is happening. For this reason I never hide my family from the world or stop going to places because of what we'll be encountering. I am trying to be a signal of change myself, so people get exposed to the fact that we exist."

I love Raul's idea. By being our authentic selves in the world, even when it flies in the face of what's "normal" today, *we* may be a clue for others.

I RECOMMEND THAT YOU PICK a few people to trade signals with regularly and make it a habit to discuss them together, over coffee, drinks, or dinner. Trading signals will expand your strangesight dramatically— because other people can pick up clues that you might have missed.

"Have you heard about the pizzly bear?" a friend asked me just this past weekend. We frequently trade signals with each other, and he had a good one to share. "It's a new hybrid species, a cross between a polar bear and a grizzly bear," he told me. "Global warming's sending polar bears south, into grizzly bear territory, and suddenly they're competing with each other for resources." This is bad for the polar bears, he explained, because polar bears are already endangered, and usually the grizzly bears can outcompete them for food. "So instead of starving to death, the female polar bears have started mating with male grizzly bears."

I quickly pulled out my phone and searched for more information. I found photos of the new species: pizzly bears have the cream-white fur of a polar bear, the body shape of a grizzly bear, and a skull size larger than a typical grizzly and smaller than a typical polar bear. The first pizzly bear was discovered and confirmed by DNA tests in 2006, I learned. They were back in the headlines now, because of a new report that their numbers in the wild are increasing. And scientists who study the animals believe the hybrid bear may be better adapted to the changing climate than either of the original species.

"So, what do you think this is a signal of?" I asked my friend, before we started riffing on the implications.

"Well, climate change, clearly," he said. "It's like a canary in the coal mine. If polar bears have to become a whole new species to survive, it makes you wonder what other species will have to do to adapt. Including us."

I was still skimming articles about pizzly bears. "Right," I said. "It's bad news, but maybe also good news? Listen to what this science journalist says." I read to him from an article: "Today's hybrids may signify more than just the erosion of biodiversity. They may signal a kind of resilience in the face of sudden environmental change."[6]

Our conversation then turned to future scenarios we might invent out of this signal of change. "I don't think we need to imagine a world full of pizzly bears, as fascinating as that is," I said. "But this clue's got me thinking about the planet shrinking. What land will, and what land won't, be inhabitable in the future—not just for bears but for people?"

Most likely, humans will be going through the same kind of migration, moving away from extreme climates and packing together into smaller environments than we're used to. We're going to have to find a way to live with a lot of people who feel like strangers to us, too, at first. But who are the polar bears—which populations will be forced to move? And who are the grizzly bears, who will have to make room?

I pulled up a scientific paper from 2020 on my phone entitled "Future of the Human Climate Niche." It was a signal I had previously found and mentally filed away for future reference. Written by climate scientists from the US, China, and Europe, the paper explains that within fifty years, as many as three billion people will be living in a Sahara Desert–like environment and "left outside the climate conditions that have served humanity well over the past 6,000 years."[7] In the coming decades, the scientists predict, these three billion people will need to leave the newly uninhabitable zones and relocate to the increasingly narrow regions of the world that can still support human life. North America, Europe, and large parts of Asia are projected to be the least hit by extreme heat (although they may experience other extreme weather or flooding), while much of Africa, South America, and Australia will face the most uninhabitable conditions.

We will need to learn how to live together on less land, and how to support essential migration safely and equitably. Today, many countries require refugees to live in camps. In the United States, we put desperate migrants in detention centers. Globally, much stricter immigration limits are enforced today than may seem humane or ethical in a future where billions of people must migrate or die. Meanwhile, in communities where legal migrants are changing the historical demographics, social scientists have documented a rise in ethno-nationalism, white supremacist activity, gun ownership (in the US), and violence against ethnic minorities.[8] If this is how we live today, then how are we going to adapt peacefully to possibly three billion people on the move by the year 2070?

The year 2070 might feel far away. It's nearly fifty years from now, and that may be longer than you've been alive. But time spaciousness will help us solve this incredibly complex problem. According to UNESCO, more than half the people who are alive today can expect to be alive in 2070, based on current age and life expectancy, including 180 million people who live in the United States now.[9] This is a future that most people alive today will experience. And it certainly won't take a full fifty years for the problem to start to boil over. According to the charity Oxfam, already over the last decade, more than twenty million people a year have been forced to leave their homes as a result of climate change.[10] Climate migration is happening now, and it will be happening more and more with each decade to come.

This is where my imagination took me, thanks to my friend's signal of change, and now I want to turn this signal over to you. Investigate this clue of the pizzly bear, from your own personal point of view. Imagine your current community dealing with mass climate migration in the future. You don't have to solve any problems today. Just warm up your mind for thinking seriously and creatively about this possible future. Here's how:

Where do you live today? Is it a part of the world that will likely become uninhabitable for humans as a result of extreme heat or a part that will remain habitable?

- **If you live somewhere today that is likely to become uninhabitable:** Take a mental time trip twenty, thirty, or even fifty years into the future, and try to envision your current community left behind, abandoned by most people, if not all, during the climate crisis. Imagine that someone has just captured drone footage of what used to be your hometown or city. As the drone flies, what do you see, or hear via the audio track? Try to imagine it as clearly as you can, as if it were real footage you could actually get ahold of and examine today. What has changed? How do you feel about having left? Where do you live now—where are you watching or listening to the drone footage from in this future scene?
- **If you live somewhere today that is likely to stay habitable:** Take a mental time trip twenty, thirty, or even fifty years into the future, and try to envision your current community with double or triple the present-day population, as a result of mass climate migration. Imagine that at least half the future residents are migrants who were forced to leave their homes. Try not to picture a worst-case scenario, where migration leads to conflict and suffering. Instead, imagine that your community has been resilient, making something new together instead of fighting each other. How has your community adapted? How have buildings and architecture, roads, parks, and public spaces changed? What has been created to support and welcome newcomers? If you had a drone to fly over this resilient town or city of the future, what kind of footage would you capture? What, exactly, would someone see or hear?

If you're not sure how climate change will affect your current hometown or city, go ahead and imagine both possible scenarios—the one where you leave and the one where you stay. (And then, maybe look for one more clue: try searching for your hometown or city, plus "extreme heat," "extreme weather," or "climate migration.")

IN THE SUMMER OF 2021, several years after I spotted my first No Drone Zone sign, I came across a headline in the news: "A Generation of Seabirds Was Wiped Out by a Drone. . . . Scientists Fear for Their Future."[11] A drone, piloted by an unknown individual who never came forward, had crash-landed into the nesting grounds of a seabird called the elegant tern at Bolsa Chica Ecological Reserve in Southern California. Mistaking the drone for a predator, thousands of mom and dad terns fled the reserve, leaving behind nearly two thousand unprotected eggs. The adult birds never returned. None of the eggs hatched. And the Bolsa Chica Ecological Reserve is one of only four known nesting grounds in the entire world for elegant terns, famous for their bright orange stiletto-like bills. It was a shocking and devastating wildlife loss. In fact, it was the single largest abandonment of incubating eggs that scientists have observed in the wild.

In the months that followed, governments up and down the West Coast of the US made plans to pass stricter "no drone zone" laws over beaches, parks, forests, and wildlife preserves. They pledged to find better ways to educate the public about these laws and to actually enforce them.[12] A future that was already here, but not evenly distributed, is about to get much more widely distributed.

What happened to the seabirds is a signal of change about drones. But it's also a signal of change about animals on the move, like the polar and grizzly bears. Sometimes, the signals you're spotting will suddenly align, and that alignment is a very special kind of clue. You might not know what this confluence means right away, or what actions it will inspire you to take. But when it happens, you'll feel it, and you'll know that your strangesight is trained in the right direction.

Interpreting a signal of change isn't a straight line. It's a winding path toward whatever possibilities capture your imagination. I'm reminded that the word "clue" comes from the archaic word "clew," meaning a ball of string. In Greek mythology, Theseus used a *clew* to successfully navigate into and back out of the heart of a labyrinth, unraveling the ball of string behind him and then following its trail back out again. Signals of change are like a *clew*. They take us on twists and turns. We may not be sure where we'll end up when we follow a new clue to the future. But if we follow our curiosity, we will usually arrive at a clearing: an open space where something new can exist, a place for us to start thinking about making a change that matters.

IMAGINATION TRAINING

RULE #6: Look for Clues.

Collect and investigate "signals of change," or real-life examples of how the world is becoming different. Let these signals spark your curiosity. Follow the trail of clues wherever it takes you.

By looking for these clues to the future, you'll develop your strangesight—a "sixth sense" for noticing surprising, strange, mind-opening examples of how your life and society could change. These clues may even inspire you to take action today.

Signals of Change—Tips and Tricks

Looking for signals of change is a habit. Here's some advice for how to practice it.

Make a commitment to spend five minutes each week finding one new signal of change. Pick a day of the week as your clue-finding day. I suggest Tuesday, Clues Day! Or how about Future Friday?

Finding signals can be as simple as doing a quick news or social media search. The easiest way to find a clue is to search "future of" plus whatever you're interested in. This week, I searched for "future of prison reform," "future of mental health," and "future of pets." (That was a particularly fun search—I learned about dinosaur chickens, therapeutic robot cushions, and "how dogs on Mars would live.") You can also throw in terms like "innovation," "experiment," "surprising," "trend," "leading-edge," "weird," "strange," "creative idea," "new phenomenon," "scientific study."

Another strategy is to ask people you know what new things they're seeing in the world that excite or worry them. Sometimes I post on social media questions like this: "What's the weirdest or most surprising thing going on in cryptocurrency right now?" "I'm looking for leading-edge projects and ideas in the future of voting—what can you share with me?" "What's happening in the world that you wish more people were paying attention to?" My students have started signals-sharing groups, in person or online. They organize monthly signals-trading snack or coffee breaks. They make it a new rule to start every team meeting with someone sharing a newly discovered signal. They trade signals on email, Facebook, WhatsApp, LinkedIn, Discord, or Slack. "It's just like starting a book club," one student told me, "but instead of reading a different book every month, we pick a different future topic, and everyone brings at least one signal of change."

Collecting signals is a way to fuel your curiosity and imagination. It's fun just to notice them and share them with others. If you want to turn a signal into a scenario, the next step is to do a little analysis of the signals, by asking these questions:

1. What kind of change is it an example of?
2. What's driving, or motivating, the change? Why is it happening?
3. What does this signal make me worry about? What does it make me excited about?

4. What would the world be like if the signal became common?

5. Do I want to wake up in that world? Is it a future I want?

These questions can spark discussion if you're collecting and sharing signals with others.

And now it's time for you to go on your own signals scavenger hunt! Before you turn another page of this book, go ahead and do a quick news or social media search. Try to find a news headline or story that makes you say, "Wow! That's weird!" or "I've never seen *that* before." Your search term can be any future topic you're interested in, but I suggest you pick as your topic *whatever unchangeable fact you named in chapter 4, when we first played Stump the Futurist.* Now that you know how to investigate signals of change, you should be able to prove yourself wrong—and find evidence that the seemingly unchangeable fact is, in at least some small way, already starting to change. And remember: when you find a new signal, write down all the questions that come up for you about it. Each question is a potential new path of investigation for you to follow.

7

Choose Your Future Forces

Let's start by acknowledging that there's no "back to normal"
future now.

—KATHI VIAN, distinguished fellow,
Institute for the Future

WHICH GLOBAL TRENDS—THINGS GOING ON IN THE WORLD THAT ARE bigger than you, and beyond your individual control—do you think will have the most influence on your life, and on your friends' and family's lives, over the next decade?

Here's my list:

1. Extreme heat and drought from climate change
2. Post-pandemic trauma (ours, and the planet's too)
3. The radicalization of young people via social media and conspiracy theories
4. The widespread adoption of facial recognition technologies

5. Universal basic income, if our city, state, or national
   government adopts it
6. The reinvention of higher education, to be more affordable
   and lifelong

When I think about my life goals, my family's safety and security,
my friends' plans and dreams, our future health and happiness—I'm
keeping this list in mind. These changes are going to make life more
challenging, or more complicated, or more interesting for us over the
next decade, and while many other forces will shape our future, these
are the ones I'm spending the most energy thinking and learning
about right now.

Of all the things I could worry about and hope for, this list is
where I'm choosing to focus my long-term imagination. These are *my*
future forces.

A *future force* is a significant trend or phenomenon that's likely to
make a disruptive or transformative impact on society. Sometimes described as a "megatrend," a "driver of change," or a "macro force," it
usually starts off as a small signal of change—and then it picks up
strength over a period of months, years, or decades.

Anything with the potential to change the world can be a future
force. It might be a quickly advancing area of *scientific research*, like human genetic modification or artificial intelligence.

It might be a *social movement*, like Black Lives Matter.

It might be a new *technology* entering the mainstream, like Bitcoin
and other cryptocurrencies.

It might be an increasingly popular *policy idea*, like lowering the
voting age to sixteen.

It might be a shift in *consumer behavior*, like the rise of plant-based diets.

It might be a growing *threat* documented by experts and researchers, like sea-level rise from climate change or the impact of noise pollution on mental health.

It might be a major *demographic shift*, like the "youth boom" in Africa,
where most countries now have an average age of fifteen to eighteen

compared to an average age of thirty-eight in the United States, thirty-nine in China, and forty in the United Kingdom.[1]

It might be a long-term *regulatory effort*, like governments attempting to limit the power and monopoly of tech companies.

Or it might be a widespread *cultural change*, like the decline of marriage rates, which have fallen in four out of five countries worldwide by an average of 34 percent over the past fifty years.[2]

If a signal of change is like a tantalizing clue that can take you surprising places, then a future force is like a giant neon blinking arrow pointing you in one unambiguous direction. It's the equivalent of thousands of signals of change combined, all hinting at the same possible future. Futurists don't often use the word "inevitable." But when it comes to future forces, it's almost certain that we're all going to have to reckon with them, one way or another.

You can work against a future force to try to minimize it, slow it down, or prevent future harm—the way climate crisis activists are working to mitigate the risks of climate change.

You can work with a future force to help it spread faster—the way universal basic income advocates are funding their own pilot programs and studies, to try to prove to governments how much the policy could help.

Or you can explore a future force with an open mind and try to find new opportunities in it—the way virtually every fast-food chain in the United States introduced at least one new plant-based version of a popular dairy or meat item in 2021.[3]

Whatever you do, know that you will never be *in control* of a future force. Neither will I, neither will anyone—not even the CEOs of the world's biggest companies, the presidents of nations, the richest billionaires, or the most influential activists. Future forces are bigger than any one person, or country, or organization. They are the most powerful, gale-force winds of change.

Yet don't underestimate the benefits of knowing which way the winds of change are blowing. As the saying goes, "You can't control the wind, but you can adjust your sail."

• • •

How do you start to think about which future forces will be most powerful in your own life? First, you have to *find* the future forces. The good news is that future forces are usually obvious—if you're willing to acknowledge reality. But powerful future forces often make us feel uncomfortable, so this is easier said than done. A future force might make us feel uncomfortable because we don't yet know enough about it to make sense of it. Or it might make us uncomfortable because it demands that we change in ways we don't want to or feel ready for yet. A force might make us feel uncomfortable, or scare us, because it seems to be blowing us straight toward disaster, and we have no idea what we can do to stop it.

The more uncomfortable a future force makes you feel, the closer you should look at it.

I've been asked many times what the secret is to making superaccurate future forecasts like Superstruct and EVOKE. The humble truth is that those crisis simulations were inspired by future forces that many global experts had been sounding the alarm about for years, but that most people were ignoring anyway. Our scenarios correctly predicted an uncontrollable respiratory pandemic, historic wildfires caused by climate change, bad actors intentionally spreading misinformation via social networks, and failing electric grids as a result of low infrastructure investment—but not because the Institute for the Future or the World Bank knew something about the future that other people didn't. Quite the opposite: our simulations were just a channel—a conduit—to communicate what was already clearly and obviously on the horizon. We compiled the biggest future forces we could find, the ones that had been gaining strength for many years and seemed to be keeping the most experts up at night. As far as I can tell, the only thing that truly set the Superstruct and EVOKE forecasts apart was our willingness to imagine *all* of the likely crises unfolding at the same time, and to consider how all of the various risks might complicate and intensify each other.

The most valuable lesson I learned from expert scenario designers at the Institute for the Future is this: when it comes to the far future, I don't have to try to figure out what's worth worrying about. Neither do you. The world is jam-packed with trustworthy experts whose full-time job is to study, analyze, and warn others of future risks and disruptions: climate scientists, epidemiologists, technology ethicists, investigative reporters, human rights activists, national security researchers, economic forecasters. We just have to listen to them.

One of the most important sources of foresight that I rely on, and that I've been using for the past fifteen years to gather up future forces, is the World Economic Forum's annual *Global Risks Report*. It's put together by a team of researchers who survey over 650 top world leaders from business, government, and global development. The leaders share which future forces they're currently most concerned about, and they rank the urgency of each risk. They also make predictions about when, exactly, each risk will have global impact—this year, next year, five years from now, ten years from now. This collective intelligence is analyzed and aggregated into a very clear road map of what is keeping some of the most informed and influential people in the world up at night.

If you read the report each year, as I do, then you realize that the same future forces keep showing up on the list. In 2021, the *Global Risks Report* identified these "usual suspects" as the most likely to have major global impact in the next decade:

- extreme weather, sea-level rise, and global warming from climate change
- infectious diseases, including long-term impacts of COVID-19, preventable diseases like malaria, and future novel pandemics
- weapons of mass destruction
- social unrest, due to lack of economic opportunity, widespread job loss, debt, and underemployment
- cyberattacks on digital networks and critical infrastructure, like water supply and the electrical power grid

No surprises here—these are widely known, well-documented threats. These forces have already demonstrably harmed humanity, and they continue to cast a long shadow on the future.

If I were planning my next large-scale social simulation, it would be a no-brainer to focus on these top five risks. I'd ask tens of thousands of people, "If this crisis really happened, what would you do?" "What would you need?" "How could you help?" I'd analyze their answers to uncover hard-to-predict social consequences and surprising ripple effects of a hypothetical disaster. These insights, as we've seen from previous simulations, can lead to more effective disaster management, harm reduction, and damage control.

A social simulation would give participants the opportunity to pre-process their shock with each other, so they could act faster, and adapt faster, in the event of a real crisis. And maybe, just maybe—there's always this hope—pre-experiencing a hypothetical global catastrophe would inspire more people to take action and demand change today, so that a real catastrophe could be avoided.

Yes, if I were creating a Superstruct 2030 simulation or an EVOKE 2035 game today, I'd just pick the top five risks from the latest *Global Risks Report*, package them into one (admittedly gloomy) super-scenario, and off to the future we'd go. I might also include a few other future forces identified by the World Economic Forum (WEF) as being of special interest in the coming decade, newer risks that haven't appeared on previous lists.

For example, the top new risk in the latest report is *digital inequality*, which refers to the gap between people who have reliable, high-speed internet access and those who don't. This gap has become increasingly problematic as society has turned to virtual and online alternatives to school, work, and staying socially connected. Today, almost three billion people worldwide, including thirty million people in the US, suffer from poor internet access. To put this risk in perspective, can you imagine having gotten through the pandemic without internet in your home or on your phone? Really try to imagine it. How different would your experience of the pandemic have been? How much more difficult?

Youth disillusionment is another force gathering strength. It's defined as "disengagement and lack of confidence and/or loss of trust with existing economic, political, and social structures at a global scale."[4] There are currently 1.21 billion young people between fifteen and twenty-four on the planet, and surveys show that they are increasingly frustrated by what they view as the corrupt, unjust, and climate-endangering actions of older generations. As a result, youth-led movements have been on the rise in the past decade—from the Arab Spring, to global climate strikes, to civil rights movements seeking more social and racial equality. This future force could be a tremendous catalyst for positive change, but only if older generations are willing to adapt and make way for younger people to lead. If young people are not given a seat at the table—a chance to make their voices heard—and if older generations are not willing to rethink some of the more damaging aspects of "business as usual," then more radical youth movements could emerge. A truly radicalized young generation could destabilize democracies and economies worldwide. Rather than leading to positive social changes, youth disillusionment could instead plunge society into chaos and extremism. The WEF ranks this risk as "a top global blind spot"—an area where the current global response severely underestimates a risk's likely future impact.

Speaking of youth: an "under-thirty" group of over ten thousand rising entrepreneurs, scientists, activists, and community leaders from 165 countries was polled by the WEF for *their* top future forces. Interestingly, this group named *mental health deterioration* just above climate change and economic inequality as their number one future force that will have the biggest global impact over the next decade. While surprising—mental health deterioration has never appeared in a *Global Risks Report* before—it also makes sense. The years 2020 and 2021 marked the largest global increases in depression, anxiety, grief, burnout, loneliness, and trauma ever observed, due to the pandemic and its long-term aftereffects. This force has hit the youngest generations hardest—studies show that during 2020 and 2021, mental health deteriorated for 80 percent of children and young adults across the globe. And there's a real possibility that these problems will linger and have ripple effects for a decade or longer.[5]

So add the digital divide, youth disillusionment, and mental health deterioration to our 2035 super-scenario. Imagine that these forces are combining with climate change, increasing economic inequality, and the other most obvious threats. If we simulated this scenario today, and then in ten or twenty years from now we were all actually living through some truly unthinkable combination of one or more of these full-blown threats—perhaps with 70 percent of global youth on a work strike, a mental health pandemic affecting one billion people, increasingly frequent cyberattacks leading to monthslong global internet shutdowns, and extreme weather forcing mass climate migration—you wouldn't say that I was a future-forecasting genius. Instead, you'd say, "Anyone could have predicted that, if they were paying attention to the future forces." And you'd be right.

It's really that simple. Not being blindsided by the future requires only that you be willing to pay attention, to pay *imagination*, when experts overwhelmingly tell you that, yes, a future is coming. You just have to look where those giant neon blinking arrows are pointing—and then not look away.

By the end of this chapter, you'll be able to make your own list of the top future forces that could disrupt your life—for better, for worse, for complicated. Just having this list will start to give you some ideas of what you want to learn more about and get better at in the coming decade, so you can be ready for whatever's next. I'll also show you how to use your list to start preparing to help others, so that instead of feeling overwhelmed by the future forces, you are energized and empowered by them. And when it comes time for you to create your own social simulation of the year 2030 or beyond (the very last thing I'll teach you in this book), your unique list of top future forces will be the inspiration for a scenario you want to game out with others.

. . .

Now I ADMIT, GLOBAL RISKS are not necessarily fun to think about, even if it's "just a game" or "just a simulation." Future forces like "weapons of mass destruction" and "the next pandemic" can make anyone's brain shut down and say, "No thanks, I'm not imagining *that* today." I wouldn't blame you if you are thinking, *Can I skip ahead to the list of happy future forces, please?* Fair enough: the happy future forces list is coming in just a few pages. But let's stay with the worrisome forces just a moment longer. I need to make sure you understand one very important thing about simulating future threats:

You don't have to spend a lot of time mentally immersed in a hypothetical crisis to get a big benefit. When it comes to dangerous future forces, even a tiny bit of imagining will help. If you can handle just twenty seconds of vividly imagining one potential disaster or catastrophe, then you can instantly overcome one of the biggest neurological obstacles to thinking effectively about the future.

The obstacle is called *normalcy bias,* and most people have it to some degree. Normalcy bias is defined by psychologists as "the refusal to plan for, or react quickly to, a disaster which has never happened before."[6] It's a state of denial that most people enter, by default, when confronted by evidence of novel or growing risks. Normalcy bias is so widespread and hard to resist, in fact, that it's responsible for roughly a quarter of CEO firings: according to a four-year study of 286 companies that forced out their CEOs, 23 percent were fired primarily for "denying reality" and refusing to recognize the need to change.[7]

Normalcy bias is a result of the brain's preference for stable patterns. It's easier to plan, strategize, and act when you can safely assume that the future will be similar to the past. The brain wants to believe that what's normal now will still be normal for the foreseeable future. And, conversely, it wants to believe that if something has never happened before, it probably won't happen anytime soon.

If we carefully scrutinize these beliefs, of course, they completely fall apart. Things happen every day that have never happened before!

History is made up of nothing but an endless series of shocking things happening for the first time: shocking scientific discoveries, shocking technological advances, shocking social progress, shocking reforms, shocking natural disasters, shocking violence, shocking government actions, shocking economic collapse. If anything, human brains should have a shock bias rather than a normalcy bias. But constantly expecting everything around us to change unpredictably would be too mentally taxing. It would wear down our nervous system. It would exhaust us emotionally. So we stick to our normalcy bias, which helps us stay sane and feel reasonably in control of our lives.

Still, we can at least, occasionally and intentionally, give ourselves a *little* shock. As the historian and activist David Swanson has said, "Almost everything important that's ever happened was unimaginable shortly before it happened."[8] We have to actively try to overcome normalcy bias, so we can think more effectively, and creatively, about the future. We have to train the brain to recognize when this cognitive bias is no longer helpful.

Fortunately, you've been training your brain to overcome normalcy bias just by reading this book. Every futures-thinking habit you've practiced, and every brainstorming game you've played, will make your mind more receptive to "not normal" ideas and information. And when it comes to fully acknowledging the reality of future forces, your new episodic future thinking (EFT) skills are especially helpful. Here's why:

Nearly fifty years ago, psychology researchers discovered something remarkable: if you want someone to believe that a future event is likely, you just have to ask them to imagine it happening, in as much vivid detail as possible.

This finding dates back to a 1976 study in which participants were asked to imagine learning the results of a real upcoming US presidential election (Ford versus Carter). They were randomly assigned one of the two candidates and told to imagine that candidate winning. They were told to fill in as many details of this future moment as possible, just as you've been doing in the EFT challenges in this book: Where are you when you hear the election results? What time is it? Whom are you with? Do you find out by TV, radio, or newspaper? What's the final electoral count? How do you feel? Later, the study participants were asked to predict who would win the real upcoming 1976 election. They overwhelmingly predicted that the winner would be whichever candidate they had imagined winning. This was true even when they strongly preferred the other candidate.[9]

A few years later, in a similar study, participants were asked to estimate the probability that they would catch a new disease in the future. Some participants were given a description of the disease that included intentionally easier-to-imagine symptoms, like headache, stomach pain, and fever. (These symptoms were considered easy to imagine because most everyone has experienced them and knows what they feel like.) Other participants were given a description of the disease that included harder-to-imagine symptoms, like "liver aches" and "paresthesia." (These symptoms were considered harder to imagine because—well, do you know what "paresthesia" means, or what liver aches feel like?!) All of the participants were asked to imagine as vividly as possible a three-week period in which they came down with the illness, suffered all of its symptoms, and then eventually recovered. They were instructed to write detailed, journal-like descriptions of exactly how they felt and what they did to treat their symptoms. After vividly imagining this potential illness, they were asked two questions: How easy was it to imagine? And how likely do you think you are to catch this disease?

As you now might guess, participants who were assigned the easy-to-imagine symptoms like headaches said it was, in fact, easy to imagine, wrote highly detailed journal entries, and rated their chances of catching the disease quite high. Participants who had to try to imagine rare symptoms like liver aches said it was hard to imagine, wrote less vivid journal entries, and rated their chances of catching the disease quite low.[10] The takeaway of this study is that *vague* imagination doesn't do much to counter normalcy bias. Vivid imagination, on the other hand, works wonders.

These two scientific studies have inspired many others. In the nearly fifty years since, hundreds more studies have shown this same effect: imagining a possible event in vivid, realistic detail convinces us that the event is more likely to actually happen.[11] And researchers pretty much all agree on why this phenomenon occurs. After you've created a memory of a possible future in your mind, you recall the details much more quickly the next time. This perceived ease of imagining tricks the brain.

Generally, psychologists explain, it's easier to recall and imagine events that are frequent and common because you have so much experience with them, and so much information about them. It's harder to recall and imagine events that are infrequent and uncommon because you just don't know as much about them. Any time a future possibility feels easy to imagine, the brain is more likely to file it away as a "normal" and likely event—*even if it's never happened before*. Moreover, the effect is cumulative: each time you reimagine a possible future event in vivid detail, you rate its probability of happening even higher. And the more details you can envision, the more likely it seems.

In short: the act of imagining an event vividly makes it *easier to imagine* the next time you try. Thanks to your imagination's hard work, a strange possibility feels quite normal to you now.

What does this research mean for you? If you don't want to be shocked or blindsided by possible future crises or disasters, you have to overcome your normalcy bias and convince your brain that these strange events can happen—no matter how "unthinkable" they seem to you today. A single act of vivid imagination today will do the trick: it will prime your brain to see a risk as normal, so you'll be more likely to notice and pay attention when the threat grows. And if the risk turns into a real crisis, you'll skip right over the shock and denial phases that keep other people stuck in old ways of thinking, and frozen in old ways of acting. You'll be able to adapt and react faster when the word "normal" no longer applies.

It doesn't take long to break down your normalcy bias. One recent fMRI study found that a new and persuasive memory of the future can be formed in just twenty seconds of active imagination.[12] So that's the good news: you don't have to spend your days wrapped up in the potential problems of tomorrow. Just take a quick mental time trip, look around a future crisis, and give your brain a few details to work with. Ask these familiar questions: What's different in this future? What's around me? How do I feel? What do I want to do? The kinds of threats that others deny, the risks others downplay, the catastrophes others refuse to imagine—you'll be able to think about them much more clearly, without normalcy bias getting in the way.

OKAY, YOU'VE CONVINCED YOUR BRAIN that a future force like youth disillusionment or global mental health deterioration is now normal and worth worrying about. What next?

Don't worry.

Literally, *don't worry*.

You can and will do the worrying later, when you're living through an actual, and not a hypothetical, crisis. Right now, you've got some time spaciousness. You can use it to do some real good.

Here's my advice: use this time now to identify *one thing* you could do to help *one person* affected by this force, now or in the future. Keep it small. Don't try to save the world. Just get ready to help a single soul.

Pema Chödrön, the Tibetan Buddhist nun and teacher, has famously written and spoken about how to stay brave and openhearted during times of personal or collective crisis. She advises: "Despite what we might think much of the time and what the news programs imply, we all wish to be sane and openhearted people. We could take our wish to be more sane and kind and put it in a very large context. We could expand it into a desire to help all other people, to help the whole world. But we need a place to start. We can't simply begin with the whole world. We need to begin by reaching out to the people who come into our own lives—our family members, our neighbors, our coworkers."[13] This is indeed the best way I know to take in a lot of challenging information about the future and not feel overwhelmed by it.

To put a twist on Chödrön's wise guidance, also expressed in her best-known book *When Things Fall Apart*: when things *might* fall apart far in the future, *get ready* to reach out to the people in your own life and in your community.

For mental health deterioration, this would mean imagining that in the next few years many of the people you know will start to suffer, or will suffer more deeply, mental health challenges like anxiety, depression, loneliness, or grief. You can pick anyone at all to imagine helping. What action could you take now to *be more prepared* to help that one person in your life, if that person becomes deeply affected by the future force?

Here's the action I decided to take when I imagined helping others during a decade-long global mental health crisis: I enrolled in a free psychological first aid course taught online by Johns Hopkins University. By teaching mental health support skills to as many community members as possible, this course is designed to increase community resilience. In the course, I learned "first responder" techniques for helping someone else during a psychological emergency. I practiced being a compassionate presence and listener. I learned what questions I can ask to determine if professional care is urgently required. My hope is that developing these skills now will prepare me to help others more effectively if and when global mental health deterioration requires "all hands on deck," including my own. And truly, I do feel more hopeful about the future as a result of having taken this small step, even if it's a future I wish we could avoid.

WE CAN ALWAYS LOOK FOR ways to turn an overwhelming future force into an opportunity to help. Let me give you a couple more examples, from my own life.

I wanted to feel more powerful in the face of digital inequality, so I decided to change how I approach online teaching. I committed to making "low-bandwidth" versions of my free online Futures Thinking classes available for anyone with an unreliable or slow internet connection. Instead of requiring students to attend a one-hour lecture live, I can divide my lectures into five- or ten-minute prerecorded videos that are easier to download and access anytime. I can hold class discussions on text-based message boards rather than in a bandwidth-hogging Zoom room. I can't solve the problem of digital inequality for everyone. I *can* be ready to help at least one student out there who might want to take my course but doesn't have access to high-bandwidth internet. So now, whenever I teach a new online course, I develop it with that one student in mind. And if someday I need to adapt to a world with increasingly widespread internet instability, my knowledge of low-bandwidth teaching will be a skill I can use to help others.

As for how to respond to the future force of youth disillusionment, I feel lucky that one of my creative colleagues at the Institute for the Future came up with a fantastic, and totally doable, idea. Typically, the institute's Ten-Year Forecast conference is an invitation-only event for our research partners and clients. But when my colleague Dylan Hendricks took over the role of planning the annual event, he had a suggestion: we should invite teenagers to attend. Ten years from now, today's teenagers will be helping to shape society. Why not give them a seat at the table now? In 2016, twenty teenagers were invited to attend the Ten-Year Forecast conference, in person or by remote-controlled Beam telepresence robots. We let them tell all of *us* what they were excited about, and what they were worried about, for the future. Twenty out of 1.2 billion young people is a very small start. But that's the best way to start—*small*, so that nothing will stop you, so that you actually do something and not *only* imagine it.

I recently asked Dylan what stood out to him about that experience. He reminded me that as part of the Ten-Year Forecast activities, we asked the teens to invent "new rites of passage" they thought would define their generation—especially if activities like getting a driver's license might no longer be something most young people do. "What really stood out was one rite they came up with," Dylan told me. "It was the most popular idea by far. They agreed the most significant rite of passage for teens of the future would be the first time you personally, directly experienced a devastating consequence of climate change. This was still two years before Greta Thunberg and three years before the school strikes for climate. It was definitely a strong early signal of that movement."

For us at the institute, this tiny experiment planted a seed for bigger possible action in the future. We've started creating more youth trainings and including teens in more of our future workshops. I recently taught my first "youth only" session of the How to Think Like a Futurist training, to thirty teenagers from across California who were nominated as leaders in their community. I feel confident that if the institute's efforts are needed to help channel a global wave of youth disillusionment, we will be ready.

IF HELPING JUST ONE PERSON sounds good to you, but you still don't know what *you* can do, just be patient. Set an intention—and then, wait for an idea or opportunity to arise. You have plenty of time. The future doesn't start today! Enjoy the time spaciousness. In the meantime, you can look for the people who are already helping.

When I attended the Planetary Defense Conference, I was amazed to discover how many people there are whose full-time job it is to defend Earth against asteroids and other near-Earth objects. It was thrilling. Over the course of a week, I learned how scientists are getting better at detecting and tracking objects in the sky. I learned how they decide which ones pose a real threat, and what their options are for dealing with it: deflecting it so it no longer is on a path to collide with our planet, using a nuclear device to obliterate it, or superaccurately forecasting the potential impact location, so that far fewer people (say one hundred thousand instead of one hundred million) need to evacuate. I watched as experts brainstormed ways to fight misinformation and communicate more effectively with the public about the risks of asteroids. They strategized how to evacuate large numbers of people safely and equitably. They debated the merits of a new convention that would allow countries to take nuclear action to deflect or destroy an asteroid, since current international space treaties ban this action, even if it's considered the only way to prevent a catastrophe. The whole five-day experience left me feeling incredibly *hopeful* about the future of humanity, even though we spent the whole time imagining potentially apocalyptic scenarios. Now that I know there are so many helpers, I feel grateful, humble, and excited to find my own small part to play in the effort. I now want to understand asteroid science well enough to explain it to others, so I can share accurate information with friends and family and fight misinformation on social media if it becomes necessary. Urgent optimism can be contagious, if we put ourselves in a position to catch it! Pema Chödrön writes: "When we look at the world around us—our immediate world and the bigger world beyond—we see a lot of difficulty and dysfunction. . . . It can be quite discouraging. Yet we could actually derive inspiration . . . from these dire circumstances. We could recognize the fact, and proclaim the fact, that *we are needed*."[14]

The possibilities of the far future are often difficult to think about. We don't want to imagine such widespread suffering or harm. But if future risks have anything to teach us, it's that we *will be* needed. And with time spaciousness, we can find our own unique ways to answer that call.

IT CAN FEEL INTIMIDATING TO try to keep track of all these dynamic forces, let alone incorporate them into your personal visions and plans. But I am here to tell you it really, truly helps. When you're willing to acknowledge the bigger forces in play, you develop the kind of confidence and clarity that can come only from being able to look at risks and revolutions head-on, and not deny or avoid them.

The *Global Risks Report* helped me anticipate the almost unimaginable world of 2019 and 2020 more than a decade in advance, and it can help you see crises years before you have to live through them. So I want you to stop reading right now and, if it's possible, search online for the latest version of the report. You don't have to read it now. But go *find* it. If you take this first step, you're more likely to actually engage with the report in the future. It won't be a thing you've heard about; it will be a thing you've made real and manifested in front of you. So go ahead and search for "WEF Global Risks Report."* You'll be opening the door to taking in difficult and challenging information. You'll be just a little more ready to imagine.

And while you're at it, go find something called *Global Trends*, a report put out every four years by the US National Intelligence Council at the start of each presidential term.[15] It's a strategic look at how future forces will influence geopolitics in the coming twenty years. The report analyzes forces from economics, technology, the environment, and demographics and combines them into future scenarios you can use as inspiration for episodic future thinking. It's not light reading, but it's fascinating, eye-opening, and convincing. And it will give you the kinds of details you need to more easily imagine how many different future forces will affect your life, and the lives of the people you care about most.

NOT ALL FUTURE FORCES ARE risks or threats, of course. Those just happen to be the ones we most commonly deny and ignore, to our detriment. Other winds of change are, generally, much easier to lift our sails for. Keeping up with new technologies can be fun. Participating in activism and social movements is exciting and meaningful. Learning about scientific breakthroughs sparks awe and wonder. Changes in culture and behavior—well, we may be one of the trendsetters ourselves, or at least curious onlookers.

Be sure to put some future forces on your list that make you feel optimistic. Need inspiration? Here are ten future forces that could make a better world in the next decade:[16]

---

* You can find the latest *Global Risks Report* right here: https://www.weforum.org /global-risks/reports.

1. **mRNA vaccines:** Ten years from now, the same technology behind the Moderna and Pfizer-BioNTech COVID-19 vaccines may be able to prevent or cure cancer, malaria, tuberculosis, and HIV, among other diseases, launching a golden age of public health.

2. **Super-inexpensive solar and wind energy:** By the end of this decade, solar and wind energy will be cheaper than fossil fuels everywhere on the planet, making it possible *and* financially lucrative to end fossil fuel use worldwide, dramatically reducing air pollution and carbon emissions.

3. **Prioritization of social safety nets over economic growth:** A global study of more than ten thousand randomly selected young adults in thirteen countries, including the US, the UK, and Canada, found that more than two in three respondents under the age of twenty-four want their governments to prioritize the health and well-being of the population over GDP. Fifty-eight percent of people aged twenty-five to thirty-four agreed, as did 54 percent of people aged thirty-four to thirty-nine. Over the long term, this trend could lead to a significant strengthening of social safety nets and decreased economic inequality.

4. **"Bioprinting" technology:** Within a decade, 3D printers may be capable of producing human organs out of biocompatible plastics. This would eliminate the need for human organ donation and make getting a new organ a viable treatment option even in the earlier stages of diseases.

5. **Living concrete:** Traditional concrete is responsible for nearly 10 percent of global carbon emissions today, but a new technology that creates living concrete bricks out of bacteria, gelatin, and sand *absorbs* carbon dioxide and releases oxygen. Living concrete self-regenerates; one brick cut in half heals and forms two bricks; those two can be cut in half to create four, and so on. Living concrete could revolutionize building in the next decade and beyond. It would be especially useful in

places where very few resources are available, such as in desert conditions (which are likely to increase on Earth if global warming trends continue) or on Mars.

6. **Direct cash transfers:** Inspired by universal basic income programs, global charities are now starting to make direct cash transfers to people instead of other kinds of handouts or donations, like food, medicine, or clothing. This dramatically reduces the overhead of charity efforts and gets more resources to people, and faster, to use however they like. A decade from now, money may flow quickly and freely to people in need, wherever they are, stimulating all kinds of new markets.

7. **Cultured meat:** Produced in a lab, without the slaughter of animals, it's meat grown in a bioreactor—and by 2030, it may be more commonly sold worldwide than meat grown inside animals' bodies. This technology is a triple win: it may help end global hunger by providing a cheap and sustainable protein source, while also reducing carbon emissions from livestock and preventing the suffering of animals.

8. **Efforts to combat social isolation:** Loneliness is a growing public health challenge linked to a range of damaging mental and physical impacts, including heart disease, stroke, and cognitive decline. To fight it, the governments of Japan and the United Kingdom have appointed "ministers of loneliness." They've launched national health initiatives that allow doctors to prescribe cooking classes, walking clubs, and art groups. They've adjusted postal worker routes to give them extra time to check in on lonely people as part of their daily rounds. And they've funded experiments in communal living, so older individuals can pool resources to own homes together and build a sense of community. Following these trends, we all may have more genuine friends in the future.

9. **Free or low-cost learning for a lifetime:** In the US, free public education has historically ended at grade twelve. But a decade from now, tuition-free community college, low-cost online certificate programs that come with job guarantees, and other learning innovations will make it possible to never stop learning.

10. **Antiaging biotech:** New technologies like "neuron reprogramming" can successfully reverse the biological clock and unwind the effects of aging in animal lab experiments today. Ten years from now, they may start to lengthen the healthy, active human lifespan by decades.

Which of these possibilities make you feel hopeful for the future? Pick one or two and take a quick mental time trip to a world in which any of these developments have achieved maximal positive impact. Spend a moment really pre-feeling the relief, excitement, joy, security, or gratitude you might experience when and if these winds of change blow through *your* community.

As with any future force, even with good intentions, there may be new ethical dilemmas to consider and potential unintended consequences. As you imagine the positive possibilities, you may be inspired to think through these uncertainties too.

If you want to give your imagination more realistic details to work with, a quick internet search will help you learn more. See if you can find any of the helpers who are pushing these forces forward today. Maybe you'll be inspired to join them.

TRACKING A FUTURE FORCE IS a continual process of educating and reeducating yourself. It doesn't have to be a crash course. Future forces move relatively slowly, and they play out over many years.

I make it a personal habit once a year to revisit the set of future forces that I'm most worried or most excited about. I do this yearly refresh in January, because that's when the WEF's *Global Risks Report* comes out. I read some articles, listen to some podcasts, watch some videos, and refresh my thinking. Sometimes I decide that a force has either fizzled out or become the "new normal," and I stop tracking it. Sometimes I start tracking a new future force I don't know much about yet. As a way to process what I'm learning, I try to come up with a new future scenario for each of my top future forces—so I can take some mental time trips and invite others to help me seriously imagine the world these forces might create.

Here's one scenario I've been playing with lately: Today, facial recognition is used in just a few contexts, like unlocking our smartphones or in airport security. But can you imagine—have you *tried* imagining yet—what your life will be like when facial recognition is used for everything?

Within the next decade, "face search apps" will likely be as common as internet search engines are today. You'll be able to get vast amounts of information about a complete stranger just by pointing your phone, smartwatch, or augmented reality glasses at them. Can you imagine how face searches will change your life? Can you imagine how your friends and family might be affected?

Future Scenario #5: Don't Face Search Me

Somewhere public, ten years from today*

You're minding your own business when you notice someone discreetly raising their phone. They're pointing the camera lens in *your* direction, at *your* face. It's just a quick flick of the wrist. It happens so fast you almost miss it. But you know what they're doing. They just *face searched* you.

---

* Realistically, this scenario could happen in the next few years; it probably won't take a full decade. If your mind is already fully open to the possibility of widespread consumer facial recognition apps, feel free to change the target date of this scenario to something much closer to today. If this scenario feels far-fetched to you, stick with the ten-year timeframe.

A couple of seconds later, they're looking at their phone screen, no doubt finding out your name, age, and whatever other personal details they've set the face search parameters for. Around here, there's a lot of face searching for "neighbor" or "stranger" status, based on whether your official home address is within the neighborhood boundaries. You know that a lot of people have been face searching for vaccination status lately too. But this is the first time you've personally been face searched—or at least, it's the first time you've noticed.

IMAGINE THIS SCENE AS VIVIDLY as you can. I've left some important details out—what kind of public space you're in, and a physical description of the person who pointed their camera at you. This is intentional. I want you to fill in those details yourself. Try to be as specific as possible. If you're in a restaurant, which one? If you're on a sidewalk, which block is it? Here are some questions to help you imagine this future moment as clearly as possible:

- Where are you?
- What time of day or night is it?
- Are you alone, or is a friend, family member, or someone else with you?
- What are you doing in the moment before you get face searched?
- Who face searched you—what's their physical description?
- How do you feel when you realize you've just been face searched by a stranger?

MOMENT OF CHOICE: What do you do about it? Do you say something to the person who face searched you? Do you ignore it? Do you stay, or do you leave? Do you quickly install a face-searching app and search them right back? What other kind of action can you imagine taking in the moment?

Here are a few more questions to play with:

- Can you think of an example of when *you* might want to use face-searching technology to find information about a stranger without their consent? When or where, and why?
- Besides name, age, and basic profile details, what kinds of information do you think people will face search each other for in the future?
- Would knowing that other people can face search you anytime and anywhere change any of your habits or behaviors? Which ones?
- If you reimagine the same scenario, but with a different location, or a different physical description of the person who face searched you, do your feelings or actions change? Try to alter the scenario details until you can imagine having a very different reaction—more positive or more negative—to what happened.

Could this scenario really happen? Technically, it's almost entirely feasible already. Companies like Facebook and Clearview AI have built massive databases of billions of facially identified photos. Hundreds of technology companies, including Intel, Microsoft, and the Chinese firm Tencent have developed their own facial recognition algorithms. And accuracy rates for facial recognition are extremely high across the industry: studies show them ranging from 90 percent at the low end to 99.98 percent at the high end.[17] Moving this technology forward is mostly a matter of building bigger databases and tweaking algorithms to improve accuracy.

You might expect increased mask wearing to complicate this scenario, whether masks are worn for health reasons or to purposefully interfere with facial recognition systems. But during the pandemic, a number of companies successfully retrained their algorithms to solve the mask problem. The Japanese firm NEC announced in January 2021 that its software was now 99.9 percent accurate for mask wearers, using just the eyes and forehead for recognition.[18] Trying to opt out of this future just by masking will be difficult indeed. Maybe we'll wear masks and dark search-blocking sunglasses too? (I can envision such a scenario clearly, and I can empathize with why people might do this, but I can't help but think how much harder it will be to connect with people if we can't see each other's faces.)

The biggest technical and ethical problem to be addressed (and it is indeed a big one) in facial recognition technology is the significant racial discrepancies in recognition error rates. Today, algorithms falsely identify Black and Asian faces between ten and one hundred times more often than Caucasian ones. Racial bias is baked into the technology—a major concern if it's being used by law enforcement, but beyond that, any technology that works well only for white people is hugely problematic. When I imagine how this future force might play out, I consider two possibilities: a scenario in which the racial bias in facial recognition is successfully eliminated and one in which it is not. These feel like two very different futures to me.[19]

Government regulation may slow down or divert this future force. US cities like Boston, Portland, and San Francisco have already banned the use of real-time facial recognition by police. The European Union proposed a similar ban in mid-2021. But so far, no government has regulated facial recognition in schools, businesses, or retail environments, or in consumer apps designed for use by the public.[20] The technology may move faster as a tool for individuals and private companies than for law enforcement.

Consider this signal of public face searching: PimEyes is a free tool that, when it launched, called itself a "face search engine for everyone."[21] According to its mission statement, "We truly believe that it is necessary to democratize facial recognition technology. It should not only be reserved for corporations or governments." I tried PimEyes recently. Within 4.56 seconds of scanning my face, it returned 453 face-matched images and websites. Of those, 452 images were actually of me; one was of my identical twin sister. Impressive.

I briefly considered using PimEyes to face search a stranger in public, as a real-world test of this scenario. But this is not a future I want to help create yet.

IF FACIAL RECOGNITION IS A future force you'd like to put on your own list, here's a set of search terms I recommend to investigate it further. Combine "facial recognition" and any of these words:

"advances," "breakthrough," "ethics," "regulation," "dilemma," "challenges," "risks," "opportunities," "benefits," "new study," "new app," "innovation," "unexpected," "unintended," "forecast," "predictions."

This set of terms will give you fuel for both your positive and shadow imagination. You can use it to track any future force across the internet and social media.

Picking just a few future forces to track over the next few years of your life is a relatively small commitment with a potentially huge positive impact. I recommend doing one search a month, to learn just one new thing. You can put a recurring appointment on your calendar or set up a monthly hangout. How about making the first Friday of each month Future Force Friday? At the very least, you'll learn a bunch of cool stuff. You might even discover a new personal purpose or mission. At the end of this chapter, I've included a list of twenty-four future forces that I recommend to inspire *your* next search for clues.

WE'VE JUST PLAYED WITH A scenario inspired by a future force that makes many people worried: facial recognition. Now let's play with a scenario inspired by a future force that makes many people hopeful: the reinvention of higher education and new opportunities for affordable, lifelong learning. This is a future force I think about a lot. Ten years from today, my twin daughters will be applying to college—if they want to go to college, that is. When I take a mental time trip to the year 2032, I wonder what kinds of colleges or programs they'll be excited about. I try to imagine what new learning paths might be available to them. And I pray that it will no longer be common for families to go into decades-long debt to pay for college. To build realistic hope, I keep track of forces and signals of change that might make their learning futures brighter when it comes to earning a degree affordably, following their curiosities, and discovering their passions. And you know what? When my kids are grown, I'll have more time to myself. Maybe I'll use some of that free time to go on a learning journey of my own. So I also try to imagine: What learning opportunities might exist for *me* ten years from now that don't exist today?

There is one possibility in particular that makes me want to stand on a mountaintop and yell, "HEY! Does anyone else think this is an amazing idea? Does anyone else want to make this future too?" It's an idea I first encountered during a One Hundred Ways Anything Can Be Different in the Future game that I led at the Institute for the Future's annual Ten-Year Forecast conference, on "the future of learning." One of the game's participants flipped the fact "Today, college students have to pick a major, like biology, business administration, English literature, or political science" to "Ten years from now, college students have to pick a grand challenge, like climate action, ending poverty, gender equality, or zero hunger." She explained the concept to our group: Students interested in all kinds of subject areas and careers—engineering, communications, teaching, political service, entrepreneurship, medicine, the arts—would come together and spend two to three years developing knowledge and skills around specific urgent global challenges. Instead of siloed majors, college learning would be more interdisciplinary and purpose driven. And careers, instead of being about choosing an industry or profession, would be more about deciding what problem you want to help humanity solve— as an engineer, mental health counselor, filmmaker, journalist, investment banker, nutritionist, marketing creative, social worker, or whatever else you might do with your days. Every type of major or career would be reimagined in service of something much, much bigger. Every course would look at a different angle of the problem—historical, economic, scientific, political, cultural—or explore possible solution spaces or interventions—technological, social, financial, behavioral. No one would worry that their major was "irrelevant" or that they would wind up in a "bullshit" job. It's all hands on deck for things that really matter.

I got goose bumps when I heard this concept. I suddenly wanted to wake up in that future *tomorrow*. I asked the participant who contributed this idea to tell me more. It turns out that she'd been part of a project by design students and faculty at Stanford University to imagine how learning might change between the years 2025 and 2100, and this was one of the top five futures they'd come up with.* She loved the idea as much as I did. But she hadn't yet seen any university, Stanford or otherwise, pick the idea up and run with it.

I want to run with it.

I've considered homeschooling my daughters around a different grand challenge each year. If I do, I'd love to get other homeschooling or unschooling families involved. I have more ambitious ideas, like pitching the concept to my local community college and offering to design a grand challenges program for them. Or maybe I'll convince the World Bank or the United Nations to partner with a major university to design and co-launch an online grand challenges degree program, for learners of any age. I will personally volunteer to help design the major or certificate program in planetary defense.

I'm right at the start of that magic ten-year timeline when it comes to thinking about my family's possible higher education future. Maybe that's why I can feel so wildly optimistic that this ridiculous, at first, idea is possible—and that I can personally help make it so. I know I can't sit around for the next decade and just hope it happens. I have to keep looking for ways to share this idea, experiment with it, get others on

---

* You can see all their ideas at http://www.stanford2025.com/. It's a fantastic example of a community-based approach to futures thinking and imagination.

board. So I'm sharing the next scenario with you as a small step toward action. If you take a mental time trip to this future, maybe you'll see something that excites you too, or expands the vision, or identifies a risk or obstacle that I haven't seen yet. Maybe you'll get as fired up as I am and put this future force on *your* list. If not, then start to think about the forces that fill *you* with hope—and the scenario *you* could invent to share with others and find your own allies for the future.

Future Scenario #6: "Have You Declared Your Challenge Yet?"

Late spring, at least several years in the future

It's that time of year again—late spring, and nearly fifty million college students and lifelong learners around the world are getting ready to declare their challenge.

It's an exciting season. Declaring a major used to feel like a personal decision, but declaring a challenge feels like joining an epic mission.

The ten most popular challenges last year were, in order of popularity:

1. Climate action
2. Good health and well-being
3. Sustainable cities
4. Gender equality
5. No poverty
6. Racial justice and equity
7. Ethical technology and innovation
8. Peace, justice, and strong institutions
9. Zero hunger
10. Responsible consumption and production

In a few weeks, the global numbers will be tallied up to see how many learners each challenge has gained. All summer long, challenge alumni will throw parties and meetups around the world to welcome newly declared learners to their global challenge community.

People pay attention during challenge season, even if they're not in school themselves. It feels good, all those people dedicating themselves to something bigger. It gives the world a boost of hope for the future. This year, you're paying extra-close attention to challenge season. That's because (pick one):

1. You're a college student about to declare your challenge. **Moment of choice:** What challenge are you going to declare? Why? Whom do you talk to, to help you make your decision? How do you share the news with friends and family?

2. You have a child, nephew, or niece in college who is trying to figure out what challenge to declare and who has asked for your advice. **Moment of choice:** What advice do you give? Picture a specific person and imagine how the conversation might go. How could you be the most helpful in this moment?

3. Your employer offers you, as a benefit, the opportunity to complete an online certificate in the challenge of your choice. You'll be given 10 percent of your work hours to dedicate to online learning for the next two years. **Moment of choice:** Do you accept this offer? If so, which challenge will you declare? Whom do you talk to, to help you make your decision?

4. You've been working on a committee to help design a brand-new challenge at your city or state community college. This program will be free to all adult learners in the community and will potentially inspire other schools to make the same challenge available to their students. **Moment of choice:** What new challenge did you help design? Why did you feel it was so important? Can you imagine what types of classes might be offered, what skills would be taught, and what projects would be completed by students in this challenge? Stretch your imagination and try to include as many subject

areas and career paths as possible, from nursing to computer programming to farming to law enforcement to franchise management to . . . (the possibilities are endless).

5. You're a teacher, and you've been given the opportunity to adapt one of your courses, or your classroom, to focus on a grand challenge. **Moment of choice:** Do you take the opportunity? If so, which challenge would you teach to? What changes would you make to your lessons? What kind of support would you need to do it?

6. You think the switch from traditional majors to grand challenges has been a terrible mistake. You're working on a video/podcast/essay about all the problems of the new system and its unintended harms. **Moment of choice:** What do you say when asked why you think it was such a mistake? What are your best arguments? What problems should have been anticipated? What do you think would make it better?

7. ??? (Add your own hypothetical future here!)

Could this scenario really happen? There are so many pieces in place already:

The United Nations' Sustainable Development Goals (SDGs) exist today as a way to build global consensus and collaboration around our most urgent challenges. The challenges in the scenario above are inspired by the latest SDGs, which were adopted by 193 countries in 2015. "Racial justice and equity" and "ethical technology and innovation" are my own additions; the other eight are taken straight from the current set of SDGs.

The growth of XPRIZEs is another trend that makes this scenario more likely. The XPRIZE organization designs and hosts public competitions intended "to catalyze innovation and accelerate a more hopeful future by incentivizing radical breakthroughs for the benefit of humanity."[22] The program famously launched in 1996 with a challenge to build private spaceships that could achieve suborbital flight, and in 2004, the $10 million prize was awarded to a winner. Since then, the foundation has launched more than a dozen challenges, including a $100 million competition currently open for a breakthrough carbon-removal technology that would help avoid the worst effects of climate change and a $15 million competition for "tomorrow's proteins"—that is, "chicken breast or fish fillet alternatives that replicate or outperform conventional chicken and fish in: access, environmental sustainability, animal welfare, nutrition, as well as taste and texture." To date, according to the organization's website, more than one million people have worked on teams officially registered to compete for an XPRIZE. In the future, challenge degree programs could certainly be inspired and motivated by such competitions.

Not to mention, there already exists a Grand Challenges Scholars Program (GCSP), created by the National Academy of Engineering in 2008 specifically for engineering students. As of 2020, roughly one hundred universities worldwide are approved as GCSP schools; they offer scholarships and custom learning paths to students who commit to focusing their education on grand challenges like "provide access to clean water," "reverse-engineer the brain," and "prevent nuclear terror." These students are so lucky! I'd like to imagine that this concept could spread beyond a single discipline to engage a much wider and more inclusive set of learners. One smaller signal of this possibility is the African Leadership University (ALU), founded in 2015, which has 1,500 students in Mauritius and Rwanda.[23] Students at ALU complete traditional undergraduate degree programs, such as in computer science or business studies, while also "declaring a mission" that forms the core of their assignments, fieldwork, and internships. The missions are inspired by challenges to transform Africa for the future, such as "urbanization," since nearly one billion Africans are expected to move from rural areas to cities on the continent by 2050. I like the twist this signal offers on the scenario—perhaps many state or city universities would focus on local grand challenges rather than global ones.

"Have You Declared Your Challenge Yet?" also imagines that as many adult continuing learners would declare a challenge as young, just-out-of-high-school college students. Is that realistic? Well, today, the largest online learning platform, Coursera, has seventy-seven million learners; edX has over thirty-five million. And user data reveals that two-thirds of them have already completed a bachelor's degree or higher, while more than half are learning while holding a full-time job. There is clearly an appetite for continuing education—for new skills, new communities, new opportunities. Other future forces will likely give this trend more momentum, whether it's automation of work, which would require that millions get connected with new learning opportunities to prepare to change careers; or free community college, which would make going back to school affordable for any adult; or universal basic income, which might give people the chance to work slightly fewer hours and take on more personal-growth opportunities.

Finally, I can't help but think that the over two billion people who play video games regularly are primed for this kind of shift in education, especially younger generations, who grow up spending nearly as many hours playing video games as they do in a formal classroom.[24] Many efforts have been made over the past decade to "gamify" education. What could be more gameful than giving learners an epic mission and connecting them with millions of people worldwide to collaborate with?

EVERY TIME YOU'VE READ A "Could this scenario really happen?" explanation in this book, you've been increasing your stockpile of signals of change and future forces. The same goes for all the evidence you collected while playing Stump the Futurist and One Hundred Ways Anything Can Be Different in the Future. Now you have a name for these kinds of clues, and a better idea of how to work with them. As you continue to train your imagination, keep in mind: both types of clues are essential for unsticking your mind.

Signals of change are like brain candy. They fuel your curiosity and spark wild thinking. They're fun to collect. And they are outrageously abundant. There are millions of signals out there every day just waiting to be discovered. When you find a new signal, it helps make your future imagination more creative, surprising, and vivid.

Future forces, on the other hand, are far fewer in number. They don't come along nearly as often. You might track the same handful of future forces for years or even decades, waiting for their full potential to be realized. Be patient and keep taking in new information. Whenever you learn more about an important future force, your imagination becomes more grounded, realistic, and convincing.

IMAGINATION TRAINING

RULE #7: Choose Your Future Forces.

Make a list of the external forces beyond your control that are most likely to affect your life and your friends' and family's lives in the next ten years. Include things that make you excited for the future *and* things that make you worry. Use this list to keep an eye on the bigger picture. Be willing to acknowledge the reality of growing risks, even when they make you uncomfortable. Keep updating your knowledge of future forces, so you can be prepared to help at least one person in your life or your community should a hypothetical future risk become a real crisis.

It's now time for you to make your own future forces list. Here's a list of some of the top future forces we're currently tracking at the Institute for the Future. These are forces that have a high probability of affecting almost any future topic you might want to investigate, or any long-term goal you might want to pursue. When you look at this list, which forces stand out as being particularly important to you personally? Which ones would you like to learn more about? I encourage you to choose at least three of your own future forces to track. Try to have a bit of balance in your list—at least one of the forces you pick should feel like a risk to you, and at least one should feel like an opportunity:

- the climate crisis
- post-pandemic trauma
- social justice movements
- increasing economic inequality
- social and political tensions caused by refugee crises and mass migration
- automation of work
- decreasing birthrates in Western countries and a "youth boom" in Africa
- shifting religious majorities and increasing theological diversity
- the global switch to renewable energy sources
- alternatives to capitalism and market-based economies
- social media–driven misinformation, disinformation, and conspiracy theories
- rise of authoritarianism and loss of faith in democracy
- widespread adoption of facial recognition and surveillance technologies
- digital currencies, cryptocurrency, and programmable money
- universal basic income and direct cash transfers
- internet shutdowns mandated by government or law enforcement
- the "right to disconnect" movement and four-day workweeks
- lifelong learning and "reskilling" at the workplace
- job guarantees
- regenerative design and the circular economy
- genomic research and CRISPR genetic modification
- the Internet of Things
- augmented and virtual reality
- satellite networks and space internet

If there's something on the institute's list above that you don't know anything about at all, this is the perfect opportunity to go find your first clue. Just do an internet search for any future force. Remember, future forces aren't secret—they're hiding in plain sight! The hard part isn't learning about them. The hard part is being willing to fully acknowledge their reality, accept how transformative they are likely to be, and keep them in mind as you go about your own work and life— even if they feel overwhelming, intimidating, or beyond your control. When you know which way the winds of change are blowing, you will be able to prepare, adapt, and positively influence your own future.

~~~~~~~~~~

Practice Hard Empathy

If I'm not imagined in your future, do I exist in it?
—HODARI DAVIS, poet, activist, and educator

OUR FUTURE SELVES ARE LIKE STRANGERS TO US.

This isn't some poetic metaphor; it's a neurological fact. When you imagine your future self, your brain does something weird: it stops acting as if you're thinking about yourself. Instead, fMRI studies show, it behaves as if you're thinking about *a completely different person.*[1]

Typically, when you think about yourself, a region of the brain known as the medial prefrontal cortex, or mPFC, powers up. When you think about other people, the mPFC powers down. And if you feel like you don't have *anything* in common with the people you're thinking about? It activates even less.

The mPFC is essential to maintaining your "continuity of self." It's how you wake up every day knowing who you are, and what you want to do next. More than one hundred brain-imaging studies have reported this effect.[2] But there's one major exception to this rule: the farther out in time you try to imagine your own life, the less activation you show in the mPFC. In other words, your brain acts as if your future self is someone you don't know very well and, frankly, someone you don't care about.

This glitchy brain behavior may make it harder for us to take actions that benefit our future selves. Studies show that the more our brains treat our future selves like strangers, the less self-control we exhibit today, and the less likely we are to make pro-social choices, decisions that will probably help the world in the long run. We're less able to resist temptations, we procrastinate more, exercise less, put away less money for retirement, give up sooner in the face of frustration or temporary pain, and are less likely to care about or try to prevent long-term challenges like climate change.[3] This makes sense. As Hal Hershfield, a researcher at the University of California, Los Angeles, who conducts fMRI studies of future self-imagination, described it to me: "Why would you save money for your future self when, to your brain, it feels like you're just handing away your money to a complete stranger?"

But some people have a little more empathy for their future selves than others. Their brains act just a little differently; their mPFCs get just a little bit more fired up. They treat their future selves as—well, if not themselves, then a dear friend or loved one. As a result, they tend to show more willpower, vote in more elections (because they want to have a say in how the future turns out), and be more successful in achieving their long-term goals (because they don't mind putting in hard work now to help their future selves).

How much empathy do *you* have for your future self? You don't need an fMRI machine to figure it out, fortunately. Psychologists have developed a scientific questionnaire, based on Hershfield's fMRI studies. It measures your relationship with your future self almost as precisely as a brain scan.[4] Here are three sample questions from this Future Self-Continuity Questionnaire:

How vividly can you imagine what you will be like in ten years from now?

1-not at all   2-not very well   3-somewhat
4-pretty well   5-very strongly   6-perfectly

How similar are you now to what you will be like ten years from now?

1-completely different   2-somewhat different   3-a little different
4-similar   5-very similar   6-exactly the same

Do you like what you will be like in ten years from now?

1-not at all   2-not very well   3-somewhat
4-pretty well   5-very strongly   6-perfectly

As you can see from these sample questions, three different factors influence your empathy for your future self: vividness of the future self, similarity to the future self, and positive affect to the future self. The higher your score along all three dimensions, the more likely you are to take action today to care for and benefit that future you. A total of fifteen or higher on these three questions shows very strong empathy for future you. Conversely, a score of six or lower would suggest quite low empathy. Anything short of a perfect eighteen suggests that there is plenty of opportunity to nurture a stronger future-you connection.

By reading this book and taking lots of mental time trips to ten years from now, you're already likely increasing your score on one of the three dimensions of future self-continuity: your vividness of imagination. Your ability to clearly envision future you is growing stronger with every ten-year scenario you play with, and with every detailed story you write about what you might think, do, or feel in the future.

But, paradoxically, the more time you spend mentally visiting strange futures, the more you may realize that future you is likely to be different, changed by choices you make, challenges you encounter, and society's own reinvention.

So the question becomes, not how do we feel more similar to our future selves, but how do we feel more connected to someone we imagine might be very different from us? And how do we build confidence that we will still like that person, no matter how changed that person is?

The solution to this dilemma requires a deeper dive into the nature of empathy itself.

IT TURNS OUT THAT THERE are two kinds of empathy.[5]

The first kind, the easy kind, happens when we can directly relate to what someone else is feeling because we've gone through the same thing ourselves. We don't have to guess. If you see a kid being bullied, for example, and you were bullied as a child yourself, empathy for that kid will probably come fast and easy for you. You might feel in your own mind and body a wave of anger or fear or humiliation, or whatever emotions you experienced when you yourself were bullied. This is your brain's way of helping you understand and relate to others more effectively. This kind of effortless empathy, like a shared emotion, pulls us back into our own feelings in a visceral way, often with a flood of neurochemicals and physical sensations. It's essentially a form of *emotional simulation*.

Emotional simulation is powerful, but it can also be exhausting to take on the feelings of others and bear them ourselves. It's "easy" empathy not because it's easy to go through but rather because it's easy to get there. It happens almost unconsciously, without thought or effort.

The second kind, hard empathy, is more effortful and creative. It's what we have to conjure up when we *don't* have any personal experience with what someone else is going through but want to understand. It's what we practice when we disagree with someone but still try to see that person's point of view and understand what life experiences led to it. It's what's happening when we say to someone after a great shock or loss, "I can't imagine how hard this is for you." When we have no firsthand knowledge to draw on, we have to make an imaginative leap. We have to quiet down our own instinctive responses based on patterns from our own personal histories. And we have to create a blank space in our mind for someone else's alternative experience to come to life. We have to invent, imagine, and fill in the blanks using whatever clues we can find. What *would* it be like to be this other person in this moment?

Hard empathy is even harder when we're not naturally inclined to connect with a particular person or group at all. We all have people who exist outside our circles of easier empathy—people with different political views, people who have made different life choices, or people who live on the other side of the world in cultures and communities that feel strange and distant to us.

And data shows that in recent years, many of us have experienced *shrinking* circles of natural empathy. We identify with "in-groups" that are more rigidly defined by political, religious, and ethnic identities. We know less about the lives of people in other groups. And we are increasingly angry, fearful, or mistrustful of people outside our inner circle.[6]

At first, the COVID-19 pandemic appeared to decrease this social polarization. People from all walks of life banded together over shared worries and sacrifice.[7] But as it wore on, studies show, partisan responses to mask wearing, stay-at-home orders, and vaccination actually increased social polarization. It created new categories of "us" versus "them": maskers versus non-maskers, social distancers versus non-distancers, pro-vaccine versus anti-vaccine.[8] Meanwhile, richer countries with successful vaccination campaigns found themselves living in a completely different reality from poorer countries without access to the vaccines or with struggling vaccination campaigns.

In short, hard empathy is getting even harder, and COVID-19 didn't help.

But we *need* hard empathy. It's essential to broadening our perspective, deepening our humanity, healing social rifts, and preparing us to be of service to others. It makes our personal relationships more resilient—we recover from disagreements faster and are less likely to give up on each other, whether it's with a family member, friend, or romantic partner.[9]

And it's not just good for individuals; the more people who practice hard empathy, the healthier a society is. Evidence from a study of more than one hundred thousand adults across sixty-three countries reveals that countries where people on average score higher on measures of hard empathy also have higher levels of subjective well-being, self-esteem, collectivism, and pro-social behavior.[10] It seems that understanding other people's hopes and worries motivates and empowers us to be more helpful and caring. This, in turn, makes us feel better about our own self-worth. It's a virtuous cycle, an upward spiral of social benefit.

And hard empathy can even help you feel more connected to your future self. If you keep extending your natural circle of empathy to strangers with unfamiliar lives, to people who seem very different from you, then *even if your brain treats your future self like a stranger, or like someone you have nothing in common with*, you will be more likely to care for and relate to that person too.

THE EASIEST WAY I'VE FOUND to practice the skill of hard empathy is to go to any news source, magazine, or social media, and look for a story about someone experiencing something radically different, almost unimaginably different, from my own life.

And then I try to imagine that my life is more like theirs.

For example, I recently read a story in the *New York Times* about two sisters in rural India. Their village is so conservative and protective of its unmarried women that when on rare occasions the sisters go into the nearest city, their male cousins and uncles come along and create a human chain around them, their hands linked, to protect the sisters from any contact with outside men.[11] Try to imagine the scene: a small group of people moving through public spaces together, two women tucked inside a protective circle of men.

Because this is a rare social custom, I'm assuming it's not something you've directly experienced—otherwise, you'd have easy empathy for the people in this village. But if this custom sounds strange to you, then I'd like you to try a thought experiment. What would it be like if, in your own life, wherever you live right now, you were expected to live by this custom? Can you imagine being considered so in need of protection that your relatives created a human chain around you whenever you went somewhere you might encounter strangers? Or, if you prefer, what if you were expected to be a protector? What if you were called upon to perform this social duty of creating a human chain around someone else?

To be clear: *do not* try to imagine that you are one of those two young women in that rural village in India. Don't put yourself in their shoes, so to speak. Stay exactly *who you are* and exactly *where you are*. What you're changing in your mental simulation are the *facts of your own life*. If you live in New York City in your real life, then you're imagining that a human chain of protection around young, unmarried women is something you commonly see in New York City. And if you are an unmarried woman in your real life, then in this alternate reality, *you* now require a human chain of protection whenever you are around groups of strangers. If you are not an unmarried woman, then in this alternate reality, you are called into service to help organize or physically make the chain.

This strategy may seem counterintuitive. After all, doesn't empathy mean being able to put yourself in someone else's shoes and see the world from their point of view? Well, yes—but research shows that when we try to imagine what it would be like to be someone else, and we have no direct experience of that person's circumstances, we're not very good at it. When we're just making up stuff in our head about what someone else might feel or do, and not basing it on any firsthand knowledge, we often get it wrong. There is often a big gap between what we imagine and what the other person describes as their experience.[12] But the hard empathy technique above helps you avoid this pitfall by blending objective facts about someone else's reality with your own subjective feelings and reactions. Instead of just guessing what someone else might feel, you're really feeling something yourself. And while this may not be the same emotions someone else would feel, it's a more authentic empathy. It's grounded in the middle space between your real feelings and the other person's real life. And studies show that when we feel this kind of "blended empathy," we feel more connected with people whom we initially identify as different or other. We feel we have more in common with them. We also feel more motivated to take action to help them, or to join a cause that might make their life circumstances better.[13]

So go ahead: get back inside your imagination and try to feel the physicality of this human chain of protection, the intimacy of it. Make the scene as vivid and specific as you can. Who, exactly, is protecting you—which relatives or neighbors? Or who are you protecting? Whose hands are you holding? Where are you going? How do you feel?

It may seem absurd to think about such a rare and unfamiliar custom becoming true in your own life. One executive in my Stanford class said in frustration during this exercise, "I literally cannot imagine this. I'm too busy to be a human chain for someone else. I would just refuse to do it." This, of course, is what makes hard empathy hard. We may have to imagine living under social pressures or expectations or limitations that we would reject if we had the power to reject them. We may have to feel, through our empathy, things we would rather not feel: anger, perhaps, or powerlessness.

Then again, I've been surprised by people who conjured up positive feelings in response to this scenario: feeling helpful, caring, or cared for, even while others imagined feeling claustrophobic, trapped, burdened, or unequal. This diversity of reactions underscores that hard empathy isn't about being right about what someone else might feel. It is about being curious about other people's lives. And it's about realizing, deeply, how many alternate realities others are already living in when compared to our own lives.

HERE'S ANOTHER SCENARIO FOR PRACTICING hard empathy, inspired by a severe water shortage that occurred in Cape Town, South Africa.

What if, by law, you had to use 75 percent less water per day than you currently do? And even with such severe restrictions, what if you were warned that your town or city might soon run out of water, and nothing would come out of the tap when you turned it on?

That's a reality many people lived through in 2018, when after three years of worsening drought, the city of Cape Town passed restrictions limiting residents to fifty liters (about thirteen gallons) of water per person per day.

To give you an idea of what you can do with fifty liters of water a day: you can flush the toilet once per day (ten liters), take a one-minute shower (ten liters), brush your teeth and wash your hands twice per day (four liters), and keep yourself and a pet hydrated (four liters). You have to save the rest of your daily ration to do one load of laundry (seventy liters) and one dishwasher cycle (thirty liters) each week. If you want to clean anything in your house with water, or cook with water, or water any plants, or take a shower that lasts longer than one minute, or wash your face at night, or wash your hands more than twice a day . . . you have to sacrifice something else. Maybe don't flush the toilet at all today? Skip brushing teeth? Wear dirty clothes next week?

The water restrictions were passed in an effort to forestall what locals called "Day Zero." On Day Zero, it was expected that the city would have to turn off all municipal water supplies. Residents would be forced to stand in line at one of 150 central water-collection points around Cape Town for a daily ration of just twenty-five liters per person. It was reported at the time that Day Zero was potentially just weeks away, as dam storage levels had dwindled to less than 15 percent total capacity.[14]

And so people in Cape Town had to make incredibly tough choices, day in and day out. They also got used to being a bit dirtier. Workplaces reportedly held "dirty shirt" contests for employees to see who could go the longest without washing their work clothes. Restaurants and bars encouraged patrons *not* to flush toilets in public restrooms, with signs that read: "If it's yellow, let it mellow." Meanwhile, wealthier people drove far outside city limits in order to buy vast quantities of bottled water and circumvent the restrictions. That quickly led to bottled water shortages.[15]

The city was able to keep postponing Day Zero through collective efforts to conserve water. When rain returned to the region months later, things went back to normal.

If you've never lived through a prolonged water crisis, then this hard empathy challenge is for you:

Imagine *you* have to live through months of a similar water restriction. Imagine that the city or state where you currently live has implemented exactly the same policy.

How would you spend your fifty liters a day?

What would you give up first? Showers? Laundry? Cooking?

What would be the hardest to give up?

Would you share any of your fifty liters with family members or neighbors?

How would you feel if a member of your household took a twenty-minute shower and burned through all your family's water for the rest of the day? Angry? Frustrated? Jealous?

How would you feel wearing the same clothing many days in a row, even if it started to smell? Embarrassed? Gross? Virtuous? Accepting?

Try to get into the physicality of the situation. And try to feel your way through the social aspects of negotiating over water decisions and helping or sacrificing for others.

Think about what emotions the prospect of your own Day Zero would bring up—anxiety, dread, or maybe motivation to help?

What actions would you take to prepare for a possible Day Zero? Would you become a water hoarder? What kind of help would you give others? What kind of help would *you* need?

Given the nature of climate change and rising drought levels worldwide, this scenario really could play out in many other cities. A little hard empathy now for people who have already lived through unprecedented government water restrictions could go a long way toward preparing you for your own future. The lived experiences of people in Cape Town set the new precedent, the new "thinkable." It could be anyone's reality going forward.

FAR-FUTURE THINKING AND HARD EMPATHY are mutually reinforcing. They are a kind of "cross-training" for your imagination. The more you practice one, the better you get at the other.

When you take a mental time trip to the far future, you have to disrupt your habitual thoughts. You have to immerse yourself in an alternate reality: What's around me? Who am I with? What do I feel in this moment? What do I really want to do? Hard empathy requires precisely the same leap of imagination. It uses the same mental simulation skills to fill in the blanks between what you know from your own experience and what *could* be true for someone else.

Likewise, when you can start to feel in your own mind and body how someone else's life experience could be different from yours, then you get unstuck and better at thinking about all kinds of change. Because if someone else can already live a completely different life from yours today, then it's possible that you yourself, and anyone around you, can lead a completely different life—tomorrow, next year, or a decade from now.

Seeing the future from *someone else's point of view*—someone whose circumstances, values, lived experiences, hopes, and worries are very different from your own—is not easy. But hard empathy is easier to practice when you're not just guessing, when you're actually getting direct information from others about what they want and need. It can be as simple as asking two questions:

1. What keeps you up at night when you think about the future?
2. What makes you leap out of bed with excitement in the morning when you think about the future?

Right now, I have a database with 9,681 different people's responses to these two questions, collected over the past two years. Whenever I'm feeling confident that I know what's worth feeling optimistic about and what's worth worrying about, I take a look at the responses and try to keep surprising myself and stretching my empathic imagination.

You don't have to build a database! But you should try asking people these questions when the occasion arises. If you're facilitating a group or meeting, try having people introduce themselves by answering one or both of these questions instead of simply sharing where they're from, job titles, or other traditional biographic details. They open up incredible conversations. And they establish a baseline of mutual understanding that makes any kind of discussion or decision-making more meaningful—even if it's not about the future.

ANOTHER WAY TO REACT TO a future scenario, besides just imagining it or talking about it, is to *freewrite* about it. Freewriting means you write whatever comes to mind, quickly, without censoring or editing yourself.

When you freewrite about a scenario, I recommend setting a timer and spending five minutes—and only five minutes!—describing what you might think, feel, and do if this scenario actually happened to you. Your goal is to visualize this future scenario *as if you've already lived through it*, as if it were a real memory you could look back on and describe to someone else in specific detail. Think of it as creating a journal entry from the future. You'll be describing some dramatic moments in your everyday life:

"I woke up today and the weirdest thing happened . . ."

"When I heard the news, the first thing I did was call my sister to ask her advice . . ."

"I immediately got in my car and started driving. I wanted to get to the store before it was mobbed . . ."

You can practice freewriting alone, but the magic happens when you freewrite with a partner or in a group. You can then swap stories (or "journal entries from the future") and have a quick chat about any surprises or differences in your reactions.

By writing down what you imagine, you're taking an important step forward—from *mental simulation* of the future, which happens in your own mind, to *social simulation* of the future, which means sharing what you imagine with others. This, too, will supercharge your hard empathy skills—because you'll be able to find out directly from others what they are likely to feel and need in the future.

In Part III of this book, as the final stage of your imagination training, you'll be invited to "Spend Ten Days in the Future," or to write ten different journal entries from the future in response to some very surprising scenarios. You'll be able to add your own stories online to a large-scale social simulation, in which thousands of others are sharing their stories too. This kind of first-person storytelling is the "core mechanic" of all social simulations that we run at the Institute for the Future.

A core mechanic, in game development terms, is whatever action players do over and over while playing the game. The core mechanic of soccer is kicking a ball. The core mechanic of playing with Legos is stacking bricks. The core mechanic of Scrabble is making words out of letter tiles. And the core mechanic of social simulations is writing quick stories that others can read, with everyone saying, "Here's what I would do," "Here's what I would feel," and "Here's what I would need," to each other, about the same scenario—so they can build mutual empathy and collective intelligence about the future.

Get some practice for social simulation now by writing your own journal entries from the future in response to these next two scenarios. One is about the future of the internet. The other is about the future of money. You can handwrite your quick reactions to the scenarios in a notebook, or write an email to yourself, or dictate it into your phone, or type it up in Notepad or in a Word document, whatever works best for you. Remember, it takes only five minutes, and you're freewriting—so you don't have to censor or edit your thoughts at all. For the most authentic social simulation experience, invite a friend to play along, so you can trade your stories and reactions.

If you're still not convinced to grab a pen or open a computer document—if you're planning to read and think about the scenarios but not actually write down your quick story—then consider this feedback I received from participants in a recent social simulation:

"Writing it down is so different from just imagining it. It makes it more concrete. I wouldn't have guessed what a difference writing makes."

"You never really know what you'll do in a crisis. Until you try to write about it. And then, suddenly, you do know. When you have to write something down, it's like your brain clicks into a different gear."

"I got really into the writing part. I filled up a few pages in a journal and took photos to send to my boyfriend, so he could read it. I wanted him to experience the scenario with me."

"The best part was reading what other people wrote. It would have been fun to do this on my own, but reading other people's stories made it much more exciting. I was so surprised by what they came up with that never crossed my mind."

This is how you start to tap into collective intelligence about the future. This is how you create collective imagination.

So—are you ready to write?

Future Scenario #7: The Great Disconnection

A Friday morning, ten years from now

Your phone buzzes twice, and then it makes a strange noise.

You check the screen and realize it's an emergency alert notification.

This is a message from the Department of Homeland Security. The president has declared a national cyber-emergency.

At 12:00:00 PM today, the internet and all cellular service within the continental United States will be temporarily shut down due to an urgent security threat.

Service will be shut down for at least fourteen days. During this time, there will be no public internet access. Mobile phones will be unable to make calls or send and receive messages.

There is no immediate threat to the public. Further information will be provided as soon as it is available. Thank you for your cooperation.

You've never seen an alert like this before. *Is it for real?*

Your mind starts racing as you think about all the things you won't be able to do without internet or cell phone service.

Then you check the time. It's 11:50 a.m. Only ten minutes until the shutdown starts!

IMAGINE THAT THIS SCENARIO IS happening to you, in your real life. How would you feel, and what would you do? Here are some prompts to help you write your journal entry from this future.

1. **Set the scene.** Where are you when you receive the emergency alert? Is anyone else with you? If so, what do you say to each other? Describe the moment in detail.

2. **Feel the moment.** What emotions are you experiencing in the moment? What physical sensations? What thoughts start running through your mind?
3. **Try to make sense of it.** What possible explanations do you come up with for what's going on?
4. **Name your worries.** What problems might you have adapting to at least two weeks—if not longer—without the internet or cellular service?
5. **Take action.** What *immediate actions* do you take after receiving the alert? What plans do you start to make?

Could a future like "The Great Disconnection" really happen? Let me tell you a little more about the signals of change and future forces that inspired this scenario, and why we at the Institute for the Future think that it's a good one to start preparing for.

First, as you probably noticed, this scenario is a bit mysterious. It's not completely clear what's going on. What, exactly, is a "cyber-emergency"? And why is it happening? How can you plan to take effective action in response to a situation that you don't fully understand?

. This uncertainty is actually an important part of the scenario's design. The lack of clarity matches our real-life experiences of "unthinkable" events and "unimaginable" challenges. When a major crisis starts to unfold, we usually don't know exactly what's happening, or why. It takes time to make sense of the changes and adjust our expectations of reality. A mysterious scenario gives you practice thinking creatively and strategically through the fog of crisis, when it's still hard to discern what's going on.

I can, however, clear away some of the fog from this scenario for you now. Here's what's really happening in "The Great Disconnection": it's about a world in which central and local governments increasingly shut down the internet and mobile communication with little, if any, advance notification. This is not a hypothetical future scenario. It is already happening.

Thirty-three countries enforced 213 internet shutdowns in 2019; in 2020, twenty-nine countries enforced 155 more. Sixty-two percent of these shutdowns affected both broadband and cellular service. The shutdowns were typically ordered by national governments and lasted anywhere from a few days to many months. (The longest known shutdown, imposed by Myanmar in nine townships where there is ongoing military conflict, has been in place for nearly two years at the time of this writing.)[16] And while you might think authoritarian regimes are the ones turning off the internet, India—the world's largest democracy—is the global leader in shutdowns, with 109 in 2020.

The most common justifications given for communications shutdowns are public safety, national security, and stopping fake news or "illegal content." In reality, according to the research and internet rights organization Access Now, shutdowns are most often used to silence protests, disrupt activism, conceal human rights violations, and influence elections. And the trend over the past few years is that internet shutdowns are lasting longer, affecting more people, and targeting vulnerable groups.

But could it happen in the United States? Just because something hasn't happened before doesn't mean it won't happen in the future. (Don't fall for that normalcy bias trap!) In the past few years, there has been considerable legal discussion and research on whether the Constitution permits a US president to shut down the internet and all other telecommunications. The legal consensus, perhaps surprisingly, is that, yes, it would be constitutionally permitted for a president to shut it *all* down, during a wartime or other public emergency, thanks to an obscure provision tucked at the back of the 1934 Communications Act (Sec. 706, codified as 47 USC 606).[17] So maybe it's not so far-fetched to imagine a US internet shutdown, perhaps to prevent dangerous misinformation from spreading during a national security crisis . . . or maybe just to prevent and interfere with public protest and political action.

The risk is significant enough that in 2021, Access Now issued a special US update in its annual global report on internet shutdowns:

"The United States [has] laws on the books that facilitate internet shutdowns and communication blackouts. . . . All that is required to trigger the president's nearly unchecked powers to shut down communications platforms nationwide is a 'state of public peril' or 'other national emergency.' . . . The threat of an internet shutdown in the U.S. remains."[18]

In recognition of this threat, there was a bipartisan effort in 2020 in both the US Senate and House of Representatives to pass a law called the Unplug the Internet Kill Switch Act, which would have reversed the earlier law and prevented the president from shutting down any communications technology during wartime, including the internet. But the act did not garner enough support to advance to a full congressional vote.

GovTrack.us, the leading nongovernmental source of legislative information and statistics, summarized opposition to the proposed law this way: "Opponents counter that an internet kill switch, even if it *sounds* Orwellian, is actually a necessary government tool in this nearly-entire-digital era, as a matter of national security."[19] They cite the growing risk of cyberattacks by foreign adversaries or terrorists on the US power grid, water systems, databases, and banking systems and argue that the president needs an internet kill switch in the event of such a cyber-emergency. Again, these risks aren't hypothetical—they are already happening, with increasing frequency. In 2021, for example, a malicious hacker took remote control of a water-treatment plant in Florida and changed the level of sodium hydroxide in the treated water from 100 parts per million to 11,100 parts per million—which would have been enough to seriously sicken residents if the water had reached their homes before the breach was detected. In 2021, Colonial Pipeline, the operator of one of the largest fuel pipelines in the US, had to shut down its 5,500 miles of pipeline, which carries 45 percent of the East Coast's fuel supplies, after its systems were hit by a cyberattack. In 2021, an attack on JBS, the world's biggest meat processor, inflated food prices and disrupted food supply chains worldwide. But hospitals are the most frequent infrastructure target, according to experts. One of the most significant health care cyberattacks in the US in 2020 shut down the University of Vermont Medical Center network for forty-two days, causing three hundred employees to be furloughed and many critical surgeries and treatments to be postponed.[20] These types of attacks are a future force that could certainly lead to network shutdowns of all kinds, as a defensive strategy.

Perhaps you'd like to feel more prepared for such a scenario. Take a moment to think about what you might do. Maybe you'll go to the AccessNow.org website and spend five minutes learning more about this risk. Maybe you'll introduce yourself to a neighbor you don't know very well, in case you need to help each other during a telecommunications shutdown. Or maybe you'll set up your own backup communications option that would still work during an internet and mobile service shutdown. Believe it or not, this is something you can easily do in five minutes or less—and I don't mean putting in a landline telephone, although that could be useful too. I mean learning how to use "mesh network" apps, which create a local internet out of whoever's phones are nearby.

In response to the growing number of telecommunications shutdowns, software developers and activists have been creating new tools to help people send messages even without cell service or internet access. One such tool, the Bridgefy app, works by using your phone's Bluetooth connection to send text messages to any other Bridgefy users nearby, within a football field's distance, or 330 feet, of your phone. That doesn't sound too helpful until you realize that those users can connect to users another 330 feet away, and *those* users can connect another 330 feet, and so on, building a mesh network that allows information to be sent and received across much greater distances. The more people using the app, the stronger and farther the communication network grows. Crucially, it works in virtually any conditions— cellular outages, internet outages, power outages—as long as your phone is charged.

Other similar apps include Signal Offline Messenger, FireChat, Briar, the Serval Mesh, and Vojer. You can find them in your phone's app store. In less than one minute, you can install one of these apps on your phone to be ready to use in the future. This is a great micro-action to take now, because you won't be able to download the apps during a shutdown. You have to get them on your phone while you still have internet!

These apps work best when there are lots of local users. So perhaps you could use your other four minutes to send a quick note to friends, family, or your Nextdoor community suggesting they install it too, in case of future internet outages. And if you're really inspired to get ready for this future, you might plan a local meetup to test out the apps, so you know how to use them in an emergency—or maybe come up with a fun use for them today.

Here's one more tantalizing clue to the future of mesh networks. In the summer of 2021, this information popped up in the news: "Amazon Sidewalk is about to create a nation-spanning 'smart network' connecting the devices of its customers, starting the rollout with select Echo speakers and Ring cameras."[21] Yes, Amazon is building its own mesh network called the Sidewalk Network. Amazon says that allowing Bluetooth connections between the smart devices in your own home and those in neighbors' homes will solve connectivity problems, help devices work faster, and even provide temporary backup internet connection during local failures. Naturally, critics of the Sidewalk Network have raised privacy and security concerns. One article that instructed readers on "Amazon Alexa features you should turn off right now to protect your privacy" trended on social media.[22] And within weeks of the project being announced, a consumer lawsuit was filed.[23]

I have no idea how far Amazon will get with this project. But I'm absolutely intrigued by the idea of a megacorporation using its smart devices to potentially counter internet shutdowns in the future. Can you imagine the great internet battles of the year 2033? A president shuts down the internet, declaring a cyber-emergency, only to have Jeff Bezos or another technology titan say, "Not so fast." It's a strange new possibility that I couldn't have imagined until I spotted this latest signal of change. Now I can't stop thinking about it.

Future Scenario #8: Double Your Money

A Tuesday afternoon, ten years from now

The Federal Cash Buyback Program is all over the news today. It's trending and going viral on every social media platform.

It sounds too good to be true. But as far as you can tell, it's legit.

Here's how it works:

The federal government has just announced the launch of a new digital currency, the digidollar.* It's worth exactly the same as a traditional dollar. It is legal tender and has the full backing of the US Treasury and Federal Reserve. Any US business or legal entity that accepts cash payments must by law now also accept the new digital dollar, at the same rate and value as a traditional dollar. Companies may choose to pay their employees in digidollars from today forward.

Unlike traditional money, digital currency has some unique features:

- It exists in electronic form only, in a digital wallet.
- You spend it via a mobile phone app or a debit card.
- Transfers and payments are instantaneous, with no fees—so it's faster and cheaper for money to reach everybody.

So far, so good. But there are some details about the new national digital currency that are raising eyebrows. Here's what else you've learned today:

- There will be no anonymous digital wallets. Government-issued ID or biometrics will be required to create one.

---

* Note that this scenario is *not* about cryptocurrencies, which use blockchain technology, are not backed by any central bank or government, and are used primarily today as investment vehicles and for speculation. This scenario, instead, is about a central bank digital currency (CBDC). A CBDC is the digital form of a country's fiat currency. Instead of printing money, the central bank issues electronic coins or an account backed by the full faith and credit of the government.

- All digidollar transactions will be tracked by the US federal government in a central database. In other words, the government will have a complete record of who paid whom, when, and for what.
- Any traditional money still in circulation will continue to be legal tender for the time being. But the US Treasury announced today that it will no longer print any new bills or mint any new coins; all future money will be digital only.

And that's where the Federal Cash Buyback Program comes in. To incentivize people to make the switch to the new digital currency, the government is making a limited-time offer for two weeks only: a *double-your-dollars* cash buyback program.

For the next two weeks, you can transfer any bills, coins, or bank holdings back to the federal government in exchange for *twice* as many digidollars.

If you have US$500 in your bank account right now, you can trade it for 1,000 digidollars. If you have US$1 million, you can trade it for 2 million digidollars.

During this two-week window, all trading will be halted on US stocks and bonds—presumably to prevent everyone from cashing out and crashing the markets. US banks will be restricted from making any new loans during the two-week window, to prevent any "gaming" of the system. (Otherwise, you'd be tempted to take out the biggest cash loan you could, trade it for digidollars, pay back the loan, and keep the surplus.)

The government says it intends to replace all traditional dollars with digidollars over the next decade. So from today forward, all payments made by the federal government—tax refunds, student loans, economic stimulus payments, paychecks to all civil servants and members of the military, payments to vendors, grants to state and local governments—will be made exclusively in digidollars, putting roughly 5 trillion new digidollars into circulation each year.

You have only two weeks to trade in any money you have for digi-dollars, starting today.

How would you feel, and what would you do, if this really happened? Here are some prompts to help you write your journal entry from the future. Imagine the cash buyback scenario is occurring in your real life. Write your own unique story, from your point of view, about how this future might start to unfold:

1. **Set the scene.** Where are you when you find out about the cash buyback program? Is anyone else with you? If so, what do you say to each other? Describe the moment of your discovery in detail.
2. **Feel the moment.** What emotions are you feeling in the moment? What physical sensations? What thoughts start running through your mind?
3. **Try to make sense of it.** What do you think is the government's motivation for launching digidollars? Why are they trying to remove traditional dollars from circulation? How do you think society will react? Do you predict that most people will make the trade or not?
4. **Take action.** What *immediate actions* do you take after finding out about the cash buyback program? What kind of information do you need? Whom do you want to talk to about your decision? What plans do you start to make?

Could a future like "Double Your Money" really happen? A hypothetical federal cash buyback is a bit of a wild card scenario. On one hand, it's quite plausible that governments will at some point try to move toward an all-digital economy. By mid-2021, more than fifty governments and central banks worldwide, including the US, were already researching, prototyping, or issuing central bank digital currencies (CBDCs).[24]

On the other hand, the chance of a dramatic financial system transformation happening so rapidly, over a two-week period, is extremely low. You might even say such a scenario is ridiculous. Much more likely is a slow, decade-long shift that plays out in such a low-key way that we barely pay attention to an otherwise radical change.

So if digital currency is likely to take years, not weeks, to change our lives, then what's the point of imagining a rapid shock to the financial system? Well, when a dramatic change happens virtually overnight, we notice it more, and we feel it more. This is just as true for the stories we tell and the scenarios we imagine as it is for the experiences we actually live through. The cash buyback scenario is dramatic because I want your brain to be primed to really pay attention to how money is already starting to change, and how it will keep changing over the next decade. I want every signal of digital currency change to jump out at you. I want you to have time spaciousness to start moving your money, adapting your own financial habits, and voicing a political opinion *before* you wake up and realize you're living in a new reality. Because that new reality is almost certainly coming.

Today, we're used to money working in a particular way—but in the future, money will be programmable to do all sorts of new and surprising things.

Digital dollars can have expiration dates set by the government, so that if the money isn't spent before it expires, it goes back to the government. This is a likely way for a government to send economic stimulus payments: with a one-time thirty- or sixty-day expiration date, to ensure the money flows quickly into the economy rather than being saved.

Digital currency can also be programmed to decay over time if it's not being spent. A digital dollar, for example, could lose half its value every thirty days that it's not spent. In this case, spending money becomes like playing a game of hot potato: you don't want to hold on to it for too long, lest it lose its value. A government might program some money to behave this way to encourage continuous spending rather than saving.

Digital currency could be programmed to be spendable only in certain ways, or at certain locations. For example, if the government wanted to stimulate use of public transportation, tourism, or local relief after a natural disaster, it could send out a stimulus programmed to be payable only to public transit authorities or travel-related businesses, or spendable only with businesses in a certain zip code to support local economic recovery. After one restricted spend, the digital dollars would revert to normal rules.

Digital currency makes it easier to implement negative interest rates during economic downturns, or to prevent gross accumulation of unspent wealth. In the scenario above, you could imagine that digidollar holdings above US$1 million for individuals and US$1 billion for companies would be subject to negative interest rates—that is, charged a small percentage each year (e.g., 1 percent) for any money that isn't spent. Any negative interest collected could be redistributed as a dividend to all other digital wallet holders.

And if the government wanted to incentivize a certain behavior—like getting vaccinated or voting—it could create digital wallets specifically for use at mass vaccination clinics or polling sites and program digital dollars to be transferable in a one-time set amount of, say, one hundred dollars to individuals at that location.

Now you see why governments are so eager to develop CBDCs. There's just so much more you can do with it to stimulate the economy and nudge behavior faster. It's also easier to combat fraud, tax underpayment, and tax avoidance, because the government already knows exactly how much income you've received in its central database. If you don't pay taxes on your digital income, the government can just go into your digital wallet and take it, or siphon off future wallet transfers until your tax liability is paid. The same goes for any fines or fees you might owe.

Of course, the rise of this kind of oversight and power will make alternatives to CBDCs very interesting to people who value privacy, or who don't want the government nudging them toward certain financial behaviors, or who want to avoid government knowledge of their financial activities. So while you're keeping CBDCs on your radar, you might also watch out for (and invest in) currencies that defy all these new powers, by design.

When most of the money in circulation becomes programmable, the creative possibilities for economic policy will explode. In some ways, the future force of digital currency is already quite far along in shaping society—it's now almost inevitable that every major government will pursue this technology. But in other ways, we're looking at just the tip of the iceberg: economists, entrepreneurs, and activists will surely devise many more ways that no one has thought of yet to take full advantage of programmable money.

A FEW YEARS AGO, A major technology company asked me to lead some futures-thinking workshops with their product team to help them anticipate any unintended consequences of their latest product. This kind of work often involves some hard empathy training—because new technologies pose more potential risks to people who have historically suffered more harms from inequality, injustice, harassment, or privacy loss: women, people of color, the LGBTQ community, people with disabilities or chronic illness.

When I do this kind of work, I sign nondisclosure agreements, so I can't tell you exactly which company, or which product, I was working on—let's call it Company X, making Product Y. I've left out the details about Company X in my story below, but as a hypothetical example, imagine that a health tech company was making a new wearable health-tracking device. I would help them ask and answer questions like: What are the potential privacy risks for users? What if the user data was leaked or stolen? Could it be used for public shaming or blackmail? What's the worst possible thing a malicious hacker could do with it? And: Could there be any mental health consequences for users of this technology? How might users get "addicted" to, or dependent on, this technology? How would that change their everyday behaviors or affect their well-being? And: If an authoritarian government wanted to access the user data, what might they do with it? Does the company have a responsibility not to collect data that could be used for government surveillance or targeted oppression?

Obviously, these aren't the kinds of questions that product designers and programmers are asked in the daily course of their jobs. But this kind of speculative futures thinking is becoming a bigger part of product design in Silicon Valley right now, and for good reason: it's hard to have a positive long-term impact on humanity if you're not looking out at least ten years ahead, for both positive and negative consequences. And more and more, technology companies are trying to practice "ethical" or "responsible" innovation, in the wake of criticism of platforms like Twitter, Facebook, YouTube, and Apple for failing to adequately predict and safeguard against phenomena like the viral spread of misinformation and conspiracy theories, the increase in hate speech and political radicalization, the coordinated abuse of individuals, and social media and smartphone "addiction."

On this particular project with Company X, after our first hard empathy workshop together, something strange happened. I was informed by my primary contact that from now on, all workshops would be attended by in-house legal counsel. And I was instructed that any email I sent them, no matter how trivial the content, should cc one of the company's lawyers and include the phrase "attorney-client privilege."

What was going on? Well, it seemed that the employees' collective imagination had revealed a few too many surprising potential consequences. And now the question arose: If a company has internal knowledge of a potential long-term risk, could it be held legally responsible in the future for not acting to prevent it?

In other words: Is it better not to know?

To its credit, the company didn't cancel the rest of our futures-thinking trainings. It didn't stop asking: If hundreds of millions of people use our technology, then what might happen? And then what? And then what? But bringing legal counsel in put a chilling effect on the conversations. And I felt less confident that the company would act on any advance knowledge of potential harms. Future imagination shouldn't be developed only behind closed doors, or only in privileged conversations. You could say one of the main reasons I've written this book is that I don't want the drawing out of future consequences, especially around technologies or policies that could affect many millions or even billions of people, to happen in secret.

If you feel so inspired, I hope you'll teach someone else the techniques you've learned in this chapter and in this book, so they can teach someone, and they can teach someone, and they can teach someone . . . and we can all be in on the secret together. No one person can anticipate everything. Together, we can foresee so much more.

Science fiction writer and technology activist Cory Doctorow has said, "Prisoners of our own time and place, it's hard not to feel like we're living in the only possible world, as if everything around us is inevitable and natural—and any change is 'unnatural.'"[25] But social imagination makes the idea of change natural. When we see others taking ridiculous, at first, ideas seriously, it gives us permission to take them seriously too—and to come up with our own.

Shared imagination will always stretch our minds more than individual imagination. When *you* take your next mental time trip, who can you invite to come along?

IMAGINATION TRAINING

RULE #8: Practice Hard Empathy.

Fill in the gaps of your own lived experiences with the stories and realities of other people whose lives are almost unimaginably different from yours. Envision your own life circumstances changing to be more like theirs, as vividly and realistically as you can. How would you feel in this alternate reality? What would you do? What kind of help would you want? This habit helps you increase your circle of natural empathy and feel more connected to others. It also improves your ability to imagine change of any kind.

You can also practice hard empathy whenever you play with future scenarios. Whenever possible, don't just guess how the future might affect others. Ask others directly: What would you be excited about in this future? What would you worry about? Write your stories down and share them, to move from *mental simulation* to *social simulation*. Fill your imagination with the real hopes and worries of people whose circumstances, values, and lived experiences are different from your own.

9

~~~~~~~~

Heal the Deeper Disease

*It's really important for us to remember how much power
we have . . . Humans made the system; humans can change
the system.*

—INGRID LAFLEUR, founder of the
Afrofuture Strategies Institute

NOW THAT YOUR MIND IS THOROUGHLY UNSTUCK—NOW THAT YOU ARE
ready to believe that almost anything can be different in the future—
the key question isn't "What *can* change in the next decade?" but
"What *should* change?"

The shock of the pandemic has created a kind of psychic rupture
in society, a space for radical ideas to seep into our collective consciousness and take root. As the activist Christine Caine has written,
"Sometimes when you're in a dark place you think you've been buried
when you've actually been planted."[1]

Coming out of the darkness of the pandemic, we have the chance
to grow into something new together. But first, we have to grapple with
the truth of what we've been through.

For nearly three decades, psychologists have studied a phenomenon called *post-traumatic growth*. It's a kind of positive personal transformation that sometimes happens in the aftermath of a trauma, when we are radically changed by our encounters with previously unthinkable challenges and previously unimaginable pain.

Post-traumatic growth can result in a better understanding of our own strengths, an openness to new possibilities and opportunities, an increased sense of connection with others who suffer, the courage to make dramatic changes in our lives that better reflect our hopes and dreams, and a newfound desire to serve a cause bigger than ourselves. It has been documented in people who have endured war, serious illnesses and injuries, natural disasters, bereavement, job loss, and economic stress.[2] It isn't universal, but it is common. Experts say that roughly 50–60 percent of people who endure a trauma will go on to experience at least one area of post-traumatic growth.[3]

Paradoxically, the best predictor of post-traumatic growth is having experienced one or more symptoms of post-traumatic stress disorder, or PTSD. That's because post-traumatic growth is not the opposite of suffering. It is the direct result of suffering deeply and *trying to make sense and meaning out of that suffering*. It happens when we are forced to rethink our core beliefs, acknowledge our own vulnerability and mortality, and decide what is truly important to us. It starts with a painful struggle to fully process and understand the traumatic past: What happened? Why did it happen? And what am I called to do now, going forward?

Post-traumatic growth is usually thought of as an individual process. But now, for the first time, we may be seeing it play out on a truly global scale.

The COVID-19 pandemic has arguably been the single largest collective simultaneous experience of trauma in human history—whether it was the trauma of frontline work, social isolation, economic loss and hardship, prolonged anxiety, severe illness, long COVID, the loss of a loved one, or the grief of being abandoned and left unprotected by your own government.

How common is trauma during a pandemic? On average, 22.6 percent of people experience symptoms of PTSD after any pandemic. Health care workers are most affected at 27 percent, followed by infected individuals at 24 percent, and the general public at 19 percent. This is according to a 2021 meta-analysis that looked at the results of eighty-eight different studies of PTSD after pandemics in the twenty-first century, including SARS, Ebola, Zika, Middle Eastern respiratory syndrome coronavirus (MERS-CoV), and COVID-19.[4] Even if we cut these percentages in half to allow for the disparity in individual and national experiences of the pandemic, that leaves nearly one billion people on earth experiencing post-pandemic trauma. And if 50–60 percent of them go on to experience some kind of post-traumatic growth, as studies suggest, that's more than half a billion people who are actively rethinking their core beliefs, opening up to new possibilities, and looking for a bigger mission to serve.

This back-of-the-envelope calculation may sound unrealistically optimistic. But more than 40 percent of three thousand people surveyed at the end of 2020 had *already* experienced at least one symptom of post-traumatic growth as a direct result of the pandemic, according to a study published by Yale School of Medicine.[5] This is why I, among many others, believe that the next decade will be the most significant opportunity most of us have in our lifetimes to create long-lasting positive change in society.

The shock of the pandemic has caused many of us to question how the world could have let so much suffering happen, despite so many resources and so much advance warning. The trauma of the pandemic has opened the door for reimagining and reinventing things we took for granted. Together, the shock and trauma have created a painful and urgent global longing for something better.

Leah Zaidi, a researcher and storyteller at the Institute for the Future, has argued that the desire to escape into fiction and virtual worlds, a common response to trauma, is the same impulse that propels us to imagine a better future. She writes, "Have you dreamt of other worlds? Another time, another place perhaps . . . universes of the mind so unlike our own. Is it because you grew tired of this one? Many of us have, at some point in our lives, asked if there is a time or place better than the one we find ourselves in—that this cannot be all that there is or the best that we can do."[6] Indeed, if there is one true thing to be said about what happened during the pandemic, it is that this cannot be the best that we can do.

So what *can* we do better? What should we do next?

"THE PRESENT WAS AN EGG laid by the past that had the future inside its shell."[7] Within this riddle, posed by Harlem Renaissance author Zora Neale Hurston, we find our answer: we must look back at our recent past to find the challenges that will define our future.

Working through a trauma requires understanding what happened, and why. In the case of COVID-19, this means acknowledging how much of our suffering was a result of long-standing systemic weaknesses in our society, vulnerabilities that the virus took advantage of and put on full display. As the Institute for the Future's executive director, Marina Gorbis, put it: "It's not just the virus that's killing us—it's our social, economic, and political systems."[8] To achieve collective post-traumatic growth for our post-pandemic planet, we will have to grapple with a difficult fact: many of the illnesses, deaths, and hardships from COVID-19 were preventable. As the virus spread through the world's population, it was accelerated by societal weaknesses that should have been addressed long ago, namely economic inequality, broken health systems, extreme political divisions, racial injustice, brittle supply chains, overworked workers, and the climate crisis. We can think of these societal weaknesses as "preexisting conditions," in the same way that old age, diabetes, and heart disease made individuals more vulnerable to the novel coronavirus. At the Institute for the Future, we call these preexisting conditions that made the effects of the pandemic so much worse, and so much harder to recover from, the "deeper disease."[9]

The deeper disease will set the stage for the next decade; and the way we address it will largely determine whether we just manage to survive COVID-19 or are transformed for the better by it. These next few pages will by no means offer an exhaustive analysis of everything that went wrong during the pandemic, or every injustice that was suffered in its wake. But I hope they can be a starting point for understanding, growth, and social healing. Let's first take a look at the symptoms of the deeper disease and how they might manifest again in the future—and then we can start to imagine a cure.

Preexisting Condition #1: Economic Inequality

Economic inequality, defined as an unequal distribution of income and opportunity between different groups in society, is a major cause of suffering in its own right. During the pandemic, its harms were turbocharged: it put many lives disproportionately at risk, and if unaddressed, it will prolong our collective suffering from the virus far into the future.

The most obvious symptom of this preexisting condition was the fact that the virus spread much faster, and took many more lives, among groups who couldn't work from home or afford to physically distance themselves. A majority of the essential jobs that put people in close contact with the virus were low-paid positions held by the economically insecure: people working in warehouses, care homes, meat plants, waste management facilities, kitchens, and grocery stores, for example. Meanwhile, people who lived in densely packed, multigenerational housing—more common in low-income neighborhoods— also suffered higher attack rates, as the virus spread more easily from person to person. Later, economic insecurity led to delayed vaccinations among low-wage workers: nearly half of adults in the US who by choice had not yet received a vaccine by the summer of 2021 identified concern about potential lost wages if unable to work due to side effects of the vaccine as the primary reason.[10]

The problem of economic inequality is likely to get worse before it gets better. A study on the economic effects of five previous pandemics found that income inequality in affected countries increased steadily for five years following the end of the pandemic. We can already see this playing out: during the first year of the pandemic, global billionaire wealth increased by $3.9 trillion. By contrast, global workers' combined earnings fell by $3.7 trillion.[11] Meanwhile, three in four households worldwide suffered declining income after the start of the pandemic, including four hundred million job losses, according to a study of thirty-seven countries published by the International Labor Organization.[12] And these jobs weren't lost equally—women and ethnic minorities were disproportionately affected. In particular, women accounted for between 80 and 95 percent of the millions of "dropouts" from the workforce (people who have voluntarily stopped working, usually to care for family). This could lead to greater long-term inequality in the workforce: data shows that an unemployment spell can result in lower lifetime earnings, as a result of lost opportunities to gain experience, skills depreciation, and scarring effects on a person's morale and self-esteem. This is particularly true for workers from poorer households and those with less education.[13]

Lost school time will have long-term consequences too. During COVID-19, more than one billion young people fell behind by an estimated average of six to twelve months of learning. In previous pandemics, such as the 1918 flu pandemic, disrupted schooling for those aged fourteen to seventeen led to lower wages throughout their lives, compared to peers who had recently graduated. Preexisting economic inequality matters, too, as expensive private schools were more likely to reopen sooner for in-person learning than public schools, and as wealthy parents hired tutors for their own at-home "learning pods."[14]

Global inequality came into play as well. While richer countries were able to minimize some of the economic hardships of pandemic shutdowns by bailing out companies and providing unemployment or cash payments to their citizens, poorer countries were unable to do this. In poorer countries, for example, half of families reported skipping meals in 2020 because of COVID-19-related lack of income. Nutritional deprivation during childhood can have lifelong impacts on mental, physical, and emotional health; widespread nutritional deprivation on a societal level means entire countries will suffer devastating consequences that last decades.[15] It's no wonder that a recent study looking at pandemics over hundreds of years of history found that the economic low point comes on average twenty to thirty years later.[16] "The pandemic is an economic wrecking ball, with intergenerational consequences," a 2020 World Economic Forum report on inequality put it.[17] And the psychological effect of growing economic inequality and insecurity may represent a new kind of underlying health risk in and of itself. Studies show that the severe mental and emotional stress of insecure, underpaid work puts physical pressure on the body, weakening heart health, undermining the immune system, and making it harder to recover from illness.[18]

To heal this deeper disease, we will have to embark on a decade of economic transformation. How will we do it? Here are some of the biggest questions that are being asked right now by governments, activists, and economists worldwide, in order to catalyze this healing:

- Could we pay a one-time, global bonus to all essential workers who labored during the pandemic? What would be a fair bonus?
- What is a fair, livable minimum wage that creates real hope for the future? Instead of incremental inching upward, is there a dollar amount that would unleash a tidal wave of economic healing?
- What about a maximum wage? What would be a fair cap on annual compensation? How might that change the kinds of jobs people are drawn to?
- Can we imagine a new era of federal job guarantees, in which the government hires unemployed workers as an "employer of last resort"? What kinds of jobs should they be? What do we need more people doing in order to make a better world?
- What if we treated secure access to food and shelter as a universal human right? How could we create a new world of guaranteed meals and guaranteed housing for all?

- Is it time to establish a universal basic income, in which the government provides every adult citizen with a set amount of money monthly to cover the basic cost of living?
- Can we provide a basic income for every human being, regardless of birthplace or citizenship? Or a minimum wage for *all* humans—not just in one city, or in one country, but as a matter of international law? What kinds of cross-border agreements and global tax policies might make this possible?
- How much debt—individual, and national—are we prepared to cancel? What loans could be forgiven?
- Should wealthy nations that have disproportionately contributed to the climate crisis pay economic reparations to poorer nations?
- Should there be a lifetime cap on the accumulation of wealth? Are we ready for a ban on billionaires?
- What do people need besides money to feel economically secure?

Take note of how these questions make you feel. What ideas do you consider, still, unthinkable? What ideas do you want to start thinking about more?

You don't personally have to have the answers to any of these questions, or to the many questions ahead, as we consider what else it might take to heal the other preexisting conditions of society. As Alice Walker writes in her 1972 poem "Reassurance," "I must love the questions / themselves / as [the poet] Rilke said / like locked rooms / full of treasure / to which my blind / and groping key / does not yet fit."[19] It's enough, for now, to invite these questions into your mind. Let them simmer. Which ones spark your curiosity? Which ones make you angry? Which give you a flicker of hope?

At my house, we have a wall next to our dining room table that we call the "question wall." Everyone in our family writes down questions that come up on rainbow-colored index cards, which we then tape to the wall. It's a way to remind ourselves what we're curious about.

Once a week or so, everyone grabs a card off the wall and starts Googling. Whenever you find a question in this chapter that really jumps out at you, write it down and hang it up somewhere you can see it often. You may be surprised at just how much this simple act can fuel your imagination.

Preexisting Condition #2: Broken Health Systems

A health system is defined by the World Health Organization (WHO) as "all organizations, people and actions whose primary intent is to promote, restore or maintain health."[20] The COVID-19 pandemic made the fragilities and inequalities in our current health systems painfully visible: a shortage of workers, uneven access to care, a focus on profit that undermines global health, a collective failure to prevent so much easily preventable disease. By the WHO's estimates, the world's supply of sixty million workers was eighteen million short of what was needed just to alleviate the strain on the system during ordinary times—and that was *before* the pandemic.[21] And the global shortage of health care workers will likely get worse, as a result of burnout and trauma. In a recent major survey, 76 percent of health workers in the United States reported feeling burnout from the pandemic, and 48 percent said they had considered either retiring, quitting their jobs, or changing careers because of the trauma of COVID-19.[22]

The shortage of workers is not evenly distributed globally. One of the biggest inequities in the system is a "brain drain" in health and medicine: citizens with medical skills leave their home countries to work in richer countries. Sierra Leone, Tanzania, Mozambique, Angola, and Liberia, for example, have expatriation rates greater than 50 percent, meaning that more than half of doctors born and trained in those countries will leave to work in richer countries. This puts poorer countries at a massive workforce disadvantage during a health crisis like the pandemic.[23]

The profit models and affordability gaps baked into global health systems also lead to needless and unevenly distributed suffering. In countries without universal health coverage—there are 124, including the United States—one in four people each year skip medical care because of the cost. During the pandemic, tens of millions of people put off seeking COVID-19 tests and care out of fear they couldn't afford it, a pattern that led to greater spread of the virus and preventable deaths.[24] The efforts of drug manufacturers to protect billions of dollars in profits also slowed the rollout of vaccines to poorer countries that couldn't afford the high cost—even as wealthy countries created stockpiles. By the summer of 2021, on average in high-income countries, almost one in four people had received a vaccine. In low-income countries, it was one in more than five hundred. This shocking disparity created what WHO director-general Tedros Adhanom Ghebreyesus described as a "vaccine apartheid."[25]

COVID-19 also put a spotlight on the epidemic of underlying preventable conditions that increased COVID-19 mortality. Heart disease, diabetes, obesity, and high blood pressure are widespread and growing globally. Preventable heart disease alone causes twenty million premature deaths annually, according to the latest *Global Burden of Disease* study. The health care burden and mortality risks of these preventable conditions are an indictment of the system's focus on treating, rather than preventing, disease. And even in the absence of a pandemic, these preventable diseases pose a growing concern: underlying health conditions make individuals more vulnerable to climate-related health crises, too, like extreme heat.[26]

Finally, during the pandemic, global health governance proved to be quite weak. When, for example, Brazil's and India's failures to protect their own citizens had devastating effects on their neighbors, or incubated dangerous new variants, there were no mechanisms to compel responsible action, no ways to hold those countries accountable.

Together, these weaknesses in our health systems set the stage for what could be a decade of global remedy and reinvention. We can expect to see unprecedented collective imagination put toward answering questions like:

- Should there be a cap on profits made by companies as a direct result of a pandemic?
- Could the excess profits be used to pay one-time bonuses to health care workers or to create a scholarship fund for medical school for the next generation of doctors?
- Should we establish access to medicine, health care, and vaccines as a human right?
- If so, should business models that violate this right be deemed illegal?
- Should countries that disproportionately benefitted from the medical brain drain fund the development of poorer countries' health care systems, as a form of economic reparations?
- Should poorer countries' international debt be forgiven if they funnel that more than US$11 trillion into developing their health systems?
- How do we bring the same urgency to reversing and preventing preventable diseases that we brought to fighting the pandemic?
- What changes to how we live, work, and eat would have the biggest, fastest positive impact on global health?
- What will it take to increase the global workforce by twenty million additional doctors and nurses in the next decade?
- How do we spread those workers across the planet more equitably?
- What might people without formal medical training be taught to do in their own communities to help meet basic health care needs?
- Can we imagine training an additional one hundred million people as "community health workers" to conduct basic health checkups, give vaccines, and administer routine health tests right in people's own homes?
- Should we create a new system for global heath governance that includes real sanctions for countries that act against our collective planetary interests?

- Should we treat a country's failure to control a virus the way we currently treat acts of aggression or nuclear weapon proliferation?
- How else can we create a more collaborative and global approach to heath, given that infectious diseases know no borders?

Even if you're not personally in a position to start reinventing the health care system, you can help stretch the global imagination: when *you* think about what could possibly change in the next decade, when *you* come up with your own ridiculous, at first, ideas, when *you* look for a way to help others heal from the pandemic. Any of these challenges would make a worthy future scenario or an epic personal mission. And you won't be going it alone: even the most surprising questions on this list are already being seriously explored and debated in leading global health policy journals and public forums.[27] The pandemic is truly a springboard for making previously unthinkable health care ideas thinkable.

So plant these questions in your mind. Take note of which ones make you uncomfortable and which give you hope. Talk about these ideas with others. See what they grow into.

Preexisting Condition #3: Extreme Political Divisions

Political polarization is the process of society becoming increasingly divided over cultural norms and policy matters, with extreme views becoming more common over time. It has been on the rise globally since the 1990s, and nowhere faster than in the United States.[28]

During the pandemic, the harms of these extreme political divisions were painfully clear. Many countries experienced the politicization of common-sense pandemic measures like mask wearing and social/physical distancing. In the US, studies revealed, political party was the best predictor of whether someone regularly wore a mask around others or practiced safe distancing. Anti-mask rallies and lockdown protests were largely organized by conservative political groups in the US, Canada, Australia, the United Kingdom, Italy, Spain, and Germany.

Conspiracy theories and misinformation about the pandemic were also more likely to spread in countries with high political polarization, researchers found. This is a result of the "post-truth" attitudes that commonly emerge from extreme political divisions. For an increasing number of people, allegiance to a political party or ideology determines what they believe to be true—rather than shared facts, evidence, or data. Early on in the pandemic, this led to harmful beliefs about whether COVID-19 was a "hoax" or no deadlier than the flu. One study found that people in the US who watched highly partisan conservative television talk shows, which regularly downplayed the risks of COVID-19, were up to 34 percent more likely to catch COVID-19 and 35 percent more likely to die from it.[29]

Later, as vaccines were developed, they too became politicized and were the subject of unfounded conspiracy theories and misinformation. Globally, researchers found that anti-vaccine movements and vaccine hesitancy were more common in countries with high political polarization. One local symptom of this extreme partisan divide: by mid-2021 in the United States, all twenty of the states with the highest vaccination rates were Democratic-leaning states, while nineteen of the twenty states with the lowest vaccination rates were Republican-leaning states.[30]

Collective action during a crisis is extremely difficult in a polarized, "post-truth" society. If we can't collectively agree on which actions are needed, we can't act on them together. And appeals to the "common good" are considerably less persuasive when people feel they have nothing in common with anyone who supports a different political party. Perhaps the most curious symptom of this preexisting condition is this: in thirteen of thirteen countries surveyed by the Pew Research Center, people who identified as supporters of the governing party were significantly more likely to say their country had "done a good job" handling COVID-19, while people who supported a different political party were more likely to say their country had "done a poor job."[31] These beliefs, researchers showed, had no correlation to actual case counts, hospitalizations, or death rates. And they had no relationship to the severity or style of measures actually taken. This partisan gap was greatest in the US, but double-digit gaps also appeared in France, Spain, the UK, Japan, Italy, the Netherlands, Canada, Sweden, Germany, and Belgium.

With such extreme post-truth polarization, how on earth will we achieve any kind of collective learning? How will we get better at fighting pandemics or any other global crises in the future if what we believe works to solve a problem is based primarily on whether we voted for the governing party—not on whether the solution actually works? And the complications complicate each other: economic inequality and broken health systems, studies show, dramatically increase mistrust of government and political polarization. It's a vicious cycle—but if we can find ways to interrupt one of these old patterns, the ripple effects may start to heal the symptoms.

Extreme political division is a challenge that will require big ideas and creative solutions in the next decade. Here are some of the questions that will fuel our collective imagination:

- How can we reestablish a basic shared reality?
- What should be the commonly agreed-upon facts, across political worldviews?
- How do we teach these facts in ways that defy political polarization?
- How will we help people recover from their belief in harmful conspiracy theories?
- What solutions could help put the brakes on quickly spreading misinformation?
- What new kinds of political parties and practices could we invent to transcend this era of extreme polarization?

- If economic insecurity and broken health systems increase political divides, should we double down on the most ambitious ideas to heal *those* symptoms?
- Should countries like the United States adopt the truth, justice, and reconciliation methods of post-conflict, post-atrocity nations like South Africa and Croatia in order to heal our political division?
- What would an American reconciliation movement look like?
- What identities will bring us together instead of dividing us?
- How can music, storytelling, and the arts help us forge these new identities?
- How can we start to see ourselves in ways that will put us all in the same group, and all on the same side?

Preexisting Condition #4: Racial Injustice

In the summer of 2020, Black Lives Matter protesters around the world held up signs reading "Racism is the real pandemic." This message was a searing commentary on the unequal risks and disproportionate suffering that people of color in the United States and ethnic minorities worldwide experience every day. The pandemic put this injustice in the spotlight: people of color and ethnic minorities, everywhere in the world, contracted and died from COVID-19 at far higher rates than their white or ethnic-majority counterparts.

In the United States, Black, Native American, and Latino people experienced three times as many cases as non-Hispanic white people, five times as many hospitalizations, and twice as many deaths. In England, death rates were twice as high for people of Chinese, Indian, Pakistani, or other Asian ethnicity, as well as Caribbean or other Black ethnicity, compared to the white population. In Canada, Indigenous people and individuals of Southeast Asian descent were anywhere between two and thirteen times more likely to be infected during various surges. In Singapore, 95 percent of confirmed cases in 2020 were among ethnic-minority migrant workers. Similarly, in Saudi Arabia and the United Arab Emirates, ethnic-minority migrant workers made up the vast majority of cases. In Brazil's hospitals, Afro-Brazilian patients were nearly twice as likely to die as white COVID-19 patients. (These statistics describe the first year of the pandemic, the most recent data available at the time of writing.)[32]

Why did COVID-19 hit these parts of society so much harder? In all the countries mentioned above, researchers were able to identify factors of structural racism that contributed to this disproportionate risk.[33]

People of color and ethnic minorities have an overrepresentation in low-paying but essential frontline work, and so they were more likely to be exposed to the virus.

They are more likely to experience crowded living conditions, with less access to outdoor spaces like patios, backyards, or gardens, because of higher poverty rates and rental market and mortgage market discrimination. This made it harder for individuals to distance or isolate during the pandemic, and easier for the virus to spread.

They are more likely to live in neighborhoods with more air pollution, because of historical redlining and discrimination in housing. Chronic exposure to pollution puts lungs and hearts at risk of COVID-19 complications. It also contributes to higher rates of medical conditions that further increase the risk of severe illness from COVID-19, like diabetes, obesity, and asthma.

Their immune systems and heart health are more likely to be compromised, because of the chronic stress of living with racism and economic insecurity.

They are less likely to receive adequate health care, for two reasons. They are more likely to work in low-paying jobs that do not offer health insurance benefits or paid sick leave. And they are more likely to have their symptoms dismissed or downplayed by doctors, or as one study put it: "Health provider ethnic bias can influence the quality and outcomes of healthcare interactions."[34]

Incarcerated individuals were infected by COVID-19 at four times the rate of the general population, because of crowded living conditions. Racism in policing and sentencing means this disproportionately affects Black men in America and ethnic minorities worldwide.

Migrant workers, who are typically ethnic minorities, live and work in extremely cramped, overcrowded conditions where the virus spread more easily. They, too, often have unequal or limited access to health care as a result of their migrant status.

And to give just one example of how structural racism showed up during the pandemic, pulse oximeters, or fingertip devices that measure oxygen levels in the blood, have been a crucial tool in detecting severe COVID-19—but in 2020, scientists reported that the technology is three times as likely to miss hypoxemia, or low oxygen levels, in people of color compared with white people. Higher levels of skin pigmentation tend to produce inaccurate results, meaning people with darker skin are more likely to miss an important warning sign that hospitalization, supplemental oxygen, or intensive care is required.

Racial injustice is a legacy of the past, a reality of the present, and an urgent challenge for the future. Here are some of the questions that will guide the global effort to right these systemic wrongs:

- What kinds of economic reparations will we make for slavery and historical discrimination?
- What is the "moon shot" for racial justice? What audacious goals can we set for political campaigns and political movements?
- What data can we collect to document where racial injustice exists and help identify targets for anti-racist interventions?
- How will we close the racial wealth gap? Is it time for government baby bonds or investment accounts for every infant? How much bigger should the bonds be for babies born to poor families and ethnic minorities who have suffered historical discrimination?
- Should we establish a federal job-guarantee program ensuring a job with a livable salary for all, which some experts argue is the most effective way to overcome racial discrimination in hiring and pay?

- How will we rethink policing and prisons to reduce racial disparities in the criminal justice system?
- Should the United States embrace the hardline approach taken by post–Nazi Germany and accept some limits to free speech in order to criminalize racist speech and symbols?
- Should we practice "defensive democracy" and ban political candidates and parties that espouse antidemocratic beliefs and racist ideologies?
- What kinds of stories will we tell, and what kinds of art can we make, to challenge the beliefs that perpetuate racist actions and ideas?
- What positive visions of the future can we create to help inspire anti-racist efforts?
- What new methods of protest, activism, and resistance can we invent?
- What does a future with people of color at the center of society, rather than at the margins, look like?
- What becomes possible in an anti-racist future that isn't possible today?

Preexisting Condition #5:
Brittle Supply Chains and Overworked Workers

For decades, companies have been optimizing their supply chains and workforces for maximum efficiency and profit: make just as much product as you can sell, and only as soon as you can sell it, with as few workers as possible. During normal times, keeping a lean workforce and taking this "just-in-time" approach to manufacturing helps companies reduce spending on storage and labor and avoid losing money on overstock that no one wants to buy.

But if something unexpected happens, a sudden shock to the supply or demand, there's no wiggle room in the supply chain, no buffer in the workforce. Inventory dries up, and people can't get what they need when they need it. Shortages, panic buying, and hoarding become much more likely. Workers can't work harder to make up for the shortages, at least not for long, because they've already been pushed to their limits. This is exactly what happened during the pandemic.

Most critically, the world found out just how unprepared it was to make more essential supplies during a crisis—whether it was personal protection equipment like N95 masks and disposable gloves for health care workers, or oxygen and medicine for sick patients. It wasn't just an increase in demand that caused a problem; it was a lack of geographic diversity and resilience in production. Most masks and PPE factories were located in China and were shut down early in the pandemic, just when they were most urgently needed. Countries realized, too late, that they had outsourced critical infrastructure. Meanwhile, patents on medicines designed to protect profits for pharmaceutical companies meant that more factories couldn't just pivot to producing what the world needed; they were actively prevented from responding to the crisis. As a result, there were critical global shortages of more than thirty drugs necessary in COVID-19 care, from anesthesia to heart medications.[35]

And it wasn't just health and medicine supply chains that shattered. All kinds of businesses found themselves unable to meet demand. "The world ran out of everything," as a *New York Times* headline put it.[36] From toilet paper to bicycles to home office equipment, many just-in-time supply chains failed because they were based on prediction models using historical data of "normal" behavior. But during a crisis, normal no longer applies.

Sudden changes in consumer behaviors showed how hard it was for companies to adapt quickly to changing needs and desires—like millions of people trying to buy a new desk for remote work, or toilet paper because they were doing all their bathroom business in their own homes instead of at schools and workplaces, or a bike because outdoor exercise was the one activity permitted by stay-at-home orders.[37] These shortages didn't have the same kind of life-or-death consequences as failures in the medical supply chain, but they put a spotlight on the larger risk companies face heading into a future where historical patterns can no longer be trusted.

Already lean workforces in manufacturing, agriculture, construction, and health care, among other industries, were laid low when employees caught the virus and couldn't work or needed to take time off to quarantine or care for others. These worker shortages caused more service and supply-chain disruptions, most notably in the meat industry, where overcrowded working conditions led to severe COVID-19 outbreaks. The resulting meat shortages led to rising prices and increased food insecurity for vulnerable populations around the world. It was just one more symptom of the underlying brittleness of business practices that seek greater efficiencies and profits at the expense of resilience and better working conditions.[38]

And although it received little public attention at the time, in 2019 the World Health Organization took notice of another emerging occupational pandemic. It wasn't a virus—it was a kind of toxic workplace stress. The WHO officially added "burnout" to its International Classification of Diseases, describing it as "feelings of energy depletion or exhaustion; increased mental distance from one's job, or feelings of negativism or cynicism related to one's job; and reduced professional efficacy," and characterizing it as "a syndrome . . . resulting from chronic workplace stress."[39] This action by the WHO proved quite prescient. One year into the pandemic, a major global survey supported by the *Harvard Business Review* analyzed the state of worker burnout and well-being across forty-six countries and a wide variety of industries and roles. An overwhelming 85 percent said their physical or mental well-being had declined as a result of overwork, 72 percent said they felt pressure to work while sick, and 51 percent said they were unable to maintain a strong connection with friends and family because of work demands.[40]

This data confirms what other studies have found: a majority of workers worldwide feel overworked, underpaid, socially isolated, and dehumanized by their employers. And the problem of overwork goes beyond physical and emotional burnout; it can be fatal. A 2021 study by the WHO found that over a one-year period (2016, the latest year for which data was available), 745,000 people died as a result of long working hours, defined as fifty-five or more hours a week. Why are long hours such a "serious health hazard," in the words of the WHO? Not getting enough rest or sleep and enduring too much stress increase the risk of heart attack by 42 percent and stroke by 19 percent. Men accounted for 72 percent of overwork fatalities, with the highest rates in the Western Pacific and Southeast Asia. To put these numbers in perspective, over the course of the next twenty years, overwork at this rate is likely to kill more people than COVID-19 has killed worldwide. Commenting on the study, WHO director-general Tedros Adhanom Ghebreyesus stated, "No job is worth the risk of stroke or heart disease. Governments, employers, and workers need to work together to agree on limits to protect the health of workers."[41]

Taken together, these risks of brittle supply chains and the harms of overwork suggest a number of challenges to building our resilience and flexibility for the next decade:

- Should we reverse the trend of globalization in favor of regional hubs and local manufacturing, at least for the most essential products, like food and medical supplies?
- How can we better anticipate what essential supplies the world might need more of during a future crisis—whether it's a new pandemic, climate emergency, nuclear attack, mass migration, emergency evacuation, or something we can hardly imagine today?
- How do we create more resilient ways of making those essential supplies?
- What are more equitable ways of distributing them during an emergency?
- How much of the current suffering and burnout around everyday work is preventable?
- What are we willing to do to prevent it?

- What kinds of work cultures and worker protections would bring more security, humanity, and dignity to our jobs?
- Are we ready for a universal four-day workweek?
- Are we ready for universal "right to disconnect" laws, which would safeguard workers against after-hours communications and work demands?
- What would a less efficient, less productive world look like? What good things might increase if global efficiency and productivity went down? Are we willing to consider those trade-offs?
- Would we be better able to respond to future crises if we were all less overworked and less burned out?

Preexisting Condition #6: The Climate Crisis

Before COVID-19 was the defining crisis of our time, climate change was at the center of most discussions of global risk. In fact, climate change was a major factor in the emergence of the novel coronavirus, and it makes pandemics of all kinds more likely.[42] As the environment changes, animals all over the planet leave their normal habitats and come into contact with new species. This creates opportunities for pathogens that usually infect one species to get into other animal hosts, or to "spill over." Occasionally, humans become the new host—which is how diseases like HIV, Ebola, SARS, and MERS emerged. And though we don't know the origin of the virus that causes COVID-19—whether it was a spillover event or was created in a lab during "gain-of-function" research, which explores how novel viruses emerge and adapt to humans—the fact remains that, either way, climate change is largely to blame. The gain-of-function field of research exists only because of climate change and its acceleration of spillover events. Labs undertake this dangerous work precisely because the climate crisis is putting us all at risk of more frequent and deadlier pandemics.[43]

Our addiction to fossil fuel burning also increased the rate of severe symptoms and mortality from COVID-19. As noted above, air pollution was associated with higher COVID-19 hospitalizations and death rates worldwide, as a result of the chronic strain that long-term exposure to air pollution puts on the lungs and heart. One major study estimated that 15 percent of all COVID-19 deaths globally were directly attributable to air pollution exposure, including 17 percent in North America, 19 percent in Europe, and 27 percent in East Asia.[44]

Climate change increases the frequency and intensity of extreme weather events, which also became a complicating factor during the pandemic. In 2020, more than fifty million people worldwide were affected by climate-change-related droughts, floods, and storms that overlapped with local COVID-19 surges, according to a report from the Red Cross, while nearly half a billion people endured extreme heat that overlapped with a virus surge.[45] More than eight million people on the West Coast were exposed to prolonged dangerous air quality as a result of wildfires that coincided with the pandemic. The overall risk of catching and dying from the virus was higher for individuals exposed to these extreme weather events, studies show, because they made social distancing harder, disrupted medical supply chains, and reduced health care access. Exposure to extreme heat and wildfire smoke in particular increased severity and mortality from COVID-19.[46]

Perhaps most damaging of all was the way the climate crisis weaponized skepticism and politicized scientific consensus.[47] Despite a near-universal consensus among scientists that human fossil fuel burning has led to long-term dangerous environmental impacts, we have allowed climate change to be debated, contested, and downplayed by the industries and elected officials who profit from our continued dependence on fossil fuels. This template for denying reality was used by political actors and partisan media to downplay the dangers of COVID-19 and to undermine confidence in public health measures and vaccines. Society's failure to effectively combat decades of attacks on climate science created an underlying weakness that not only made it harder to control the pandemic but also sets us up for future inabilities to respond collectively to *any* kind of global risk that requires scientific understanding and guidance.

The climate crisis poses innumerable challenges for the future. We know that we must break our addiction to fossil fuels, reduce consumption and waste, grow our sustainable energy sources, undo the damage to our water, land, and air. But there are other open questions that will require more rethinking, and more imagination, to help us heal from this preexisting condition:

- What new kinds of frontline climate workers and emergency climate responders will we need as we try to solve the climate crisis?
- Who will do this work? How will we compensate them?
- What should the future of science look like if we want it to be understood and trusted by all?
- What can we do to increase our physical resilience, individually and collectively, so we can better withstand extreme heat, novel diseases, and other health shocks in the future?
- What can we do to increase our social resilience so we can trust each other more and protect and help each other more effectively during future health or climate crises?
- What can we do to increase our mental resilience so we can better endure the compounding stress and anxiety of relentless, overlapping crises?
- What can we do to increase our emotional and spiritual resilience so we have the inner resources required to stay engaged with these long-term climate challenges, even when we are exhausted by what we've already endured?

Economic inequality, broken health systems, extreme political divisions, racial injustice, brittle supply chains, overworked workers, and the climate crisis—all of these are problems in their own right. During a crisis, they become complicating factors that deepen and prolong our suffering. As my institute colleague Kathi Vian says, "When a large disturbance shakes a complex system, the weakest parts of the system collapse first."[48]

It's clear that the problems we refuse to solve today will complicate and intensify the crises we face tomorrow. Fortunately, once we've diagnosed a deeper disease, it's easier to predict future symptoms. Going forward, we now have the opportunity to think about how these same preexisting conditions might manifest again. Whatever future we're imagining or predicting—the future of food, the future of voting, the future of learning, the future of cities—we can consider how these same systemic weaknesses might undermine our goals and create new risks. At the Institute for the Future, we're asking these "deeper disease" questions about every future scenario we imagine:

- Who gets sick in this future? What will they need to be healed or protected?
- Who might be left behind or left out in this future? How do we prevent economic inequality from leading to unjustly diverging experiences?
- What behaviors might be politicized in this future? What facts might be disputed? Who will try to bridge these divides to create consensus or common ground?
- How will racial injustice show up in this future? What will anti-racist efforts look like in this world?
- What will people need dramatically more of in this future? Which supply chains might snap? What could make them more resilient?
- Who will experience burnout and overwork in this future? What kinds of support can we give them? What happens if we don't?
- How are people adapting to the adverse impacts of climate change in this future? What are people doing to slow down or reverse its effects? How might extreme weather events and extreme heat add to the overall risk and unpredictability of this world?

Even if you believe you're thinking about a future that has little to do with, say, health care or worker burnout or climate change, you should still ask these questions. Until society is fully healed from the deeper disease, its symptoms will be felt in *every* future we can imagine.

Finding future vulnerabilities, and predicting ways we might try to protect each other, is a skill. You can practice it by looking for future complications of the deeper disease with any of the scenarios you've already played with in this book.

Take, for example, "Have You Checked the Asteroid Forecast?" and "The Global Emergency Sperm Drive." In the case of scientists announcing a potential asteroid impact in the near future, you might think about the preexisting condition of extreme political divisions. How might the scientific forecasts be politicized, disputed, and down-played? What could go wrong if half of society rejected the forecasts outright, on political grounds? Or you might think about the preex-isting condition of economic inequality. If an asteroid were predicted to land somewhere within a specific geographic region, who could afford to pack up well in advance and relocate just in case? And what would happen to those who couldn't afford an extended relocation? In the case of a global emergency response to a fertility crisis, you might consider the preexisting condition of brittle supply chains. If demand spiked and resources were diverted for this global effort—say, because of a massive long-term need for liquid nitrogen, which is used to preserve frozen sperm—what ripple effects would that have on other industries? Well, if that resource were diverted, the global food supply chain could snap, since the food industry uses liquid ni-trogen to freeze and transport bakery products, meat, poultry, fish, prepared meals, vegetables, and fruits. We might have to shift our entire food economy toward eating fresh, local foods. Or think about the preexisting condition of racial injustice. Would people of color and ethnic minorities be less likely to participate in an emergency sperm drive for the same structural reasons they were less likely to be tested or vaccinated for COVID-19? What might be some long-term consequences of creating a racially biased fertility bank? What would it take to counter this risk and ensure equity in genetic material pre-served for the future?

As is always the case when we play with future scenarios, the goal here is not to perfectly predict what might happen in the next decade, or to imagine only the most likely events. By playing with the "deeper disease" model, you're training your imagination to make connections and to see the relationships between different domains. You're improving your general ability to notice interdependencies and risks that others might overlook. Every time you ask yourself how one symptom of society's deeper disease might reemerge in a hypothetical future, you get better at recognizing that symptom in *any* scenario—whether in the far future or in the present. You might never wake up in the wildest future scenarios you imagine. But you will be more ready to help today.

SHOULD WE BE ON THE lookout for *other* preexisting conditions that might complicate our future?

Yes. And here's how.

I recently revisited the original pandemic forecast from Superstruct, the social simulation that we ran at the Institute for the Future in the year 2008 to imagine the world of 2019.[49] I was struck by one of the central elements of the scenario: our fictional illness, respiratory distress syndrome (ReDS), had a low mortality rate but a high rate of long-term, persistent symptoms. In our scenario, tens of millions of people were surviving their initial illness, only to go on to suffer chronic fatigue, brain fog, pain, and breathing difficulties.

One of the main questions we asked participants to consider as they imagined this future was: How do you think the world might adapt to a sudden increase in chronic illness? How would workplaces and schools respond? Who would become new caregivers? How would society need to change to meet the needs of this new, chronically ill population? We also asked them to imagine how their own lives might change if they, or someone in their family, developed this new invisible disability.

During the real COVID-19 pandemic, in contrast, the possibility of chronic disease was downplayed from the beginning. Early reports of long-term symptoms were generally ignored or dismissed by doctors, according to the patients who struggled to be taken seriously or get treatment. They formed online support groups for "long-haulers" and told their stories on social media. Studies eventually would show that anywhere from 5 to 20 percent of previously healthy people continue to experience at least one symptom of the disease six months after their initial illness. But it took an entire year for the medical world to start taking patient reports of this new chronic illness seriously, to give it an official name ("post-acute sequelae of COVID-19"), or to establish special medical clinics to treat it.[50]

Given how under-anticipated and under-appreciated the risk of long COVID was for most of 2020, I was curious about how my fellow researcher at the institute had gotten this detail right. While I designed the Superstruct simulation interactions and mechanics, the initial pandemic scenario was written by then Ten-Year Forecast director Kathi Vian. It turns out that Kathi had a good reason to include chronic illness, the kind often dismissed and downplayed by the medical field, front and center in the Superstruct scenario: in 2008, she herself was living with the long-term, mysterious, debilitating symptoms of chronic Lyme disease. And as a resident of Woodstock, New York, which had one of the highest infection rates of the tick-borne Lyme disease in the world, Kathi knew plenty of other people who also had persistent brain fog, fatigue, and joint pain in the months and years after their initial diagnosis.

"Lyme was considered an epidemic in that area," she told me recently when we made time to dig through the old Superstruct data together. "Most of my friends were dealing with some form of Lyme. Even my doctors and dentist had it. But there was all the controversy about the chronic form of it." Indeed, some doctors today still consider the question of whether Lyme disease symptoms can persist for years as unsettled, despite research suggesting that at least two million people in the United States are living with chronic "post-treatment Lyme disease," the clinical name for the syndrome.[51]

Chronic Lyme is more widely accepted as a valid diagnosis today than when Kathi first imagined the fictional future world of ReDS.

But back then, her future imagination was informed by her own lived experience of what now might be referred to as "medical gaslighting." It's when patients are told that symptoms are all in their head, and health care providers fail to seriously investigate or try to treat them.[52] Medical gaslighting is most commonly experienced by people of color and middle-aged women, who tend to suffer hard-to-treat autoimmune illnesses and hard-to-diagnose post-acute infection symptoms at a much higher rate than the general population. This is the shameful history of chronic fatigue syndrome, or myalgic encephalomyelitis, which an estimated twenty-five million people live with currently. It was dismissed for decades by the medical field as a primarily psychological disorder before finally being recognized as a real, physical illness with detectable root physiological causes, including a genetic predisposition, most likely triggered by a viral infection.[53]

"I was part of a larger community of people trying to come to terms with future uncertainty in the midst of an uncertain disease," Kathi said. "And I think we filter all our future visions through our personal experience. How could it be otherwise?"

It can't be otherwise, and that's a good thing. Our lived experiences give us our future-forecasting superpowers. They help us anticipate future possibilities that others can't see.

Kathi identified an important part of what would happen during a real pandemic because she had already experienced a preexisting condition of society that many others overlooked: the long-standing medical injustice of patients, especially women and people of color, having their chronic illnesses under-diagnosed, under-treated, and under-studied. Today, she is optimistic that the attention now being paid to long COVID will mean that this pattern of the past can finally be disrupted and healed for good. But I can't help but wonder how much suffering could have been avoided for long-COVID patients if more people had been able to see the future from Kathi's point of view.

When it comes to the deeper disease, the six preexisting conditions of society in the Institute for the Future's model speak to some, but certainly not all, of the long-standing weaknesses that society has failed to address. You may have your own perspective on systemic failure, your own lived experience of injustice, that goes beyond what we've addressed in this chapter. That wisdom is essential. I urge you to bring it with you when you imagine the future.

What symptom would *you* add to the deeper disease?

What pattern of the past have you been personally affected by, that you urgently hope we can heal for the future?

Whatever you have lived through, whatever your community has endured, if you choose, you can help others imagine how that suffering might arise again.

Or, you might prefer to help others envision a future in which we no longer suffer in the same way. You can present your own vision for a transformed society. Positive visions of the future are an essential part of the healing. As activist and futurist Iris Andrews said at a 2021 Skoll World Forum panel on collective imagination: "Everything clearly is not fine. It is absolutely not fine. But I do feel that we can authentically and deeply feel and learn from and heal the pain of the present and the past, without necessarily assuming we have to carry or project it into the future."[54]

THIS FEELS LIKE A GOOD moment to exhale and take a break from analyzing the patterns of the past.

Let's take a mental time trip to the future.

Almost all the scenarios in this book are set ten years from now. But this next one is *near future*: it could start playing out as soon as a few months from now.

Think of it as a "bridge scenario." Between today and a decade from now, how will people express their anger and grief over what has happened? How will they demand change?

To get from the present moment to a world of social transformation, it may help first to imagine new kinds of social movements and collective action.

Future Scenario #9: The Howl

The near future

howl \ 'haủ(-ə)l \ *verb*

1. to make a loud, long mournful cry or sound, in distress, pain, rage
2. to utter with unrestrained outcry[55]

Twice a day, the world stops everything and howls.

Not the *whole* world. But many, many millions of people. It happens first at noon, and then again after dark. The howl is the opposite of a moment of silence. It's a moment of *noise*.

It started three months ago, when Anshu Bhide, twenty-three, of Mumbai, howled out her window and posted a video of it online. She posted another, and then another. In the videos, she would stop whatever she was doing and howl for one full minute. She would do it twice a day, wherever she was, no matter who else was around or what they were doing. She howled in a park, on the train, at the market, in a café, in her bedroom, at a temple. Sometimes she wept. Sometimes she crouched like an animal. Sometimes she stood still. Sometimes she danced. She was loud. She was unapologetic. In the videos, people stared, tried to avoid her, or tried to help her. Occasionally, bystanders would join in and howl with her.

She posted the same message online with each video:

I am howling to say that everything is not okay.

I am howling to say, the people in power failed us.

I am howling to say, you will not ignore me.

I am howling to say, we can do better.

At noon I am howling out my pain and my grief.

At night I am howling so you can hear my hope and my power.

Can you hear the difference?

I will howl until the whole world howls.

Howl with me.

Other people started posting their own howling videos. In some of them, the person filming would pan the camera, and you could see they weren't alone. Small groups were gathered, howling together.

Howling became the number one trend on TikTok.

Signs began appearing in public spaces. Some read, "Gather here to howl." Others read, "Howling is not allowed. Please do not disturb our neighborhood."

Some restaurants and stores put up notices welcoming howlers. Others kicked them out.

The noon howl sounded a certain way. It was sorrowful, mournful, heartbroken, angry, and wild. It was the sound of a world in pain.

The night howl was different. It was joyful, defiant, melodic, playful. People echoed each other's distinctive howls back to them, as if to say, "I hear you. I'm here for you."

Students howled at school. Employees howled at work. It was allowed, it was not allowed, it was debated whether it should be allowed—as free speech, as protest, as civil disobedience.

What are your demands, journalists wanted to know of the howlers. How long do you plan to keep this up? What are you trying to achieve?

It was described as a social movement. It was described as a fad. It was art, it was politics, it was collective action, it was selfish, it was awe-inspiring, it was annoying, it was global. It was soon illegal in certain places.

IMAGINE YOURSELF IN THIS FUTURE. Try to envision the scene as vividly and realistically as you can: tens of millions of people howling twice a day, in every kind of private and public location.

What are the sights of this future? What are the sounds? In a word, what emotion do you feel at noon when it happens? In a word, what emotion do you feel at night when it happens? What does it sound like to you the very first time you hear it? When you've immersed yourself in this future, it's time to make a decision.

~~~~~~~~

MOMENT OF CHOICE: Do you join the howl? Why or why not?

If you join, where do you howl for the first time? Who else is around? How do they react?

If you don't join the howlers, what do you do instead during the twice-daily howls? Does the howling cause problems for you? Does it affect you in any way, or are you able to ignore it?

Now that you've made your move, let's keep playing with this possible future.

Here are some additional questions to consider. Let your mind wander through the possibilities:

- Which of your friends, family, and other people you know do you predict would join the howling? Who do you think would not join? Why?
- Are there any places howling should be prohibited in this future? Where?
- If it were prohibited, do you imagine that people would practice civil disobedience and do it anyway? Should they? Why or why not?
- Pick a social space you often find yourself in: your school, your workplace, public transportation, a hospital, a care home, a theater, a sporting venue, a place of worship, a retail location, a restaurant. How might that specific location start to adapt to, acknowledge, or work around the howling?
- If people made T-shirts or buttons for this movement, what might be on them?
- Can you picture graffiti from this future? What messages might get spray-painted onto buildings or written on bathroom walls?
- What good might come out of a howling movement?
- What harms could it cause?

- If you could change the ritual or rules of the howling to make it more meaningful, or effective, or respectful, or anything else you might want it to be, what change would you make? (If you absolutely hate the idea, can you think of anything that would make you more likely to participate?)
- How might symptoms of the deeper disease show up in this future? For example, would racial injustice or economic inequality affect who felt safe or secure enough to participate in howling?
- Imagine this is the beginning of a movement. Where could it go next? What comes *after* the howling?

You might not have ideas for some of these questions right away—that's fine. As you build your skills at playing with future scenarios, I'm challenging you to fill in bigger blanks, stretch your imagination a bit further. Whatever questions you can't answer now, just tuck this scenario in the back of your mind and see what ideas pop up another day.

Could this near future really happen? On a very small scale, it already did.

On March 22, 2020, a neighbor of mine, Hugh, made a suggestion on our community message board. He was inspired by a recent pandemic ritual: people in cities around the world were opening their windows and celebrating frontline workers each evening with cheering, applause, and singing. He suggested that our town, which had just been put on lockdown, do the same, but with a local twist: "Let's howl."

We live on a mountain, and coyotes are endemic here; their howls often fill the night air. The idea of howling alongside them seemed to suit folks. That night, you could hear human howls echoing across the valley. It became a nightly practice, with its own Facebook group and instructions: "Every night at 8pm, take a minute to step outside and let out a cathartic howl! Howl with compassion - for those affected by COVID-19. Howl for community - we may be sheltering but we are not alone."

The howl spread across the San Francisco Bay Area. Soon thousands of people were howling each night. Sister howling groups formed in other towns in the western United States, and news articles about the phenomenon started appearing.[56] In one article, Robert Faris, a professor of sociology at the University of California, Davis, said that he could see the appeal "for stress relief and solidarity," and yet: "If you come back to me in May and say there are still people howling, I'll be surprised."[57]

But people in our neighborhood *were* still howling in May, and June, and July. By summer, the howling had taken on a different mood, as compassion and catharsis evolved into activism and outcry. "Howl for Black Lives Matter," "Howl for People of Color in our community," neighbors started posting. The howling moved, at times, out of homes and into the public eye: "Take a knee in the street when we howl tonight at 8," an update to the Howl group announced.

By the end of the summer of howling, by my estimate, more than a million people had joined in. The howl died away by the fall, but it has periodically reemerged in our community, on election night, for example, on the evening of the January 6 violent attack on the US Capitol, and on the anniversary of our first COVID-19 lockdown.

My family howled every night for months. It helped us feel less alone during the long lockdown. I personally howled to say, "I'm still here," and to say, "I hear you," and sometimes to say, "What the hell is wrong with our country?" and to say, after recovering from a COVID-19 illness I thought was going to kill me, "There is air in my lungs, and I can breathe without gasping again, and I am grateful to be alive, and I hope I never forget this gratitude."

There were so many different kinds of howls expressed in our community over the course of 2020—playful, heartfelt, hopeful, and sometimes, it seemed, pained. But looking back on it now, even after hundreds of collective howls, I still feel that there is more to howl about, and maybe a different sound that needs to come out.

Scientists who study emotion have observed that the sounds associated with grief are distinct from other outcries. Cries of grief have a distinct vocal signature, an almost animalistic desperation and vulnerability that are impossible to ignore, literally: they trigger an evolutionary instinct in others who hear them, to soothe and to help.[58]

The worst sound I ever heard was one of these outcries. It was the cry of a stranger.

My twin daughters were born in the winter of 2015, nine weeks premature. They spent two months in the hospital's neonatal intensive care unit, gathering their strength to come home. Several families were cared for in each NICU room, our babies incubating next to each other. We often saw the same familiar faces, other parents coming to hold and help feed their babies, in whatever ways were allowed; usually it was less time and touching than we craved.

Curtains were sometimes drawn between the families for privacy. One day, a doctor drew the curtain, and my husband and I heard him deliver terrible news to the parents next to us. Their prematurely born daughter was "failing to thrive," in the medical parlance, he said, and would not survive. She would be taken off life support as soon as the parents said their goodbyes.

I will never forget the cries of the mother in that moment. Unrestrained, forsaken. I think of her grief so often; it feels like the vibrations of those sound waves are still happening in my mind.

We left the NICU to give the family privacy during their final moments together, and I did not see them again. I would describe her pain as unimaginable, but I try to imagine it. I carry it with me still. Seven years later I catch myself still wondering, impossibly, if I might somehow find her and do something to help.

When that kind of pain enters our minds, when it travels from someone's mouth into our ears, I do believe it changes us. When you are a witness to another human's full-bodied, full-throated, unrestrained grieving, it stays with you. So when I think about what it might take to heal our global traumas, I wonder if we will be able to give people time and space to make those sounds—and if we will be willing to listen. I wonder if people will *demand* that time and space— not with an orderly howl but with howling that refuses to be confined or ignored. I don't know if a scenario like "The Howl" is probable. But I want to at least imagine it. I want to explore the possibility of tens of millions of people making the kinds of sounds that tap into our powerful evolutionary instincts to soothe and help each other, creating mutual witnesses out of us all.

Ocean Vuong, the poet and novelist, has said, "We often tell our students, 'The future's in your hands.' But I think the future is actually in your mouth. You have to articulate the world you want to live in first."[59] And yet, maybe before we can put the future we want into words, we have to say the wordless things first.

THIS CHAPTER HAS BEEN FULL of questions. Why so many? As we say at the Institute for the Future, "There are no facts about the future." Nothing can be proved about it, since it hasn't happened yet. And so, when it comes to the future, a statement is less useful, less *truthful*, than a question.

The truth of the future isn't what *will* happen; it's what *could* happen. From where we stand today, we can only provably say: Here is the potential, or the momentum, for certain kinds of change. But the future is always uncertain, in flux, and changeable; it is a perpetually expanding and collapsing set of possibilities. We have to sneak up on the truth of the future sideways. We ask: Is this possible? Well, what about that—is it possible? And how about this? What can we do to make it more possible? Each question about what could possibly be different sneaks us up a little bit closer to the truth. And what is that truth? Well, it's different for everyone.

The truest truth of the future is personal. It's whatever we feel deep in our bones that we really want to be different, whatever we really *need* to be different, whatever we are willing to howl twice a day about until it is different. It's whatever we are willing to spend not just a week, or a month, or a year, but a whole decade of our lives trying to make different.

And so I have a few more questions for you.

The Urgent Futures Questionnaire

I developed the Urgent Futures Questionnaire as a way to help my students and my fellow futurists get to their own future truth. Here's how it works:

First, pick any urgent challenge you feel strongly about, such as economic inequality, broken health systems, extreme political divisions, racial injustice, brittle supply chains, overworked workers, the climate crisis, or any other "preexisting condition" of the future you have in mind.

Next, pick a specific community that you're a part of. It could be your town or city, your school or workplace, the religious community you belong to, the political party you identify with, the industry you work in, or the country you live in.

Now, thinking about this challenge within your own community, answer these four questions, on a scale of 1 to 10:

1. **How urgent** do you think it is to address this problem in your own community? (1 = not urgent at all, 10 = extremely urgent)
2. What percentage of people in your community do you think **agree with you?** (1 = almost nobody, 10 = almost everybody)
3. **How optimistic** are you that this problem will be significantly improved in your community in the next ten years? (1 = extremely pessimistic, 10 = extremely optimistic)
4. **How much power** do *you* personally have to influence whether or how this problem is significantly improved in your community in the next ten years? (1 = no power at all, 10 = a huge amount of power)

You should have four numbers at the end of this questionnaire, for example: 8, 5, 6, 3. Don't add the numbers up—you're not giving yourself an "overall score." Instead, you're looking at the relationships among the four numbers. These relationships measure four different dimensions of how you relate to the future: your calling, your belonging, your hope, and your power:

1. **Your calling to the future:** Do you have a strong inner impulse toward a particular course of action that can change the future, like helping solve a global problem, preparing for a crisis, or inventing something new?

2. **Your belonging to the future:** Do you have a strong sense of community and fellowship around your calling? Do you feel like you're going it alone or like you have plenty of allies?

3. **Your hope for the future:** Do you feel that positive change around your calling is both possible and realistic?

4. **Your power to shape the future:** Are you confident that your actions matter when it comes to making positive change, and that you have an important role to play in helping others?

Your *calling score* is your answer to question #1 (example: 8). Whenever there is a high number (a score of 8 or more), there is a strong and urgent calling to the future. You've found a specific long-term challenge that you feel passionate about and are highly motivated to help solve. The higher the number, the stronger the calling.

If you can't think of any social problem or global challenge that you would rate 8 or higher, then finding one that calls to you is the first step to becoming urgently involved in making the future. (Keep reading, there are many more challenges to choose from in this book!)

On the other hand, if you're rating *every* long-term challenge 8 or higher, then look for the one or two challenges that you rate the very highest. Are there any 10s? This will help you focus your future energy.

Your *belonging score* is the number you get when you *subtract* your answer to question #2 from your answer to question #1 (example: 8 − 5 = 3).

When your numbers for #1 and #2 are more closely aligned (a difference ≤2; or it may even be a negative number, if you think your community cares about the issue even more than you), there is *belonging* to the future: a sense that the future will be full of people who share your calling to make it better. But when there is a significant gap in values between question #1 and question #2 (a difference >2), there can be *alienation* from the future. That's the painful feeling that others aren't invested in the same change you want to help make.

Closing this gap is a powerful way to change how you relate to the future. This may mean seeking out people in your community who are already working on this problem and joining them, or educating yourself about their efforts. Finding these helpers will give you a place to belong.

Or it may mean picking a different community to try to create change in. Is there another group where your calling might be better appreciated? Look around and consider all the groups you belong to. One of them may be more ready for change.

Or it may mean actively working to increase the community of people who share your urgency by becoming an advocate for the challenge to your friends, family, neighbors, colleagues, and others. Even finding just one other person who shares your future calling can make a huge impact on how much energy and optimism you bring to that future.

Your *hope score* is the number you get when you subtract your answer to question #3 from your answer to question #1 (for example: $8 - 6 = 2$).

When your numbers for #1 and #3 are more closely aligned (a difference ≤2; it may even be a negative number if you are very confident that positive change is coming), there is strong *hope for change* in the future about the challenge you've chosen.

When there is a significant gap in numerical values for #1 and #3 around the same issue (a difference >2), there is *anxiety* or *hopelessness* about the future, an unease that something you care passionately about changing for the better may not, in fact, be possible to change.

The best way to increase hope for change around a particular challenge is to use the imagination skills you've been practicing already in this book: zoom out to a ten-year timeline, look for evidence that anything can change by playing Stump the Futurist and One Hundred Ways Anything Can Be Different in the Future, and take mental time trips to imagined future worlds where positive change has already happened. The more vividly and realistically you can imagine positive change, the better prepared your brain will be to spot real opportunities to make it.

Your *power score* is the number you get when you subtract your answer to question #4 from your answer to question #1 (example: $8 - 3 = 5$).

When #1 and #4 are well aligned (a difference ≤ 2; it may even be a negative number if you are confident that your actions matter), there is a feeling of *power to make change and help others* in the future, a confidence that your efforts can and will make a positive impact.

When there is a significant gap in numerical values for #1 and #4 around the same issue (a difference > 2), there is a *powerlessness or helplessness* toward the future.

Part III of this book will suggest a variety of types of actions you can take to increase your power to shape the future. After you've read those chapters, you may wish to revisit this questionnaire and see if you feel just a little more powerful, and just a little more helpful.

There's no "good score" or "bad score" on the Urgent Futures Questionnaire, no homework to "improve" your score. Instead, it's a framework for understanding how you (and others) relate to different future challenges, and for exploring where you (and others) may have the most powerful opportunity to make change.

Someone with a score that suggests high calling, belonging, hope, and power is likely to be actively engaged in making the future in a way that feels authentic, energizing, motivating, and meaningful. Someone with a score that suggests low calling, belonging, hope, or power may have a harder time feeling energized by that future; it may feel too abstract, far away, or impossible to change.

But a person's scores can change day to day, week to week; they can be affected by current events, conversations, personal setbacks, and exposure to new ideas and information. A person can also have high scores for one future challenge or community and low scores for others— that's natural and suggests which challenges and communities a person may have the most energy and opportunity for engagement with.

You may find these questions helpful as a way to give a more concrete form to the swirling whirlwind of feelings you have as you imagine different futures. You may want to ask yourself all four questions for each of the preexisting conditions we've examined in this chapter. Which one do you have the strongest calling for? The most belonging? The most hope? The most power? As we look at other future challenges in this book, you may want to revisit the Urgent Futures Questionnaire and score yourself on them too.

You can also try using the questionnaire when discussing urgent challenges with a larger group, whether it's at a town hall, team meeting, volunteer training, or classroom discussion. You don't have to calculate scores; just share and compare your numbers for each question. This is a great way to connect with others who can increase your hope and sense of power around your calling. Who has a higher answer to question #3 or #4 than you? Ask them why they chose the numbers they did; they may have good news or useful strategies to share.

Most importantly, just the very act of asking these questions can help nudge someone toward more optimistic engagement with the future. As one respondent to the Urgent Futures Questionnaire put it: "It was actually kind of empowering just to ask myself these questions. Just reading these questions I felt, well yeah, there are more possibilities open to me than what I normally consider in my day. I could be someone who really thinks about and helps solve these kinds of challenges. Why not me?"

AUTHOR AND ACTIVIST WALIDAH IMARISHA writes: "Futures we want don't exist as untouchable distant points out of our reach. When we focus on collective action, mutual aid, self-determination, and centering the leadership of the marginalized, we live the change we want and we defy linear time. We pull those liberated futures into the present. . . . Let's keep pulling liberated futures into the present over and over again until we reach the day when that's all there is."[60]

Imagination is the first act of pulling the future into the present. It builds urgency, motivation, and a community for action when we share our imagination with others. Questioning also pulls the future into the present. Every question we ask makes space for new ideas, new possibilities. When we frame future possibilities as questions, instead of predictions, we can be braver and bolder in our thinking. We don't have to be certain; we can be curious. We can reveal our curiosities to others. We can start asking the same questions, together.

So let's keep going. What other futures can we imagine? What other futures *should* we imagine?

Are you ready to defy linear time?

Are you ready to start pulling?

IMAGINATION TRAINING

RULE #9: Heal the Deeper Disease.

Find the social challenges that fill you with the most urgent optimism. Which inequalities, injustices, and vulnerabilities do you personally feel called to help heal? These challenges will connect you to our collective post-pandemic, post-traumatic transformation. They can be a springboard for your own personal growth and meaning making. So look for the preexisting conditions of society that made us suffer more deeply in the past. Then imagine how they might create the complications of the future. What might happen over the next decade if we fail to remedy them? What might be possible if we heal them?

PART III

〜〜〜

IMAGINE THE UNIMAGINABLE

After tragedies, one has to invent a new world, knit it or embroider, make it up. . . . You have to imagine something that doesn't exist and dig a cave into the future and demand space. It's a territorial hope affair. At the time, that digging is utopian but in the future it will become your reality.

—BJÖRK, singer-songwriter

<u>How much control or influence</u> do you feel <u>you</u> personally have in determining how the world and your life change over the next ten years?

. . . .

Rate your outlook on a scale of 1 to 10.

1 is almost no control or influence,
10 is almost complete control or influence.

$\sim\!\sim\!\sim$

Answer the Call to Adventure

*The "call to adventure" signifies that destiny has summoned
the hero.*

—JOSEPH CAMPBELL, mythologist

IN 1967, A TEAM OF RESEARCHERS AT THE UNIVERSITY OF PENNSYLVANIA
conducted a controversial psychology experiment in which dogs
were given electric shocks. The goal of the study was to find out how
animals—and perhaps, by extension, humans—learn from adverse
experiences. The dogs were restrained in a hammock, their legs dan-
gling through four of its holes. The researchers then delivered a series
of painful electric shocks to the dogs' hind legs. For some of the dogs
in the experiment, there was also a lever that they could reach with
their nose. If the lever was nudged, it would stop the shocks. Most dogs
quickly figured out how to stop the shocks. But for some of the dogs,
the lever purposefully did not work. No matter what they did, the
shocks would continue.

Twenty-four hours after the dogs endured their initial round of shocks, they were placed in a different test environment, called a "shuttle box." The box was divided into two sections by a low barrier that the dogs could easily jump over if they tried. On one side of the box was a metal plate that could deliver more electric shocks; the other side was safe. The dogs first spent five minutes in the shuttle box, unrestrained and free to move around. Then the shocks began. To escape, all the dogs had to do was jump from one side of the box to the other.

The researchers observed that the two groups of dogs—those who in the hammock the day before had been able to stop the shocks by nudging a lever, and those who had no way to stop the shocks—reacted very differently to the second trial. The first group of dogs all figured out how to jump over the barrier and escape the shocks quickly. But most of the dogs in the second group didn't even *try* to escape the shocks. They simply lay down and endured them until the researchers ended the experiment.[1]

Today, this kind of cruel animal research would be forbidden. But it yielded an important theory that became a cornerstone of animal and human psychology: the theory of *learned helplessness*. According to this theory, if we learn that outcomes are independent of our responses—that nothing we do matters—then we will internalize that lesson and carry it with us to other situations. Even if, objectively, we are not helpless, we will *feel* helpless. And so we will be less likely, whatever future problems we face, to take actions to better our circumstances.

This theory held up for decades, through repeated experiments with mice, monkeys, and people. The same helpless behavior appeared again and again, in animals and humans alike. It became one of the most cited explanations for clinical depression: if we experience an inability to control outcomes in multiple areas of our lives—at home, at school, at work, in our health, in our finances, in our love lives—then we learn to stop trying. Our brains tell us, "Don't bother." We get depressed and turn inward; we become passive, just like the dogs in the shuttle box.[2]

But then, something unexpected happened in the field of psychology. One of the original researchers on the University of Pennsylvania experiment, Steven F. Maier, then a graduate student, switched fields and became a neuroscientist. He decided to revisit the theory he helped establish, but this time from a neurological perspective. He started investigating which circuits, receptors, and neurotransmitters were involved with learning helplessness. And when he watched what was actually going on in the brain, he discovered that the original theory had it all backward: We don't *learn* helplessness. The brain *assumes* helplessness when exposed to adverse conditions. If we want to feel that we have any control over our own outcomes, we have to *learn that we have power.*

This newer research is complicated, but the most important thing to understand is that psychologists now know that a passive, defensive strategy—or simply trying to endure the worst until it ends—is actually the most hardwired, instinctive biological response we have to bad experiences. You've probably heard of the "fight or flight" reaction to stress, and that's real too. (Psychologists have updated the theory recently to include a third instinctive reaction to stress: "tend and befriend," in which we seek and give social support.) But before fight or flight, before tend and befriend, "freeze" is actually the most primal response, the reaction that evolution initially favored. If we don't want to freeze, we have to learn that we can fight back. We have to learn that we can take flight. We have to learn that we can ask for and give others support.[3]

How do we learn our own power? We have to activate pathways in the ventromedial prefrontal cortex (vmPFC) region of the brain that *turn off* the instinctive, helpless response—our default freeze response—which, as it turns out, is driven by a region of the brain called the dorsal raphe nucleus. The dorsal raphe nucleus responds to aversive stimuli like painfully loud noises, blinding bright lights, threats of violence, shame, or electric shocks by directing neurotransmitters to two *other* regions of the brain, the amygdala and the sensorimotor cortex, which stimulate fear and tell the body to "freeze." The vmPFC only turns off the dorsal raphe nucleus response *if and when we have direct experience of taking purposeful action that leads to a desired result in the face of aversive stimuli*. In other words, we have to learn that we can, in fact, turn down the noise, turn off the lights, flee the threat, soothe the shame, or escape the shocks. We have to be like the animals in the University of Pennsylvania experiment who noticed that by accidentally nudging a nearby lever, they could escape the shocks. We have to discover all the levers (whatever they might be) that allow us to exert our will and make a positive difference in our own lives, and in the lives of others, even when under duress.

This study explains something I observed when I was doing my PhD research in the psychology of games at the University of California, Berkeley. I was fascinated by how much control frequent gamers perceived—not just in the video games they liked to play but in their everyday lives as well. My research, and many others' since, has shown that gamers set higher goals for themselves in their everyday lives and are less likely to quit in the face of real-world setbacks. They are more likely to ask for help from, and offer real-world assistance to, friends and family they play games with regularly than non-gamers do from their friends and family. And they are more likely to volunteer to help with a social problem that others might feel is beyond their abilities or control.[4]

Where does this extreme sense of agency come from? Well, video games are like psychological experiments, designed to teach control over outcomes. Every game starts with a challenge or obstacle that is difficult to overcome, or a threat that is difficult to escape. (Think of the fast-moving ghosts in *Pac-Man*.) Players must experiment to discover for themselves what actions they can take, what resources they can collect, which allies they can recruit, what strategies they can adopt to deal with the aversive conditions of the game. Eventually, as players figure out the game, improve their skills, and achieve their goals, they build a powerful confidence in their ability to determine what happens next. And crucially, fMRI studies of gameplay show that all of this happens along the same neurological pathways in the vmPFC that teach us we have control over aversive stimuli.[5] Gamers are, essentially, unlearning the freeze instinct and learning to fight, flee, or help others more effectively every time they play.

The title of the now-famous 1967 scientific paper that laid the groundwork for these findings in the *Journal of Experimental Psychology* was "Failure to Escape Traumatic Shock." These words could just as aptly describe our own experiences today. It's not electric shocks we've endured but rather social ones. We've been battered by a pandemic, protests, wildfires, extreme heat, attacks on democracy and the truth. The question becomes, will we lie down like the dogs and simply wait to be shocked again?

I wouldn't blame anyone who, after the tumultuous past few years we've lived through, decided: "There's no way to control what happens next, so why bother trying?" But there is another way to process the trauma and shock. We can overcome the natural, hardwired neurological response to adverse experiences. We can train our brains, instead, to detect the possibility of exerting control over outcomes in the future—by exposing ourselves to future scenarios and imagining how we might successfully react to them.

Playing with a future scenario, it turns out, can be a uniquely therapeutic practice. It can give us a chance to practice the opposite of learned helplessness: *learned helpfulness.*

Learned helpfulness simply means building our own confidence and sense of control when it comes to solving problems for ourselves and others. Every time we successfully help ease someone's suffering, or fill an unmet need, or lighten someone's burden, we learn our own helpfulness. We strengthen the neurological pathways that allow us to believe that, yes, we do in fact have power over the way things turn out. It might not be ultimate power—we might not solve everyone's problems or heal the whole world—but knowing that we can take action to make something better guarantees that when we face a future shock, we won't freeze. We won't assume our own helplessness. We will look for a new way to help.

Each future scenario in this book, by design, delivers its own kind of mental or emotional shock. A future scenario describes a world that is meant to be surprising and, in many cases, hard to think about—either because it's so strange and unfamiliar that we can hardly imagine it or because the crisis or potential trauma we encounter there makes us feel anxious and we don't *want* to think about it. But like any other kind of game, a scenario or simulation is a safe place to experiment. There are no real-world consequences for whatever actions or strategies we might imagine ourselves trying. And we can consider the possibility that in the future, we will be even braver, smarter, stronger, kinder, more skillful, more heroic versions of ourselves. We can imagine ourselves doing anything—inventing something, launching a business, moving somewhere new, running for office, starting a charity or nonprofit, earning an unexpected degree, taking up a new profession, leading a social movement, following a lifelong dream— things we might feel underprepared or ill-equipped to try today.

So far, you've practiced many different ways of playing with future scenarios. You've vividly imagined waking up in a new world and asking yourself: What would I feel in this future? What actions would I take? You've expanded your empathy for how a scenario might affect other people differently, by playing with scenarios with others. You've written journal entries from the future about how you might react to a shocking event, in order to get better at thinking through the fog of crisis. You've diagnosed the symptoms of a deeper disease to find preexisting conditions of the present that will become the complications of the future. Now it's time to practice the single most important future imagination skill: finding your own unique way to help.

I describe this as "answering the future's call to adventure."

IN HIS FAMOUS MODEL OF the hero's journey, mythologist Joseph Campbell writes that in countless myths and legends, the adventure begins when an otherwise ordinary person receives the "call to adventure." It's a challenge to embark on a journey to "a zone unknown," a "fateful region of both treasure and danger," somewhere that "the familiar life horizon has been outgrown; the old concepts, ideals, and emotional patterns no longer fit."[6] Upon arrival to this faraway place, the hero is given the chance to solve a difficult problem, or learn an extraordinary truth, or collect a powerful resource. The hero then returns to the ordinary world with this reward and uses it to make that world better.

For those of us living out our lives in the real world, the zone unknown that we are most urgently called to, where everything seems strange and upside down, is the future. And like the archetypal hero, we too may choose to visit that strange world, through mental time trips—to imagine how we might solve problems there, to see what opportunities or treasures await in that world, to find the risks or dangers that exist there. And we can bring what we discover on our trip to the future back to the present moment: foresight and insights that we too can use to improve our world.

In Campbell's model, only one hero receives the call to adventure. The hero is a special person, and only he or she has the necessary skills and character strengths to rise to the heroic occasion. But we are *all* called to the future. And because time is the great equalizer, we all travel through life together at exactly the same speed, live in exactly the same present moment, are all exactly equidistant from ten years from now, and will all arrive at the future at exactly the same time. When it comes to the future, there is not just one hero; any one of us may answer the future's call to adventure. In fact, the more of us who answer the call, the better.

What is that call? It is an urgent invitation for us to pre-think and pre-feel how we might help ourselves and others adapt and thrive in unfamiliar scenarios and crises.

In the archetypal hero's journey, the call to adventure is sometimes followed by "refusal of the call." Instead of rising to the occasion, the potential hero refuses to go. As Campbell writes in *The Hero with a Thousand Faces*, "In actual life, and not infrequently in the myths and popular tales, we encounter the dull case of the call unanswered." Refusal may occur when the potential hero is "walled in boredom, hard work, or 'culture'"—that is, mentally stuck in the trappings of the status quo by the desire for the "present system . . . to be fixed and made secure." In my work as a professional futurist, I have seen many such refusals—even by individuals and organizations who have hired me specifically to challenge their assumptions and help them imagine strange new worlds. In my experience, there are four different ways people refuse the urgent call of the future: with distancing, denial, fatigue, or surrender.

Distancing means answering the call to seriously imagine the future this way: "That's a long way off, we don't have to think about it now." Or: "It won't affect me personally, it's someone else's issue." Or: "That's a problem for the other side of the world to worry about."

Denial means answering the call this way: "That will never happen"; "If it happens, it's not going to be a big deal"; "The risk is exaggerated."

Fatigue means responding: "I have too many real problems today to worry about a hypothetical future one." Or "I'm burned out from trying to get other people to pay attention to this long-term risk. I can't do it anymore."

Surrender means thinking: "I can't personally do anything about this; it's beyond my control, so why bother?"

Do these "refusals to imagine" sound familiar? We heard so many of them during the COVID-19 pandemic, even when the unimaginable future we were being asked to imagine was potentially just days or weeks away.

Can you recall those early days, when regions first hard hit by COVID-19 tried, urgently, desperately, to show us our future? From China, then from Italy, then from Spain, then from New York City, videos and social media posts and op-eds all tried to warn the world what was coming.[7] One of the most striking calls to future imagination was a March 17, 2020, essay by Ida Garibaldi titled: "Hello from Italy. Your Future Is Grimmer than You Think":

> Writing this from Italy, I am also writing to you from your own future. From our state of emergency, we have been watching the crisis unfold in the United States with a terrible sense of foreboding. . . . Stay away from restaurants, gyms, libraries, movie theaters, bars and cafes, yes. But also: Don't invite people over for dinner, don't let your kids go on playdates, don't take them to the playground, don't let your teenagers out of your sight. They will

sneak out with their friends, they will hold hands, they will share their drinks and food. If this seems too much, consider the following: We are not allowed to hold weddings or funerals. We can't gather to bury our dead. For us, it might be too late to avoid an incredible loss of life. But if you decide against taking actions because it seems inconvenient, or because you don't want to look silly, you can't say you weren't warned.[8]

These people were sending messages from the future because, despite all the evidence that the unthinkable could happen, so many of us simply couldn't believe it could happen to *us*. We couldn't really imagine the future until it happened in our own communities.

The future's call won't always be this explicit. We won't often be shown such a clear, detailed vision of what's coming. But if we keep an ear to the ground—if we look for signals of change and follow the future forces—then we *will* hear the call of the future, and it will be up to us to choose whether or not to answer it.

You've answered the call to adventure. You're now about to take a mental time trip to an upside-down world. What will you bring with you to better face the challenges you encounter there? Learning your own surprising power to help shape the future begins with a quick challenge that I call Pack Your Bags for the Future.

In myths and legends, every hero brings a unique combination of skills, character strengths, knowledge, and tools that help the hero rise to the occasion and solve the problem at hand. You, too, have your own signature strengths that suggest how *you* might be of service to others in the future. As author and leadership coach Tara Mohr has written, "The world was made with a you-shaped hole in it. / In that way you are important. / In that way you are here to make the world. / In that way you are called."[9]

So: What are you good at? What do you know a lot about? What communities are you part of? What's something you're more passionate about than most people? What values drive you forward in your own life, no matter what obstacles or setbacks you face? I'll help you draw out your answers to these questions in a moment. But first, I want to encourage you to answer them with a very open mind.

Some strengths and abilities may seem, on the surface, to be more helpful than others when it comes to future crises. Depending on the scenario, "essential" might describe medical skills, or an ability to translate languages, or to organize protests, or to fundraise, or to model data, or to innovate in a laboratory, or to provide spiritual care and comfort, or to keep the power grid up and running. If you lack these "essential" skills, then you might feel underqualified to do something that really matters. But I want you to keep an open mind as to what might be needed, by whom, in the future. Fashion savvy, long-time participation in a Bible study group, gun safety knowledge, manga drawing skills, knowing most people in your neighborhood by name, a habit of writing timely thank-you notes, the ability to identify constellations in the sky and tell their stories, a commitment to being the best parent you can be, an unrivaled determination to get ten thousand steps each and every day, adventurous eating habits—truly, there is no skill or strength too small or too random to potentially make you of service to someone else in the future, as you will shortly see.

So as you pack your bags, don't prejudge any of your skills as unimportant, or any kind of knowledge as trivial, or any community as nonessential, or any character strength as unhelpful. After you come up with a list of everything *you* bring to the future, we'll take a trip to a future scenario, and you'll have a chance to creatively work out what you might do with all your own unique strengths. For now, your task is simply to pack a bag.

HERE'S HOW TO PLAY PACK Your Bags for the Future:

I'm going to ask you several questions about your skills, abilities, knowledge, passions, communities, and values. You may find it helpful to write down your answers on a blank piece of paper so you can hang the list up somewhere to inspire your future imagination. Try to come up with at least one answer for each question. (If you have more than one idea per question, write them all down! The more ideas, the merrier.)

You may find that comparing answers with others is fun and eye-opening. In fact, if you can't think of an answer, ask a friend or family member to suggest answers for you. Other people often have a knack for pointing out personal skills and strengths we never really notice about ourselves.

Skills and abilities. What are you good at? What do you know how to do that many people don't?

This might be a professional skill, a life skill, a hobby, something you get paid to do, or something you do for your own enjoyment. It might be something you learned at school or work or received special training in. Or it might be something you've picked up on your own. Don't limit yourself to what you think might be useful in a crisis; it can be anything at all. For my own list, for example, I would include: making up new games, planning trips, explaining scientific research to non-scientists, trail running, and keeping wildfire smoke out of my house.

When you get to the future, you may find that these skills and abilities will be powerful clues as to how you might help.

Deep knowledge and passions. What topic or activity do you know a lot about, more than most people? What do you spend a lot of time thinking about, more than most people?

Here are some answers I've seen in the past: dog agility training, nutrition, Bollywood movies, DIY Halloween costumes, military history, traditional Persian cooking, Zumba dance, project management, the enneagram of personality types, Stoicism philosophy, the ethics of artificial intelligence, party planning, self-care, digital photography.

When you get to the future, you may find that you can make creative connections between your knowledge and passions and the crisis at hand.

Communities. What communities are you a part of? What groups are you a member of? You might consider your neighborhood, your school, your workplace or wider industry, a religious community, a diaspora, a support group, a political party, a music or art scene, an athletic or gaming community, a patient or health community online, a discussion forum or channel or social network you're very active on, a recovery group, any kind of club or team, or even your extended family if that's a big part of your identity.

When you get to the future, you may be able to mobilize this community, or advocate for their interests, or play an important role in keeping them informed.

Values. What are your core values? A value is a way of being that brings purpose and meaning to life. It's a strength you want to exhibit, a virtue you want to uphold, a quality you want to embody, or a way of being in service to something bigger than yourself. Here are some examples of values you might hold: to never stop learning; to be the best parent possible; to always challenge your physical limits and be an inspiration to others; to be a loving and caring person who is there whenever a friend needs you; to connect with and respect nature; to enjoy everything, and never be bored, because life is short; to serve God faithfully and, through your actions, be an example to others; to explore the whole world and understand as many different cultures as possible; to stand up for others and fight for what's right; to bring beauty to the world wherever you can; to document truth and spread it widely. (You know you've identified a core value when you can complete this sentence with it: "I vow to . . ." or "My purpose in life is to . . ." or simply, "I feel like the best version of myself when I spend my time and energy on . . .")

When you get to the future, you may find that these values guide your actions and help you focus your attention on what will keep you motivated and resilient during a challenging time.

Superstruct and EVOKE players completed this same activity, identifying their skills and abilities, knowledge and passions, communities, and values, at the very start of each simulation. Back then, we called it creating your "super-empowered hopeful individual" profile. I believe that listing these specific signature strengths was an essential step toward being able to imagine how they might rise to the heroic occasion of those hypothetical future pandemics. As one player I recently reconnected with told me, "The experience had a major impact on me. Maybe the biggest impact was imagining what skills I have now that I could bring into the future. The ability to imagine myself helping in the future, rather than just picturing a scenario with me as a passive observer, has given me the courage and confidence to step into the real future."

Now it's your turn to put *your* strengths in service of a possible future crisis. The world of 2035 faces another pandemic, but it's nothing like the one you've already lived through.

You've answered the call. You've packed your bags. A future scenario awaits. As you read through the scenario, which is based on a real disease that exists today, let the wheels in your mind start spinning: Which of your signature strengths that you've just listed would be most helpful in this future?

Future Scenario #10: The Alpha-Gal Crisis

The year 2035

Today, the news reported a milestone: "Alpha-gal syndrome, or AGS, has affected fifty million people in the United States, a previously unthinkable number."

You haven't seen the words "unthinkable" and "unimaginable" in so many headlines since the COVID-19 pandemic fifteen years ago.

You know how AGS works by now: a carrier tick bites a human, injecting the person with the sugar molecule galactose-α-1,3-galactose, or "alpha-gal," which is commonly found in the blood of animals that ticks feed on, like cows and sheep. Then the person's immune system goes crazy, overreacting as if the sugar molecule were a deadly virus. The person develops severe, life-threatening allergies to most mammalian animal products, including beef, pork, dairy, cheese, lard, and gelatin. From that point forward, any exposure to the alpha-gal sugar could be fatal.

This means that fifty million previously healthy Americans, or one in eight, must now avoid all kinds of animal products. One taste of a hamburger, a handful of gummy bears, cow milk in their coffee instead of oat milk, and they'll likely wind up in the hospital. All because of a tick bite. Even just smelling the fumes of meat cooking on a grill can trigger respiratory distress and a dangerously elevated heart rate. You'd never heard of "airborne meat" before the AGS crisis, but now it's a real thing people have to avoid.

And a second or third tick bite makes AGS worse. For those people, skin contact with common household products can send them into fatal anaphylactic shock. You never realized just how many nonfood items—crayons, toilet paper, condoms, plastic bags, and toothpaste—are "held together" or softened up by beef fat or gelatin. Thanks to the CDC's public service announcements, part of its Meat Is Everywhere campaign, now you know.

Since the start of the crisis, emergency room visits for allergic reactions are up from 125,000 a year in the US to over ten million a year.

When you put it that way—it really is unthinkable.

You've lost count of how many of your friends and family are living with alpha-gal syndrome. Twenty, maybe? Thirty? At least. You feel lucky that, so far, you've avoided it, especially since there is no known treatment or cure.

You can still remember when AGS was unusual. Back then, a story like "Forced Vegetarian Reveals Tick Bite Left Them Allergic to Red Meat" might appear in your "Weird News: The Source for All Things Bizarre, Strange, and Odd in the World" feed. That was in 2009, when only a dozen or so cases had been detected. But by 2019, over thirty-four thousand people had been diagnosed with AGS in the United States, and thousands more were affected across northern Europe, Australia, and sub-Saharan Africa.[10] Suddenly, the news coverage became less "weird" and more alarming:

"Rare Tick Is Becoming Common, and It Could Give You a
Potentially Fatal Meat Allergy."

"It's Not Just the Woods Anymore: Lone Star Tick Populations
Are Rising to Previously Unimaginable Levels in Cities, Putting
Global Health at Risk."

Almost overnight, it seemed, people were catching AGS from ticks
in Central Park in New York City and on beaches in Southern California. Kids were catching it from ticks on soccer fields in all fifty
states. Soon, alpha-gal syndrome was found on every continent except
Antarctica.

In 2034, by the time over 250 million people worldwide had been
affected, the World Health Organization declared AGS the first tick-
borne pandemic on record. And things started changing, fast:

"Twenty-Five Percent of People in the World Will Eat a Fully
Vegan Diet This Year, Due to Life-Threatening Meat Allergy;
Meat Manufacturers, Food and Restaurant Industries Face an Era
of Unimaginable Change."

"Parks, Beaches, and Athletic Fields Empty Out, Despite Beautiful
Weather, as People This Year Plan to Do the Unthinkable to
Avoid Ticks: Stay Indoors All Summer Long."

"Is It the End of Dogs? Pet Owners Are Abandoning Their Dogs
in Record Numbers, to Reduce Exposure to Ticks."

"The World Is Running Short of Epinephrine, an Essential Drug
to Reverse Life-Threatening Allergic Reactions of All Kinds;
Seven Hundred Million More People with Non-AGS Allergies
Now at Risk."

"Monoclonal Antibodies, the Most Successful Treatment
Option for SARS-CoV-2, 3, 4, and 5, Are No Longer an Option
for People with AGS. The Lifesaving Medicine Is Produced
in Mammalian Cell Lines. Voluntary Lockdown for All People
with AGS during Any Local Virus Outbreak Is Now
Recommended."

Now that AGS is a pandemic, the world seems to have divided into
five kinds of people:

1. People with AGS: If you have AGS, your life revolves around
avoiding the alpha-gal molecule by any means necessary. You are now
mostly vegetarian, whether you like it or not. You have to do things
like bring your own vegan toilet paper everywhere, to avoid contact
exposure with beef gelatin. And you're extra cautious about ticks, because if you get another tick bite, your symptoms could get even worse:
faster and harder-to-treat allergic reactions, joint pain, severe abdom-
inal pain, brain fog.

2. People afraid of getting AGS: You're anxious about being in
outdoor spaces. When you do go to parks, beaches, or athletic fields,
you cover as much skin as possible. You drench yourself in DEET or
whatever tick repellent you can find that isn't sold out. You ask friends
and family members to give you extensive, full-body tick checks every
time you walk in the door; this new ritual reminds you of the
COVID-19-era ubiquitous temperature checks, but it takes a lot longer and is certainly more intimate.

**3. People without AGS, but who start living as if they have
it—just in case:** You preemptively stop eating meat. You buy
all-vegan household products. You avoid breathing meat fumes. This
way, if you do get AGS, you won't be at serious risk. Taking these actions now also helps you keep your family safe. It gives you peace of
mind to live this way.

4. People who double down on the outdoors and the "meat life": You're not going to worry until you have to. You're savoring all the meat you can get your hands on. You're outside as much as possible. Better enjoy it while you can.

5. People who are convinced AGS is a hoax: You think it's a lie perpetrated by the plant-based industry to increase profits. Or it's the work of a "feminist militant vegan" global secret society called the Alpha Gals, designed to scare people into adopting a vegan lifestyle and possibly lowering their testosterone by eating less red meat. Whatever your reasoning, you don't believe AGS is really a dangerous or widespread illness. No one is going to make you scared of the outdoors. You definitely aren't changing your diet. And if you listen to the advice of the most influential AGS deniers online, you may decide to start spiking people's drinks with bone broth to reveal the hoax and prove to them that they are not at real risk.

Imagine yourself living in this world. You're whatever age you would be in the year 2035, possibly with different life circumstances—living in a different town or city, working a different kind of job, newly married or unmarried, a parent for the first time, or a parent whose kids are fully grown now; maybe you've been able to build up your wealth or savings, maybe not. Think of who you might be in 2035, and how that person might be different from you today. And then answer this question:

~~~~~~~~

MOMENT OF CHOICE: How do you think you would react to the AGS crisis? Would you be someone who worries about getting it and takes every precaution possible? Or would you "live for the moment" and start eating more meat and spending more time in nature, to enjoy it while you can? Would you preemptively make major life changes, just in case, or to protect family members who might catch it? Would you be likely to join the deniers? What other kind of reaction can you imagine having? I'll ask you to come up with a more detailed action plan for living through a hypothetical AGS crisis in a moment. For now, just stretch your imagination and think about what your overall reaction or response style might be. (Because AGS is a real syndrome affecting hundreds of thousands of people worldwide, you may already be living with AGS. If so, how would you imagine your experience guiding you to react to an AGS pandemic on the scale of the COVID-19 pandemic?)

Now that you've had a chance to immerse yourself in the possibilities, let's focus on detecting opportunities to make a positive difference in this future.

There are three key questions to ask about any scenario, to spark the "learned helpfulness" process that allows us to feel (and actually be) more in control of how the future turns out:

1. What will people want and need in this future?
2. What kinds of people will be particularly useful in this future?
3. How will *you* use your unique strengths to help others in this future?

Let's brainstorm some answers for "The Alpha-Gal Crisis." When you imagine a world with a tick-borne pandemic that leads to a life-threatening allergy to meat products, what becomes the new "essential"?

What will people want and need in this future?

What supplies?

What kinds of advice and information?

What sorts of support or protection?

What new ways of doing things would be necessary? In other words, what would no longer work the old way and have to be reinvented in this new world?

These are brainstorming questions—the more answers, the better. If you're feeling game, go ahead and think up a few ideas on your own before reading my suggestions.

In a world living through an alpha-gal crisis . . .

There would probably be a huge increase in demand for tick repellant; EpiPens to stop anaphylactic reactions; plant-based meats, poultry, and seafood; vegan toilet paper; and vegan versions of most household products. There would be increased demand for tick-safe indoor pets like fish and lizards. What else would you add to this list?

People would need to learn how to perform thorough tick checks on themselves and their pets. Other helpful information might include public maps showing the highest-risk areas for tick bites; instructions on how to spot anaphylaxis and deliver lifesaving EpiPen injections (in fact, people without allergies might start carrying them to help others); and, for people with AGS, or people who have friends and family with AGS, cooking tips and nutritional advice for switching to a plant-based diet. It could be helpful to have a public awareness campaign of what products have hidden meat ingredients, like toothpaste and vitamins. Or perhaps PSAs for how to perform a "tick drag," which is an inexpensive, homemade way to identify tick infestations (according to *Consumer Reports*: "Cut a 5-inch-square swatch of fabric and tie it to an 18-inch-long pole or stick. Holding the pole, drag the fabric along tall grass or weeds, particularly near woodland edges of your lawn. Ticks will typically transfer themselves to the swatch."[11]) What else might people want to know in this future?

People might need mental health support to deal with the anxiety of living with AGS, or the fear of developing it. And people who work in high-risk jobs—those associated with an increased risk of exposure to carrier ticks, like construction, farming, oil field work, forestry, and utility line work—might need special protections or support, whether it's hazard pay or prioritized personal protection equipment. Meanwhile, workers in meat production or dairy might need job training and placement programs, if those industries shrink because of a dramatic decline in meat and dairy consumption. Who else might need support or protection?

Recreation and outdoor activities of all kinds might need to be rethought, or temporarily redesigned, to take place safely indoors away from ticks—essentially, the opposite of the COVID-19 pandemic strategy, which was to move as many things outdoors as possible. Restaurants might reinvent themselves to offer safer dining experiences for people with AGS. Dog shaving might become the norm, because it's easier to spot and remove ticks on a dog with shaved hair than one with a full coat. Yards, lawns, and gardens might be reimagined to emphasize tick control, the way they've already been reimagined for wildfire prevention in high-risk areas today. What other things can you imagine changing dramatically as society adapts to this future?

By the way, the best way to expand your thinking on this question is to ask lots of different people what *they* might want or need in a given future.

What kinds of people will be particularly useful in this future?

Who are the new experts?

Who are the people with essential skills?

Who would you feel comforted having around you?

Who provides a service that will be more important than ever before?

Go ahead and think up a few ideas on your own before reading my suggestions.

In a world living through an alpha-gal crisis, the most helpful people would be . . .

People who have previous experience living with life-threatening allergies, to offer advice to the newly diagnosed.

Health care professionals who can treat severe allergic reactions.

Ordinary people who can spot allergic reactions and provide care until emergency medical help is available.

Longtime vegetarians or vegans who can help people with AGS transition to a new way of eating.

Plant-based chefs.

Anyone who can do yard, lawn, and garden work to help with tick control.

Outdoorsy people with practical suggestions for avoiding ticks.

People who manage indoor sports and activity centers, like rock-climbing walls, spin studios, and indoor playgrounds.

"Exit counselors," or experts who specialize in helping people recover from false conspiracy theory addiction and disinformation campaigns, to deal with "Alpha Gals" conspiracy theories and disinformation.

Whom else would you add to this list?

Finally, how will you *use your unique strengths to help others in this future?*

Think about the skills, abilities, knowledge, passions, communities, and values you identified as your own signature strengths. Can you imagine one or more of them being a springboard for action in this scenario?

This question may be a bit more of a creative stretch than the previous two, especially if your own strengths aren't a direct or obvious match for the wants and needs of this future. Most people, I find, need a little time to think about this question before an idea sparks. So don't force it—let the scenario roll around in the back of your mind for a few hours or days and see what pops up when you're least expecting it. In the meantime, here are some unique ideas for helping that popped up for others when I playtested this scenario:

"One of my passions is fashion. I try to have a unique style and post my outfit every day on Instagram. In this future, I could try to make anti-tick fashion cool. Like tucking your pants into your socks. That is not cool today, but I could try to make it look good and inspire a new trend."

"The public gardens community could help create safe, beautiful indoor garden spaces that nurture your spirit like the outdoors but are safe from ticks."

"This might be a weird idea, but I'm active in our neighborhood Nextdoor community, and I've noticed the same people who used to post conspiracy theories about 5G were the same people who posted misinformation about COVID-19 and vaccines. Maybe I could reach out to them and get solid information about alpha-gal syndrome in their heads before the new conspiracy theories take off. Give them a chance to get in on the facts early, ask them for help spreading the word, help them feel included."

"I'm an assistant football coach. If any of our players developed meat and dairy allergies, they would need a different strategy for building muscle and increasing body mass. I could help with that. Maybe there's a new movement for 'athletes with AGS.'"

"Anyone who hunts will tell you that this future needs help thinning out the deer and rabbit population. The bigger those populations, the more ticks. I would see myself helping organize a community effort to increase the number of hunting licenses and extend the hunting season and see if we can handle the problem that way."

"This is a small thing, but as an entrepreneur, I'd probably start a new line of EpiPen holsters. They already exist, but there's not a lot of variety. If everyone is going to start carrying EpiPens, it would be nice to have some options, something fun, a way to express yourself. And if they were colorful and interesting to look at, it could raise awareness of what's going on with AGS and how to help people in allergic shock."

"Preschool teachers could teach our little ones a new song for doing tick checks. Something like the song 'Head, shoulders, knees and toes, knees and toes,' but helping you learn where ticks like to hide. I actually looked this up. It's 'Scalp, neck, armpits, back of knees, back of knees.'"

Are you getting the idea? Your unique way to help will stem from whatever you already know, love, and do. In a global crisis, almost every community, industry, neighborhood, social ritual, and daily activity will be affected. You don't have to reinvent yourself to be useful for the future; use whatever you naturally bring with you. That said, you may also be inspired by answering these three helping questions to add a few more skills or knowledge topics to the bag you're packing for the future.

What could you quickly pick up that would make you more prepared if a scenario like this actually happened? Learning how to perform a tick check, do a tick drag, spot signs of anaphylaxis, use an EpiPen, and cook a plant-based version of a favorite meal might all be quick wins that will give you more control over outcomes in the future.

COULD A SCENARIO LIKE "THE Alpha-Gal Crisis" really happen? It's certainly possible. Here are the future forces that make this future worth seriously imagining and preparing for:

Alpha-gal syndrome (AGS) is real, and it's currently on the rise worldwide.[12] The fastest documented growth is in the United States, where allergy blood tests of the general population suggest that 10 percent of the entire US population *already* have an increased allergic sensitivity to the alpha-gal sugar molecule, most likely from a single tick bite. In the southeastern US, where alpha-gal carrier tick exposure is more common, this number is even higher: an estimated 20 percent of people have been sensitized to the sugar molecule. Pet owners and outdoorsy people are at the highest risk. And in some parts of the world, and in certain professions, sensitivity to AGS is truly widespread right now. Among hunters and forest workers in Germany, 35 percent have alpha-gal sensitivity; in the Esmeraldas Province of Ecuador, it's 37 percent of the entire population, and in rural Kabati, Kenya, it's 76 percent of the population.[13]

Fortunately, not everyone who develops an allergic sensitivity from a single tick bite will go on to experience full-blown AGS. Most of these people currently have no symptoms in their daily lives, and just 9 percent have experienced severe anaphylactic reactions. But, as medical scientists point out, it's an evolving situation. Continuing to eat a diet high in the alpha-gal molecule can turn a mild sensitivity into a severe allergy. And every additional bite by a carrier tick makes future severe reactions more likely.[14] With an estimated thirty-three million Americans already sensitive to alpha-gal, it's plausible to imagine that many of them will go on to develop life-changing AGS.

And because climate change is dramatically increasing the tick population worldwide, the number of alpha-gal-sensitive individuals will surely go up. Meanwhile, deforestation is bringing animals that ticks feed on, like deer and rabbits, into more frequent contact with humans.[15] Ticks are also showing up in new places, like city parks and beaches. One study published in 2019 by the Centers for Disease Control found disease-carrying ticks in seventeen out of twenty-four parks that it examined in New York City's five boroughs.[16] Another study found that one in five tick bites now happen in urban areas.[17] In California, beachgoers are now warned that up to 40 percent of ticks are disease-bearing and that tick populations in coastal shrub are at all-time highs.[18] As a result, tick-borne diseases of all kinds are on the rise—not just AGS but also Lyme disease, babesiosis, anaplasmosis, and Rocky Mountain spotted fever. Tick-bite protection will undoubtedly be a growing concern for most people in the next decade. And figuring out how to help people avoid ticks? It will be a major area for creativity, research, and innovation.

At the same time, there are reasons to hope that the world will be able to avoid a crisis quite as extreme as the one imagined in this scenario. Early research suggests that AGS may be reversible in some people after two to three years, if they completely avoid all exposure to the alpha-gal molecule during that time. Researchers are also making excellent progress on a new kind of drug called Bruton's tyrosine kinase inhibitors (BTKis) that, if taken shortly before exposure to an allergen, completely prevents a reaction—even among people with life-threatening allergies. People with AGS could use this as a "free pass" to occasionally enjoy red meat. It could even, potentially, be taken daily to live an allergy-free life—although there may be side effects from chronic use. Finally, the field of tick research is rapidly turning out new ideas for disease prevention and tick control, on the order of more than ten thousand peer-reviewed scientific publications a year as of 2020. If you'd like to learn more and get involved, there's an app for that: the Tick App (thetickapp.org). If you live in the United

States, you can report tick encounters and submit photos of ticks you find, to help build a better picture of how and where tick populations are growing. By joining the Tick App, you'll be helping scientists prevent a tick-borne pandemic now—you definitely don't have to wait until the year 2035 to make a positive difference.

So, YES—A GLOBAL ALPHA-GAL CRISIS could happen. By planting this scenario in your mind and paying attention to these future forces now, you can lower your risk of being affected by AGS and other life-changing tick-borne diseases. And if alpha-gal syndrome really does become as widespread as many scientists predict? You won't be shocked by it. You'll recognize this future. You'll be ready to help yourself, and others, faster. You'll have more control over how the crisis plays out, in your community and in your own life.

THERE'S ONE MORE IMPORTANT BENEFIT to answering the question, How will I use my unique strengths to help others in this future?

Imagining yourself as helpful can increase empathy for your future self.

Remember the Future Self-Continuity Questionnaire from chapter 8? It's the psychologist-developed tool that measures how much empathy you have for your future self, or the person you will be ten years from now, along three different dimensions: how *vividly* you can imagine your future self, how *similar* you feel to your future self, and how much you *like* the future self you expect to be. Imagining all the ways you will be helpful, heroic even, makes your future self more likable. When you see yourself as capable of doing positive things in a future scenario, you build a positive emotional connection with yourself. And this teaches your brain to treat your future self less like a stranger, someone you hardly know and don't care about at all, and more like someone you know well and love.

• • •

"FUTURE ME IS AMAZING!" THAT'S how Mita Williams, a research librarian in Windsor, Ontario, and mom to two teenagers, explains why she frequently joins social simulations of the future. I first met Mita online when she was one of several thousand people helping to imagine a global oil crisis back in 2007. I ran into her again when she joined our Institute for the Future efforts to imagine a pandemic in 2008, and then again during our World Bank simulation of cascading emergencies, including extreme weather and a massive power grid failure. We spoke recently about what brings her back, again and again, to the future—what makes her keep answering the call to adventure.

"People have said to me, 'Mita, isn't that stressful? Why do you enjoy thinking about these kinds of things?' But I really like who I am in the future. That's the best way I can explain it. Future me gets involved in solving important problems. Future me helps others. And that experience really changed me. Now I really am someone who gets involved, when I wasn't that person before."

Mita explained to me that telling stories about how she might help during a fictional global crisis gave her a new kind of identity. "I started to see myself as someone who does things, who looks at issues that might be bigger than me and says, 'What can I do to help?' I might not be the most powerful person in the world, but let me see what I can do for my family, my friends, my neighbors, my city."

Mita gave me an example of a recent action she took—not in an imagined future but in her present-day neighborhood. "There's an annual festival called Jane's Walk, where people give free guided walks in their local communities. Anyone can volunteer to give a walk, to share neighborhood stories or reveal interesting facts about the area that people might not otherwise know."

The Jane's Walk festival happens each May in hundreds of cities around the world, in honor of urbanist and activist Jane Jacobs, who is remembered for her pioneering research on what makes for vibrant, healthy cities. This year, Mita decided to give a Jane's Walk inspired by some of the challenging future scenarios she has spent time imagining—such as disruptions to the power grid due to extreme weather and climate change. "I gave a tour of the local power infrastructure," she said. "I'm not an expert on it, but I did some research." *Of course she did some research!* I thought as she told me this story—she's a research librarian. It's a signature strength she brings to any challenge.

Mita's guided walk was called "The Electric Slide: A Tour of Windsor's Electric Grid." The invitation to the walk read: "Do you know where your electricity comes from or where the wires that connect your home end up? Take this big-picture tour of the invisible and in-plain-sight electrical grid that connects us to the power that we rely on, to find out." One hundred sixty-two people joined her on the tour, which was virtual because of COVID-19. "Highlighting where our power comes from is one small way I can make my community more resilient," Mita said.

"Future you *is* amazing," I told her. "Present you is amazing too."

Hearing about Mita's action inspires me. I'd like to get involved in Jane's Walks. What if researchers at the Institute for the Future led people on guided walks through future scenarios? We could challenge our students: Take at least one person in your neighborhood on a guided walk to talk about how a future scenario might play out in your local community. I'd love to try it myself. Maybe I could create a guided hike set in the fictional alpha-gal crisis!

Now I have an idea for a new action I could take—and that's the thing about learned helpfulness: it's contagious. Courage, creativity, agency—it spreads. When one person finds his or her future power, it inspires others to find their power too.

I'VE OFTEN BEEN ASKED, WHY not just look around the world, see the real problems facing us, and help someone today? What's so magical about imagining future challenges ten years out? I recently asked my cocreator on EVOKE, Robert Hawkins, these same questions. He has a unique perspective on the matter, having helped bring future imagination to an organization that's dedicated to tackling problems on the ground, today. Hawkins is the World Bank's global lead for technology and innovation in education. Since our first global play of the game in 2010, Hawkins has led regional versions of EVOKE with new future scenarios alongside research studies of the game's impact in South Africa, Brazil, Mexico, and Colombia. And he has seen firsthand the ways that imagining how you might help in a fictional future scenario can change how you think about yourself today, particularly in communities where resources and opportunities can be scarce. "For young people in these communities, being able to think about the future is a way to break out of what often is a limiting reality," he told me. "Limited expectations, low self-esteem, and maybe limited options too. Looking ten years out helps them imagine alternative scenarios. It allows them space and creativity, more liberty and freedom to imagine who they might become, as well as maybe to analyze who they are today.

"One young woman who participated in the Colombia game described EVOKE as 'a bridge between what I thought my limitations were and what my potential could be.' And I do think it's a way to illuminate opportunities for action, to make a bridge between these grand challenges that seem insurmountable and overwhelming and impossible for one individual to tackle, to helping people feel they are the kind of person who can actually get out and address these problems." He pointed me to a study of EVOKE's impact on players in South Africa, the first such study of the impacts of EVOKE. For 60 percent, the game had a "strong effect" on their personal identity, as they became significantly more likely to agree with these statements: "I'm someone who thinks big thoughts about the future" and "I can picture myself starting something new."[19]

THERE'S A SAYING: "IF YOU'RE not the hero of your own story, then you're telling yourself the wrong story." To which I would add: "If you're not the hero of your own future, then you're imagining the wrong future."

You don't have to be everyone's hero in the future—but be *someone's* hero. Whether you're serving a community you belong to, or making your local neighborhood safer, or setting your family up for success, or spreading the truth when others undermine it, or inventing a new way to do things, or helping just one person who might otherwise struggle—these are the very things you are called by the future to do.

By taking mental time trips to the future now, you can discover opportunities for action long before your help is urgently needed. You can learn your own power in any scenario, and avoid feeling shocked or helpless—so that if and when that future arrives, you're creatively and mentally prepared to do something that matters.

IMAGINATION TRAINING

RULE #10: Answer the Call to Adventure.

Treat every future scenario as an invitation to imagine yourself doing something important. Ask yourself three questions to better understand the opportunities for action: What will people want and need in this future? What kinds of people will be particularly helpful in this future? How will *you* use your unique strengths to help others in this future? Look for ways to use your own skills, abilities, and knowledge to take helpful action. Consider how your values might motivate you to do hard things. Think of how you might serve or mobilize the communities you belong to, if the scenario really happened. Be someone's hero, in whatever future you imagine.

〜〜〜〜〜

Simulate Any Future You Want

If there's one lesson to take away from the pandemic, it's the importance of looking ahead. And not just "looking ahead," but "feeling ahead." By imagining together in structured ways, and creating the experience of change before it happens, rather than while it's happening, we have a hope of planning, and even affecting our future.

—Filippo Cuttica, designer and artist

Why do we dream such strange things when we sleep? Philosophers, artists, and psychologists have long pondered this question. More recently, scientists have also started asking this question—and it turns out that it's not just humans who dream during sleep. Over the past twenty years, scientists have documented brain activity that looks just like human dreaming in cats, dogs, birds, lizards, and even cuttlefish.[1] That dreaming is so common among living things suggests that it isn't just an accidental by-product of how our human brains work. When something shows up again and again across many different species, it must deliver a strong evolutionary advantage. But what is that advantage? How does dreaming help us survive?

Computer scientists may have the answer. They've discovered that the most effective method of teaching humanlike intelligence to machines is to give computer programs their own kind of dreams. These dreams, called "noise injections," make the programs more flexible and adaptive in their thinking. Here's how a noise injection works: First, an AI program is given a real-world data set to analyze and interpret. It learns to process and make accurate predictions based on that data. Then, when the program is working well, it gets fed *purposefully weirder versions* of the same data. These new data sets are dreamlike by design. In computer science, "noisy data" refers to data that is meaningless, that cannot be easily understood or interpreted correctly by machines. And so noise injections randomly warp and recombine the real-world information in novel ways that are designed to surprise and temporarily confuse the AI program. They show the program things it has never seen before, things that don't make sense. These weird data sets are also often more "sparse," or less detailed, than the original data sets. They remove essential data points and require the program to stretch and strain to try to fill in the blanks of what's missing.

The purpose of noise injections is to make sure that an AI program learns how to handle stuff it has never seen before, things it's harder to make sense of. They ensure that the program doesn't assume all future real-world data will look exactly like whatever it has already seen. In other words, they safeguard the machine version from future shock: they teach the AI program to expect the unexpected and not freeze up when never-before-seen data comes in. And, studies show, they work incredibly well: programs trained with noise injections learn much faster and perform much better than programs trained only on real-world data sets.

Recently, Erik Hoel, a neuroscientist at Tufts University, noticed how similar these machine-learning techniques are to the surreal and hard-to-interpret nature of human dreams.[2] When we dream, Hoel suggested in a 2021 paper in the data science journal *Patterns*, it often feels like a "noise injection" into our brains. Our dreams rarely repeat the exact details of our real-world experiences. Instead they recombine real people, places, experiences, and events in bizarre and seemingly random ways. Human dreams also have the same sparseness, or missing data, as noise injections, a kind of narrative fuzziness. We recognize this lack of coherent detail as soon as we try to explain a dream to someone else—only to realize it doesn't make sense.

Hoel's research led him to propose a brand-new universal theory of dreaming. Dreams must be weird, he posited, because *all brains benefit in the same unique way from that weirdness*—whether it's a human brain, an animal brain, or a computer-based artificial "neural network." The benefit is that in repeatedly encountering things in dreams we've never directly experienced or even imagined before, our brains help us get "unstuck" from the specific details of what we've lived in the past and think more flexibly, so we are better prepared for whatever strange new things we encounter in the future. Dreams, it may turn out, are an ingenious method of counterbalancing the brain's other most important hardwired, evolutionary adaptation: the pattern-recognition capacity that leads to normalcy bias, or the expectation that the future will largely be like the present.

Normalcy bias, on most days, is helpful. It lets us expend less mental energy trying to figure things out, so we can react faster to predictable events. As long as things continue as normal, normalcy bias works great! But when the environment or our circumstances change dramatically, a normalcy bias can be harmful, even deadly. It keeps us stuck in our old ways and unable to adapt. And so it may be necessary for our survival that dreams counterbalance this bias. Their evolutionary purpose may be to ensure that we have the imaginative capacity to deal with and make sense of things that are not "normal."

Hoel's hypothesis is an intriguing explanation that has garnered tremendous interest from neuroscientists and AI researchers. As a futurist and game designer, I am drawn to it for another reason. I believe it helps explain the unique brain-training power of future scenarios and mental simulations of the future—especially when those simulations are social.

A future scenario describes the strange new facts of a possible future. It asks us to explore what is happening in this future that, for better or for worse, has never happened before. A mental simulation is an invitation to live, briefly, in that future—to visit that possible world in our minds and have an immersive first-person experience of it. So far in this book, you've been running your own quick mental simulations of the future. You've been answering questions like: What would I feel in this future? What would I do? What would I need? How would I help others? Your trips to the future have so far been quick thought experiments. But mental simulations can last longer than just a few minutes. They can play out over many hours, days, or even weeks—and not just in your own mind but in conversation with others. That's the kind of social simulation I specialize in creating, like Superstruct and EVOKE. It's the kind of simulation I want to invite you to experience now in this final part of the book—like a noise injection for your conscious, waking mind.

During a long-form future simulation, we go about our daily lives with an alternative reality running through our minds. We imagine in vivid detail what we would do, think, feel, want, and need in a future scenario *by superimposing that imagined future onto our real-life events*. If we go to school today, we're challenged to imagine how schools might be different in the future scenario. If we go to work, we're challenged to imagine how our jobs might be different. If we see that people are going hungry in our present community, we are challenged to imagine how this problem might be solved or intensified in the future scenario. If we go out for coffee, or to a party, or take the dog for a walk, or pick up a book at the library, or get medical treatment, or worry about money, or comfort a loved one, we may choose to imagine how all of these things would be happening differently if the future scenario were real.

In this way, the simulation purposefully blurs the line between our present real lives and our imaginations. It warps and weirdens the facts of our everyday lives with hypothetical possibilities. These facts and possibilities blend together into combinations that we must try to make sense of, and fill in the narrative gaps of, despite our expectations of what's "normal." The scenario unsticks our minds from the patterns of the past and gives our brains the opportunity to practice encountering the unexpected—just as dreams can do.

In other words, a mental simulation is a *waking dream* of a possible future.

Say you were simulating the "Alpha-Gal Crisis" scenario from the previous chapter. In that possible future, hundreds of millions of people worldwide have developed life-threatening allergies to red meat and other animal products as a result of the first-ever tick-borne pandemic. How might you experience the real world differently with this hypothetical future in mind? What would you see, hear, and encounter in your everyday life that isn't there today?

If you were walking by a vegan café in reality, for example, you might imagine this scene from the year 2035: a crowd spilling out of the now mostly empty café, owing to increased future demand for plant-based dining. You'd see that real-world location differently in your mind—as a possible resource for the future.

Alternatively, you might imagine protesters blocking the entrance to the same café, shouting about the "vegan mafia" and holding signs that promote unfounded conspiracy theories: "Trust your gut! Alpha-gal syndrome is NOT REAL!" You'd reframe that real-world location, in your mind, as a possible site of conflict in the future.

If you found yourself at a backyard barbecue, you might envision guests wearing N95 masks to protect themselves from airborne meat fumes. You might take a moment to consider how those same friends and family might feel different in the future about social gatherings and meals if they were afflicted by alpha-gal syndrome. You might wonder how the mood of the party might be different, or whether you would even attend such a gathering in the future.

These hypothetical scenes would exist only in your mind. They are quick acts of mental simulation. They bring the scenario to life in vivid and realistic detail, as if you could already actually feel and experience it. They feel like a hallucination of the future, but one you control and direct with your own imagination.

What else might you imagine during a weeks-long simulation of "The Alpha-Gal Crisis"? When you're getting dressed one morning, you might imagine yourself strapping on an EpiPen holster. What style did you pick? What material is it made of? What color is it? Do you wear it as an armband, on your waist, or strapped to your thigh? You might make a quick sketch of it later, to capture your mental image. Or, if you feel like really getting into the scenario, maybe you actually tuck your pants into your socks—which is the style in your imagined future, part of the anti-tick fashion scene—and wear them that way, all day, in your real life. It's just one small detail, but you might find it really helps you "feel" that future.

If you follow the stock market, when you're checking the financial news, you might think about how the market would respond to the alpha-gal crisis: Which stocks go up in this future, and which go down? If you work in advertising, you might zone out during your commute and try to imagine a new kind of client you would work with, or a new campaign you might develop for an existing client in response to the crisis. If you work in book publishing, you might look at the current best-seller lists and try to imagine the list of best-selling books ten years from now, inspired by the crisis. What are they titled, what genre are they, and what kind of author might write them?

Any moment of your waking life could be transformed by your awareness of the scenario into a vivid glimpse of a possible future. You might find yourself at a routine doctor's appointment. While waiting to be seen, you might play out in your mind, just for a moment, an alternate future version of your reality: that you are actually there to get a blood test to find out if you have alpha-gal sensitivity. You might try to imagine what emotions you would feel over the forty-eight hours while you were waiting for the results.

Or maybe you're getting the flu shot in real life. With the scenario in mind, you might imagine that it's not a flu shot but an injection of the Bruton's tyrosine kinase inhibitor (BTKi) medicine that can squash allergic response. You might briefly imagine that you have AGS, and you've just paid one hundred dollars for the shot so you can have a seventy-two-hour meat pass. Later, this fleeting idea could become a bigger story, an opportunity for you to fill in the blanks of the future: Why and when would you choose to get a BTKi shot? What, exactly, would you do with your seventy-two hours of meat freedom?

Even the smallest things can become opportunities to bring future scenarios to life. If you're watching a cooking show or an episode of *Top Chef*, for example, you might try to imagine how that show would be produced differently in an alpha-gal crisis. If you're reading international news, you might write your own future news headline about different countries' approaches to the tick-borne pandemic. If you're checking out your social media feeds, you might feel inspired to draft a Facebook post or tweet from this future. What kind of help or information would you ask for during an alpha-gal crisis, or offer to others? When you're cooking dinner, you might find yourself wondering how the meal you're making would be different if you had a friend or family member with AGS. How would it change what you do together?

It might sound a bit trippy to be walking around projecting an alternate reality on top of normal life. And it *is* trippy—it really does have that surreal, hyper-creative quality of a dream. It likely has the same neurological benefits too. By actively imagining strange ways the world around you could change, you're training your brain to respond to real change with less shock and more flexibility. If you're someone who doesn't think of yourself as having an active imagination, after you play through a long-form social simulation, that will change.

As you get deeper into the simulation, you might want to bring the scenario to life in a more hands-on way. You could create real physical objects from the imagined future, or what futurists call "artifacts from the future." These are everyday objects that might exist in a future scenario, such as signs, posters, household products, or clothing items.

After you make these objects, you can put them in your real-world personal surroundings, and sometimes even in public spaces, as visual and tactile clues to the future.

For example, you could download and print a "How to check for ticks" poster (you can find them easily on the internet today), and then make it an artifact from the future by writing "YOU ARE IN AN ALPHA-GAL HOT ZONE! Please check yourself before entering" in red marker across the top. Put this sign up by your front door to help yourself feel immersed in the scenario. Or you could make some protest signs. Perhaps you would want to protest pharmaceutical companies' practice of charging high prices for lifesaving drugs: "EPIPENS for ALL! Saving a life should be free" and "DON'T PROFIT FROM MY CRISIS." You don't actually have to organize a real protest for a fictional scenario, obviously, but being in a space where you can see the future not just in your mind but in the actual world really enhances the "waking dream" nature of a social simulation.

What else could you make? You could "future-fy" an ordinary household object by adding a sticker or label from the future. You could add a label to an unopened package of toilet paper, for example, that reads "AGS ALLERGY WARNING! This product contains beef gelatin for extra-cushy softness." Or you could mark up a plain white T-shirt with a slogan that captures some of the emotions or controversies of the scenario. In an alpha-gal crisis, people who have tested positive for sensitivity to the sugar molecule might want to destigmatize their status by boldly proclaiming "I'm sensitive." Can you picture yourself making and wearing a real "I'm sensitive" T-shirt—and then explaining the scenario if asked about it?

Not everyone wants to be an ambassador for the future! But if you do like sharing what you're learning with others, artifacts like a sign, poster, sticker, or shirt are a fantastic opening for conversations about future scenarios and the signals of change that inspired them. The magic of a simulation really happens when you document and share your dreamlike future ideas with others, and they share their waking dreams with you.

Sharing makes it feel more real. It becomes a world you're visiting together. When Superstruct, a six-week simulation, ended, one player wrote on a discussion forum: "It feels like waking up from a dream, but a dream I had with thousands of strangers." Indeed, by choosing what scenario to simulate, we're choosing what future to dream about. And when our simulations are social, they allow us to dream the future together.

To dream the future together, we need to document and share what we imagine. This is the most crucial part of social simulations: we must *record all the strange things we've conjured up in our minds*, giving narrative form to the surreal thoughts and imagery. This social imagining can take the form of two people keeping their own handwritten journals in separate notebooks, writing down a few thoughts each day, and then trading the journals at the end of the simulation to compare the futures they dreamed. Or it can take the form of a group email, with all participants replying daily or weekly with a new thought about what else might happen in the scenario, what they would worry about, what they would do to help.

It can take the form of an online discussion forum, with hundreds or even thousands of people all imagining the same future scenario, contributing myriad different personal stories and possibilities and building on each other's ideas. Or it can take place "in the wild," as we say at the Institute for the Future. Participants can post their thoughts and stories about how the scenario might affect their lives and communities wherever they normally share online—Twitter, Facebook, Instagram, TikTok, YouTube, Medium, Twitch, any-where!—and include a scenario hashtag, for example, #AlphaGalCrisis. This creates a distributed story, bits of future scattered across the internet in a way that evokes William Gibson's observation quoted earlier: "The future is already here. It's just not evenly distributed." The simulation becomes a kind of scavenger hunt across social media platforms to find fellow future travelers and their stories. A whole alternate universe can be constructed out of small, personal moments imagined and shared by individuals.

Social documentation, in any format, allows us to revisit and reflect on our imaginings, so our insights aren't fleeting and lost. And it gives us access to other people's experiences of the same scenario, so we can dream the future from their points of view. Much of what we encounter will be possibilities that our own brains would never conjure up. Think of it as an exponential "noise injection" for our waking imagination, with data collected from many other brains and many other lived experiences.

The current all-time record for an Institute for the Future simulation is more than sixty-four thousand stories and ideas shared by nearly nine thousand participants over the course of a two-day simulation. At such an epic scale, no one person can possibly take in all of this content. Instead, it becomes an immersive flow of ideas you exist in, picking up threads and following your curiosity. If you collect everything in a database, you can search and analyze it all later for trends and patterns, which is what we do at the institute. But I always say: The *experience* of the simulation is the most important thing. The most valuable output is the way it stretches participants' imaginations and builds real skills for adapting to unthinkable change. Whatever research you get out of social simulation, whatever predictions it helps you make—that's a bonus.

The more people who participate in a social simulation, the more the collective imagination grows. But you don't have to play with scenarios at such a big scale. Two people, sharing stories and ideas back and forth for a few days or weeks, can also create a universe of the mind.

IF THIS SOUNDS A BIT abstract to you still, then my goal in this chapter is to make it more concrete. I'm going to break down my own creative process of designing a social simulation and walk you through all six steps you need to take if you want to create and run your own long-form social simulation—using one of the scenarios in this book or inventing your own. Once you know how to do it, you might decide to run a simulation for a club, a work team, a support group, an online community, a class, a conference, your whole neighborhood, or a special event.

But if you think you get it, and you feel ready to play right now, I invite you to *skip ahead to the final chapter*, "Spend Ten Days in the Future (The Game)." There, you'll find three future scenarios to play with. Pick one of the scenarios, and then go about your regular life for ten days with the scenario running in the back of your mind. You'll be guided to imagine how each place you visit, each activity you do, each interaction you have with another person *in your real life* might be different if that future scenario were actually happening. You'll be challenged to keep a "future journal" of all the weirdest things you think, all the most surprising things you imagine, in whatever format you want—in a notebook, emails, a video diary, audio recordings, social media posts, visual sketches, a Google or Word document, or in whatever way you want to capture it all. And you'll be encouraged to share the experience with at least one other person, to dream the future together.

To get started, just turn to the next chapter, read the simulation instructions—there's a different imagination prompt for each of the ten days—and then pick someone to start simulating the future with you. Play through one of the scenarios together. Share your ideas and stories with each other. See how many of the daily challenges you can complete.

Start small: play with one other person, or with a book-club-sized group. If you have fun, maybe invite a bigger group to play. Eventually, you might feel more ambitious, inspired to invent your own scenario or run a very large-scale simulation of your own. If so, the rest of the information in this chapter can help you do just that.

If you're ready to play now, feel free to skip the rest of this chapter, and I'll see you in the year 2033—to spend ten days in the future together.

Six Steps to Simulate Any Future You Want

To plan your own social simulation, you'll need to decide:

1. **What** scenario do you want to simulate?
2. **Who** will you invite to participate?
3. **When** will you start and end the simulation?
4. **Where** will the social sharing happen?
5. **How** will you explore different dimensions of the future?
6. **Why** are you simulating this future?

I'll walk you through these six steps using a real example of a social simulation that the Institute for the Future created for high school students in 2016, in partnership with the educational nónprofit Facing History and Ourselves.

Step 1. What scenario do you want to simulate? At the heart of any social simulation is a future scenario that describes a specific world we might wake up in someday, usually ten years from today. Your first step is to pick *which* possible world you want to spend time imagining with others. For the institute's 2016 collaboration with Facing History and Ourselves, we wanted to explore the future of social technologies. We were curious: What might the next version of social media look like? What would we share online in the future that we can't share today?

Future Scenario #11: Feel That Future

The year 2026

More than a billion people have joined a new social network called FeelThat.

It's like any other social network—but instead of sharing words, photos, or videos, you share your physical sensations and emotions.

Members of the FeelThat network wear biotracking, hormone-detecting, and neuro-sensing devices. Heart rate, stress level, physical energy, mood, and oxytocin scores are all reported to friends and followers in real time. It's considered the most authentic way to share your true self online—totally uncensored and unfiltered.

Whatever you're feeling, your followers on the FeelThat network can feel it too—if they have the neuro-stimulating peripheral. It's a noninvasive device that stimulates the vagus nerve and regions of the brain involved in mood control. Click the "*really* feel that" button, and the stimulating peripheral will alter your own energy and emotions to more closely match those of the individual you're following—or "feeling." The technology isn't quite perfected yet, but it's the closest thing to mind melding that humans have yet invented.

If you want, you can zoom out from individuals' feelings and watch as emotions, stress, love, and energy spread across neighborhoods and cities. You can check the "trending feelings" for your school, workplace, family circle, or neighborhood.

With one billion members and counting, the biggest social impact of the FeelThat network so far is that many members are seeking out and spending more time with the people and places that spread positive emotions, raise physical energy, and increase the love-and-trust hormone oxytocin. More and more, FeelThat members are avoiding people and places that raise stress levels, drain physical energy, and spread negative emotions.

Not everyone uses the network this way. Some members intentionally seek out the sad or the anxious, the low-energy or the low-oxytocin, the most stressed-out people and places—either because misery loves company or because it's a chance to try to help someone else feel better.

MOMENT OF CHOICE: Would you join the FeelThat network? Why or why not?

In addition to a brief written scenario, we created a ten-minute video showing how people might use the fictional FeelThat network, to help participants feel more immersed in this future. You can watch this video, which includes an "unboxing" and live demo of the neuro-stimulating peripheral, by visiting the Institute for the Future's You-Tube channel and searching for "Face the Future."

We also shared links to a dozen news articles describing real neuro-sensing, biotracking, and neuro-stimulating technologies that are already being invented today, signals of change that make this scenario plausible. (If you're curious, check out these clues: Kernel, Emotiv, Neurable, Neuralink, Facebook Reality Labs, NeoRhythm, Openwater.) Whatever scenario you pick or invent, you may wish to collect and share some signals of change with participants, too, to help them understand why the scenario is plausible and worth imagining.

So what possible world will you invite others to imagine together? For your first experience organizing and playing through a social simulation, I recommend that you pick one of the scenarios from this book. Feel free to adapt or modify the scenarios however you like, as long as it's for a noncommercial purpose. After you get the hang of it, you may wish to invent your own scenario to simulate. At the end of this chapter, I provide some tips for how to do just that.

The scenario I want to simulate first is: _____

_____.

Step 2. Who will you invite to participate? A social simulation can be as intimate as an experience between two people or as epic as a collaboration of many thousands of participants.

It's certainly easier to start small. I suggest you aim for three to thirty participants for your first simulation. Think in terms of the size of a book club, work team, meetup, or class. Later, you may wish to run a larger-scale simulation, for an entire company, school, conference, event, city, or for the global public.

Many of the Institute for the Future's simulations are completely open to the public—anyone, anywhere. For "Feel That Future," however, we worked with our partner organization to limit participation to high school students, mostly from the United States. The "who" was especially important for this simulation, for two reasons. From a social impact perspective, we wanted to teach futures-thinking skills to young people, who are too often left out of conversations about society's future. And from a research perspective, we wanted to explore what might happen if a technology like the FeelThat network were really available. When it comes to popular new technologies, it's most often young adults who drive early adoption, and who set the norms and cultural expectations for how the new technology will be used. By inviting participants aged thirteen to eighteen, we were engaging young people who would be twenty-three to twenty-eight years old when the imagined neuro-sensing, biotracking social network would hypothetically exist. This was exactly the demographic that would be in the best position to actually shape a future in which this emerging technology existed, through their own decisions and actions about how to use it.

And if you're inviting people who might not be familiar with the idea of social simulations, it's helpful to have some language to share, like this, which we used to invite teachers and their students to simulate the "Feel That Future" scenario:

This is a game of ideas, hopes, concerns, and predictions. In the game, you'll be asked to imagine a world where a new technology, called the FeelThat network, tracks and shares information about our state of mind and body. It's like any other social network—but instead of sharing words, photos, or videos, we're sharing our physical sensations and emotions. The scenario is make-believe, and while it's based on real technology that is being developed today, it takes place in an imagined future.

To play the game, you'll be asked to share your ideas about what you, personally, would do if the FeelThat network were real. Would you join the network? Who would you "friend"? Who would you block? Who would you follow? What would you be excited about, if this technology were real? What would you worry about? How might a day in your life unfold if you were on the FeelThat network instead of Instagram, Snapchat, Facebook, or Twitter? You'll be able to discuss these questions in your classroom and add your thoughts to a global online discussion.

Join us to imagine how you might use social technologies in the future—to think about what's possible and to be in conversation with other people across the globe about how the world is changing and how we want to respond to, prepare for, or try to affect or alter those developments.

In total, we had over 8,500 high school students and more than 300 teachers participate in the live global simulation. Facing History and Ourselves has also made the scenario and discussion prompts permanently available to any educator or youth group, anywhere worldwide, to run a smaller, local version of the simulation. (If you have a group of young people you'd like to run this simulation with, you can access the materials at https://www.facinghistory.org/face-future-game-videos.)

One more tip about the "who" of a social simulation: you may want to run the same simulation multiple times, with different social groups or age groups, or in different countries or communities, to create alternative visions of how the future might play out.

The person or group I'm going to invite to play first is: _____
_____.

Step 3. When will you start and end the simulation? A social simulation can be as short as a few hours, or it can unfold over a much longer period of time. I prefer simulations that last for at least two to three days. I find that creative ideas about the future come more easily when there's a chance to let the scenario really sink in, and to let the subconscious work on it. I always want to give participants a chance to "sleep on it." A few days is usually enough time for genuinely surprising ideas to emerge.

The "Feel That Future" simulation was a two-day live experience, and we gave students and teachers the scenario a week in advance to let it simmer a bit in their imaginations before they joined the global conversation. Superstruct, on the other hand, ran for six weeks, and EVOKE for ten weeks. But my favorite length for a simulation is ten days. It's long enough to feel that you're really living through the scenario and not just giving it a quick consideration. And it's short enough that more people can reasonably make a commitment to play for at least ten minutes a day, all the way through from start to finish. By play, I mean actively think about the scenario at least once during the day, tell a quick story or capture an idea about how they might personally be affected by the scenario, and then share it with the group.

Many participants play for longer than ten minutes a day, especially if they're taking in other people's stories and ideas and getting involved in ongoing discussions. The average "Feel That Future" participant spent thirty-one minutes each day on the global online discussion forum, according to our data analysis. (We weren't able to track how much time they spent thinking or talking about the scenario offline!)

There are reasons to run simulations longer than ten days—for example, if you want to explore multiple scenarios with the same group. We explored five different scenarios over six weeks in Superstruct, and ten scenarios over ten weeks in EVOKE. Daily play is harder to sustain the longer a simulation lasts. During these longer simulations, participants might share just one story or idea each week.

The biggest benefit of these longer simulations is that participants tend to become more comfortable and more imaginative as they get more practiced at playing with scenarios. They also have more time to investigate signals of change related to the scenario, to help make their imaginings more realistic and convincing. Also, a longer simulation can create a tighter-knit community and have a deeper psychological impact on participants. No one has ever told me that a two-day simulation was "life-changing," but many people say that about multi-week simulations—because it helped them realize what they really wanted to do with their own future or what global challenge they felt called to help solve.

The number of days or weeks I want us to spend together imagining this future is:

_____

_____.

Step 4. Where will the social sharing happen? To run a social simulation, you need a place where participants can share their thoughts and stories. This might be online or in person, depending on the group you're inviting, or some combination of the two.

If you're playing with just one partner, kick it off with a conversation to make sense of the scenario together. Plan to send each other one idea or personal story from the future each day—by email or text message or however you normally talk. If you're lucky enough to live with the person you're simulating the future with, share your daily story over dinner, or go for a walk to discuss what you imagined today! If daily sharing sounds too intense, you can plan to trade your completed "journals from the future" at the end of the ten days (or however long you play). Be sure to have one final conversation about it all, at the end of the simulation. What was most surprising or interesting about the experience? Are you planning to take any actions to feel more prepared for the scenario if it were really to happen?

If you're running a slightly larger simulation, say thirty or fewer participants, you should schedule at least one live meetup. Live meetups might take the form of a club meeting, an afternoon happy hour, a weekly work team or class meeting, or an evening social Zoom. Invite participants to take turns sharing their favorite imagined future moments. This may spark conversation and perhaps some further drawing out of consequences: "If that happened, then this might happen . . ." You can also encourage participants to bring one signal of change related to the scenario, or one idea for a micro-action to take to prepare for this future, to share with the group. Depending on the group and the length of the simulation, you might want to do this kind of meetup more than once; personally, I love a regularly scheduled weekly simulation meetup!

In addition to a meetup, you will probably want to set up an email list, Facebook group, Slack channel, Discord channel, social media hashtag, or online discussion forum for people to post their ideas and stories throughout the simulation. This allows for deeper-dive discussions and gives people plenty of opportunities to check out other people's contributions. Most importantly, it gives you a way to collect all the content if you want to curate it for sharing to a wider community, or analyze it for trends and patterns, or simply revisit it in the future.

For very large-scale simulations, an online platform is where most of the action will happen, although participants may choose on their own to meet up socially in small, local groups as well.

Don't go crazy trying to figure out the best online platform— pick one you're familiar with already, and that you think many or most participants will be comfortable with. I've tried so many different platforms—if you're not sure what to go with, I recommend asking participants what they'd prefer!

If you run a simulation at a multi-day conference or event— which is one of my favorite ways to do it—then you might schedule three or four in-person meetups over the course of the event *and* offer a social media hashtag or discussion forum for 24/7 idea sharing and storytelling.

For "Feel That Future," teachers organized in-person classroom and after-school discussions, while the Institute for the Future hosted a global online discussion where all the students were able to share and respond to each other's ideas.

One important tip: I always encourage the host or organizer of the simulation to do some curation and spotlighting of their favorite ideas and stories throughout the simulation, so that the most interesting stories and most surprising ideas get seen by all. The simplest way to do this is to pick one "moment from the future" each day or each week to share with all the participants, by email, pinned post, or social media. This helps create a common narrative and a universal experience for the group. It can also inspire participants to up their game, if they want to be chosen as the story or idea of the day! And it helps participants who may be drawing a blank or running out of their own ideas—they can follow the creative lead of others.

During "Feel That Future," for example, we highlighted the following beautiful idea for the whole group: "With the FeelThat network, we could have feelings that we record and pass down the generations: 'Grandma was proud of you, can you feel that?' 'Mom loved you, even if you don't remember her.'" We then asked participants to build on this idea: What's a feeling *you* would want to pass on to future generations? What's a feeling from the past you wish could have been recorded and passed on to you?

Finally, depending on the size of the online group, you may need to plan for active moderation of posts and comments. When I have many thousands of participants in a public simulation, I usually put together a team of five to ten part-time online moderators to make sure no one is harassing, insulting, spamming, or otherwise affecting the social experience in a negative way. These moderators can also help you dig through and find the most interesting stories and surprising ideas to share back with the larger group—which is essential when, in large-scale simulations, participants may be contributing many hundreds or thousands of ideas and stories a day. During "Feel That Future," for example, the high school students and their teachers contributed 64,012 ideas and stories over a two-day period! When that much imagining is happening so quickly, no individual will be able to keep up with it all—and having a team and a plan to pull out and highlight your favorite content will be essential. At the end of "Feel That Future," the institute published a twenty-page summary of the most interesting themes and ideas. At the end of the simulation, you may want to plan to share with participants a summary of big ideas, favorite stories, most surprising predictions, and your own reflections.

This will help participants zoom out of their own personal experience and make sense of the bigger picture—and give people who didn't participate a chance to learn what you collectively discovered.

The place for sharing ideas, stories, and "moments" from this future will be:

_____

_____.

Step 5. How will you explore different dimensions of the future? At their best, social simulations have a rhythmic quality, a kind of "call-and-response" vibe. Participants are invited to return to the scenario multiple times over the course of hours, days, or weeks, with fresh thoughts and deeper insights. To achieve this kind of engagement, you may find it helpful to plan a series of discussion questions or creative prompts that will "refresh" everyone's imagination and guide participants to explore the scenario in new ways.

For example, during "Feel That Future," which was a two-day experience, every hour we posted a new guiding question on the online discussion forum to keep the conversation moving in different directions. How might families and parents use FeelThat? How might FeelThat be used in education? How might FeelThat be used in policing and in the criminal justice system? How might FeelThat be used in elections, political action, and democracy? How might FeelThat be used in art, storytelling, and entertainment? How might FeelThat be used in romantic and other intimate relationships? We shared this list of nearly fifty different questions with teachers in advance, to pick from and incorporate into their classrooms however they wanted. If you're using the scenarios in this book for your simulation, discussion questions are already provided. Feel free to add your own!

For shorter simulations, a new prompt each hour will keep energy high and encourage participants to come back and check in on what's happening. For longer simulations, you might give one new imagination prompt each day, or one each week.

Another way to explore different dimensions of the future is to encourage people to collaborate on a challenge together. Two of my favorite group challenges during a simulation are: What are one hundred things people will *need help with* in this future? And: What are one hundred ways people will *help each other* in this future? Make a space for participants to contribute to a collective brainstorm and see how many different ideas you can collect. You can organize or curate your favorite one hundred ideas later. If no other insights come out of a social simulation, these two lists alone make for a powerful and inspiring takeaway from the experience.

You might want to put out a call for artifacts from the future, physical objects that bring the scenario to life in the real world. During Superstruct, participants at one meetup covered the walls with handmade protest signs lamenting the failure of the future government to adequately control the fictional virus and demanding more economic support for individuals with the "long" version of the fictional respiratory distress syndrome. "Keep your feelings to yourself" and "Feel Me @ [username]" T-shirts were popular fashion statements in the imagined world of the FeelThat network. During "Feel That Future," some participants shared "selfies from the future"—photographs they took of themselves wearing homemade headsets and wristbands that were meant to evoke what neuro-sensing and emotion-stimulating technology might look like in the year 2026. And during Superstruct, participants took photos wearing masks in different social settings (which turned out to be uncannily accurate visual predictions of their future). What kinds of selfies could your participants take to capture the unique "stuff" and "vibe" of the scenario you're simulating?

Depending on how far you want to take it, there are countless creative and social approaches to bring a scenario to life. You could host a real dinner party with a menu inspired by the future scenario. You could make a start-up company "pitch deck" in PowerPoint to describe a new venture you might form in the future. You could compose and record a new protest song that might become popular in the future. You could design an advertisement for a new product that might exist in the future.

You could even invent and practice a new ritual or tradition—a new kind of welcome party for climate emergency migrants, or a neighborhood potluck to use up all the refrigerated and frozen foods that would go bad during rolling power outages. During a 2007 social simulation called World Without Oil, for example, a team of art students at the San Francisco Art Institute designed a collection of new children's playground games that might arise during an energy crisis. They were inspired by the popular story that the nursery rhyme "Ring around the rosie, a pocket full of posies, ashes, ashes, we all fall down" arose from the 1665 Great Plague of London, so they imagined how kids living with unreliable power and energy might transform that experience through rituals and play. And then they hosted a small playground festival and taught others to play the new games they'd invented.

Which is to say, social simulations truly are an invitation to play and to create in whatever way you're inspired.

One question I'd like to ask others to answer during this simulation is: _____
_____.

One way I could "make" the future is by (e.g., creating a protest sign, making a T-shirt, taking a selfie that looks like it's from the future . . .): _____
_____.

Step 6. Why are you simulating this future? If you're planning to invite a few friends or colleagues to simulate a scenario together, your motivation might be simply to have fun, learn a new skill, follow your curiosity, and do something creative. Those are perfectly good reasons for inviting several thousand people to simulate the future too! But if you do want to plan a larger simulation, for a community, organization, or event, or for anyone online who wants to join in, it helps to think about your larger goals.

Defining one or more big goals for your own simulation can help set participant expectations and build excitement. People will want to know: Why are we doing this? What will I get out of it? How am I helping a bigger cause by participating?

Here are some of the reasons I've decided to run a large-scale social simulation:

To take a possible future crisis seriously now, so we'll all be better prepared to help ourselves and others when and if it actually happens.

To investigate how a proposed policy or new law might affect our lives, so we can all decide with more clarity and empathy whether to support it.

To find out how people might use a future technology—and leverage the wisdom of the crowd to anticipate potential risks, unintended harms, or ethical dilemmas.

To give an underrepresented group or community the opportunity to share their hopes and fears for the future and have more of a say in how the future turns out.

To figure out what surprising things people might do, what irrational behaviors might turn out to be quite common, during a particular kind of crisis or emergency, so we can better predict the "hard-to-predict" social consequences of future events.

To optimistically engage people who are worrying about worst-case scenarios (think: climate change), so we can come up with creative solutions to handle whatever comes our way.

To create an opportunity for collaborative creativity, a way for many different people to tell a story together and share a vision of the future as a kind of public art.

To "stress test" an idea that I think could create change for the better: Could it really work? Which groups or communities am I leaving out of the solution? What possible unintended consequences am I overlooking?

To stretch a team's imagination to get better at believing that anything could be different in the future, so we can discover our power to make change today.

For "Feel That Future," we wanted to help young people feel more in control of their future. From a research perspective, we had another goal: to find out how likely it was that neuro-sensing and neuro-stimulating would become a "normal" social activity. We would get a sense of whether young people wanted access to this kind of technology and, if so, what they would do with it. Would they be willing to share such intimate biological and neurological data, or would they see it as an intrusion on privacy, even a kind of dystopian or dangerous possibility? In the end, I was surprised by how open the young participants were to the FeelThat network. While they identified many potential risks and harms, they also had so many exciting ideas for new forms of personal expression, art, activism, volunteering, scientific research, and social experiences.

One of the factors that makes a future scenario more likely is a high level of favorable interest: a lot of people who really *want* it to happen and are willing to help make it happen. Likewise, a future scenario is less plausible if most people seem to want to actively avoid it. Before the "Feel That Future" simulation, I would have said neuro-sensing and neuro-stimulating social technologies were unlikely to be widely embraced. But after the simulation, it's a future I fully expect to be living in someday.

Fun, learning, curiosity, creativity, and readiness are always at the heart of a future simulation. If you have an even bigger mission, research question, or purpose in bringing people together to imagine what they would think, feel, and do in a possible future, let that mission, question, or purpose be known!

My goals for this simulation are to: _____

_____.

Now THAT YOU KNOW THE six steps to planning your own simulation, let me share a little more advice. A social simulation is a springboard toward making a better world. Always keep in mind that its *primary* purpose is to give people a chance to stretch their imagination and build their confidence for the future. It's a way to prepare mentally for "unthinkable" events, to get better at reacting to shocks, and to discover small actions we can take today to prepare to help ourselves and others. When someone asks me what the "result" of a particular simulation was, they usually mean: What did we find out? What can we now confidently predict about the future? But I always say that the result of a simulation was a whole bunch of newly super-empowered hopeful individuals. Whatever positive impact a social simulation might have, it is primarily each participant's increased sense of urgent optimism and readiness for whatever's next.

A *secondary* purpose of a social simulation is to learn from the participants: to create collective wisdom that reveals what is *likely* to happen if the future scenario actually occurs, and to find out which hopes and fears most people share about the future.

If you want to learn from the participants, you'll have to plan a way to make sense of all the shared stories and ideas. This is a challenging research activity, which takes a certain kind of analytical mind and patience—it's not for everyone! You may prefer instead to send a survey to participants afterward, asking them questions about what actions they predict they would take, and what needs they would have, in this future. Now that they've considered this future, what is their biggest hope? Their biggest worry? What's one action they plan to take today to feel more ready for the future they've imagined? An online survey tool like Google Forms or SurveyMonkey can help you collect, analyze, and share these results, no special research team required.

My last piece of advice: social simulations of the future are a relatively new idea. I'm always trying new approaches, and my own "best practices" are still evolving. In fact, I've never run a simulation in exactly the same way twice. I hope you'll take inspiration from what I've shared, but you don't have to approach simulations the way I do. You may have your own unique vision, a different style, a way to adapt social simulations for a different purpose. Go for it! The future is a place where anything can be different, including *how* we simulate it. Feel free to invent your own rules. Email me and tell me all about *your* approach to simulating the future with others: jmcgonigal@iftf.org.

IMAGINATION TRAINING

RULE #11: Simulate Any Future You Want.

When the future becomes a shared dream, it does more than stretch our own individual imaginations; it expands our collective imagination. Invite someone else, or a team, or a whole community, to spend a few hours, days, or weeks actively thinking about a future scenario with you. Encourage everyone to describe how their own lives might be affected by the scenario. What would they feel? What would they do differently? What would they need? How could they help? Collect the ideas and stories to build an alternate reality, imagined from many different points of view.

Tips for Inventing a New Scenario

1. Focus on a few favorite signals of change and future forces.

Your scenario should be inspired by real things already happening today. Start by identifying some signals of change and future forces you're either really excited about or really worried about. They will be the backbone that makes your scenario plausible and worth imagining.

To brainstorm a scenario, ask yourself: What would the world be like if this signal were widespread and commonplace? What would the "new normal" be if the signal became a global trend? Ask yourself: What's the biggest positive change this future force could lead to? What's the worst thing this future force could lead to? There are no right or wrong answers. This is where your creativity, intuition, and unique perspective come into play. Spin up a few different possibilities and pick one or more to draft into a compelling scenario. See which possible future feels the most exciting to imagine, or the most urgent to prepare for. Remember: as long as you have a few solid signals and at least one powerful future force, you can spin them into a scenario as dramatic and extreme as you want. If the scenario doesn't strike you as surprising or provocative enough, then dial it up to an even bigger version of that change or crisis. Make your future world as wild or surprising as you like. Ban something. Have the world run completely out of something. Proclaim that no fewer than *one billion* people are using a new technology, or have adopted a strange new behavior, or have joined a new movement. Pass a radical law that some might say is politically unthinkable today. Have the most shocking version of a future crisis you can imagine come to pass. Whatever you do, be ridiculous, at first—because to stretch the imagination, you need to create strong emotions like curiosity, awe, horror, hope, or wonder.

2. Pick an archetype. Or pick four!

What kind of story do you want to tell about the future? Professional futurists often classify scenarios into one of four kinds of stories or archetypes: growth, constraint, collapse, or transformation.[3] When you're inventing your own scenario, you may find it helpful to start by considering which type of story you're most inspired to imagine.

Growth is a story of more. In a growth scenario, current trends and conditions, both good and bad, continue to grow as they have in the past—but now, at a faster rate. "The Alpha-Gal Crisis," a tick-borne pandemic, is a dramatic acceleration of existing health and environment trends; it's a growth scenario. So too is "Medicine Bag," which imagines what might happen if present-day local "food is medicine" programs were scaled up to the entire country.

Constraint is a story of accepting new limits. In a constraint scenario, we respond to a threat or problem by agreeing to new restrictions and new kinds of self-discipline. Often, it's the story of desperate times that call for desperate measures, coordinated global efforts, and a reordering of priorities. It's a story of individual sacrifices for the greater good. The story of Cape Town's water crisis invites you to consider how you would adapt to severe water restrictions; it's a constraint scenario. So too is the pizzly bear–inspired scenario, which imagines new limits on where it's safe to live, with as many as two billion people on the move, adapting to extreme heat and rising sea levels.

Collapse is a story of a sudden shutdown or a tragic failure. It's when something we take for granted is no longer reliable or available, its absence leading to shock and sometimes chaos. In a collapse scenario, major social systems are strained beyond the breaking point, causing new kinds of suffering and social disarray. "The Great Disconnection," a government-mandated internet shutdown, is a collapse scenario that explores what happens when an essential utility disappears overnight.

Transformation is the story of a world-changing innovation or breakthrough. It stretches our imagination, challenging our assumptions and suggesting that what was once impossible can now be realized. Transformation is often aspirational, setting a new course for individuals and society alike. "Thank You Day," a new kind of economic stimulus that combines universal cash payments with gratitude for essential workers, is a radical policy experiment; it's a transformation scenario. So are "Double Your Money" (central bank digital currency) and "Feel That Future" (biotracking and neuro-stimulation tech), scenarios that imagine a transformative technology being adopted at massive scale.

Any future topic can be explored through all four archetypes. If I were imagining the future of shoes (as I so often do!), I could look for signals of change that might inspire a growth story, a constraint story, a collapse story, and a transformation story for shoe culture or the shoe industry. In fact, often futurists will create all four alternative scenarios about the same topic, in order to explore and hold multiple, diverging possibilities in mind. Consider your options. See which archetype helps you tell the most previously unimaginable, or otherwise unthinkable, story.

3. Get feedback before you play.

When I create a new scenario, I'll share it with at least a few other people to get some crucial feedback before I ask a larger group to play. Here are the questions I ask when I first come up with a new scenario:

- On a scale of 1 to 10, how interesting is this scenario to you personally?
- Is there anything in the scenario that's confusing or doesn't make sense?
- Is there anything you want to be explained better, or in more detail?
- Can you think of at least one way your life would be affected by this scenario? How?
- On a scale of 1 to 10, how plausible or likely do you think it is that this scenario could really happen sometime in the next decade?

If a scenario isn't interesting to most people (average score lower than 6), I'll scrap it and start over with a new idea. If there are any confusing parts, I'll clarify them. And if there's something people want to understand better, I'll expand upon it.

If people generally have a hard time relating to the scenario, then I'll rethink it and rework it so that the impacts on our lives and society are more obvious. Conversely, I get very excited when people give diverse answers to how they imagine the scenario affecting their own lives. A simulation is more interesting and productive when different people imagine different things.

If the plausibility scores are low (less than 5), that's fine with me—good scenarios often sound absurd at first. But in that case, I make sure to introduce the scenario with lots of signals of change and future forces before asking anyone to play with it—because I do want people to be invested in the possibility that, yes, we really might wake up in a world like this someday.

~~~~~~~~

Spend Ten Days in the Future (The Game)

We have to free our mind, imagine what has never happened before and write social fiction.

> —MUHAMMAD YUNUS, social entrepreneur
> and winner of the Nobel Peace Prize

Breathe. Don't panic and flee. Sink. Feel it all. . . . Imagine. Let it burn.

> —GLENNON DOYLE, author and activist

WELCOME TO THE YEAR 2033, WHERE STRANGE THINGS ARE HAPPENING.

Strange new weather patterns. Strange political alliances. Strange behaviors, and not just by other people—*you're* doing things you never thought you'd do.

No wonder people are starting to call the 2030s "the unthinkable thirties." It's like the whole world woke up at the start of the decade and decided to try something different. All those potential solutions to global challenges that were previously considered too radical, too weird, too expensive, too difficult to implement? Well, they're happening now.

You're sure that in the future, people will look back on the year 2033 as a turning point in human history. Hopefully, a turn for the better—although with all the weird stuff the world is trying there are bound to be unexpected consequences. You're doing your best to keep up. To adapt, make the best of it, be ready for whatever opportunities come your way. You're keeping a journal to capture your thoughts, feelings, and experiences. When the world looks back with fascination and awe at everything that happened in 2033, you want *your* story to be a part of it.

Year 2033—the Simulation

It's time to spend ten days in the future. Which world will you wake up in first?

- **"The Road to Zerophoria":** Wake up in a world where a public service you take for granted disappears virtually overnight. Get ready to rethink every aspect of your daily life.
- **"Welcome Party":** Wake up in a world that is working together to move one billion people across borders. Get ready to pick your new destination.
- **"The Ten-Year Winter":** Wake up in a world that has just voted, as a planet, to take the biggest risk in human history— will it pay off? Get ready to find out.

These three scenarios, all set in the year 2033, are fictional, but plausible: They're based on real signals of change and future forces that already exist today. They may sound extreme to you, or ridiculous, at first. They may feel shocking, hard to imagine, full of "unthinkable" possibilities. That's intentional. They are designed to help you get better at thinking the unthinkable and imagining the unimaginable *before* they happen—so you can respond more creatively and strategically to whatever future challenges you might face.

These hypothetical futures are a little chaotic, and a lot uncertain. They explore transition periods, worlds we might have to *move through* to get to the futures we want. They might not seem like "happy end-ings." And they're not—because the future isn't a final destination. It's an ever-unfolding process. And we may have to live through challeng-ing times, in order to achieve our most optimistic visions.

Read through the scenarios. Talk about them with others. Tell some stories about what you would think, feel, and do in these futures. Let them run wild in your imagination. I may be the author of this book, but I can take you only so far in this story.

This last chapter, I need you to write with me.

How to get started

1. **Pick one of the three 2033 scenarios to simulate.** Start with the future that intrigues you most.
2. **Set up your "journal of the future."** Decide where and how you'll capture your thoughts and ideas about it: in a notebook, emails to a friend, a computer document, a video diary, an online discussion forum, or whatever feels most natural to you.
3. **Choose a day to start the simulation.** Each simulation takes ten days to play through, from start to finish. Plan to spend *at least ten minutes each day* imagining what you might think, feel, do, and experience in the scenario—and capturing what you imagine in your journal of the future. There will be creative prompts to guide you. You don't have to journal for ten days in a row. If it takes you two weeks, or a month, to complete all ten days in the future, that's fine.
4. **Bring someone to the future with you.** You can simulate the future on your own, but I encourage you to invite at least one other person to simulate it with you. Sharing what you imagine is at least half the fun—and at least half the learning, as you get to see the future from someone else's point of view. Share from your journals of the future with each other daily, or just at the start and end of the ten days, or however often

works best for you. (If you'd like to play with a larger global community, visit iftf.org/imaginable.)

Now you're ready to go on a trip to a strange new world. As you play, you might come up with your own ideas for how to bring the year 2033 to life. Feel free to go beyond what I've suggested and make up your own challenges! I'd love to see what you come up with. Send any future journaling prompts or creative challenges you invent for yourself to jmcgonigal@iftf.org, or share them on social media with the hashtag #imaginable2033.

How to return to the present

After you've spent ten days journaling about the future, you'll be ready to return to the present day. Here are some "reacclimating" activities I recommend to help you reflect on your journey:

- **Collect signals of change:** What are some real-world events and headlines that suggest how we might eventually wind up in a world like one described in the scenario? Search the news and social media for clues. Try to find at least three signals of change related to the scenario. (For pointers on how to look for clues to the future, see chapter 6.)
- **Commit to tracking a future force:** Each scenario is inspired by real future forces that are already changing what's possible today. Pick one of the forces listed in the scenario and make a commitment to learn more about it in the coming year. Find at least one book, podcast episode, TED talk, downloadable trend report, expert you can follow on social media, or newsletter you can subscribe to that will increase your understanding of this future force. (For more guidance on how to track a future force, see chapter 7.)
- **Plan a micro-action:** What's one thing you could do to feel at least a little more prepared for this scenario if it were really to

happen? Pick an action that you're confident you can realistically take in the next few weeks. The smaller the better, so there are no obstacles in your way.

- **Debrief with someone:** Discuss your experiences with a fellow future traveler. What was the most interesting part of this experience for you? What was the most challenging part? What was the biggest "aha" moment? What are you more worried about now than you were before you imagined this scenario? What are you more hopeful about? If you've collected signals of change or planned any micro-actions, share them with each other. You can debrief one-on-one or host a group conversation. (Or, if you have lots of fellow future travelers, send a post-simulation survey!)

When you're ready for another trip to the future, pick another scenario and do it all over again. When you finish the 2033 simulations, you can go back to any scenario in this book and come up with your own future journaling prompts. Soon, you'll be creating your own scenarios and inviting other people to simulate a future *you've* invented. (For tips on how to create a scenario and design your own simulations, see chapter 11.)

Before you travel to the year 2033 . . .

Create a quick bio or profile for future you. Who could you be in the year 2033? Feel free to make your 2033 life as different from your life today as you want, as long as it feels realistic and authentic to you. (Remember: you're still *you* in 2033—don't adopt a fictional persona!)

- How old are you in the year 2033?
- Where do you live?
- Whom do you live with, if anyone?
- How do you spend your days?
- What are your passions and interests?

Include as many details as you can imagine. Don't just think your answers to these questions. *Write your bio/profile as the first entry in your journal of the future:*

Decide what you will bring to the future. Make a quick list of the strengths and connections you already have today that might be useful in the year 2033:

- **Skills and abilities.** What are you good at? What do you know how to do that many people don't? In the year 2033, you may find that these skills and abilities are powerful clues as to how you might help yourself and others.
- **Deep knowledge and passions.** What topic or activity do you know a lot about, more than most people? What do you spend a lot of time thinking about, more than most people? In the year 2033, you may find that you can make creative connections between your knowledge and passions and the crisis at hand.
- **Communities.** What communities are you a part of? In the year 2033, you may be able to mobilize these groups, or advocate for their interests, or play an important role in keeping them informed.
- **Values.** What are your core values? A value is a way of being that brings purpose and meaning to life. It's a strength you want to show, a virtue you want to uphold, a quality you want to embody, or a way of being in service to something bigger than yourself. In the year 2033, you may find that these values guide your actions and help you focus your attention on what will keep you motivated and resilient during a challenging time.

Make your list as the second entry in your journal of the future, so you can refer to it when you need to.

The Road to Zerophoria

Really, to get along on this Earth, we must do just one thing:
Stop wasting so much of it.

—ROBERT KUNZIG, science journalist

TODAY, WE ALL HAVE TO DEAL WITH GARBAGE. IT'S ONE OF THE MOST basic and universal facts of life. But like any fact about today, we can flip it upside down for the future. Let's consider a ridiculous, at first, possibility: a world in which the word "garbage" is obsolete.

Can you imagine this future? Disposable packaging no longer exists. Most people go weeks, even months, without throwing anything out. Kids grow up not knowing what it was like to "take out the trash." You don't even have a trash can in your home anymore!

The endless, mindless accumulation of stuff is over. People spend most of their money on experiences, not things. And whatever you temporarily own, you quickly pass on to the next person who needs it. Or you send it back to the company that sold it to you, to be recycled into something new.

Zero waste is the new normal, and it feels good. So good, in fact, that psychologists have invented a new word, "zerophoria," to describe the positive emotion that defines life in a zero-waste society. Zerophoria is a combination of joy, pride, and resourcefulness. It's a lightness of being that comes from wasting nothing and leaving no trace behind. This new feeling is a healing balm for the days of climate change anxiety. And the trillions of dollars that governments previously spent every year to bury and burn trash is now spent instead on better things: education, health care, infrastructure, and universal basic income.

It's certainly a future I'd like to wake up in. But how could we get to a world like this? What sudden "shock" to the system might lead us there? What would it feel like to live through that transition period? How could we help each other adapt? And when, exactly, does the zerophoria kick in?

That's what we're going to try to find out in future simulation #1: "The Road to Zerophoria."

Let's play.

THEY TOOK YOUR GARBAGE CAN away today.

Your recycling bin too. All that's left is the compost bin.

Neighbors are standing at the curb watching the trucks drive off, looking a bit in shock.

It sounded impossible when the federal government first announced it last year. But now it's really happening.

It's the end of garbage as we know it.

All the landfills are full. The waste-to-energy plants have been shut down; it turned out that burning trash was making too many people sick. And recycling wasn't really working after all. Less than half of what people put in their bins actually got recycled, including less than 10 percent of the plastic. The US was exporting 80 percent of its garbage, shipping it to other countries with more landfill space. China, the Philippines, Indonesia, Kenya—they took US trash for a price for decades. But then those countries realized, one by one, that in the long run it wasn't healthy for them to bury and burn the world's waste. They started turning away the massive shipping containers full of plastic bottles and old clothes and sending them back to US shores. The president declared a national emergency. The Environmental Protection Agency took federal control of municipal waste collection. And then they shut it all down.

The new rules have been explained countless times, in mailings, in town hall meetings, in live-streamed public addresses, in messages sent over the Wireless Emergency Alerts system to everyone's mobile phone, and even in a star-studded television special.

The rules for a post-trash society are as follows:

1. There will be no more curbside garbage or recycling pickup. The days of expecting someone else to deal with your waste are over.

2. All trash cans will be removed from public spaces, schools, workplaces, and retail environments. Wherever you go from now on, national park rules are in effect: "Leave no trace" and "Pack out all trash, leftover food, and litter." Yup—you have to take it with you.

3. If you absolutely need to throw something out, you can take it to a local pay-as-you-throw center, where you'll be charged one hundred dollars for each bag's worth—and the bags are small, about the size of a grocery paper bag. Yes, it's ridiculously expensive. The government doesn't want you throwing anything out anymore—and if you do, you're going to pay a lot for that privilege.

4. Starting immediately, there's a 1,000 percent sales tax on any items sold with non-compostable, non-disposable packaging. If you want a two-dollar cup of coffee in a disposable cup, it will cost you twenty-two dollars with the new tax. That ten-dollar book you ordered on Amazon? If they deliver it using non-compostable shipping materials, the price goes up to $110. The government has a theory: The best way to

achieve extreme sustainability isn't through top-down
regulation of business. It's through an overwhelming
consumer demand for sustainable products and services.
"Companies and businesses will adapt, if consumers demand
it," the president said. "So we're going to generate some
demand."

5. It's not all sticks, there's a carrot too. If the country reduces its
annual collective waste by 80 percent, or back to 1960s levels
of garbage per person, by the end of the year, then every
resident—children too—will receive a $10,000 cash payment.
"If it costs $3.5 trillion to break our nation's addiction to
garbage once and for all, then it will be a small price to pay in
the long run for the good of our planet's health and our own
well-being," the president said. The payment will be in the
form of digidollars that must be spent within sixty days, or
they expire. You have to admit: it's kind of fun to imagine the
whole country going on a $10,000-per-person spending spree.

Weirdly, a lot of people seem really excited by all this—especially
the younger generations, who have been waiting for the world to wake
up and actually do something about the environment. And with the
government out of the recycling business, entrepreneurs are stepping
in to fill the void. Thank goodness composting is still being picked up
weekly. You've already memorized everything on the list of "One
Hundred Weird Things You Can Actually Compost," including fur,
hair, cardboard boxes, vacuum debris, and dust.

But not everyone is on board with the program. People are already
trying to figure out what they can get away with flushing down the
toilet, or putting down the garbage disposal, or hiding in their compost
bins. Protesters are planning bonfires to burn their trash. Companies
are looking for loopholes. Some people are joking that the billionaires
will just send their garbage up to space—but maybe it's not a joke.
Illegal dumping and littering will definitely be a problem—drones,
facial recognition systems, and other surveillance technologies will be

put to the test as the new rules are enforced. But maybe social norms will evolve quickly, if enough people want to get their hands on $10,000 in cash—and, of course, save the planet. After all, as the environmentalist Bill McKibben says, "If we're really going to change, sooner or later we'll have to actually make a change."[1] And who knows? It might feel good to do something different. Maybe you'll start shopping at the "package-free" grocery store that's just opened up. It's part of a new chain. You have to bring your own reusable containers—but surprisingly, the prices are cheaper than what you're used to paying for individually wrapped everything. Maybe you'll check out the new local "swap shop," where people leave unneeded items that can't be recycled, for others to take for free. Maybe you'll even become an "upcycling consultant" who gives people creative ideas for how to repurpose old things.

It's a new world. You're going to have to change your habits. You could think up new ways to help others adapt to a post-trash society. Or you could rise up, join the resistance, and try to make the new system fail. Or you could be a reformer and propose ways to make the rules fairer and easier to follow. That's up to you.

CAPTURE YOUR FIRST REACTIONS TO this scenario or talk it over with a friend. Here are some questions you might want to answer in your first conversation or journal entry about this future:

- In one word, what emotion are you feeling?
- What thoughts run through your mind as you take in the new rules?
- What questions do you have about what's allowed and not allowed?
- What's one habit you could change that would instantly reduce your trash?
- What's the hardest thing to imagine giving up or changing?

- How do you predict others will react? Your family? Friends? Neighbors?
- Is there anything that's exciting to you about this new reality?
- What worries you most about this future moment?

~~~~~~~~~

MOMENT OF CHOICE: In this future post-trash society, will you embrace the new system and try your best to adapt? Or do you plan to resist it? Or reform it? Why? Record your answers, and your overall reactions to the scenario, in your journal of this future.

Journaling ideas

Your challenge is to create a total of ten journal entries about daily life in this future. Try to imagine it in as much vivid and specific detail as you can: How is your life changing? What are you doing differently? What good things are happening? What problems have come up? Be sure to write from your own unique point of view—about the places you know, the people you spend time with, the work and activities you do, the causes you care about, the communities you belong to.

Below are some ideas for what you might journal about in this future. Pick and choose whichever ones you like, guided by your own curiosity and creativity. If you really like a prompt, you can respond to it more than once, with different stories or ideas. And don't feel limited by these suggestions—however you're inspired to explore "The Road to Zerophoria," go for it!

1. **Be a journalist and report on what's going on in the year 2033,** somewhere you spend a lot of time in the present day: a park, a school, a workplace, a place of worship, public transportation, a store, a gym, a restaurant or coffee shop, a site you volunteer at. How does the scenario show up in this place? What do you see, hear, feel,

encounter, or experience in the year 2033 that's different from today? Maybe the post-trash society rules have been implemented success- fully. How so? Or maybe it's not going very well so far. What problems are popping up? You may find it easier to imagine if you are physically in the location you're thinking about.

2. **Find a small moment in your daily life where the scenario could show up.** How would that moment be different in the year 2033 as a result of the new post-trash rules? It could be a tiny moment, like a daily habit (getting dressed), a meal (making breakfast), a chore or errand (walking the dog), a hygiene ritual (brushing your teeth), an act of self-care (what are you doing to relax or center yourself in this future?), or a phone call to your mom (what do you talk about in this future?). Pick something that's routine today—and then describe the small moment in your journal in a way that captures what's new and different in the post-trash world of 2033.

3. **Imagine what's happening on social media.** What topics or hashtags are trending in this future? What products are influencers promoting? What messages would you post? What opinions would you express? What would you vent or complain about? What kinds of in- formation, advice, or help would you ask for? What exciting news or happy thoughts would you share? Go ahead and make your own social media posts from this future—as if you were sharing thoughts, feel- ings, and news with your friends, family, or followers in the year 2033.

4. **Experiment with a zero-waste mindset.** To get a sense of how much this scenario might affect you, for the next twenty-four hours, keep a list of everything you put into a trash can in your real, present-day life. Tally it up—how many things in total did you throw out today? What would have to change, in your habits, in how compa- nies package and sell things, and in the way society works, for you not to throw out any of these things in the future? Write about what feels possible to change, and what seems impossible to change.

5. **Describe what it's like to go to a swap shop in 2033.** What do you bring to give away, and what do you hope to find?

6. **Practice creative upcycling and reuse:** Look for something in your home that you'd likely throw away in the near future. What creative new thing could you do with it instead, if throwing things away were no longer an option?

7. **Make an artifact of the future.** What everyday object might exist in this world that doesn't exist today? Bring the scenario to life with a physical object that can help you really pre-feel this future. Maybe it's a sticker you could place on a disposable coffee cup that reads: "WARNING: A $20 surcharge is applied to beverages served in disposable cups." Maybe it's a T-shirt encouraging people to join the collective effort to achieve 80 percent reduction in annual waste to unlock the cash bonus: "Team $10,000," the shirt might read on the front. "I didn't throw anything out today. How about you?" on the back. Maybe it's a local flyer announcing an upcoming bonfire to protest the new rules: "NEIGHBORHOOD TRASH-IN! Fight back against government overreach. Bring your trash! We'll burn it for you!" Making an artifact of the future is a quick, proven trick to overcome your brain's normalcy bias. It turns an abstract, hypothetical possibility into something more tangible and "imaginable." It plants a clue in your everyday physical environment to remind you of the scenario and keep your imagination sparking. So whatever you imagine existing in the post-trash world, try to make it, for real, and put this new object somewhere you'll see it often.

8. **Think of the special days you look forward to:** a favorite holiday, a family tradition, a fun vacation, an important day of worship, an annual sporting event, a party or celebration, a performance, a trip to a theme park, a big festival or convention. Pick one to imagine. How might the post-trash rules affect this special occasion or event? How might you adapt it in 2033?

9. **Use your skills, knowledge, and passions.** What do you feel called to do in this future? What could you make or create? What business or service might you start? How would you mobilize your community? What could you teach others to do? What idea do you have to make this future better?

10. **Look for the deeper disease.** Who is having a harder time adapting in this new world? What inequality or injustice might make it harder for people to comply with the new post-trash society rules? What personal and social factors would make people more likely to resist the new system? Make some suggestions for how you would change the post-trash society rules that might make the system more fair, more popular, more effective, or easier to adopt.

11. **Go as far into this future as you want.** What are the biggest positive changes in society or in your own life that have come about, a year or more into the new rules? What changes to the post-trash rules have been made, to make them more fair or easier to adapt to? How have big companies stepped up to completely change how they do things, to make it easier for people to live a zero-waste lifestyle?

12. **Feel good and celebrate a positive outcome.** Imagine the day that everyone gets the promised $10,000 bonus for achieving the collective year-end goal of 80 percent waste reduction. How do people celebrate? How do you spend your $10,000? (Remember, everyone has to spend the bonus in sixty days, or it goes away!) Or, describe a moment in this future world when you felt a rush of that new positive emotion, zerophoria. Where and why did you feel it? What's it like to experience?

Journaling tips

- You might get creatively inspired and want to spend all ten days going deep on just one prompt, or a few prompts. If so, that's great! Feel free to spend all ten days in the future creatively repurposing things in your home, or making artifacts from the future, or imagining trending topics on social media in the year 2033, or coming up with ideas for making this future more fair and equitable . . . Whatever feels fun, interesting, and meaningful to you, that's the best way to spend ten days in the future.

- Limit yourself to a maximum of one journal entry per day, and keep the simulation going for at least ten days, to make sure the scenario has plenty of time to simmer and develop in your imagination.

Could a future like this really happen? Let's take a look at the signals of change and future forces behind "The Road to Zerophoria." The problems that inspired this scenario are certainly real and growing— but fortunately, so are the potential solutions.

Let's start with the global waste crisis. Currently, the world produces over two billion tons of trash every year. To put that number in perspective, if you were to line up trash cans full of two billion tons of garbage, they would stretch out for twenty-five thousand miles, more than the circumference of the earth. That's how much trash we produce *every year*. According to the World Bank, that number will likely double in the next twenty-five years.[2] Dealing with all this waste is becoming a major contributor to climate change and health problems worldwide.

Rotting trash now accounts for 5 percent of total carbon emissions worldwide, which is more than the entire aviation, rail, and shipping industries combined.[3] That's because landfill waste leaks methane and carbon dioxide as it breaks down. The more we throw out, the faster sea levels rise, and the wider extreme heat waves spread. And research shows that people living closer to landfill sites suffer from medical conditions such as asthma, cancer, chronic fatigue, and other long-term health problems at a higher rate than those living far from landfills, a result of continuous exposure to chemicals, toxic fumes, and dust.[4] The more trash we bury, the sicker we get.

Meanwhile, if we continue to dump nearly half the plastic we produce each year, it's expected that there will be more plastic than fish in the oceans by the year 2050. Toxins from dumped plastics are already entering the oceanic food chain today, killing more than one million fish, turtles, birds, and sea mammals every year and putting our health and our global food systems at risk.[5]

Many countries, as they run out of landfill space and try to minimize environmental impact, are turning to waste-to-energy plants that burn trash for fuel. The upside is that incinerated trash doesn't wind up rotting in the ground or floating in the oceans. The downside is that these plants create significant air pollution and can also release lead, mercury, and hazardous ash into nearby communities. These health risks, like those of landfills, aren't equally borne. Waste-to-energy plants tend to be located in lower-income communities with higher concentrations of ethnic minorities.[6] Burning trash for fuel may seem viable in the short term, but in the long term, it's unlikely to be sustainable, equitable, or acceptable to most communities.

Finally, it's expensive to deal with so much trash. In high-income countries, 5 percent of all municipal budgets is spent managing trash. It's 10 percent in middle-income countries, and 20 percent in low-income countries. If some of that money were freed up, it could be spent on health care, education, infrastructure, climate adaptation. Anything would be better than literally throwing it away.[7]

If the global waste crisis is going to reach peak emergency anywhere, it's in the United States. Americans produce the most trash by far—on average, five pounds per person *every day*.[8] For decades we've been paying other countries to take it—more than ten thousand shipping containers' worth every month in recent years. Until late 2018, the US was shipping *more than half* its total recyclable plastics and paper waste to China.

It turned out that roughly a third of what we were sending to China was too contaminated by food waste to recycle; it needed to be landfilled or burned instead. In 2018, China decided that the income from importing all this garbage wasn't worth the environmental and health impacts and closed its borders to international trash.[9] Soon after, most of the world's leading importers of trash—Malaysia, Indonesia, Vietnam, the Philippines, and India—followed suit, banning trash imports or severely limiting what they would take. As a result, countries like the US, Japan, Germany, and the UK are increasingly stuck having to deal with their own mounting garbage.

That's the current state of the crisis. Garbage is very much a real and growing future risk. But will our future *solutions* to the global waste crisis look anything like the dramatic measures imagined in "The Road to Zerophoria"? Likely, yes—even if the actual policies we adopt aren't quite so extreme. Many of the waste management ideas described in the hypothetical scenario are already being experimented with today.

Pay-as-you-throw programs, for example, already exist in many parts of the world. In South Korea, all food waste must be separated from other trash and weighed in community "smart bins" equipped with scales and radio frequency identification (RFID) readers. Individuals must scan an RFID card to open the bin and throw something out, and they are automatically charged per pound of trash. As a result, the country now recycles an astonishing 95 percent of its food waste—up from 2 percent in 1995. In other pay-as-you-throw programs, such as in the city of Taipei, trash is collected only in special blue bags, which individuals must purchase if they want to throw anything out. It's a flat fee per bag—so people tend to squeeze as much into each bag as possible. Still, the city has seen overall garbage volume reduced by 35 percent since switching to this program in 1999. Can you imagine if all public trash bins, everywhere in the world, were designed this way—and there was always a cost to throwing something out?

Even in the US, roughly 10 percent of municipalities have already implemented some kind of "variable rate pricing," which most commonly offers residents a choice of garbage bin size and charges a higher monthly collection fee for larger trash bins. Studies suggest these programs have resulted in more modest reductions of garbage—on average 10–15 percent.[10] It's not too much of a stretch to imagine that variable rate pricing might evolve to include smaller bin sizes in the future. Would you be willing to swap your current trash bin for one the size of a shoebox, with the right economic incentive?

None of these existing pay-as-you-throw programs charge anywhere near the exorbitant fees imagined in the 2033 scenario. But treating waste removal like a utility, where you pay more the more you use it, is already a well-tested idea. And in a true global waste crisis, it's plausible that the average fees would increase exponentially.

Some governments have successfully enacted even stricter waste policies, with the goal of becoming "zero-waste communities." In the village of Kamikatsu, Japan, for example, residents are required to bring all their waste to a community sorting facility, where they sort their trash into forty-five different garbage bins. This approach allows the town to recover forty-five different types of metal, plastic, paper, and food waste, and recycle a world-leading 81 percent of its trash. To further reduce garbage, the town also provides residents with free products that make a zero-waste lifestyle easier. All new parents, for example, get a free supply of cloth diapers. Most uniquely, Kamikatsu has a swap shop in the center of town, where residents leave all their unneeded items that can't be recycled, for others to take for free.[11] Can you imagine swap shops becoming an essential part of everyday life worldwide in the year 2033?

In fact, there are already a growing number of local Buy Nothing groups on social media platforms like Nextdoor and Facebook that allow neighbors to post items they want to give away, and to ask for the items they need. Facebook has more than six thousand of these groups, with an estimated four million active participants in at least forty-four countries. And the first official Buy Nothing app launched in 2021. This type of informal local gifting network would certainly be essential infrastructure in a post-trash world.[12]

Even without government intervention, zero-waste lifestyles may become more popular in the coming decade. Already today, social media is full of influencers living their best zero-waste lives. The most followed zero-waste influencers have figured out how to reduce their personal trash output to just one bag or less per year, despite living in garbage-rich countries like the US and the UK. They post photos of their impressively tiny annual trash output, often squeezed into a single mason jar for a family of four, to inspire others. And they share practical tips for zero-waste cooking, cleaning, traveling, parenting, beauty, and fashion on sites like Going Zero Waste, the Zero Waste Family, and Trash Is for Tossers. (If you're looking for ideas to inspire your journal entries from the future about how you might adapt to the 2033 scenario, these sites are a great place to spark your imagination.)[13]

It takes a certain amount of privilege to live a zero-waste lifestyle today. You need to have abundant free time to do things in a less convenient, less prepackaged way. In the future, however, it could become a more accessible lifestyle, especially if zero-waste infrastructure grows more common—for example, if a new kind of grocery store emerges to sell entirely unpackaged foods. It's not impossible to imagine; in fact, in Hong Kong, a grocery store called Live Zero already sells only zero-waste, packaging-free bulk food and cleaning products, and similar stores exist in Brooklyn, Sicily, Malaysia, and South Africa.[14] These shops are small experiments today. But can you imagine what the first successful global chain of zero-waste groceries might be like a decade from now?

If the Whole Foods and Walmarts of the future are all package-free, then strict limits on residential and commercial garbage become much easier to follow, and the policies more equitable. And a popular new kind of law may make package-free shopping even more common. In 2021, Maine and Oregon became the first US states to pass a law requiring manufacturers to cover the cost of recycling any packaging they produce by paying a fee to a nonprofit "producer responsibility organization" that contracts with local governments.[15] The fee is determined by the total tonnage of packaging a company puts into the marketplace. This isn't the same as charging individuals for their trash, but it's comparable: *You make the waste, you pay for it.* Laws like this are already popular in the European Union, Japan, South Korea, and parts of Canada, countries that have made their recycling programs more resilient after China and other countries stopped importing the world's waste. Companies may decide they'd rather just create less packaging, if they're going to have to pay for it.

Other types of businesses are experimenting with zero-waste models today, in big and small ways that could add up to major transformation by the year 2033. Consider these further signals of change:

- In 2020, Starbucks, McDonald's, and Burger King started testing reusable coffee cups and burger packaging. Customers in these trial runs were given five days to return the reusable containers, which had unique QR codes. Customers who didn't return the containers within five days were automatically charged a fifteen-dollar "keep it" penalty. Trials of this kind have shown a 90–95 percent return rate so far.[16]
- The fashion retailer Eileen Fisher will now buy back any item of used Eileen Fisher clothing, in any condition, for five dollars, to resell, repurpose as art materials, or donate to women in need.[17] Meanwhile, IKEA recently opened its first-ever secondhand store, in Stockholm, where shoppers can buy used IKEA furniture.[18] Most major brands and retailers will likely experiment with ways to extend the life cycle of their products. Can you imagine shopping at the official secondhand shop of your favorite brand or retailer in the future?
- Electronics are increasingly getting a second life too. The US company HYLA Mobile partners with telecom companies to collect more than twenty thousand traded-in, old, and broken mobile phones every day, over one hundred million in total so far, that would have otherwise been sent to a landfill. HYLA Mobile repairs and redistributes them in emerging and

developing markets where individuals might not otherwise be able to afford a mobile phone.[19]

- The Australian company Close the Loop recycles old printer cartridges by combining them with traditional asphalt to make a more durable road surface. Every mile of newly paved road contains the waste toner from 20,000 recycled printer cartridges.[20]
- In 2022, the Swiss shoe company On Running plans to launch the first fully recyclable sneaker, made from castor beans. You cannot buy the shoe—you can only *subscribe* to it. When you wear it out, you send the sneaker back to the company for recycling, and they send you a new pair.[21] You may never own or throw out a pair of shoes again.

Driving many of these innovations is the concept of a *circular economy*. In a circular economy, all resources, products, and materials are kept in use for as long as possible and are never simply discarded. Most big companies are already working toward circular economy solutions, with the expectation that within a decade or two, it will be the norm. So if you do find yourself waking up in a world like "The Road to Zerophoria," the good news is that you won't be figuring out how to adapt on your own. Many companies will have strategies in place that make it possible for us all to live a life without trash.

And that imagined $10,000 cash payment to all citizens if the most ambitious national waste reduction goals are achieved by the end of the program's first year? Even that isn't as far-fetched as it might seem. A $10,000 payment is equivalent to the amount that would be paid each year through a universal basic income program, an idea that is gaining popular support and political traction in many parts of the world. In the future, governments could make the adoption of such a program contingent on societal progress in other measures—like reduced carbon emissions, universal vaccination, or the end of garbage as we know it. Can you imagine governments increasingly offering universal cash prizes and other rewards to motivate healthy and sustainable behaviors? I can.

Keep looking for clues to this future. Stay one step ahead of this scenario. You can find experts to follow on social media and discover new signals of change by investigating these search terms:

- "the circular economy"
- "pay-as-you-throw programs"
- "the global waste crisis"
- "the zero-waste movement"

FUTURE SIMULATION #2

~~~

Welcome Party

*We can continue to think of [climate migration] as a
catastrophe. Or we can reclaim our history of migration and our
place in nature as migrants like the butterflies and the birds.*

—SONIA SHAH, science journalist

TODAY, WE FACE A GROWING CLIMATE MIGRATION CRISIS. BUT WHAT IF
we flipped our way of thinking upside down? Let's imagine another
ridiculous, at first, possibility: a world in which climate migration is no
longer seen as a great crisis but as an urgent solution.

In this future, it no longer makes sense for most people to live in
one country their whole lives just because they were born there. The
freedom to move is recognized as a fundamental human right, and
keeping people trapped behind borders is considered a barbaric, out-
dated practice. Financial support is available to anyone who needs to
relocate because of climate change.

It's not just a matter of what's fair. It's also about fueling economic
growth and innovation. More migration gets more people to where

they can maximize their potential and make the biggest contributions to society. And most countries need more workers, not fewer. In this world, governments no longer ask how we limit migration. They ask how we maximize its benefits.

Some of the smartest and most creative people in the world are putting all their energy into figuring out the logistics of a mass migration: How do we quickly help hundreds of millions of people move somewhere they can be happier and healthier? Which places will have the safest climates? How can we make room there for all of us?

Not everyone is on the move in this future. The rest of humanity is learning how to make others feel welcome and at home somewhere new. In fact, the art of welcoming is now ranked by online learners as the most useful and desirable practical skill to master, ahead of computer programming, data science, and even health care. It turns out that a "soft" skill may be the most essential one for humanity's future.

Migration in this future is no longer an individual burden or a dangerous, illegal journey. It's coordinated, intentional, and strategic—the whole world working together to build vibrant, thriving societies. The climate journey *you* choose to take, if you do move, will bravely make your family's new history for generations to come.

How might we get to a world like this, where a crisis becomes a solution? What new kinds of political actions and social movements could lead us there? What would it feel like to live through the first waves of coordinated, intentional mass migration? What will be our greatest sources of happiness, comfort, and resilience, if we decide to do the hard work necessary to make a climate-safer life for all?

That's what we're going to try to find out in simulation #2: "Welcome Party."

Let's play.

JUST NOW, FOR THE FIRST time in history, more than four billion mobile phones buzzed at the same time. And twelve hours from now, as soon as the other side of the world wakes up, another four billion plus will buzz. Eight billion phones. That's not all the mobile phones on earth. But it's most of them.

You look down at your own phone. It's an emergency alert notification. You're not panicking, because you were expecting it, and you know it's not a real emergency—at least, not in the traditional sense. There's no immediate danger. It's an emergency alert about something that's expected to happen *ten years from today*. Yes, plenty of people have argued that a ten-year warning is not an appropriate use of the global wireless emergency alert system. And they have a point. But after decades of talking about the climate crisis, maybe it's not such a bad idea to actually treat it as a crisis.

The alert is from the Welcome Party. The subject: "It's party time!" That doesn't sound too ominous. But you know, from all the news coverage, that it's a big deal. "It's party time!" was the slogan that thousands of political candidates ran on worldwide, as part of the new Welcome Party coalition platform. And they achieved their goal: they harnessed enough law-making power worldwide to launch a comprehensive humanitarian response to the growing demand for climate relocation. They did it thanks in no small part to three years of unrelenting social protests and general work strikes from the We Are All Immigrants to the Future movement.

However you choose to respond to this emergency alert will help determine the fate of a billion people. And given what's been going on where you live—longer and more extreme heat waves, more frequent power and water outages—it might decide your fate too.

EMERGENCY ALERT—IT'S PARTY TIME!

CONGRATULATIONS! You have been selected to participate in the First Global Census of Climate Risk Tolerance and Migration Intent.

Ten years from today, the world will begin the largest human migration ever attempted. Up to one billion people are expected to request relocation from regions that have been severely affected by climate change.

The Welcome Party, a coalition of thirty-three national governing parties, is preparing models and forecasts to help plan migration routes and to prepare climate-resilient destination cities for a rapid population influx.

Your responses to the following ten questions will be factored into our data models, so we can more accurately predict the locations and timing of climate relocation requests.

You have ten days to submit your responses. You may wish to consult family, friends, and neighbors on your answers. Depending on your responses, you may be offered early migration opportunities and financial support.

The data we collect will help build the readiness of the United States, Canada, China, Japan, Russia, Australia, New Zealand, the United Kingdom, and all thirty-three countries in the European Economic Area (EEA) to welcome new residents to the most climate-safe regions on earth.

Tap the link now to begin the questionnaire.

You tap the link and scroll quickly through the questions to get a better sense of what information they want from you. No wonder they gave you ten days to think it over. Some of these questions you honestly have no idea how to answer. You start weighing your choices . . .

The First Global Census of Climate Risk Tolerance and Migration Intent

1. On a scale of 1 to 10, how free do you feel to move to a safer climate if you need to?

   (Not free at all) 1 2 3 4 5 6 7 8 9 10 (Completely free)

2. What might cause you to STAY in your current home, even if the climate became extremely unsafe? Mark all that apply.

   I lack the financial resources to move.

I don't know where I would go.

If my extended family doesn't want to leave, I won't go
   without them.

I have deep roots in my community, I cannot abandon it.

I worry about violence and discrimination against migrants.

I believe there must be a way, with technology, to make any
   place livable.

I can't imagine living anywhere else.

Other _____

3. If you are forced to leave your current home due to unsafe
   climate, do you have a preferred climate-safer destination?
   Where would you want to move to? It might be to a different
   country, or to a new region in your home country, or to a
   specific city somewhere else on earth. Please give at least three
   options.

   First choice _____
   Second choice _____
   Third choice _____

4. Would you prefer *seasonal migration* or *permanent relocation*?
   Seasonal migration requires you to evacuate for several
   months each year during the annual "leave season," to avoid
   extreme heat, storms, flooding, etc. Permanent relocation
   means making a full-time home somewhere new.

5. How many extreme heat days (110 degrees F or higher) would
   you tolerate annually before seeking to move to a climate-safer
   destination?

6. How many severe air pollution days (AQI 200 or higher, at
   which it is unsafe to breathe outdoor or unfiltered air for
   longer than five minutes) would you tolerate annually before
   seeking to move to a climate-safer destination?

7. How many days without running water or under extreme water rations (25 L per person, per day) would you tolerate annually before seeking to move to a climate-safer destination?

8. How many total days without electricity or internet would you tolerate, due to instability of the power grid during extreme weather, before seeking to move to a climate-safer destination?

9. On a scale of 1 to 10, how worried are you currently about infrastructure collapse (buildings, roads, bridges) where you live due to rising sea levels, flooding, and extreme weather? How much imminent danger do you feel you are in?

   (No danger at all) 1 2 3 4 5 6 7 8 9 10 (Extreme danger)

10. On a scale of 1 to 10, how welcoming would you be to newcomers if your current home area remains climate-resilient?

   (Not welcoming at all) 1 2 3 4 5 6 7 8 9 10 (Extremely welcoming)

The Welcome Party Platform

Humans are a migratory species. We started in Africa. Now we cover the whole planet. No one stopped us then. We must not stop each other now.

Thousands of years of history show that human movement across the earth is natural and beneficial to our survival. Today, we are on the move again, leaving behind extreme heat, droughts, unrelenting storms, rising sea levels, and flooding. And we are not alone. Birds, frogs, butterflies, moose, bears, sharks, funguses, trees—scientists have found that over 50 percent of all species of life on earth are following changes in the climate, seeking out safer homes, and living where they've never lived before.

Human movement toward climate safety cannot be prevented, and it is nothing to be afraid of.

We believe it is time for "the climate underground railroad" to come aboveground.

As members of the Welcome Party coalition:

We vow to promote and protect the fundamental human right to flee deadly dangers, and to seek out environments compatible with life.

We acknowledge that some nations have historically contributed more carbon emissions than others and are therefore more responsible for climate change. These nations have a moral responsibility to take in the vast majority of climate migrants as a form of climate reparations. The United States, which has contributed 25 percent of all carbon emissions over the past three hundred years, will be encouraged to take in 250 million climate migrants; China (15 percent) 150 million migrants; Japan (4 percent) 40 million migrants; and so on for all thirty-three member nations.

We will give ourselves a full decade to build up the infrastructure of climate-resilient destination cities. With planning and preparation, there will be less social shock and more economic growth when our massive relocation gets underway.

Today, we encourage all people, everywhere:

Be ready to move. Places that seem climate-safe today may change dramatically over the next decade. We must all prepare ourselves, our families, and our communities, practically and mentally, to leave if and when it becomes necessary.

Be ready to welcome. How we treat each other along our journeys will determine whether we live the next century in peace or suffer needlessly. Let us prepare now: to share our local knowledge, to offer aid however we can, and to warmly welcome newcomers. Any one of us could become a climate migrant in the future.

TAKE A FEW MINUTES TO capture your first reactions to the scenario in your journal or talk it over with a friend:

- In one word, what emotion do you feel when you receive the questionnaire?
- What thoughts run through your mind as you read it?
- How prepared do you feel to answer the questions?
- How do you predict others will react to receiving the questionnaire?
- Is there anything that's exciting to you about this future moment?
- What worries you most about this future moment?
- What questions do you have about the Welcome Party's plans and the logistics of helping up to one billion people migrate?

～～～～～

MOMENT OF CHOICE: If this really happened, whom would you most want to talk to about the questionnaire before submitting your response—to get their perspective and advice, to compare answers, or to make a plan together? Why? Record your answer, and your overall reactions to the scenario, in your journal of this future.

Journaling ideas

Below are some ideas for what you might journal about as you spend ten days in the world of "Welcome Party." Pick and choose whichever ones you like (or invent your own prompts, guided by your own curiosity and creativity):

1. **Spend some time taking the Welcome Party's First Global Census of Climate Risk Tolerance and Migration Intent.** Answer just one question each day. Remember, you're answering the questionnaire as future you. Keep in mind where you might live, with whom, and what your life circumstances might be like in the year 2033—they might be the same as today, or they might be quite different. Make some notes in your journal about any information you

looked up or conversations you had to help you answer each question. Share some quick thoughts about why you chose the answers you did.

2. **Pick a destination.** Imagine a few details about what your life might be like if you really moved to your top-choice destination to escape dangerous climate change. You might find it helpful to consult real forecasts of which countries and cities will be most at risk from climate change, and which will be most resilient. The Notre Dame Global Adaptation Initiative Country Index summarizes each country's vulnerability to climate change in combination with its readiness to improve resilience. The top ten countries as of 2021 were Norway, New Zealand, Finland, Switzerland, Sweden, Austria, Denmark, Iceland, Singapore, and Germany. You can view the current ratings at https://gain.nd.edu/our-work/country-index/rankings/. The Cities at Risk series ranks the world's 576 largest urban centers on their future exposure to a range of environmental and climate-related threats. The least risky cities, and best bets for long-term relocation as of 2021, were Krasnoyarsk in Siberia; Glasgow, Scotland; and Ottawa, Canada. Other highly resilient cities included Memphis, Montevideo, and Cairo. Asia's lowest-risk cities were Mongolia's Ulaanbaatar and Shizuoka in Japan. You can see more rankings by searching online for the "Verisk Maplecroft Environmental Risk Outlook" reports.

3. **Define "home" for you.** What are the sights, sounds, smells, tastes, experiences, traditions, people, and places that define "home" for you today? How could you bring them with you if you have to relocate because of climate change? Brainstorm some ideas for bringing home with you as you move in the future. (If you're inspired, create something real today that would help you take a feeling of home with you wherever you go.)

4. **Practice fitting into a new culture.** Imagine what you would do to feel at home somewhere new. You might learn a language, make a new recipe, change your name, become a fan of a new sport, or join

a local exercise or art group where you don't have to speak the same language to participate. Tell a story about what you might do. (If you're inspired, do it for real and write about your experience!)

5. **Welcome someone.** What could you do to make climate migrants feel welcome—in your neighborhood, school, workplace, or home? What has made *you* feel welcome somewhere new in the past? Could you do something similar for climate migrants? Brainstorm ideas and tell a story about an action you might take. (If you're inspired, try out your welcoming skills in the present day and write about your experience!)

6. **Make an artifact of the future.** What everyday object might exist in this scenario that doesn't exist today? Maybe it's a handmade tally sheet, or scorecard, by your front door or on your refrigerator, keeping track of the number of climate-unsafe days so far in the year 2033. How many tally marks might there be for unsafe air days? Unsafe temperature days? Power outage days? Or maybe it's a sign or visual symbol that local residents and businesses could put in their windows to warmly welcome climate migrants. Maybe it's a T-shirt encouraging people to join the Welcome Party: "It's Party Time!" Maybe it's a poster from a We Are All Immigrants to the Future social protest. Maybe it's a card signed by all your new neighbors, welcoming you to your new climate-resilient city. Whatever you imagine existing in the "Welcome Party" world, try to make it, for real. Then put this new object somewhere you'll see it often, to keep sparking your imagination.

7. **Tell a story about seasonal migration.** Imagine that "leave season" is the new normal in many parts of the world, including where you live. For several months each year, virtually everyone who is able relocates to a climate-safer region to avoid suffering through the annual season of extreme heat, storms, flooding, wildfire smoke, water restrictions, or power outages. During the other three seasons, when

things are more stable and temperate, everyone returns and lives their ordinary lives. Not everyone is able to relocate, but the vast majority does. What might it be like to be expected to pack up and relocate for leave season? Where would you go? Whom might you stay with? How would you afford it? Could you work or study remotely, or would you need to find seasonal work away from home? Would you go back to the same place every leave season or go to different places? What services and support systems might exist in this world to help people who would otherwise be unable to leave get safely away each leave season? You might search the internet for the interactive map "Every Country Has Its Own Climate Risks. What's Yours?" created by the *New York Times*, which maps risks of flooding, heat stress, drought, wildfires, hurricanes, and sea-level rise, to a get a better idea of what you might be leaving.[1]

8. **Go as far into this future as you want.** What would you *like* to see happen as a result of billions of people answering the First Global Census of Climate Risk Tolerance and Migration Intent? What's the best possible outcome you can imagine? What's a best-case scenario news headline from the year 2043, when the billion-person planned migration and global "welcome party" finally get underway? Or what might happen that makes a mass climate migration unnecessary after all? How might one of your favorite cities, or hometown, make itself more climate-resilient between now and then? Tell a story of climate migration or climate resilience that describes the world you *want* to wake up in.

Could this future really happen? Let's take a look at the signals of change and future forces behind "Welcome Party."

Climate migration is one of the biggest future forces of the century. Experts estimate that climate change will force anywhere from 200 million to 1.5 billion people to move within and across borders by the year 2100.[2] Most of this migration will be driven by extreme heat and drought and its impact on power grids, water supply, and infrastructure. One major study published in the *Proceedings of the National Academy of Sciences* predicted that by the year 2070, as many as three billion people will find themselves living in "conditions unsuitable for human life."[3] It's not unthinkable, given these numbers, that world leaders might soon start to proactively plan for the movement of *at least* one billion people to more climate-resilient regions.

This planned migration could take two forms. The most likely solution is one recently recommended by experts from Harvard Law School, Yale Law School, and the University Network for Human Rights: lawmakers could create a temporary visa for people displaced by climate change that would offer a pathway to a green card or citizenship.[4] Such a program, if implemented by dozens of countries, might create a limited, ten-year window of opportunity for an unprecedented number of individuals from the hardest-hit regions—Southeast Asia, Central and South America, and sub-Saharan Africa—to move across borders and change citizenship.

In policy papers about this kind of large-scale planned migration, the term "climate reparations" has started appearing more frequently. It's the idea that countries that have historically contributed the most carbon emissions should now take in a proportional number of climate migrants. The countries making reparations would also pay many of the costs of resettlement. This idea may seem like a political nonstarter today, with so much focus on strengthening border control and growing anti-immigration sentiment on the political right. But there is likely to be a generational shift on this issue, as almost half of people in the US under thirty-five today favor the idea of government reparations for past injustices, whether for slavery, economic exploitation and colonization, or climate harm.[5]

As we witness more dramatic humanitarian crises and their ripple effects on geopolitical stability and the global economy, climate reparations may become a more widely agreed-upon moral responsibility, regardless of political party. Consider that in 2020 there were more than five million global deaths attributed to extreme temperatures caused by climate change; COVID-19, by comparison, caused an estimated 3.5 million deaths that same year.[6] It's reasonable to hope that, as climate change becomes an even bigger threat to global health, the world will rise to the occasion and not choose to leave people trapped behind borders.

Or the solution may be even more radical than climate reparations. There's a growing political movement in support of permanently open borders worldwide, in recognition of the fundamental human right to move freely and seek out safe environments. Advocates of open borders propose a system in which individuals who pass a criminal background check are able to move as freely from nation to nation as people in the United States can move from state to state today. Individuals would be able to work and receive social services such as education and basic health care anywhere, regardless of citizenship, although some rights and services—such as voting or a universal basic income—would be limited to citizens. Some economists argue that an open borders policy is not only a matter of human rights and equity; it would also lead to a vast increase in global productivity and wealth by moving people to where they could thrive and make the best contribution to society.

Temporary visas by the billion or completely open borders—both options are already on the table today.[7] Whatever the policy, human migration will almost certainly be considered more as a solution than feared as a "crisis." Many countries with aging populations and more deaths than births—the US, Japan, China, Russia, and the UK, to name a few—will actually find themselves competing for migrants, and not just "skilled" ones. These countries will be happy to provide education and skill training to young people—and perhaps free housing too—because without vastly higher numbers of young migrants to fill the workforce and care for elders, these countries will be unable to sustain their current standard of living.[8]

To this end, some leaders are calling for extremely ambitious immigration goals. Century Initiative, a diverse nonpartisan network of Canadians from the business, academic, and charitable sectors, calls for Canada to triple its population from thirty-eight million to one hundred million people by the year 2100, in order to increase Canadian innovation, economic stability, and influence on the world stage.[9] Best-selling books also advocate for this shift in thinking, such as Matthew Yglesias's *One Billion Americans: The Case for Thinking Bigger*, which proposes that the US open its doors to welcome nearly seven hundred million new immigrants in the interest of global competitiveness, and *The Next Great Migration* by Sonia Shah, which argues that all living organisms migrate in response to environmental pressure and that humans should embrace this evolutionary adaptability wholeheartedly as we deal with climate change.[10] These new ways of thinking about the benefits of mass migration are reflected in the Welcome Party's imagined platform, and they are likely to become more mainstream.

The First Global Census of Climate Risk Tolerance and Migration Intent in the scenario is inspired by a recent real-world phenomenon. Many people who never thought they would be affected by unlivable weather are beginning to realize they are at risk. The historic and deadly "heat dome" in the summer of 2021 made it painfully clear to residents of the Pacific Northwest that previously unimaginable temperatures for that region—multiple days in a row over 120 degrees Fahrenheit in some parts—were not only possible but likely to happen more often in the future. A friend of mine who fled Portland, Oregon, temporarily with her family texted me, "Is this what our lives are going to be like from now on? Always be ready to leave?" And as one central California resident said in an interview with the *Guardian* about the state's increasing number of extreme heat days, "Everything is wet with sweat. Sometimes my head starts to hurt, and I get dizzy. That is when I start to have doubts, so many doubts: why are we even here?"[11] The reality is that over the next decade many hundreds of millions of people worldwide will be assessing just how much they can bear. In the United States, ninety-three million people are forecast to face severe, potentially unlivable climate harms.[12] And they will all have to make strategic calculations about relocating.

On the other hand, climate futurist Alex Steffen has argued, "in the planetary crisis, relocation is not refuge"—and he makes an excellent point.[13] Trying to predict climate-safer regions may be a fool's errand, as places once thought safe turn out to be at new risk, and ripple effects from one local crisis spread globally. Think of how toxic wildfire smoke from Oregon choked the supposedly climate-safer skies of the Midwest and Northeast thousands of miles away in the summer of 2021, creating the most polluted air in the world in cities that had zero risk of wildfires. Even so, people with the economic resources and freedom to move will surely *try* to get ahead of the risks. Mass migration might not work as a long-term strategy to escape climate change, especially in the absence of radical global sustainability measures. But it will surely happen.

For those who have already decided they have no choice but to leave, even if they lack resources or legal options, the "climate underground railroad" does in fact exist today. It's a form of humanitarian aid and activism designed to facilitate the movement of people across borders, and to support and hide those threatened by deportation or anti-immigrant violence. The name, used by activists to describe their own work, is a reference to the nineteenth-century underground railroad in the United States, a network of secret routes and safe houses that helped enslaved African Americans escape to free Northern states and Canada.

As migration scholar Maurice Stierl writes:

Growing mass displacement caused by conflict, persecution, poverty or environmental destruction has coincided with tightening visa regimes and enhanced border controls. In response, forms of support and sanctuary for those on the move have spread. . . .

Today, the spirit of [the original underground railroad] lives on in countless ways, ranging from direct interventions along deadly borders, such as the Mediterranean Sea, the Sonoran desert along the US border and Saharan desert in Africa, to providing guidance to those still trying to move. It also lives on in anti-deportation and anti-detention campaigns, and in networks creating sanctuary spaces and cities after arrival.[14]

If governments don't massively increase immigration to help those suffering in conditions unsuited for human life, the climate underground railroad could grow to become a formidable global social movement, on the order of Black Lives Matter.

What might that social movement look like? One example of a large underground network is the All Hands AZ volunteer group in Phoenix, Arizona, which coordinates housing, food, clothing, and travel arrangements for migrant families who have been arrested or detained by US Immigration and Customs Enforcement and released pending a court hearing. In a media interview, the director of the volunteer group asked to be identified only by the first name Jen, because of hateful messages and death threats she has received. They keep the locations of where they shelter families secret to avoid protesters and have a constantly changing password of the day. There are more than five hundred volunteers in the All Hands AZ group, many of whom have welcomed literally hundreds of migrant families into their own homes, to stay a night or two while figuring out their next move.[15] Can you imagine if this kind of volunteer activity, or welcome party, were scaled up in the future and went aboveground, so that every climate migrant was met by a host family ready to offer advice, resources, and a warm welcome?

The global We Are All Immigrants to the Future social movement imagined in the world of 2033 isn't real yet. But it's inspired by an essay written by the Institute for the Future's executive director, Marina Gorbis, herself an immigrant to the US from the former Soviet Union. She writes:

> We are all immigrants to the future; none of us is a native in that land. . . . The very underpinnings of our society and institutions— from how we work to how we create value, govern, trade, learn, and innovate—are being profoundly reshaped. . . . We are indeed all migrating to a new land and should be looking at the new landscape emerging before us like immigrants: ready to learn a new language, a new way of doing things, anticipating new

beginnings with a sense of excitement, if also with a bit of under-standable trepidation.[16]

There are no facts about the future, but this is about as close to a fact as you can get: we will all wake up one day in a world that feels strange and unfamiliar to us, because that is how the future works. Even if we don't ourselves become climate migrants, we will all need to learn, adapt, ask for help, and help each other through whatever shocks the future holds for us. "Welcome Party" imagines a world in which a majority of people have the humility to recognize that it may be their turn to ask for help next. Can *you* imagine waking up in that future?

Keep looking for clues. Stay one step ahead of this scenario. You can find experts to follow on social media and discover new signals of change by investigating these search terms:

- "climate migration"
- "climate reparations"
- "climate underground railroad"
- "climate-resilient cities"

The Ten-Year Winter

While humanity is currently on a trajectory to severe climate change, this disaster can be averted if researchers aim for goals that seem nearly impossible. We're hopeful, because sometimes engineers and scientists do achieve the impossible.

—DAVID FORK AND ROSS KONINGSTEIN,
research engineers

TODAY, GLOBAL WARMING IS THE BIGGEST CLIMATE CHALLENGE THAT WE face. But what if we woke up in an upside-down future where we faced *global wintering* instead?

Imagine it: in this future, the world has access to a breakthrough geoengineering technology that can partially block the sun's rays and cool the planet. It could potentially reverse decades of global warming. It could give the world time to achieve a full transition to 100 percent renewable energy. But it will require living for years with dramatically less sunlight, and more rains and potential flooding. The technology has never been used before at global scale. No one knows exactly how cool or wet the earth might get—or what complications might arise when it's time to turn the technology off and let the sun back in again.

Scientists are optimistic. They're urging governments and the United Nations to approve a full-scale global wintering effort. It really could be the end of our climate nightmare and the beginning of climate healing. But who should have the legal and moral authority to make extreme geoengineering decisions like this? What voice should ordinary people have in the process? How can the science be communicated to the public—and will it be trusted? Will most people be in favor of taking the risk, or against it? And what would it feel like to live through a decade, at least, of global wintering?

That's what we're going to try to find out in simulation #3: "The Ten-Year Winter."

Let's play.

YOU'VE BEEN STARING AT THE screen all night. You've refreshed it more than a hundred times. It still says the same thing:

"Results pending."

Refresh. The same two words.

Refresh. Still no news.

Refresh. You have to remind yourself to breathe.

Refresh.

There it is:

"YES."

So that's it. We're really doing this.

The world voted yes. Yes to dimming the sun. Yes to geoengineering our way out of the climate crisis.

In 2016, there was Brexit. In 2029, there was Calexit. And now, in 2033, the Sun Exit.

It had to be a supermajority decision, more than 60 percent, because you don't do something as drastic as inject sulfate particles into the stratosphere without the consent of the people. And it was close:

according to the results page, out of the 7.1 billion people who voted, 62 percent went yes, 38 percent no.

It took nearly a year to get all the votes in. That in itself was a historic achievement: a secure election, in nearly two hundred countries, including places with no previous history of democracy, and with kids eligible to vote, too, because they had more on the line than anyone.

Now there's a countdown clock on the screen. The ten-year winter begins in ten days.

Surely people will protest. Hackers will try to crash the solar radiation management system. But as far as you can tell, this vote is binding. A global coalition of climate scientists and engineers are going to put into action the plan that they've been simulating and risk-mitigating since the UN General Assembly authorized the first local sun-dimming experiments in 2027.

Here's what they've told you to expect: the sulfate particles will mimic the effect of a volcanic eruption and reflect sunlight back into space. "It's a natural process, that we're assisting with technology," the YES campaign explained. "All of the cooling benefits, with none of the harmful ash that makes people sick." But if you like bright blue skies and feeling the sun on your skin, you're not going to like the next decade. The skies will be gray. Rains will happen more often, and last much longer. Temperatures will cool significantly. In most places, the new average *high* temperature will be the previous average *low* temperature. That's a swing of potentially twenty degrees. It's a much more dramatic intervention than geoengineers were talking about earlier in the twenty-first century when the field was first getting underway. But ultimately, it's what all the most powerful climate supercomputers wound up predicting would be required to keep most of the planet inhabitable—from the NASA Center for Climate Simulation to the Earth Prediction Innovation Center to the Department of Energy's Energy Exascale Earth System Model.

It won't be a permanent winter, thank goodness. It will end, hopefully, sometime in 2043. Geoengineers will stop seeding the clouds with sulfate as soon as the planet recovers from its mega-drought, extreme heat, and endless wildfires—all of which got so much worse, so much faster, in the early 2030s than even the most dire climate forecasts had predicted. If it had been even just a little less severe, maybe geoengineering would still be off the table. But, "it's this or Mars," or so went the popular joke leading up to the Sun Exit vote. Realistically, only one in ten thousand people have a hope of joining a Mars settlement in their lifetime. For most people, anyway, a ten-year winter on Earth sounds a lot better than trying to settle a new planet 234 million miles away.

In the meantime, humans still have to get their sustainability act together. As you've heard a million times: "Geoengineering is not an alternative to cutting carbon emissions. It's a way to buy precious time." And the YES campaign has promised to use that time wisely. "A ten-year winter will give the world enough time to finish our total transition to clean energy, and once and for all, to end all man-made carbon emissions on Earth." By the time full sun is restored, every country must be 90 percent powered by renewable energy. Goodbye fossil fuels, hello solar plants and wind turbines. Wave energy converters will capture the energy of the oceans' movement. Heat from volcanoes, geysers, and hot springs will be extracted and used for heating. The aviation industry committed to switching to 70 percent food waste, or volatile fatty acids, as jet fuel.[1] Trade sanctions will likely be applied to countries that don't manage to shrink their meat and dairy industries in half. The last holdout countries will be pressured to ban new construction and sales of vehicles that aren't fully powered by renewable energy sources. After all, what's the point of buying a few more years with sun dimming if humanity goes right back to warming the earth?

Will it work? Is it safe? Real volcanic eruptions in the past have cooled the whole earth by as much as three degrees Fahrenheit, for two to three years. In 1815, the eruption of Mount Tambora in Indonesia led to the "year without summer."[2] There were famines from crop loss, disease outbreaks from flooding around the world, and reports of mental health crises from the unrelenting gloom. "But our transportation, food, and humanitarian infrastructure are much better now than they were in the early 1800s," promised the YES campaign. Plans have been made to reinvent agriculture and food chains, to flood-proof high-risk regions, to provide free vitamin D supplements to everyone, and to build a global network of "sun centers" offering artificial light therapy. Everyone will be asked to step up and help others adapt. Enduring ten years of a world without summer is going to take a lot of sacrifice and resilience.

So many emotions are already swirling on social media now that the election results are in. Anger, from people who voted no. Gratitude, from people who voted yes, that humanity made the tough choice to act and not let the planet burn. Panic, that the planet won't be able to feed itself if the cooling actually works. Worry, that there will be unintended health side effects from the sulfate particles. Grief, that children face a decade without natural seasons. An almost manic creative energy, to start remaking communities to help each other get through the next decade. And hope, that if the world can get through the ten-year winter, the planet will be healed.

No more debating. No more campaigning. Sun Exit is a done deal. You've got ten days before the atmospheric seeding begins. Ten days to make plans, get supplies, start figuring out how you can help others, and enjoy the sun while you still can.

CAPTURE YOUR FIRST REACTIONS TO this scenario or talk it over with a friend. Here are some questions you might want to answer in your first journal entry or conversation about this future:

- How would you have voted in the Sun Exit election?
- In one word, what emotion are you feeling as the election results come in?
- What thoughts run through your mind?
- What questions do you have about what happens next?
- How do you predict others will react? Your family? Friends?

- What actions do you take immediately after learning the results?

～～～～～

MOMENT OF CHOICE: Tell a story about how you voted in the Sun Exit election, and your reaction to hearing the results. Record your answers in your journal of this future.

Journaling ideas

Below are some ideas for what you might journal about as you spend ten days in the world of "The Ten-Year Winter." Pick and choose whichever ones you like (or invent your own prompts, guided by your own curiosity and creativity):

1. **Imagine what's happening on social media immediately after the Sun Exit results are announced:** How are people reacting? What topics and hashtags are trending? What information are people asking for? What messages do *you* post? Create your own social media posts, as if you were sharing your thoughts, feelings, and news with friends, family, and followers in 2033.

2. **Tell a story about getting ready for winter:** What do you do in the ten-day period after the announcement of the Sun Exit election results leading up to the first day of sun dimming? Whom do you talk to about what's coming? What do you try to experience while you can? Try to envision the practical things *you* would do, right away, to start readying yourself, your family, or your community for the ten-year winter. Capture the imagined details in your journal: "Today, I . . ."

3. **Describe your new local climate:** To get a better sense of how this scenario would play out for you, look up the seasonal average highs and lows where you live. The new average *high* temperature during the ten-year winter will be whatever the average *low* is today.

(Where I live in California, the new average high in this scenario would be forty-three degrees Fahrenheit in January and fifty-two degrees Fahrenheit in August.) Add to your journal whatever information you find, and any thoughts about your new climate reality. What does it feel like to look ahead to a whole decade of this kind of cooler, wetter, gray weather? What will you miss? What will you do more of? How do you anticipate coping with it?

4. **Make an artifact of the future:** What everyday object might exist in this scenario that doesn't exist today? Maybe it's an informational flyer explaining how solar geoengineering works (you can easily download and print one online today), with a handwritten message across the top: "Science is real! Vote YES on Sun Exit." Maybe it's a sticker on a bottle of vitamin D gummies that reads, "Courtesy of the Solar Radiation Management Global Task Force. Take one daily until 2043." Maybe it's a poster announcing that the public library has a dozen light therapy boxes that can now be used for free fifteen-minute sessions. Maybe it's an ironic T-shirt: "The sun will come out tomorrow in ten years." Maybe it's a couple of leftover campaign signs from the Sun Exit election: "VOTE NO ON SUN EXIT" and "Please don't take my sunshine away." Whatever you imagine existing in the world of "The Ten-Year Winter," try to make it, for real. Then put this new object somewhere you'll see it often, to keep sparking your imagination. Describe what you made, and where you put it, as your journal entry for today.

5. **Be a journalist and report on what's going on in the year 2033:** Imagine how the ten-year winter might affect what people are doing in a specific location. Pick a place where you spend a lot of time in the present day: a park, a school, a workplace, a place of worship, public transportation, a grocery or other store, a gym, a restaurant or coffee shop, a site that you volunteer at. How does the scenario show up in this place? What do you see, hear, feel, encounter, or experience there in the year 2033 that's different from today?

You may find it easier to imagine if you are physically in the location you're thinking about.

6. **Make a list of what people will need and want during a ten-year winter.** As society adjusts to its new reality, and the effects of geoengineering are felt worldwide . . .

- What new problems will be common?
- What help or support will people ask for?
- What mental health challenges will people have?
- What kinds of information will people be seeking out?
- What will be the essential supplies in this scenario?
- What might the world suddenly run short of?
- Who will have a harder time adapting, or who will suffer more, during a ten-year winter?
- What community or group of people might need extra help?

Add this list of new needs and wants to your journal. Feel free to brainstorm any actions or policies that might help. And if you feel inspired, tell a quick story about a new problem or need you or your family might have during a ten-year winter:

7. **Use your unique skills, knowledge, and passions.** Now that you've spent some time in this new world, what do you feel called to do in this future? What could you make or create? What business or service might you start? How would you mobilize your community? What could you teach others to do? What ideas do you have to make this future better?

8. **Write a letter to the present from the middle of the ten-year winter, the year 2038.** Imagine that you've lived through the first half of the global cool-down. (Congratulations!) How are you coping? How is the rest of the world coping? What do you feel when you look ahead to the next five years? Write a letter to your present-day self, or

to a family member or loved one, your town, or the whole world. What do you want them to know about life on a geoengineered planet? How would you encourage them to prepare for a future like this? What words of wisdom or advice can you share from the year 2038?

9. **Go as far into this future as you want.** What's the best possible outcome of a global wintering that you can imagine? What progress has been achieved during these ten years to make the world more sustainable and climate-resilient? What's the good news in this future? How do you celebrate when the technology gets turned off and full sunlight is restored, and what are your biggest hopes for the future now?

Could a future like this really happen? Let's look at some of the signals of change and future forces behind "The Ten-Year Winter."

Geoengineering, once considered a fringe idea, is becoming a serious scientific discipline. The Oxford Geoengineering Programme defines it as "the deliberate large-scale intervention in the Earth's natural systems to counteract climate change."[3] In the past five years, more than 13,500 peer-reviewed scientific papers on geoengineering ideas have been published.[4] Proposals include sending a giant mirror into orbit to reflect sun away from the earth; using genetically engineered *E. coli* bacteria to produce enzymes that convert carbon dioxide into a less harmful substance; and spraying salt water into the clouds above the sea so that they become just a little bigger and brighter, enough to cool specific areas of the planet while leaving the rest unchanged.[5]

The geoengineering idea that's furthest along, with the biggest potential impact, is solar radiation management (SRM), in which sulfate particles are injected into the atmosphere—just as described in "The Ten-Year Winter." It's also called "sun dimming," and it's gaining support among scientific governing bodies. In March 2021, the National Academies of Sciences, Engineering, and Medicine recommended that the US government establish a $200 million federal research program to investigate solar geoengineering.[6]

The Solar Radiation Management Governance Initiative is another signal: it promotes and funds geoengineering research in the most climate-vulnerable countries in the global south. Since 2018, it has funded half a million dollars' worth of SRM research in eight countries: Argentina, Bangladesh, Benin, Indonesia, Iran, Ivory Coast, Jamaica, and South Africa.[7] Meanwhile, Y Combinator, Silicon Valley's largest incubator, is requesting proposals from geoengineering-focused start-ups.[8] And in the summer of 2021, *IEEE Spectrum*, the flagship magazine and website of the IEEE, the world's largest professional organization devoted to engineering and the applied sciences, published an article under the headline: "Engineers: You Can Disrupt Climate Change; Decarbonization, Carbon Capture, and Solar-Radiation Management Will Provide Work for Decades to Come." It's another clear signal that SRM is no longer a radical idea but rather a respectable one with career-building potential.[9]

That said, governments are just barely beginning to try to figure out how to regulate and coordinate geoengineering efforts. In 2015, the UN Convention on Biological Diversity established a moratorium on geoengineering activities, with 196 countries signing on. It cited the moral hazard of one country acting unilaterally to change the planet's climate, as well as potential risks like unintended health and environmental impacts. Crucially, SRM isn't the kind of action you can just "undo" if you don't like the results. But the moratorium made an exception for "small scale scientific research studies that . . . are justified by the need to gather specific scientific data and are subject to a thorough prior assessment of the potential impacts on the environment."[10] The first such study almost got underway in 2020, when Harvard University scientists working on the Stratospheric Controlled Perturbation Experiment planned to launch a test balloon over the northernmost town in Sweden—the kind of balloon that would be needed to inject particles into the atmosphere. The purpose of the experiment was to find out how well the balloon operated in the thinning atmosphere while carrying a heavy load. If it worked, the test balloon would then be used to scatter mineral dust into the atmosphere and create the first

SRM sun-dimming cloud one kilometer long and 100 meters in diameter. But the test faced opposition from environmentalists and was suspended until further research can be carried out on potential risks.[11]

The Carnegie Climate Governance Initiative (C2G), an advocacy group based in New York City, is working to have solar geoengineering discussed again at the UN General Assembly in 2023. It has an eye toward advancing a framework for approving and risk-mitigating larger, strategic experiments. In a statement on stratospheric injection, C2G proposes: "It could be relatively cheap to deploy, and quick acting. But it also brings big risks. And there are no effective global systems in place to govern it. We have no time to waste. The window may be closing to create effective governance that looks at all tools potentially available. . . . We need to learn more and create governance before events overtake us."[12]

I must underscore one important fact: the radical sun-dimming plan described in "The Ten-Year Winter" is far more extreme than what any SRM researchers are proposing today. When I talked to experts in the field, they described a much more modest, less noticeable daily impact on the quality of light and weather. The global temperature swing from well-controlled SRM would, ideally, be closer to one to two degrees, not twenty. In that regard, the 2033 scenario is a significant and fantastical departure from what geoengineers think would actually happen if they could implement their desired plans. In a best-case scenario, SRM wouldn't dramatically cool the planet. It would simply stop the advancing global warming, temporarily, while other long-term sustainability measures were put in place. So when you think about actually preparing yourself for this future, you can dial back the drama of the scenario and imagine a much milder winterization effect. That's the more likely future, as long as geoengineers continue to call for conservative climate intervention.

But it's certainly possible that SRM recommendations will evolve. In 2021, precedent-shattering flooding in Germany and record-breaking heat in the US Pacific Northwest prompted some climate scientists to suggest the field should be less conservative in its forecasts and recommendations. Michael Wehner, who studies extreme weather at Lawrence Berkeley National Laboratory, told the online publication Axios that climate scientists tend to err on the side of being cautious in their "projection and attribution statements," to avoid being seen as alarmist. But as the climate crisis deepens, he said, they may become less conservative.[13]

Of course, even if we *did* think a decade of full-throttled sun dimming might be necessary to save the planet, it likely would take decades longer of climate suffering before humanity agreed to give it a try. In the end, 2033 is probably too early for this scenario to be plausible. But 2043? Or 2053? That's a less ridiculous, at first, idea. If you can stretch your imagination that far out, it's worth playing with the possibilities.

How *would* scientists know when it's finally time to undertake the kind of dramatic geoengineering efforts described in "The Ten-Year Winter"? The climate supercomputers mentioned in the scenario are real, and many more like them are being developed. They can run billions of calculations per second, computing in a few hours what it would take nearly 150 years to compute on an average computer. The planet's climate change can be simulated at an incredible level of detail: every individual twenty-five-kilometer section of the planet's ocean, atmosphere, and land can be represented by a different set of real-world data points. Supercomputers analyze all the interactions among these data points simultaneously, across the entire planet, combined with sophisticated models of temperature change, atmospheric gases, sunlight, and wave movement, among thousands of dynamic and variable factors.[14]

These AI-powered simulations often result in surprising predictions about how Earth's complex systems will interact in the long run, potentially in catastrophic ways. Over the next decade, the public will be increasingly expected to understand and trust the forecasts developed by these supercomputing systems. Just how comfortable will most people be taking real-world action based on hard-to-explain super-computer data models? That remains to be seen. Today, there's a growing resistance to scientific consensus of all kinds, stoked by partisan media and social media conspiracy theories. In the future, supercomputers and their super-forecasts will likely be a new domain for misinformation and partisan divide. *Do you really trust the supercomputer? Are you going to act on its recommendations, even if it contradicts your own intuition?* You can expect these kinds of debates, alongside coordinated efforts from researchers and governments to increase supercomputer trust, to become commonplace in the next decade.

Would geoengineering ever be put to a public vote, as it is in "The Ten-Year Winter"? I don't know of any mechanisms in place yet for a global democratic vote on urgent planetary problems. But more and more, I'm running into experts who want to create new ways to gain the consent of the public for extraordinary scientific actions that could affect the long-term fate of humanity. For example, the "gain-of-function" virus research that some believe may be the source of the original COVID-19 outbreak has raised tricky ethical questions. This type of research genetically alters naturally occurring animal viruses to be more transmissible or more pathogenic, in order to discover what causes novel diseases to emerge in humans. It's supposed to help prevent future pandemics, but ironically it may actually cause them. Is such risky science truly necessary? And given the potential global consequences of a lab accident leading to a new virus outbreak, shouldn't there be a way for the rest of the world to weigh in on whether the potential benefits outweigh the potential harms?[15]

Likewise, CRISPR genetic modification technologies could change what it means to be human. Shouldn't more than just a few scientific bodies or government officials have a chance to weigh in on what kinds of experiments and modifications we feel comfortable with, and which ones go far beyond our moral boundaries?[16]

Or consider the work of the Search for Extraterrestrial Intelligence (SETI) and its offshoot Messaging Extraterrestrial Intelligence. METI, a very small coalition of scientists, has already started sending messages into deep space in the hopes of alerting other life forms in the universe to our existence. But a growing number of astrophysicists and ethicists are calling for a ban on such deep-space messaging—at least until humans can collectively agree on it. They argue that before we intentionally say hello to aliens, we need to answer questions like: Should we reach out to extraterrestrial societies who may be far more advanced than we are, and might not be benevolent? If so, who speaks for our species? And who will decide what to communicate in response to any extraterrestrial messages we receive?[17]

These debates are part of a growing interest in new approaches to global governance of global challenges. Today, we have the United Nations, the International Criminal Court, the World Trade Organization, the World Health Organization, the World Bank. But as both problems and their potential solutions become more planetary in scale, we will need to create new and more inclusive systems for making difficult decisions, and giving the public a say. What other frameworks for political, economic, social, and environmental cooperation can you imagine being created in the coming decades? To be clear, we're not talking about the emergence of a "one-world government," that staple of unfounded conspiracy theories. But surely in the future there will be opportunities for democratic voting beyond national borders—especially when local actions have global consequences.

In 2016, an online project called the Global Vote tested out this very idea by inviting citizens of any country to cast their hypothetical votes in both the UK European Union membership referendum (a.k.a. Brexit) and the US presidential election between Hillary Clinton and Donald Trump. Over one hundred thousand global voters from 149 countries considered how the results might affect their own lives. Then they cast mock online votes in the weeks leading up to the real elections. In the Global Vote's alternate reality, the UK remained in the EU, and Clinton became president.[18]

"The Ten-Year Winter" is perhaps most plausible in the sense that it finds us all living on a fundamentally different planet in ten years and leading entirely different lives as a result. As climate futurist Alex Steffen writes in his newsletter *The Snap Forward*: "When we first see what it means to say that climate change is not an issue, but an era, we can feel dizzy with vertigo. After all, to say we no longer live on the planet we once knew also means we no longer have the lives we once lived."[19] Whatever the actual climate future holds, whether we geoengineer the results or not, it is essential that we practice pre-feeling that vertigo now. Imagining ourselves living through a dramatic scenario like "The Ten-Year Winter" is one way we can learn how to move more confidently forward, into a world that no humans have ever moved through before.

Keep looking for clues to this future. Stay one step ahead of this scenario. You can find experts to follow on social media and discover new signals of change by investigating these search terms:

- "solar radiation management"
- "climate supercomputers"
- "global governance"
- "geoengineering ethics"

YOU'VE JUST EXPLORED THREE POSSIBLE versions of the year 2033: Trash becomes illegal, virtually overnight—and garbage removal as we know it is officially over. The richest countries on earth embark on a ten-year project to carefully, thoughtfully, and equitably move one billion people across borders to climate-safer homes. A global vote approves an unprecedented geoengineering effort, and the whole world voluntarily enters into a decade-long winter.

No futurist would seriously predict these things—if by "predict," we mean to confidently declare something is likely to happen.

Even if we wouldn't predict these futures, we should imagine them anyway.

Simulating the year 2033 isn't about getting ready for a specific crisis. It's about strengthening mental resilience, increasing psychological flexibility, and powering up learned helpfulness for when *any* unthinkable event occurs. The neuroscientist Erik Hoel writes in "The Overfitted Brain," his AI-inspired explanation of why humans dream such strange and hallucinatory things: "It may seem paradoxical, but a dream of flying may actually help you keep your balance running."[20] So, too, mental simulations of impossible futures may help you stay calm, steady, and urgently optimistic in the face of real future shocks.

You might experience an uncanny sense of déjà vu when you get to the real year 2033, having played with "The Road to Zerophoria," "Welcome Party," and "The Ten-Year Winter." Not because those scenarios will happen, but because the feelings of the future will be recognizable to you: The sudden lurching of society into extreme action, because there isn't any other choice. The hope that a solution is at hand, mixed with uncertainty about whether it will really work. The dawning recognition that momentous decisions affecting all human beings should not be made at the whim of a few scientists or elected officials from just one or two countries but rather should be subject to global public discussion and vote. The heavy weight of a long, collective sacrifice. The peace and clarity that come with doing the right things, even when they are hard.

A bit of déjà vu when you face a new challenge is a good thing. That experience of precognition gives you a boost of confidence. *I saw it coming. I felt it coming.* You're more likely to feel prepared to rise to the heroic occasion, ready to help yourself and others.

I've imagined a moment as strange as this.

I've trained for a world as unthinkable as this.

The future, whatever it is, will be different from anything you've lived through before. That's unavoidable. But by playing with these final three scenarios, and the others in this book, you will have imagined strange new worlds of all kinds, seriously and vividly. You will have dreamed them with others. You will have adapted your brain to their wildest possible configurations.

So give yourself the gift of simulating the future. Whatever world you wake up in, you won't get stuck in old ways of doing things. You'll be ready for something different.

CONCLUSION

I go to scale the Future's possibilities! Farewell!
—Henrik Ibsen, playwright

All the mental time travel you've done, all the scenarios you've played with, all the ridiculous, at first, ideas you've come up with, all the signals of change you've collected, all the future forces you've tracked, all the social simulation skills you've practiced—these habits and exercises are the essential building blocks of urgent optimism.

So take a moment now to feel that urgent optimism, nurture it.

Yes, there are great challenges and risks ahead in the next decade. But you have something important to contribute to how we meet them. You're ready to help others through whatever unthinkable events happen next. You have agency and the ability, using your unique talents and skills and life experiences, to create a world you want to live in.

At the beginning of this book, you answered three questions about your future mindset. It's time for you to answer those same three questions again, now with the benefit of your imagination training.

When you look ahead to the next ten years, do you think things will mostly *stay the same and go on as normal*? Or do you expect that most of us will *rethink and reinvent how we do things*? Rate your outlook on a scale of 1 to 10. 1 is almost everything stays the same, 10 is almost everything will be dramatically different.

When you think about how the world and your life will change over the next ten years, are you *mostly worried or mostly optimistic*? Rate your outlook on a scale of 1 to 10. 1 is extremely worried, 10 is extremely optimistic.

How much control or influence do you feel *you* personally have in determining how the world and your life change over the next ten years? Rate your outlook on a scale of 1 to 10. 1 is almost no control or influence, 10 is almost complete control or influence.

Compare your answers now to your original answers, if you made a note of them.

Have any of your numbers gone up? Can you find that "+1" of urgent optimism that I promised you?

Maybe you're expecting at least +1 more dramatic change.

Maybe you're at least +1 more optimistic about how the next decade will turn out.

Maybe you feel at least +1 more in control of what happens next.

Or maybe, I would wager, you're at least +1 on all three counts.

I hope so. I *expect* so. Because you've done more than just imagine the future. You've learned to see in the dark.

We often say the future is bright, as in full of reasons to be hopeful. But the future is also dark, as in unforeseeable, unknowable. And that's a wonderful thing, because if we can't know exactly what the future will be, then it can be anything. We can still change it, we can shape it, we can actively make it whatever we can imagine.

It's a waste of what the future is really good for to try to predict it. The gift of the future is creativity.

As we try to tackle the biggest challenges we face, personally and collectively, we don't want to be limited by what seems normal or reasonable today. That's why we take mental time trips and run social simulations of the future. To create something new, or make a change, we first have to be able to imagine how things can be different.

· · ·

L ET'S TAKE JUST ONE MORE quick trip ten years into the future together.

Imagine that it's Thursday, September 29, 2033. You're logging in to an online book club meeting. It's not just any book club meeting. It's the official *Imaginable* book club, and I'm hosting it.

September 29, 2033, is the day you and I will meet again and say to each other, "Well done. We made it through a decade of unthinkable change. And the change didn't just happen to us. We were anticipating it, shaping it, influencing it, every step of the way."

Envision our future book club meeting as vividly as you can. Where, exactly, might you be when you log in to our meeting? What kind of room or outdoor space? What technology are you using? Who might be with you? What's the weather like? What were you doing today, before the book club? And in one word, how do you feel as you join the meeting?

Whatever you've just imagined, store it as a memory of the future—so we can see how it compares to the actual year 2033. Because there really will be an official book club meeting for *Imaginable* on September 29, 2033, hosted by me, and you really are invited. In fact, you can go right now to iftf.org/imaginable and RSVP. I've created a calendar event for the official *Imaginable* book club, and you can add it to your Google, Apple, or Outlook calendar. Sure, it takes a bit of urgent optimism to plan an event ten years in advance. But it's not just a fun idea; there's a purpose behind it. Having a real, concrete event scheduled for the far future helps you feel more connected to your future self—who I hope will never feel like a stranger to you again.

When we meet again for the book club in 2033, I'll ask you two questions. Maybe you can even start to imagine your answers to these questions now.

What's one "surprising" thing you saw coming and felt ready for?

What's one important change you made, or helped make—in your life, or in your community, or in the world?

I can't wait to hear your stories.

I'll try my best to have some good stories to tell you too.

And if you want to make a difference in the world and in other people's lives between now and then, keep playing with future scenarios. Keep taking those mental time trips. Remember: the phrase "to make a difference" literally means *to make something different*. And as you've proved with your own imagination, the future is a place where anything, or one hundred things, or *everything*, can be different—even things that seem impossible to change today.

ACKNOWLEDGMENTS

It was an honor, a privilege, and a wonderful learning experience to work with Celina Spiegel and Julie Grau on this book. Thank you so much for your vision, brilliant editing, and confidence that we could make this book faster than the future could unfold. Finding a home for this book at the new Spiegel & Grau is the best outcome I could have possibly imagined. You fuel my urgent optimism for the future of books and storytelling!

I am so grateful to all the futurists I have learned from, especially my colleagues at the Institute for the Future, and to everyone who collaborated on the games and simulations described in this book. Special thanks to Kathi Vian and Jamais Cascio, who cocreated Superstruct, and Robert Hawkins and Kiyash Monsef, who cocreated EVOKE.

Thank you also to everyone at Stanford Continuing Studies and Coursera for the opportunity to teach; and to all the students of the How to Think Like a Futurist and Futures Thinking courses and all the players of Superstruct, EVOKE, and other Institute for the Future games and simulations, thank you for sharing your future hopes and worries with me.

I am so lucky to have the guidance of my agent, Chris Parris-Lamb, who is truly the best ally any writer could have. Thank you for the support of everyone at the Gernert Company, especially Rebecca Gardner and Will Roberts, who so successfully brought this book to the wider world. Many thanks also to Susanna Wadeson, Stephanie Duncan, and Andrea Henry at Transworld in the UK, and Caspian Dennis at Abner Stein Ltd.; Jens Dehning and Karen Guddas at DVA Verlag in Germany, and Christian Dittus at the Paul & Peter Fritz Agency; Yan HAN at Cheers Publishing Company in China, and Yu-shiuan Chen and Chang-Chih Tsai at Bardon-Chinese Media Agency; Random House in Korea, and Jackie Yang.

I want to sing the praises of Anne Horowitz, who provided invaluable copyediting and fact checking for this book. Anne, you made the prose stronger, the ideas clearer, and the details more accurate. Thank you!

Thank you, Kelly, for telling me to write this book. Thank you, Sibley and Tilden—you helped me so much, and you were just learning to read and write yourselves this year in Secret Kindergarten! You really do have great ideas for how to prepare for the future! Thank you, Mom and Dad, for all the love and support, and for Secret Kindergarten; thank you, Bibi Paula and Papa Mike; and to Kiyash, this book wouldn't exist without your encouragement and support, especially your brilliant idea to set EVOKE ten years in the future in an upside-down world where ridiculous, at first, ideas are true and anyone can help solve global challenges.

SOURCE NOTES

Introduction

1   Based on Google News search tracking of stories containing the words "unthinkable" and "unimaginable," between March 2020 and September 2021.

2   Joni Sweet, "Why Weddings Are Becoming Superspreader Events," Healthline, November 25, 2020, https://www.healthline.com/health-news /why-weddings-are-becoming-superspreader-events; Cleveland Clinic, "What Are 'Superspreader' Events and Why Should You Avoid Them?," Health Essentials, November 17, 2020, https://health.clevelandclinic.org /coronavirus-covid-19-superspreaders-pandemic/; "How to Recognize Superspreader Events," Nebraska Medicine, November 9, 2020, https:// www.nebraskamed.com/COVID/what-do-covid-19-super-spreader-events -have-in-common.

3   Megan Cerullo, "Nearly Three Million U.S. Women Have Dropped Out of the Labor Force in the Past Year," CBS News, February 5, 2021, https:// www.cbsnews.com/news/covid-crisis-3-million-women-labor-force/.

4   Rabail Chaudhry et al., "A Country Level Analysis Measuring the Impact of Government Actions, Country Preparedness and Socioeconomic Factors on COVID-19 Mortality and Related Health Outcomes," *EClinicalMedicine* 25 (August 1, 2020): 100464, https://doi.org/10.1016/j.eclinm.2020.100464.

5   Bryan Walsh, "SARS Made Hong Kong and Singapore Ready for Coronavirus," Axios, March 25, 2020, https://www.axios.com/sars-hong -kong-and-singapore-ready-for-covid-19-46444868-2550-4d90-ab92 -a3cc90635cb4.html.

6   Karen Attiah, "Africa Has Defied the Covid-19 Nightmare Scenarios. We Shouldn't Be Surprised," *Washington Post*, September 22, 2020, https://www .washingtonpost.com/opinions/2020/09/22/africa-has-defied-covid-19 -nightmare-scenarios-we-shouldnt-be-surprised/.

7   Alvin Toffler, *Future Shock* (New York: Random House, 1970).

8 Arundhati Roy, "The Pandemic Is a Portal," *Financial Times*, April 3, 2020, https://www.ft.com/content/10d8f5e8-74eb-11ea-95fe-fcd274e920ca.

9 Barbara Freeman and Robert Hawkins, "Evoke—Developing Skills in Youth to Solve the World's Most Complex Problems: Randomized Impact Evaluation Findings," World Bank Education, Technology and Innovation: SABER-ICT Technical Paper Series no. 19 (Washington, DC: World Bank, 2017), https://openknowledge.worldbank.org/handle/10986/29167.

Chapter One

1 Elaine Wethington, "Turning Points as Opportunities for Psychological Growth," in *Flourishing: Positive Psychology and the Life Well-Lived*, eds. Corey L. M. Keyes and Jonathan Haidt (Washington, DC: American Psychological Association, 2003), 37–53; Anat Bardi et al., "Value Stability and Change During Self-Chosen Life Transitions: Self-Selection versus Socialization Effects," *Journal of Personality and Social Psychology* 106, no. 1 (January 2014): 131–47, https://doi.org/10.1037/a0034818; Claudia Manzi, Vivian L. Vignoles, and Camillo Regalia, "Accommodating a New Identity: Possible Selves, Identity Change and Well-Being across Two Life-Transitions," *European Journal of Social Psychology* 40, no. 6 (October 2010): 970–84, https://doi.org/10.1002/ejsp.669; Sharan B. Merriam, "How Adult Life Transitions Foster Learning and Development," *New Directions for Adult and Continuing Education* 2005, no. 108 (November 2005): 3–13, https://doi .org/10.1002/ace.193.

2 Hal E. Hershfield and Daniel M. Bartels, "The Future Self," in *The Psychology of Thinking about the Future*, eds. Gabriele Oettingen, A. Timur Sevincer, and Peter M. Gollwitzer (New York: Guilford Press, 2018), 89–109.

3 Joan Meyers-Levy and Rui Zhu, "The Influence of Ceiling Height: The Effect of Priming on the Type of Processing That People Use," *Journal of Consumer Research* 34, no. 2 (August 2007): 174–86, https://doi.org/10.1086 /519146; Trine Plambech and Cecil C. Konijnendijk Van Den Bosch, "The Impact of Nature on Creativity: A Study among Danish Creative Professionals," *Urban Forestry & Urban Greening* 14, no. 2 (2015): 255–63, https://doi.org/10.1016/j.ufug.2015.02.006.

4 Ginger L. Pennington and Neal J. Roese, "Regulatory Focus and Temporal Distance," *Journal of Experimental Social Psychology* 39, no. 6 (November 2003): 563–76, https://doi.org/10.1016/S0022-1031(03)00058-1.

5 Carol Kaufman-Scarborough and Jay D. Lindquist, "Understanding the Experience of Time Scarcity," *Time and Society* 12, no. 2–3 (March 2003): 349–70, https://doi.org/10.1177/0961463X030122011; John De Graaf, ed., *Take Back Your Time: Fighting Overwork and Time Poverty in America* (San Francisco, CA: Berrett-Koehler, 2003).

6 Jane McGonigal, *The American Future Gap* (Institute for the Future: Palo Alto, CA, April 13, 2017), https://www.iftf.org/americanfuturegap.

7   C. Neil Macrae et al., "Turning I into Me: Imagining Your Future Self," *Consciousness and Cognition* 37 (December 2015): 207–13, https://doi.org/10.1016/j.concog.2015.09.009.

8   Ethan Kross, "When the Self Becomes Other," *Annals of the New York Academy of Sciences* 1167, no. 1 (June 2009): 35–40, https://doi.org/10.1111/j.1749-6632.2009.04545.x; Yaacov Trope and Nira Liberman, "Construal-Level Theory of a Psychological Distance," *Psychological Review* 117, no. 2 (April 2010): 440–63, https://doi.org/10.1037/a0018963; Valeria I. Petkova, Mehmoush Khoshnevis, and H. Henrik Ehrsson, "The Perspective Matters! Multisensory Integration in Ego-Centric Reference Frames Determines Full-Body Ownership," *Frontiers in Psychology* 2, no. 35 (March 2011), https://doi.org/10.3389/fpsyg.2011.00035; Emily Pronin and Lee Ross, "Temporal Differences in Trait Self-Ascription: When the Self Is Seen as an Other," *Journal of Personality and Social Psychology* 90, no. 2 (February 2006): 197–209, https://doi.org/10.1037/0022-3514.90.2.197; Cheryl J. Wakslak et al., "Representations of the Self in the Near and Distant Future," *Journal of Personality and Social Psychology* 95, no. 4 (October 2008): 757–73, https://doi.org/10.1037/a0012939; Michael Ross and Fiore Sicoly, "Egocentric Biases in Availability and Attribution," *Journal of Personality and Social Psychology* 37, no. 3 (1979): 322–36, https://doi.org/10.1037/0022-3514.37.3.322.

9   Scott F. Madey and Thomas Gilovich, "Effect of Temporal Focus on the Recall of Expectancy-Consistent and Expectancy-Inconsistent Information," *Journal of Personality and Social Psychology* 65, no. 3 (October 1993): 458–68, https://doi.org/10.1037/0022-3514.65.3.458.

10 Yosef Sokol and Mark Serper, "Temporal Self Appraisal and Continuous Identity: Associations with Depression and Hopelessness," *Journal of Affective Disorders* 208 (January 2017): 503–11, https://doi.org/10.1016/j.jad.2016.10.033.

11 Brandon Schoettle and Michael Sivak, "The Reasons for the Recent Decline in Young Driver Licensing in the United States," *Traffic Inj Prev.* 15, no. 1 (2014): 6–9. doi: 10.1080/15389588.2013.839993. PMID: 24279960.

12 Edie Meade, "American Teens Are Driving Less, and the Reasons Are More Than Economic," January 13, 2020, https://medium.com/swlh/american-teens-are-driving-less-and-the-reasons-are-more-than-economic-4cf6217375a1.

Chapter Two

1   Howard Ehrlichman and Dragana Micic, "Why Do People Move Their Eyes When They Think?," *Current Directions in Psychological Science* 21, no. 2 (March 2012): 96–100, https://doi.org/10.1177/0963721412436810; Joshua M. Ackerman, Christopher C. Nocera, and John A. Bargh, "Incidental Haptic Sensations Influence Social Judgments and Decisions," *Science* 328, no. 5986 (June 2010): 1712–15, https://doi.org/10.1126/science.1189993.

2   David Stawarczyk and Arnaud D'Argembeau, "Neural Correlates of Personal Goal Processing during Episodic Future Thinking and Mind-Wandering: An ALE Meta-Analysis," *Human Brain Mapping* 36, no. 8 (August 2015): 2928–47, https://doi.org/10.1002/hbm.22818.

3   Brittany M. Christian et al., "The Shape of Things to Come: Exploring Goal-Directed Prospection," *Consciousness and Cognition* 22, no. 2 (March 2013): 471–78, https://doi.org/10.1016/j.concog.2013.02.002; Pennington and Roese, "Regulatory Focus and Temporal Distance," 563–76.

4   Emily A. Holmes and Andrew Mathews, "Mental Imagery in Emotion and Emotional Disorders," *Clinical Psychology Review* 30, no. 3 (April 2010): 349–62, https://doi.org/10.1016/j.cpr.2010.01.001; Janie Busby Grant and Neil Wilson, "Manipulating the Valence of Future Thought: The Effect on Affect," *Psychological Reports* 124, no. 1 (February 2020): 227–39, https://doi.org/10.1177/0033294119900346; Torben Schubert et al., "How Imagining Personal Future Scenarios Influences Affect: Systematic Review and Meta-Analysis," *Clinical Psychology Review* 75 (February 2020): 101811, https://doi.org/10.1016/j.cpr.2019.101811.

5   According to a timebound Google Scholar search for scientific papers with the terms "episode future thinking" (4,310) and "episodic foresight" (831), over the period 2000–21.

6   Andrew K. MacLeod, "Prospection, Well-Being and Memory," *Memory Studies* 9, no. 3 (June 2016): 266–74, https://doi.org/10.1177/1750698016645233; Beyon Miloyan, Nancy A. Pachana, and Thomas Suddendorf, "The Future Is Here: A Review of Foresight Systems in Anxiety and Depression," *Cognition and Emotion* 28, no. 5 (2014): 795–810, https://doi.org/10.1080/02699931.2013.863179; Anne Marie Roepke and Martin E. P. Seligman, "Depression and Prospection," *British Journal of Clinical Psychology* 55, no. 1 (March 2016): 23–48, https://doi.org/10.1111/bjc.12087.

7   Cristina M. Atance and Daniela K. O'Neill, "Episodic Future Thinking," *Trends in Cognitive Sciences* 5, no. 12 (December 2001): 533–39, https://doi.org/10.1016/S1364-6613(00)01804-0; David J. Hallford et al., "Psychopathology and Episodic Future Thinking: A Systematic Review and Meta-Analysis of Specificity and Episodic Detail," *Behaviour Research and Therapy* 102 (March 2018): 42–51, https://doi.org/10.1016/j.brat.2018.01.003; Jordi Quoidbach, Alex M. Wood, and Michel Hansenne, "Back to the Future: The Effect of Daily Practice of Mental Time Travel into the Future on Happiness and Anxiety," *Journal of Positive Psychology* 4, no.5 (September 2009): 349–55, https://doi.org/10.1080/17439760902992365; David J. Hallford et al., "Impairments in Episodic Future Thinking for Positive Events and Anticipatory Pleasure in Major Depression," *Journal of Affective Disorders* 260 (January 2020): 536–43, https://doi.org/10.1016/j.jad.2019.09.039; David J. Hallford, Manoj Kumar Sharma, and David W. Austin, "Increasing Anticipatory Pleasure in Major Depression through Enhancing Episodic Future Thinking: A Randomized Single-Case Series Trial," *Journal*

of Psychopathology and Behavioral Assessment 42, no. 4 (January 2020): 751–64, https://doi.org/10.31234/osf.io/9uy42.

8 Jan Peters and Christian Büchel, "Episodic Future Thinking Reduces Reward Delay Discounting through an Enhancement of Prefrontal-Mediotemporal Interactions," *Neuron* 66, no. 1 (April 2010): 138–48, https://doi.org/10 .1016/j.neuron.2010.03.026; Sara O'Donnell, Tinuke Oluyomi Daniel, and Leonard H. Epstein, "Does Goal Relevant Episodic Future Thinking Amplify the Effect on Delay Discounting?," *Consciousness and Cognition* 51 (May 2017): 10–16, https://doi.org/10.1016/j.concog.2017.02.014; Lars M. Göllner et al., "Delay of Gratification, Delay Discounting and Their Associations with Age, Episodic Future Thinking, and Future Time Perspective," *Frontiers in Psychology* 8 (January 2018): 2304, https://doi.org /10.3389/fpsyg.2017.02304; Fania C. M. Dassen et al., "Focus on the Future: Episodic Future Thinking Reduces Discount Rate and Snacking," *Appetite* 96 (January 2016): 327–32, https://doi.org/10.1016/j.appet.2015 .09.032; Jillian M. Rung and Gregory J. Madden, "Experimental Reductions of Delay Discounting and Impulsive Choice: A Systematic Review and Meta-Analysis," *Journal of Experimental Psychology: General* 147, no. 9 (September 2018): 1349–81, https://doi.org/10.1037/xge0000462; Pei-Shan Lee et al., "Using Episodic Future Thinking to Pre-experience Climate Change Increases Pro-environmental Behavior," *Environment and Behavior* 52, no. 1 (January 2020): 60–81, https://doi.org/10.1177 /0013916518790590; Hal E. Hershfield, "Future Self-Continuity: How Conceptions of the Future Self Transform Intertemporal Choice," *Annals of the New York Academy of Sciences* 1235, no. 1 (October 2011): 30–43, https:// doi.org/10.1111/j.1749-6632.2011.06201.x; Brent A. Kaplan, Derek D. Reed, and David P. Jarmolowicz, "Effects of Episodic Future Thinking on Discounting: Personalized Age-Progressed Pictures Improve Risky Long-Term Health Decisions," *Journal of Applied Behavior Analysis* 49, no. 1 (March 2016): 148–69, https://doi.org/10.1002/jaba.277; Jessica O'Neill, Tinuke Oluyomi Daniel, and Leonard H. Epstein, "Episodic Future Thinking Reduces Eating in a Food Court," *Eating Behaviors* 20 (January 2016): 9–13, https://doi.org/10.1016/j.eatbeh.2015.10.002.

9 Reece P. Roberts and Donna Rose Addis, "A Common Mode of Processing Governing Divergent Thinking and Future Imagination," in *The Cambridge Handbook of the Neuroscience of Creativity*, eds. Rex E. Jung and Oshin Vartanian (New York: Cambridge University Press, 2018), 211–30, https:// doi.org/10.1017/9781316556238.013; Daniel L. Schacter, Roland G. Benoit, and Karl K. Szpunar, "Episodic Future Thinking: Mechanisms and Functions," *Current Opinion in Behavioral Sciences* 17 (October 2017): 41–50, https://doi.org/10.1016/j.cobeha.2017.06.002; Jens Förster, Ronald S. Friedman, and Nira Liberman, "Temporal Construal Effects on Abstract and Concrete Thinking: Consequences for Insight and Creative Cognition," *Journal of Personality and Social Psychology* 87, no. 2 (August 2004): 177–89, https://doi.org/10.1037/0022-3514.87.2.177; Fa-Chung Chiu, "Fit

between Future Thinking and Future Orientation on Creative Imagination," *Thinking Skills and Creativity* 7, no. 3 (December 2012): 234–44, https://doi.org/10.1016/j.tsc.2012.05.002.

10   Thomas Suddendorf and Jonathan Redshaw, "The Development of Mental Scenario Building and Episodic Foresight," *Annals of the New York Academy of Sciences* 1296, no. 1 (August 2013): 135–53, https://doi.org/10.1111/nyas.12189.

11   Janani Prabhakar and Judith A. Hudson, "The Development of Future Thinking: Young Children's Ability to Construct Event Sequences to Achieve Future Goals," *Journal of Experimental Child Psychology* 127 (November 2014): 95–109, https://doi.org/10.1016/j.jecp.2014.02.004; Cristina M. Atance, "Future Thinking in Young Children," *Current Directions in Psychological Science* 17, no. 4 (August 2008): 295–98, https://doi.org/10.1111/j.1467-8721.2008.00593.x; Tessa R. Mazachowsky and Caitlin E. V. Mahy, "Constructing the Children's Future Thinking Questionnaire: A Reliable and Valid Measure of Children's Future-Oriented Cognition," *Developmental Psychology* 56, (2020): 756–72, http://www.brockdmclab.com/uploads/3/7/8/2/37821089/mazachowsky_mahy_cftq_final.pdf.

12   Beyon Miloyan and Kimberley A. McFarlane, "The Measurement of Episodic Foresight: A Systematic Review of Assessment Instruments," *Cortex* 117 (August 2019): 351–70, https://doi.org/10.1016/j.cortex.2018.08.018.

Chapter Three

1   Michael Dimock and Richard Wike, "America Is Exceptional in the Nature of Its Political Divide," Pew Research Center, November 13, 2020, https://www.pewresearch.org/fact-tank/2020/11/13/america-is-exceptional-in-the-nature-of-its-political-divide/.

2   John R. Allen, "Reconciling and Healing America," Brookings Institute, February 8, 2021, https://www.brookings.edu/president/reconciling-and-healing-america/; Rachel Kleinfeld and Aaron Sobel, "7 Ideas to Reduce Political Polarization. And Save America from Itself," Carnegie Endowment for International Peace, July 23, 2020, https://carnegieendowment.org/2020/07/23/7-ideas-to-reduce-political-polarization.-and-save-america-from-itself-pub-82365; Lee De-Wit, Sander Van Der Linden, and Cameron Brick, "What Are the Solutions to Political Polarization?" *Greater Good Magazine*, July 2, 2019, https://greatergood.berkeley.edu/article/item/what_are_the_solutions_to_political_polarization.

3   Kristina Cooke, David Rhode, and Ryan McNeil, "The Undeserving Poor," *Atlantic*, December 20, 2012, https://www.theatlantic.com/business/archive/2012/12/the-undeserving-poor/266507/.

4   NASA Jet Propulsion Laboratory, "Sentry: Earth Impact Monitoring," Center for Near Earth Object Studies, https://cneos.jpl.nasa.gov/sentry/.

5   Francesco Bassetti, "Environmental Migrants: Up to 1 Billion by 2050," Foresight: The CMCC Observatory on Climate Policies and Futures, May

22, 2019, https://www.climateforesight.eu/migrations-inequalities /environmental-migrants-up-to-1-billion-by-2050/; John Englander, *Moving to Higher Ground: Rising Sea Level and the Path Forward* (Boca Raton, Florida: Science Bookshelf, 2021); Chi Xu et al., "Future of the Human Climate Niche," *Proceedings of the National Academy of Sciences* 117, no. 21 (May 2020): 11350–355, https://doi.org/10.1073/pnas.1910114117.

6   Clara Chaisson, "Fossil Fuel Air Pollution Kills One in Five People," Natural Resources Defense Council, February 19, 2021, https://www.nrdc .org/stories/fossil-fuel-air-pollution-kills-one-five-people; Nita Bhalla, "U.N. Warns of Millions of Premature Deaths by 2050 Due to Environmental Damage," Reuters, March 13, 2019, https://www.reuters.com/article/us -global-environment-pollution/u-n-warns-of-millions-of-premature-deaths -by-2050-due-to-environmental-damage-idUSKCN1QU2WD.

7   United Nations, "Global Issues: Water," https://www.un.org/en/global -issues/water; World Health Organization, "Fact Sheets: Road Traffic Injuries," https://www.who.int/news-room/fact-sheets/detail/road-traffic -injuries.

8   World Health Organization, "WHO releases country estimates on air pollution exposure and health impact." September 27, 2016, https://www .who.int/news/item/27-09-2016-who-releases-country-estimates-on-air -pollution-exposure-and-health-impact.

Chapter Four

1   Jessica Hamzelou, "Exclusive: World's First Baby Born with New '3 Parent' Technique," *New Scientist*, September 27, 2016, https://www.newscientist .com/article/2107219-exclusive-worlds-first-baby-born-with-new-3-parent -technique/#ixzz6rkYu5Kjl.

2   Shami Sivasubramanian, "Children with Two Genetic Fathers? It's Possible," SBS, July 14, 2016, https://www.sbs.com.au/topics/science /humans/article/2016/07/13/children-two-genetic-fathers-its-possible.

3   Maya Wei-Haas, "Same-Sex Mouse Parents Give Birth via Gene Editing," *National Geographic*, October 11, 2018, https://www.nationalgeographic.com /science/article/news-gene-editing-crispr-mice-stem-cells.

4   Elie Dolgin, "Making Babies: How to Create Human Embryos with No Egg or Sperm," *New Scientist*, April 11, 2018, https://www.newscientist.com /article/mg23831730-300-making-babies-how-to-create-human-embryos -with-no-egg-or-sperm/#ixzz6rkam5LuX.

5   Gina Kolata, "Scientists Grow Mouse Embryos in a Mechanical Womb," *New York Times*, March 17, 2021, https://www.nytimes.com/2021/03/17 /health/mice-artificial-uterus.html.

6   Elizabeth Chloe Romanis, "Artificial Womb Technology and the Frontiers of Human Reproduction: Conceptual Differences and Potential Implications," *Journal of Medical Ethics* 44, no. 11 (November 2018): 751–75, http://dx.doi.org/10.1136/medethics-2018-104910.

7   Shanna H. Swan with Stacey Colino, *Count Down: How Our Modern World Is Threatening Sperm Counts, Altering Male and Female Reproductive Development, and Imperiling the Future of the Human Race* (New York: Simon & Schuster, 2021).

8   Lixiao Zhou et al., "PM2.5 Exposure Impairs Sperm Quality through Testicular Damage Dependent on NALP3 Inflammasome and miR-183 /96/182 cluster Targeting FOXO1 in Mouse," *Ecotoxicology and Environmental Safety* 169 (March 2019): 551–63, https://doi.org/10.1016/j.ecoenv.2018 .10.108.

9   NASA, "NASA Announces US Industry Partnerships to Advance Moon, Mars Technology," press release no. 19-063, July 30, 2019, https://www .nasa.gov/press-release/nasa-announces-us-industry-partnerships-to -advance-moon-mars-technology.

10   Elon Musk, March 25, 2019, on Twitter as @elonmusk. https://twitter.com /elonmusk/status/1110329210332053504.

11   Justin Bachman, "New Space Race Shoots for Moon and Mars on a Budget: QuickTake," *Washington Post*, February 21, 2021, https://www.washingtonpost .com/business/new-space-race-shoots-for-moon-and-mars-on-a-budget -quicktake/2021/02/18/661c1c0a-7243-11eb-8651-6d3091eac63f_story .html; Dave Mosher, "Elon Musk Says SpaceX Is on Track to Launch People to Mars within 6 Years—Here's the Full Timeline of His Plans to Populate the Red Planet," Business Insider, November 2, 2018, https:// www.businessinsider.com/elon-musk-spacex-mars-plan-timeline-2018-10; "UAE Aims to Establish Human Settlement on Mars by 2117," SpaceWatch.Global, February 2017, https://spacewatch.global/2017/02 /uae-aims-establish-human-settlement-mars-2117/.

12   "Governance Futures Lab—Reinventing Civic Society," Institute for the Future, accessed August 27, 2021, https://www.iftf.org/govfutures/.

13   Alan Taylor, "Mars in the Gobi Desert," *Atlantic*, April 17, 2019, https:// www.theatlantic.com/photo/2019/04/photos-mars-gobi-desert/587353/.

14   Jason Pontin, "The Genetics (and Ethics) of Making Humans Fit for Mars," *Wired*, August 7, 2018, https://www.wired.com/story/ideas-jason-pontin -genetic-engineering-for-mars/.

15   Swan, *Count Down*, 2–3.

16   Nathaniel Scharping, "Sperm Counts Are on the Decline. Is the Human Race in Danger?," *Discover*, May 1, 2012, https://www.discovermagazine .com/health/sperm-counts-are-on-the-decline-is-the-human-race-in-danger.

17   Marion Boulicault et al., "The Future of Sperm: A Biovariability Framework for Understanding Global Sperm Count Trends," *Human Fertility* (2021): 1–15, https://doi.org/10.1080/14647273.2021.1917778.

18   "High-Impact-Low-Probability (HILP)," Asset Insights, 2013, https://www .assetinsights.net/Glossary/G_High_Impact_Low_Probability_HILP.html.

19   "Our Vision, Mission Statement and Key Aims," Frozen Ark, accessed August 27, 2021, https://www.frozenark.org/vision-and-mission-statement.

20   "Millennium Seed Bank," Royal Botanic Gardens Kew, accessed August 27, 2021, https://www.kew.org/wakehurst/whats-at-wakehurst/millennium

-seed-bank; Karin Kloosterman, "The Blueprint for Noah's Coral Ark," *Green Prophet*, November 17, 2020, https://www.greenprophet.com/2020/11/living-coral-biobank/.

21 Angus Fletcher, *Wonderworks: The 25 Most Powerful Inventions in the History of Literature* (New York: Simon & Schuster, 2021), 22–24.

Chapter Five

1 Sam Byford, "Fitbit Will Supply 'Free' Trackers to Singapore's Public Health Program," *Verge*, August 22, 2019, https://www.theverge.com/2019/8/22/20827860/fitbit-singapore-healthcare-free-fitness-tracker-deal.

2 Heidi Shierholz, "Low Wages and Few Benefits Mean Many Restaurant Workers Can't Make Ends Meet," August 21, 2014, *Economic Policy Institute*, https://www.epi.org/publication/restaurant-workers/.

3 One Fair Wage and Raise, *Roadmap to Reimagine Restaurants: A New Path Forward after COVID-19*, May 2020, http://www.highroadrestaurants.org/wp-content/uploads/2020/06/RoadmapToReimagineRestaurants.pdf.

4 Emma Belcher, "Transforming Our Nuclear Future with Ridiculous Ideas," *Bulletin of the Atomic Scientists* 76, no. 6 (2020): 325–30, https://doi.org/10.1080/00963402.2020.1846420.

5 Jamais Cascio and N Square, "Crossroads: Five Scenarios for the End of Nuclear Weapons" *Journal of Nuclear Security Innovation* (March 20, 2015): 1–21, https://issuu.com/nsquarecollab/docs/nsquare_crossroads.

6 Elisabeth Eaves, "Why Is America Getting a New $100 Billion Nuclear Weapon?," *Bulletin of the Atomic Scientists*, February 8, 2021, https://thebulletin.org/2021/02/why-is-america-getting-a-new-100-billion-nuclear-weapon/; Kingston Reif, "CBO: Nuclear Arsenal to Cost $1.2 Trillion," Arms Control Association, December 2017, https://www.armscontrol.org/act/2017-12/news/cbo-nuclear-arsenal-cost-12-trillion.

7 Terence Babwah et al., "Exercise Prescriptions Given by GPs to Sedentary Patients Attending Chronic Disease Clinics in Health Centres—the Effect of a Very Brief Intervention to Change Exercise Behavior," *Journal of Family Medicine and Primary Care* 7, no. 6 (November 2018): 1446–51, https://doi.org/10.4103/jfmpc.jfmpc_84_18; Falk Müller-Riemenschneider et al., "Long-Term Effectiveness of Interventions Promoting Physical Activity: A Systematic Review," *Preventive Medicine* 47, no. 4 (October 2008): 354–68, https://doi.org/10.1016/j.ypmed.2008.07.006.

8 Scott H. Kollins et al., "A Novel Digital Intervention for Actively Reducing Severity of Paediatric ADHD (STARS-ADHD): A Randomised Controlled Trial," *Lancet Digital Health* 2, no. 4 (April 2020): e168–78, https://doi.org/10.1016/S2589-7500(20)30017-0.

9 Sujata Gupta, "Microbiome: Puppy Power," *Nature* 543 (March 30, 2017): S48–S49, https://doi.org/10.1038/543S48a.

10 Genevieve F. Dunton and Margaret Schneider, "Perceived Barriers to Walking for Physical Activity," *Preventing Chronic Disease* 3, no. 4 (October

2006), https://www.ncbi.nlm.nih.gov/pmc/articles/PMC1779280/; Kristen A. Copeland et al., "Flip Flops, Dress Clothes, and No Coat: Clothing Barriers to Children's Physical Activity in Child-Care Centers Identified from a Qualitative Study," *International Journal of Behavioral Nutrition and Physical Activity* 6, no. 74 (2009), https://doi.org/10.1186/1479-5868 -6-74.

11 Katie Garfield et al., *Mainstreaming Produce Prescriptions: A Policy Strategy Report* (Center for Health Law and Policy Innovation of Harvard Law School and the Rockefeller Foundation, March 2021), 1, https://www.chlpi.org/wp -content/uploads/2013/12/Produce-RX-March-2021.pdf.

12 Yujin Lee et al., "Cost-Effectiveness of Financial Incentives for Improving Diet and Health through Medicare and Medicaid: A Microsimulation Study," *PLOS Medicine* 16, no. 3 (March 2019): e1002761, https://doi.org /10.1371/journal.pmed.1002761.

Chapter Six

1 Tate and Lyle Sugars and the Future Laboratory, "Cakes of the Future: The Full Report," Tate and Lyle, accessed August 27, 2021, https://www .wearetateandlylesugars.com/cakes-future-full-report.

2 Peter Holley, "Meet 'Mindar,' the Robotic Buddhist Priest," *Washington Post*, June 22, 2019, https://www.washingtonpost.com/technology/2019/08 /22/introducing-mindar-robotic-priest-that-some-are-calling-frankenstein -monster/.

3 Sam Keen, *Fire in the Belly: On Being a Man* (New York: Bantam Books, 1991), 132.

4 Alan Watts, *The Wisdom of Insecurity: A Message for an Age of Anxiety*, 2nd ed. (New York: Vintage, 2011), 43.

5 Beth DeCarbo, "Drones Are Poised to Reshape Home Design," *Wall Street Journal*, December 5, 2020, https://www.wsj.com/articles/drones-are -poised-to-reshape-home-design-11607194801.

6 Ben Turner, "'Pizzly' Bear Hybrids Are Spreading across the Arctic Thanks to Climate Change," Live Science, April 23, 2021, *https://www.livescience .com/pizzly-bear-hybrids-created-by-climate-crisis.html*; Moises Velasquez-Manoff, "Should You Fear the Pizzly Bear?" *New York Times*, August 14, 2014, https://www.nytimes.com/2014/08/17/magazine/should-you-fear-the -pizzly-bear.html.

7 Chi Xu et al., "Future of the Human Climate Niche," *Proceedings of the National Academy of Sciences* 117, no. 21 (May 2020): 11350–355; https://doi .org/10.1073/pnas.1910114117.

8 Eric Kaufmann, "'It's the Demography, Stupid': Ethnic Change and Opposition to Immigration," *Political Quarterly* 85, no. 3 (October 2014): 267–76, https://doi.org/10.1111/1467-923X.12090; James Laurence, Katharina Schmid, and Miles Hewstone, "Ethnic Diversity, Ethnic Threat, and Social Cohesion: (Re)-evaluating the Role of Perceived Out-Group

Threat and Prejudice in the Relationship between Community Ethnic Diversity and Intra-community Cohesion," *Journal of Ethnic and Migration Studies* 45, no. 3 (2019): 395–418, https://doi.org/10.1080/1369183X .2018.1490638; Sjoerdje van Heerden and Didier Ruedin, "How Attitudes towards Immigrants Are Shaped by Residential Context: The Role of Ethnic Diversity Dynamics and Immigrant Visibility," *Urban Studies* 56, no. 2 (2019): 317–34, https://doi.org/10.1177/0042098017732692; Lindsay Pérez Huber, "'Make America Great Again!': Donald Trump, Racist Nativism and the Virulent Adherence to White Supremacy amid US Demographic Change," *Charleston Law Review* 10 (2016): 215–48; Brandon Hunter-Pazzara, "The Possessive Investment in Guns: Towards a Material, Social, and Racial Analysis of Guns," *Palgrave Communications* 6, no. 79 (2020), https://doi.org/10.1057/s41599-020-0464-x.

9   "World Radio Day 2013: Statistics on Youth," UNESCO, accessed August 27, 2021, http://www.unesco.org/new/en/unesco/events/prizes-and -celebrations/celebrations/international-days/world-radio-day-2013 /statistics-on-youth/; "United States Demographic Statistics," Infoplease, accessed August 27, 2021, https://www.infoplease.com/us/census /demographic-statistics.

10   Oxfam International, "Climate Fuelled Disasters Number One Driver of Internal Displacement Globally Forcing More Than 20 Million People a Year from Their Homes," December 2, 2019, https://www.oxfam.org/en /press-releases/forced-from-home-eng.

11   Alex Wigglesworth, "A Generation of Seabirds Was Wiped Out by a Drone in O.C. Scientists Fear for Their Future," *Los Angeles Times,* June 7, 2021, https://www.latimes.com/california/story/2021-06-07/thousands-of-eggs -abandoned-after-drone-crash-at-orange-county-nature-reserve.

12   Zach Urness, "Drones Are Harassing Nesting Birds on the Oregon Coast. There's a Plan to Stop Them," *Statesman Journal,* June 30, 2021, https:// www.statesmanjournal.com/story/news/2021/06/30/oregon-coast-drones -nesting-birds-endangered-oystercatcher/5351369001/.

Chapter Seven

1   Joe Myers, "19 of the World's 20 Youngest Countries Are in Africa," World Economic Forum, August 30, 2019, https://www.weforum.org/agenda /2019/08/youngest-populations-africa/.

2   Jay L. Zagorsky, "Why Are Fewer People Getting Married?" *Conversation,* June 1, 2016, https://theconversation.com/why-are-fewer-people-getting -married-60301.

3   Dane Rivera, "All the Fast Food Chains and Grocers Serving Plant-Based Meat in 2021," Uproxx, February 14, 2021, https://uproxx.com/life/fast -food-chains-serving-plant-based-meat-2021/.

4   "Pandemials: Youth in an Age of Lost Opportunity," World Economic Forum, accessed August 27, 2021, https://reports.weforum.org/global

-risks-report-2021/pandemials-youth-in-an-age-of-lost-opportunity/; *The Global Risks Report 2021*, 16th ed. (Geneva, Switzerland: World Economic Forum, 2021), 88, http://www3.weforum.org/docs/WEF_The_Global _Risks_Report_2021.pdf.

5   Jamie Ducharme, "COVID-19 Is Making America's Loneliness Epidemic Even Worse," *Time*, May 8, 2020, https://time.com/5833681/loneliness -COVID-19/; Philip Jefferies and Michael Ungar, "Social Anxiety in Young People: A Prevalence Study in Seven Countries," *PLOS One* 15, no. 9 (2020): e0239133, https://doi.org/10.1371/journal.pone.0239133; "The Impact of Covid-19 on Young People with Mental Health Needs," Summer 2020 Survey, Young Minds, accessed August 27, 2012, https://youngminds.org .uk/about-us/reports/coronavirus-impact-on-young-people-with-mental -health-needs/.

6   Haim Omer and Nahman Alon, "The Continuity Principle: A Unified Approach to Disaster and Trauma," *American Journal of Community Psychology* 22, no. 2 (April 1994): 273–87, https://doi.org/10.1007/BF02506866.

7   Mark Murphy, "Leadership IQ Study: Mismanagement, Inaction Among the Real Reasons Why CEOs Get Fired," Cision, June 21, 2005, http:// www.prweb.com/releases/2005/06/prweb253465.htm.

8   Ann Garrison, "Should California Secede? An Interview with David Swanson," *Free Press*, February 12, 2017, https://freepress.org/article /should-california-secede-interview-david-swanson.

9   John S. Carroll, "The Effect of Imagining an Event on Expectations for the Event: An Interpretation in Terms of the Availability Heuristic," *Journal of Experimental Social Psychology* 14, no. 1 (January 1978): 88–96, https://doi .org/10.1016/0022-1031(78)90062-8.

10   Steven J. Sherman et al., "Imagining Can Heighten or Lower the Perceived Likelihood of Contracting a Disease: The Mediating Effect of Ease of Imagery," *Personality and Social Psychology Bulletin* 11, no. 1 (1985): 118–127, https://doi.org/10.1177/0146167285111011.

11   Other highly cited studies in this area of research include: Richard J. Crisp and Rhiannon N. Turner, "Can Imagined Interactions Produce Positive Perceptions?: Reducing Prejudice through Simulated Social Contact," *American Psychologist* 64, no. 4 (May 2009): 231–40, https://doi.org/10.1037 /a0014718; Maryanne Garry et al., "Imagination Inflation: Imagining a Childhood Event Inflates Confidence That It Occurred," *Psychonomic Bulletin and Review* 3, no. 2 (1996): 208–14, https://doi.org/10.3758/BF03212420; Scott Eidelman, Christian S. Crandall, and Jennifer Pattershall, "The Existence Bias," *Journal of Personality and Social Psychology* 97, no. 5 (November 2009): 765–75, https://doi.org/10.1037/a0017058; Hazel Markus and Paula Nurius, "Possible Selves," *American Psychologist* 41, no. 9 (September 1986): 954–69, https://doi.org/10.1037/0003-066X.41.9.954; Shelley E. Taylor et al., "Harnessing the Imagination: Mental Simulation, Self-Regulation, and Coping," *American Psychologist* 53, no. 4 (1998): 429–39, https://doi.org/10 .1037/0003-066X.53.4.429; Gillian Butler and Andrew Mathews, "Cognitive

Processes in Anxiety," *Advances in Behaviour Research and Therapy* 5, no. 1 (1983): 51–62, https://doi.org/10.1016/0146-6402(83)90015-2.

12 Lisa Bulganin and Bianca C. Wittmann, "Reward and Novelty Enhance Imagination of Future Events in a Motivational-Episodic Network," *PLoS ONE* 10, no. 11 (November 2015): e0143477, https://doi.org/10.1371/journal.pone.0143477.

13 Pema Chödrön, "Smile at Fear," *The Best Buddhist Writing 2012* (Boulder, Colorado: Shambhala, 2012).

14 Ibid.

15 National Intelligence Council, *Global Trends 2040: A More Contested World*, March 2021, https://www.dni.gov/files/ODNI/documents/assessments/GlobalTrends_2040.pdf.

16 Recommendations for learning more about these future forces: Antonio Regalado, "The Next Act for Messenger RNA Could Be Bigger Than COVID Vaccines," *MIT Technology Review*, February 5, 2021, https://www.technologyreview.com/2021/02/05/1017366/messenger-rna-vaccines-COVID-hiv/; Bill McKibben, "Renewable Energy Is Suddenly Startlingly Cheap," *New Yorker*, April 28, 2021, https://www.newyorker.com/news/annals-of-a-warming-planet/renewable-energy-is-suddenly-startlingly-cheap; Kaitlin Love, "Majority Favors Social Progress over Economic Growth in the Wake of the Coronavirus Pandemic," Ipsos, September 10, 2020, https://www.ipsos.com/en-us/news-polls/Majority-Favors-Social-Progress-over-Economic-Growth-in-the-Wake-of-the-Coronavirus-Pandemic; Matthew Shaer, "Soon, Your Doctor Could Print a Human Organ on Demand," *Smithsonian Magazine*, May 2015, https://www.smithsonianmag.com/innovation/soon-doctor-print-human-organ-on-demand-180954951/; Amos Zeeberg, "Bricks Alive! Scientists Create Living Concrete," *New York Times*, January 15, 2020, https://www.nytimes.com/2020/01/15/science/construction-concrete-bacteria-photosynthesis.html; Ron Lieber, "How to Get Your Money to Those Who Need It More Than You," *New York Times*, May 30, 2020, https://www.nytimes.com/2020/05/30/your-money/philanthropy-charity-giving-coronavirus.html; Azeem Azhar, "The Future of Meat," April 21, 2021, in *Exponential View*, season 5, episode 26, 37:56, *Harvard Business Review* Podcasts, https://hbr.org/podcast/2021/04/the-future-of-meat; Gov.UK, "PM Launches Government's First Loneliness Strategy," press release, Prime Minister's Office, October 15, 2018, https://www.gov.uk/government/news/pm-launches-governments-first-loneliness-strategy; Katie Warren, "Japan Has Appointed a 'Minister of Loneliness' after Seeing Suicide Rates in the Country Increase for the First Time in 11 Years," Insider, February 22, 2021, https://www.insider.com/japan-minister-of-loneliness-suicides-rise-pandemic-2021-2; Udacity Team, "The Future of the Workforce: Hiring Will Be Based on Skills Rather Than Degrees," Udacity, October 20, 2020, https://www.udacity.com/blog/2020/10/the-future-of-the-workforce-hiring-will-be-based-on-skills-rather-than-degrees.html; Sean Gallagher, "It's Time to Digitally Transform

Community College," EdSurge, August 12, 2020, https://www.edsurge
.com/news/2020-08-12-it-s-time-to-digitally-transform-community-college;
Nicholas St. Fleur, Chloe Williams, and Charlie Wood, "Can We Live to
200?," *New York Times*, April 27, 2021, https://www.nytimes.com/interactive
/2021/04/27/magazine/longevity-timeline.html.

17 William Crumpler, "How Accurate Are Facial Recognition Systems—and
Why Does It Matter?," Center for Strategic and International Studies, April
14, 2020, https://www.csis.org/blogs/technology-policy-blog/how-accurate
-are-facial-recognition-systems—-and-why-does-it-matter.

18 James Clayton, "Facial Recognition Beats the COVID-Mask Challenge,"
BBC News, March 25, 2021, *https://www.bbc.com/news/technology-56517033*.

19 "Facial Recognition Fails on Race, Government Study Says," BBC News,
December 20, 2019, https://www.bbc.com/news/technology-50865437;
Alex Najibi, "Racial Discrimination in Face Recognition Technology,"
Special Edition: Science Policy and Social Justice (blog), Harvard University,
October 24, 2020, https://sitn.hms.harvard.edu/flash/2020/racial
-discrimination-in-face-recognition-technology/.

20 Will Knight, "Europe's Proposed Limits on AI Would Have Global
Consequences," *Wired*, April 20, 2021, https://www.wired.com/story
/europes-proposed-limits-ai-global-consequences/.

21 PimEyes, accessed August 27, 2021, https://pimeyes.com/en.

22 XPRIZE, accessed August 27, 2021, https://www.xprize.org/.

23 African Leadership University. https://www.alueducation.com/.

24 Jane McGonigal, *Reality Is Broken: Why Games Make Us Better and How They
Can Change the World* (New York: Penguin, 2011).

Chapter Eight

1 Hal E. Hershfield, "Future Self-Continuity: How Conceptions of the Future
Self Transform Intertemporal Choice," *Annals of the New York Academy of
Sciences* 1235, no. 1 (October 2011): 30–43, https://doi.org/10.1111/j
.1749-6632.2011.06201.x.

2 Pengmin Qin and Georg Northoff, "How Is Our Self Related to Midline
Regions and the Default-Mode Network?," *Neuroimage* 57, no. 3 (August
2011): 1221–33, https://doi.org/10.1016/j.neuroimage.2011.05.028.

3 Ed Yong, "Self-Control Is Just Empathy with Your Future Self," *Atlantic*,
December 6, 2016, https://www.theatlantic.com/science/archive/2016
/12/self-control-is-just-empathy-with-a-future-you/509726/; Cynthia Lee,
"The Stranger Within: Connecting with Our Future Selves," UCLA
Newsroom, April 9, 2015, https://newsroom.ucla.edu/stories/the-stranger
-within-connecting-with-our-future-selves.

4 Yosef Sokol and Mark Serper, "Development and Validation of a Future
Self-Continuity Questionnaire: A Preliminary Report," *Journal of Personality
Assessment* 102, no. 5 (May 2019): 677–88, https://doi.org/10.1080/002238
91.2019.1611588.

5   Adam Smith, "Cognitive Empathy and Emotional Empathy in Human Behavior and Evolution," *Psychological Record* 56, no. 1 (2006): 3–21, https://doi.org/10.1007/BF03395534; Simone G. Shamay-Tsoory, Judith Aharon-Peretz, and Daniella Perry, "Two Systems for Empathy: A Double Dissociation between Emotional and Cognitive Empathy in Inferior Frontal Gyrus versus Ventromedial Prefrontal Lesions," *Brain* 132, no. 3 (March 2009): 617–27, https://doi.org/10.1093/brain/awn279.

6   Andrew Reiljan, "'Fear and Loathing across Party Lines' (Also) in Europe: Affective Polarisation in European Party Systems," *European Journal of Political Research* 59, no. 2 (May 2020): 376–96, https://doi.org/10.1111/1475-6765.12351; Shanto Iyengar et al., "The Origins and Consequences of Affective Polarization in the United States," *Annual Review of Political Science* 22 (2019): 129–46, https://doi.org/10.1146/annurev-polisci-051117-073034; Shanto Iyengar, Gaurav Sood, and Yphtach Lelkes, "Affect, Not Ideology: A Social Identity Perspective on Polarization," *Public Opinion Quarterly* 76, no. 3 (September 2012): 405–31, https://doi.org/10.1093/poq/nfs038.

7   Levi Boxell et al., "Affective Polarization Did Not Increase during the Coronavirus Pandemic," working paper no. 28036 (October 2020), National Bureau of Economic Research, https://doi.org/10.3386/w28036.

8   Sebastian Jungkunz, "Political Polarization During the COVID-19 Pandemic," *Frontiers in Political Science* 3 (March 2021): 622512, https://doi.org/10.3389/fpos.2021.622512; Hunt Allcott et al., "Polarization and Public Health: Partisan Differences in Social Distancing During the Coronavirus Pandemic," *Journal of Public Economics* 191 (November 2020): 104254, https://doi.org/10.1016/j.jpubeco.2020.104254; Christos Makridis and Jonathan T. Rothwell, "The Real Cost of Political Polarization: Evidence from the COVID-19 Pandemic," June 29, 2020, available at SSRN: http://dx.doi.org/10.2139/ssrn.3638373; Ariel Fridman, Rachel Gershon, and Ayelet Gneezy, "COVID-19 and Vaccine Hesitancy: A Longitudinal Study," *PloS One* 16, no. 4 (April 2021): e0250123, https://doi.org/10.1371/journal.pone.0250123; Wändi Bruine de Bruin, Htay-Wah Saw, and Dana P. Goldman, "Political Polarization in US Residents' COVID-19 Risk Perceptions, Policy Preferences, and Protective Behaviors," *Journal of Risk and Uncertainty* 61 (November 2020): 177–94, https://doi.org/10.1007/s11166-020-09336-3.

9   Mark H. Davis, "Empathy, Compassion, and Social Relationships," in *The Oxford Handbook of Compassion Science*, eds. Emma M. Seppälä et al. (New York: Oxford University Press, 2017), 299–316; Deborah R. Richardson et al., "Empathy as a Cognitive Inhibitor of Interpersonal Aggression," *Aggressive Behavior* 20, no. 4 (1994): 275–89, https://doi.org/10.1002/1098-2337(1994)20:4<275::AID-AB2480200402>3.0.CO;2-4; Minet De Wied, Susan J. T. Branje, and Wim H. J. Meeus, "Empathy and Conflict Resolution in Friendship Relations among Adolescents," *Aggressive Behavior* 33, no. 1 (January 2007): 48–55, https://doi.org/10.1002/ab.20166.

10 William J. Chopik, Ed O'Brien, and Sara H. Konrath, "Differences in Empathic Concern and Perspective Taking across 63 Countries," *Journal of Cross-Cultural Psychology* 48, no. 1 (January 2017): 23–38, https://doi.org/10.1177/0022022116673910.

11 Ellen Barry, "Young Rural Women in India Chase Big-City Dreams," *New York Times*, September 24, 2016, https://www.nytimes.com/2016/09/25/world/asia/bangalore-india-women-factories.html.

12 Nicholas Epley, "Be Mindwise: Perspective Taking vs. Perspective Getting," *Behavioral Scientist*, April 16, 2014, https://behavioralscientist.org/be-mindwise-perspective-taking-vs-perspective-getting/; Tal Eyal, Mary Steffel, and Nicholas Epley, "Perspective Mistaking: Accurately Understanding the Mind of Another Requires Getting Perspective, Not Taking Perspective," *Journal of Personality and Social Psychology* 114, no. 4 (April 2018): 547–71, https://doi.org/10.1037/pspa0000115.

13 C. Daniel Batson, Shannon Early, and Giovanni Salvarani, "Perspective Taking: Imagining How Another Feels versus Imagining How You Would Feel," *Personality and Social Psychology Bulletin* 23, no. 7 (July 1997): 751–58, https://doi.org/10.1177/0146167297237008.

14 Zaheer Cassim, "Cape Town Could Be the First Major City in the World to Run Out of Water," *USA Today*, January 19, 2018, https://www.usatoday.com/story/news/world/2018/01/19/cape-town-could-first-major-city-run-out-water/1047237001/; Richard Poplak, "What's Actually Behind Cape Town's Water Crisis," Atlantic, February 15, 2018, https://www.theatlantic.com/international/archive/2018/02/cape-town-water-crisis/553076/; Geoffrey York, "Cape Town Residents Become 'Guinea Pigs for the World' with Water-Conservation Campaign," *Globe and Mail*, March 8, 2018, https://www.theglobeandmail.com/news/world/cape-town-residents-become-guinea-pigs-for-the-world-with-water-conservationcampaign/article38257004/; Patricia de Lille, "Day Zero: When Is It, What Is It, and How Can We Avoid It?," City of Cape Town, November 15, 2017, https://www.capetown.gov.za/Media-and-news/Day%20Zero%20when%20is%20it,%20what%20is%20it,%20and%20how%20can%20we%20avoid%20it.

15 Christian Alexander, "Cape Town's 'Day Zero' Water Crisis, One Year Later," Bloomberg CityLab, April 12, 2019, https://www.bloomberg.com/news/articles/2019-04-12/looking-back-on-cape-town-s-drought-and-day-zero.

16 Global statistics gathered and reported by Access Now, as part of its #KeepItOn campaign to raise awareness of, and action against, government communications shutdowns. AccessNow.org, March 21 2021.

17 Tom Wheeler, "Could Donald Trump Claim a National Security Threat to Shut Down the Internet?," Brookings TechTank, June 25, 2020, https://www.brookings.edu/blog/techtank/2020/06/25/could-donald-trump-claim-a-national-security-threat-to-shut-down-the-internet/.

18 Berhan Taye, *Shattered Dreams and Lost Opportunities: A Year in the Fight to #KeepItOn* (New York: Access Now, March 2021), 28, https://www

.accessnow.org/cms/assets/uploads/2021/03/KeepItOn-report-on-the
-2020-data_Mar-2021_3.pdf.

19 "S. 4646 (116th): Unplug the Internet Kill Switch Act of 2020," GovTrack, updated November 27, 2020, https://www.govtrack.us/congress/bills/116 /s4646/summary.

20 David E. Sanger, Clifford Krauss, and Nicole Perlroth, "Cyberattack Forces a Shutdown of a Top U.S. Pipeline," *New York Times*, May 8, 2021, https:// www.nytimes.com/2021/05/08/us/cyberattack-colonial-pipeline.html; Frances Robles and Nicole Perlroth, "'Dangerous Stuff': Hackers Tried to Poison Water Supply of Florida Town," *New York Times*, February 8, 2021, https://www.nytimes.com/2021/02/08/us/oldsmar-florida-water-supply -hack.html; Laura Dyrda, "The 5 Most Significant Cyberattacks in Healthcare for 2020," Becker's Health IT, December 14, 2020, https:// www.beckershospitalreview.com/cybersecurity/the-5-most-significant -cyberattacks-in-healthcare-for-2020.html.

21. Scott Ikeda, "Amazon Sidewalk's 'Smart Neighborhood' Vision Raises Serious Privacy Concerns," CPO Magazine, June 29, 2021, https://www .cpomagazine.com/data-privacy/amazon-sidewalks-smart-neighborhood -vision-raises-serious-privacy-concerns/.

22 Linda Howard, "Amazon Alexa Features You Should Turn Off Right Now to Protect Your Privacy," *UK Daily Record*, July 12, 2021, https://www .dailyrecord.co.uk/lifestyle/money/amazon-alexa-features-to-disable -24516564.

23 Christina Tobacco, "Consumer Lawsuit Filed against Amazon over New 'Sidewalk' Network," Law Street, July 9, 2021, https://lawstreetmedia.com /tech/consumer-lawsuit-filed-against-amazon-over-new-sidewalk-network/.

24 "The Digital Currencies That Matter," *Economist*, May 8, 2021, https:// www.economist.com/leaders/2021/05/08/the-digital-currencies-that -matter.

25 Cory Doctorow (@doctorow), "A key idea from sf is 'all laws are local, and no law knows how local it is,'" Twitter, May 16, 2021, 12:03 p.m., https:// twitter.com/doctorow/status/1393960274256822273.

Chapter Nine

1 Christine Caine (@ChristineCaine), "Sometimes when you're in a dark place you think you've been buried when you've actually been planted. You will bring forth life!!," Twitter, February 28, 2015, 6:27 p.m., https://twitter .com/ChristineCaine/status/571814033780682752?s=20.

2 Lawrence G. Calhoun and Richard G. Tedeschi, eds., *Handbook of Posttraumatic Growth: Research and Practice* (New York: Routledge, 2014).

3 Kai Yuan et al., "Prevalence of Posttraumatic Stress Disorder after Infectious Disease Pandemics in the Twenty-First Century, Including COVID-19: A Meta-Analysis and Systematic Review," *Molecular Psychiatry* (February 2021): https://doi.org/10.1038/s41380-021-01036-x.

4   Ibid.

5   Robert H. Pietrzak, Jack Tsai, Steven M. Southwick, "Association of
Symptoms of Posttraumatic Stress Disorder with Posttraumatic
Psychological Growth among US Veterans During the COVID-19
Pandemic," *JAMA Network Open* 4, no. 4 (April 2021): e214972, https://doi
.org/10.1001/jamanetworkopen.2021.4972.

6   Leah Zaidi, "Building Brave New Worlds: Science Fiction and Transition
Design" (master's thesis, Ontario College of Art and Design, 2017), 2,
https://www.researchgate.net/publication/321886159_Building_Brave
_New_Worlds_Science_Fiction_and_Transition_Design.

7   Zora Neale Hurston, *Moses, Man of the Mountain* (1939; repr., New York:
Harper Perennial, 1991), 194.

8   Marina Gorbis and Kathi Vian, "Post-COVID-19 Futures: What Can We
Build after the Global Pandemic?," Urgent Futures, Institute for the Future,
May 6, 2020, https://medium.com/institute-for-the-future/post-COVID
-19-futures-what-can-we-build-after-the-global-pandemic-3cac9515ef20.

9   "After the Pandemic: A Deeper Disease," Institute for the Future, September
15, 2020, https://www.iftf.org/whathappensnext/.

10   Molly Kinder and Martha Ross, "Reopening America: Low-Wage Workers
Have Suffered Badly from COVID-19 so Policymakers Should Focus on
Equity," Brookings Institute, June 23, 2020, https://www.brookings.edu
/research/reopening-america-low-wage-workers-have-suffered-badly-from
-COVID-19-so-policymakers-should-focus-on-equity/; Alyssa Fowers,
"Concerns about Missing Work May Be a Barrier to Coronavirus
Vaccination," *Washington Post*, May 27, 2021, https://www.washingtonpost
.com/business/2021/05/27/time-off-vaccine-workers/.

11   Oxfam International, *The Inequality Virus: Bringing Together a World Torn Apart
by Coronavirus through a Fair, Just and Sustainable Economy* (Cowley, Oxford:
Oxfam GB, January 2021), https://oxfamilibrary.openrepository.com
/bitstream/handle/10546/621149/bp-the-inequality-virus-250121-en.pdf.

12   International Labor Organization, *ILO Monitor: COVID-19 and the World of
Work*, 5th ed., June 30, 2020, https://www.ilo.org/wcmsp5/groups/public
/---dgreports/---dcomm/documents/briefingnote/wcms_749399.pdf;
Courtney Connley, "Women's Labor Force Participation Rate Hit a 33-Year
Low in January, According to New Analysis," CNBC Make It, February 8,
2021, https://www.cnbc.com/2021/02/08/womens-labor-force
-participation-rate-hit-33-year-low-in-january-2021.html; Catarina Saraiva,
"Women Leaving Workforce Again Shows Uneven U.S. Jobs Recovery,"
Bloomberg News, May 7, 2021, https://www.bloomberg.com/news/articles
/2021-05-07/women-leaving-workforce-again-shows-uneven-u-s-jobs
-recovery.

13   Till von Wachter, "Lost Generations: Long-Term Effects of the COVID-19
Crisis on Job Losers and Labour Market Entrants, and Options for Policy,"
Fiscal Studies 41, no. 3 (September 2020): 549–90, https://doi.org/10.1111
/1475-5890.12247; Kenneth Burdett, Carlos Carrillo-Tudela, and Melvyn

Coles, "The Cost of Job Loss," *Review of Economic Studies* 87, no. 4 (July 2020): 1757–98, https://doi.org/10.1093/restud/rdaa014.

14 "The Impact of COVID-19 on Student Equity and Inclusion: Supporting Vulnerable Students during School Closures and School Re-openings," OECD, November 19, 2020, https://www.oecd.org/coronavirus/policy -responses/the-impact-of-COVID-19-on-student-equity-and-inclusion -supporting-vulnerable-students-during-school-closures-and-school-re -openings-d593b5c8/.

15 "UN Report Finds COVID-19 Is Reversing Decades of Progress on Poverty, Healthcare and Education," United Nations Department of Economic and Social Affairs, July 7, 2020, https://www.un.org/development/desa/en /news/sustainable/sustainable-development-goals-report-2020.html; "America's Huge Stimulus Is Having Surprising Effects on the Poor," *Economist*, July 6, 2020, https://www.economist.com/united-states/2020 /07/06/americas-huge-stimulus-is-having-surprising-effects-on-the-poor; Ian Goldin and Robert Muggah, "COVID-19 Is Increasing Multiple Kinds of Inequality. Here's What We Can Do about It," World Economic Forum, October 9, 2020, https://www.weforum.org/agenda/2020/10/covid-19 -is-increasing-multiple-kinds-of-inequality-here-s-what-we-can-do-about-it/.

16 Davide Furceri et al., "COVID-19 Will Raise Inequality If Past Pandemics Are a Guide," VoxEu, Centre for Economic Policy Research, May 8, 2020, https://voxeu.org/article/COVID-19-will-raise-inequality-if-past -pandemics-are-guide.

17 Goldin and Muggah, "COVID-19 Is Increasing Multiple Kinds of Inequality," https://www.weforum.org/agenda/2020/10/covid-19-is -increasing-multiple-kinds-of-inequality-here-s-what-we-can-do-about-it/.

18 Jack P. Shonkoff, Natalie Slopen, and David R. Williams, "Early Childhood Adversity, Toxic Stress, and the Impacts of Racism on the Foundations of Health," *Annual Review of Public Health* 42 (April 2021): 115–34, https://doi .org/10.1146/annurev-publhealth-090419-101940; David R. Williams, Jourdyn A. Lawrence, and Brigette A. Davis, "Racism and Health: Evidence and Needed Research," *Annual Review of Public Health* 40 (April 2019): 105– 25, https://doi.org/10.1146/annurev-publhealth-040218-043750; Ralph Catalano, "The Health Effects of Economic Insecurity," *American Journal of Public Health* 81, no. 9 (September 1991): 1148–52, https://doi.org/10.2105 /AJPH.81.9.1148; Barry Watson and Lars Osberg, "Healing and/or Breaking? The Mental Health Implications of Repeated Economic Insecurity," *Social Science and Medicine* 188 (September 2017): 119–27, https://doi.org/10.1016/j.socscimed.2017.06.042; Evelyn Kortum, Stavroula Leka, and Tom Cox, "Psychosocial Risks and Work-Related Stress in Developing Countries: Health Impact, Priorities, Barriers and Solutions," *International Journal of Occupational Medicine and Environmental Health* 23, no. 3 (2010): 225–38, https://doi.org/10.2478/v10001-010-0024-5.

19 Alice Walker, *In Search of Our Mothers' Gardens: Womanist Prose* (New York: Houghton Mifflin Harcourt, 2004), 40.

20 World Health Organization, *Everybody's Business: Strengthening Health Systems to Improve Health Outcomes* (Geneva, Switzerland: WHO Press, 2007), 2, https:// www.who.int/healthsystems/strategy/everybodys_business.pdf.

21 "Health Workforce," World Health Organization, accessed July 7, 2020, https://www.who.int/health-topics/health-workforce#tab=tab_1; Jenny X. Liu et al., "Global Health Workforce Labor Market Projections for 2030," *Human Resources for Health* 15, no. 11 (February 2017), https://doi.org/10 .1186/s12960-017-0187-2.

22 "The Mental Health of Healthcare Workers in COVID-19," Mental Health America (MHA), accessed August 27, 2021, https://mhanational.org /mental-health-healthcare-workers-COVID-19.

23 Ehui Adovor et al., "Medical Brain Drain: How Many, Where and Why?," *Journal of Health Economics* 76 (March 2021): 102409, https://doi.org/10 .1016/j.jhealeco.2020.102409; Natalie Sharples, "Brain Drain: Migrants Are the Lifeblood of the NHS, It's Time the UK Paid for Them," *Guardian*, January 6, 2015, https://www.theguardian.com/global-development -professionals-network/2015/jan/06/migrants-nhs-compensation-global -health-brain-drain.

24 "Universal Health Coverage (UHC)," World Health Organization, April 1, 2021, https://www.who.int/news-room/fact-sheets/detail/universal -health-coverage-(uhc); Megan Leonhardt, "Nearly 1 in 4 Americans Are Skipping Medical Care Because of the Cost," CNBC Make It, March 12, 2020, https://www.cnbc.com/2020/03/11/nearly-1-in-4-americans-are -skipping-medical-care-because-of-the-cost.html.

25 Emma Frage and Michael Shields, "World Has Entered Stage of 'Vaccine Apartheid'—WHO Head," Reuters, May 17, 2021, https://www.reuters .com/business/healthcare-pharmaceuticals/world-has-entered-stage -vaccine-apartheid-who-head-2021-05-17/; "Low-Income Countries Have Received Just 0.2 Per Cent of All COVID-19 Shots Given," United Nations, April 9, 2021, https://news.un.org/en/story/2021/04/1089392.

26 "The Lancet: Latest Global Disease Estimates Reveal Perfect Storm of Rising Chronic Diseases and Public Health Failures Fuelling COVID-19 Pandemic," Institute for Health Metrics and Evaluation, October 15, 2020, http://www.healthdata.org/news-release/lancet-latest-global-disease -estimates-reveal-perfect-storm-rising-chronic-diseases-and; George Luber and Michael McGeehin, "Climate Change and Extreme Heat Events," *American Journal of Preventive Medicine* 35, no. 5 (November 2008): 429–35, https://doi.org/10.1016/j.amepre.2008.08.021.

27 Sriram Shamasunder et al., "COVID-19 Reveals Weak Health Systems by Design: Why We Must Re-make Global Health in This Historic Moment," *Global Public Health* 15, no. 7 (April 2020): 1083–89, https://doi.org/10.1080 /17441692.2020.1760915; Lawrence O. Gostin, Suerie Moon, and Benjamin Mason Meier, "Reimagining Global Health Governance in the Age of COVID-19," *American Journal of Public Health* 110, no. 11 (November 2020): 1615–19, https://doi.org/10.2105/AJPH.2020.305933; "COVID-19

Is Showing Us How to Improve Health Systems—Sometimes by Disrupting
Them," Bill & Melinda Gates Foundation, https://www.gatesfoundation.
org/ideas/articles/health-systems-coronavirus-workers-women; Stuart M.
Butler, "After COVID-19: Thinking Differently about Running the Health
Care System," *JAMA* 323, no. 24 (June 2020): 2451–51, https://doi.org
/10.1001/jama.2020.8484; Axel Baur et al., "Healthcare Providers:
Preparing for the Next Normal after COVID-19," McKinsey & Company,
May 8, 2020, https://www.mckinsey.com/industries/healthcare-systems
-and-services/our-insights/healthcare-providers-preparing-for-the-next
-normal-after-covid-19.

28 Jill Kimball, "U.S. Is Polarizing Faster Than Other Democracies, Study
Finds," Brown University, January 21, 2020, https://www.brown.edu/news
/2020-01-21/polarization.

29 Leonardo Bursztyn et al., "Misinformation during a Pandemic" (working
paper no. 2020-44, Becker Friedman Institute for Economics, University of
Chicago, September 2020), https://bfi.uchicago.edu/wp-content/uploads
/BFI_WP_202044.pdf.

30 Danielle Ivory, Lauren Leatherby, and Robert Gebeloff, "Least Vaccinated
U.S. Counties Have Something in Common: Trump Voters," *New York
Times*, April 17, 2021, https://www.nytimes.com/interactive/2021/04/17
/us/vaccine-hesitancy-politics.html.

31 "Most Approve of National Response to COVID-19 in 14 Advanced
Economies," Pew Research Report, August 27, 2020, https://www
.pewresearch.org/global/wp-content/uploads/sites/2/2020/08/PG_2020
.08.27_Global-Coronavirus_FINAL.pdf.

32 Simon Ostrovsky and Charles Lyons, "Inequities in Care, Misinformation
Fuel COVID Deaths among Poor, Indigenous Brazilians," PBS News Hour,
May 25, 2021, https://www.pbs.org/newshour/show/inequities-in-care
-misinformation-fuel-COVID-deaths-among-poor-indigenous-brazilians;
Ruth Sherlock, "Migrants Are Among the Worst Hit by COVID-19 in
Saudi Arabia and Gulf Countries," NPR, May 5, 2020, https://www.npr
.org/sections/coronavirus-live-updates/2020/05/05/850542938/migrants
-are-among-the-worst-hit-by-COVID-19-in-saudi-arabia-and-gulf-countries;
Pete Pattisson and Roshan Sedhai, "Qatar's Migrant Workers Beg for Food
as COVID-19 Infections Rise," *Guardian*, May 7, 2020, https://www
.theguardian.com/global-development/2020/may/07/qatars-migrant
-workers-beg-for-food-as-covid-19-infections-rise; Ian Austen, "The
Coronavirus Is Raging in Manitoba, Hitting Indigenous People Especially
Hard," *New York Times*, May 26, 2021, https://www.nytimes.com/2021/05
/26/world/the-coronavirus-is-raging-in-manitoba-hitting-indigenous
-people-especially-hard.html.

33 Rashawn Ray, "Why Are Blacks Dying at Higher Rates from COVID-19?"
Brookings Institute, April 9, 2020, https://www.brookings.edu/blog/fixgov
/2020/04/09/why-are-blacks-dying-at-higher-rates-from-COVID-19/;
"Why Have Black and South Asian People Been Hit Hardest by

COVID-19?," UK Office for National Statistics, December 14, 2020, https://
www.ons.gov.uk/peoplepopulationandcommunity/healthandsocialcare
/conditionsanddiseases/articles/whyhaveblackandsouthasianpeoplebeen
hithardestbyCOVID19/2020-12-14; Alissa Greenberg, "How the Stress
of Racism Can Harm Your Health—and What That Has to Do with
COVID-19," PBS, July 14, 2020, https://www.pbs.org/wgbh/nova/article
/racism-stress-covid-allostatic-load/.

34 William J. Hall et al., "Implicit Racial/Ethnic Bias Among Health Care
Professionals and Its Influence on Health Care Outcomes: A Systematic
Review," *American Journal of Public Health* 105, no. 12 (2015): e60–76.

35 Sonu Bhaskar et al., "At the Epicenter of COVID-19—the Tragic Failure of
the Global Supply Chain for Medical Supplies," *Frontiers in Public Health* 24,
no. 8 (November 2020): 562882, https://doi.org/10.3389/fpubh.2020
.562882.

36 Peter S. Goodman and Niraj Chokshi, "How the World Ran Out of
Everything," *New York Times*, June 1, 2021, https://www.nytimes.com/2021
/06/01/business/coronavirus-global-shortages.html.

37 Diane Brady, "COVID-19 and Supply-Chain Recovery: Planning for the
Future," October 9, 2020, in *The McKinsey Podcast*, 29:09, https://www
.mckinsey.com/business-functions/operations/our-insights/COVID-19
-and-supply-chain-recovery-planning-for-the-future.

38 Sarah Gibbens, "These 5 Foods Show How Coronavirus Has Disrupted
Supply Chains," *National Geographic*, May 19, 2020, https://www
.nationalgeographic.com/science/article/covid-19-disrupts-complex-food
-chains-beef-milk-eggs-produce; "Food Security and COVID-19," World
Bank, August 17, 2021, https://www.worldbank.org/en/topic/agriculture
/brief/food-security-and-covid-19.

39 "Burn-Out an 'Occupational Phenomenon': International Classification of
Diseases," World Health Organization, May 28, 2019, https://www.who
.int/news/item/28-05-2019-burn-out-an-occupational-phenomenon
-international-classification-of-diseases.

40 Jennifer Moss, "Beyond Burned Out," *Harvard Business Review*, February 10,
2021, https://hbr.org/2021/02/beyond-burned-out; Anitra Lesser, "The
Impacts of COVID on Rising Burnout Rates," Employers Council, October
23, 2020, https://blog.employerscouncil.org/2020/10/23/the-impacts-of
-COVID-on-rising-burnout-rates/.

41 "Long Working Hours Increasing Deaths from Heart Disease and Stroke:
WHO, ILO," World Health Organization, May 17, 2021, https://www
.who.int/news/item/17-05-2021-long-working-hours-increasing-deaths
-from-heart-disease-and-stroke-who-ilo.

42 Maria Cristina Rulli et al., "Land-Use Change and the Livestock Revolution
Increase the Risk of Zoonotic Coronavirus Transmission from Rhinolophid
Bats," *Nature Food* 2 (June 2021): 409–16, https://doi.org/10.1038/s43016
-021-00285-x; "Coronavirus, Climate Change, and the Environment: A
Conversation on COVID-19 with Dr. Aaron Bernstein, Director of Harvard

Chan C-CHANGE," Harvard T. H. Chan School of Public Health, accessed August 27, 2021, https://www.hsph.harvard.edu/c-change /subtopics/coronavirus-and-climate-change/.

43 Institute of Medicine and National Research Council, *Potential Risks and Benefits of Gain-of-Function Research: Summary of a Workshop* (Washington, DC: National Academies Press, 2015), https://doi.org/10.17226/21666.

44 Andrea Pozzer et al., "Regional and Global Contributions of Air Pollution to Risk of Death from COVID-19," *Cardiovascular Research* 116, no. 14 (December 2020): 2247–53, https://doi.org/10.1093/cvr/cvaa288.

45 Dan Walton and Maarten van Aalst, *Climate-Related Extreme Weather Events and COVID-19: A First Look at the Number of People Affected by Intersecting Disasters* (Geneva, Switzerland: International Federation of Red Cross and Red Crescent Societies, September 2020), https://media.ifrc.org/ifrc/wp -content/uploads/2020/09/Extreme-weather-events-and-COVID-19-V4 .pdf.

46 James M. Shultz, Craig Fugate, and Sandro Galea, "Cascading Risks of COVID-19 Resurgence during an Active 2020 Atlantic Hurricane Season," *JAMA* 324, no. 10 (August 2020): 935–36, https://doi.org/10.1001/jama .2020.15398.

47 Shanto Iyengar and Douglas S. Massey, "Scientific Communication in a Post-Truth Society," *Proceedings of the National Academy of Sciences* 116, no. 16 (2019): 7656-61, https://doi.org/10.1073/pnas.1805868115.

48 Kathi Vian, "The Deeper, Longer Disease," Institute for the Future, June 10, 2020, https://medium.com/institute-for-the-future/the-deeper-longer -disease-13e859de2d16.

49 "Superstruct Superthreat: Quarantine," Institute for the Future, video, 3:59, September 21, 2008, https://www.youtube.com/watch?v=r _HxFSY581U&t=2s.

50 Ed Yong, "Long-Haulers Are Redefining COVID-19," *Atlantic*, August 19, 2020, https://www.theatlantic.com/health/archive/2020/08/long-haulers -COVID-19-recognition-support-groups-symptoms/615382/; Shayna Skarf, "Denied Treatment, Some COVID Long-Haulers Could Become Lifelong-Haulers," STAT, January 28, 2021, https://www.statnews.com /2021/01/28/stop-ignoring-undocumented-long-haulers/; Judy George, "Study Puts Numbers to 'Long COVID' Duration, Prevalence—High Frequency of Debility Lasting for Months," MedPage Today, February 19, 2021, https://www.medpagetoday.com/infectiousdisease/COVID19 /91270; Alvin Powell, "A Pandemic That Endures for COVID Long-Haulers," *Harvard Gazette*, April 13, 2021, https://news.harvard.edu /gazette/story/2021/04/harvard-medical-school-expert-explains-long -COVID/; "One in 20 People Likely to Suffer from 'Long COVID', but Who Are They?," Zoe COVID Study, October 21, 2020, https://covid .joinzoe.com/post/long-covid.

51 Allison DeLong, Mayla Hsu, and Harriet Kotsoris, "Estimation of Cumulative Number of Post-Treatment Lyme Disease Cases in the US,

2016 and 2020," *BMC Public Health* 19, no. 352 (April 2019), https://doi
.org/10.1186/s12889-019-6681-9.

52 Sarah Fraser, "The Toxic Power Dynamics of Gaslighting in Medicine,"
Canadian Family Physician 67, no. 5 (May 2021): 367–68, https://doi.org
/10.46747/cfp.6705367; Maya Dusenbery, *Doing Harm: The Truth about How
Bad Medicine and Lazy Science Leave Women Dismissed, Misdiagnosed, and Sick* (New
York: HarperCollins, 2018); Rita Rubin, "As Their Numbers Grow,
COVID-19 'Long Haulers' Stump Experts," *JAMA* 324, no. 14 (September
2020): 1381–83, https://doi.org/10.1001/jama.2020.17709; Monica
Verduzco-Gutierrez et al., "In This for the Long Haul: Ethics, COVID-19,
and Rehabilitation," *PM&R* 13, no. 3 (March 2021): 325–32, https://doi
.org/10.1002/pmrj.12554.

53 "How Many People Have ME/CFS?," American Myalgic
Encephalomyelitis and Chronic Fatigue Syndrome Society, accessed August
27, 20121, https://ammes.org/how-many-people-have-mecfs/; Chris
Ponting, "Analysis of Data from 500,000 Individuals in UK Biobank
Demonstrates an Inherited Component to ME/CFS," *ME/CFS Research*
(blog), June 11, 2018, https://mecfsresearchreview.me/2018/06/11/analysis
-of-data-from-500000-individuals-in-uk-biobank-demonstrates-an-inherited
-component-to-me-cfs.

54 "Building Imagination Infrastructure to Shape Better Futures," Skoll World
Forum, video, 49:56, April 15, 2021, https://www.youtube.com/watch?v
=gUQYwWwwUyw.

55 Definition adapted from *Merriam-Webster*, s.v. "howl (v.)," accessed August 27,
2021, http://www.merriam-webster.com/dictionary/howl.

56 Paulina Cachero, "When the Clock Strikes 8, Some Americans in Isolation
Are Howling in the Night for Health Workers Battling the Coronavirus,"
Insider, April 1, 2020, https://www.insider.com/americans-in-isolation-howl
-8-night-health-workers-solidarity-2020-4.

57 Will Schmitt, "North Bay Residents Howl into the Night to Release Stress,
Support First Responders during Coronavirus Shutdown," *Press Democrat*,
April 10, 2020, https://www.pressdemocrat.com/article/news/north-bay
-residents-howl-into-the-night-to-release-stress-support-first-re/?sba=AAS.

58 Emiliana R. Simon-Thomas et al., "The Voice Conveys Specific Emotions:
Evidence from Vocal Burst Displays," *Emotion* 9, no. 6 (December 2009):
838–46, https://doi.org/10.1037/a0017810; Marc D. Pell et al., "Preferential
Decoding of Emotion from Human Non-linguistic Vocalizations versus
Speech Prosody," *Biological Psychology* 111 (October 2015): 14–25, https://
doi.org/10.1016/j.biopsycho.2015.08.008; A. S. Cowen et al., "Mapping 24
Emotions Conveyed by Brief Human Vocalization," *American Psychologist 74*,
no. 6 (September 2019): 698–712, https://doi.org/10.1037/amp0000399;
Disa A. Sauter et al., "Cross-Cultural Recognition of Basic Emotions
through Nonverbal Emotional Vocalizations," *Proceedings of the National
Academy of Sciences* 107, no. 6 (February 2010): 2408–12, https://doi.org
/10.1073/pnas.0908239106.

59 Ocean Vuong, "Ocean Vuong: A Life Worthy of Our Breath," interview by
Krista Tippett, *On Being*, April 30, 2020, https://onbeing.org/programs
/ocean-vuong-a-life-worthy-of-our-breath/#transcript.

60 Walidah Imarisha, "To Build a Future without Police and Prisons, We Have
to Imagine It First," OneZero, October 22, 2020, https://onezero.medium
.com/black-lives-matter-is-science-fiction-how-envisioning-a-better-future
-makes-it-possible-5e14d35154e3.

Chapter Ten

1 M. E. Seligman and S. F. Maier, "Failure to Escape Traumatic Shock,"
Journal of Experimental Psychology 74, no. 1 (May 1967): 1–9, https://doi.org
/10.1037/h0024514.

2 William R. Miller, Robert A. Rosellini, and Martin E. P. Seligman,
"Depression: Learned Helplessness and Depression," in *Psychopathology:
Experimental Models*, eds. J. D. Maser and M. E. P. Seligman (New York: W.
H. Freeman, 1977), 104–30; Lauren B. Alloy and Lyn Y. Abramson,
"Learned Helplessness, Depression, and the Illusion of Control," *Journal of
Personality and Social Psychology* 42, no. 6 (1982): 1114–26, https://doi.org
/10.1037/0022-3514.42.6.1114; Steven F. Maier, "Learned Helplessness
and Animal Models of Depression," *Progress in Neuro-Psychopharmacology and
Biological Psychiatry* 8, no. 3 (1984): 435–46, https://doi.org/10.1016
/S0278-5846(84)80032-9.

3 Steven F. Maier and Martin E. P. Seligman, "Learned Helplessness at Fifty:
Insights from Neuroscience," *Psychological Review* 123, no. 4 (July 2016): 349–
67, https://doi.org/10.1037/rev0000033; Shelley E. Taylor et al.,
"Biobehavioral Responses to Stress in Females: Tend-and-Befriend, Not
Fight-or-Flight," *Psychological Review* 107, no. 3 (July 2000): 411–29, https://
doi.org/10.1037/0033-295X.107.3.411.

4 For a detailed study of the psychological impacts of gaming on frequent
gamers' mindset, everyday behaviors, social interaction styles, and
problem-solving styles, see Jane McGonigal, *Reality Is Broken: Why Games
Make Us Better and How They Can Change the World* (New York: Penguin, 2011)
and Jane McGonigal, *SuperBetter: The Power of Living Gamefully* (New York:
Penguin, 2015).

5 Jari Kätsyri et al., "Just Watching the Game Ain't Enough: Striatal fMRI
Reward Responses to Successes and Failures in a Video Game during Active
and Vicarious Playing," *Frontiers in Human Neuroscience* 7, no. 278 (June 2013),
https://doi.org/10.3389/fnhum.2013.00278.

6 Joseph Campbell, *The Hero with a Thousand Faces*, 3rd ed. (Novato, California:
New World Library, 2008), 41–48.

7 "Italians Record Messages for 'Themself from 10 Days Ago' during
Coronavirus Pandemic," A Thing By, video, 3:30, March 15, 2020, https://
www.youtube.com/watch?v=o_cImRzKXOs&feature=youtu.be&fbclid
=IwAR1FCqCPhC0TvWY1KV--hl3uxKTLywTx8QDwQHRHPf5eR8

wDsk-RpqWWBOk; Ignacio Escolar, "Opinion: I'm in Spain, but This Is a Message from the Future," *Washington Post*, March 16, 2020, https://www .washingtonpost.com/opinions/2020/03/16/im-spain-this-is-message -future/; Jane McGonigal, "During a Pandemic, We Urgently Need to Stretch Our Imagination," *Urgent Futures*, Institute for the Future, March 18, 2020, https://medium.com/institute-for-the-future/during-a-pandemic -we-all-need-to-stretch-our-imagination-a9295cfcd1f8.

8   Ida Garibaldi, "Hello from Italy. Your Future Is Grimmer Than You Think," *Washington Post*, March 17, 2020, https://www.washingtonpost.com /outlook/2020/03/17/hello-italy-your-future-is-grimmer-than-you-think/.

9   Tara Mohr, "You-Shaped Hole," Tara Mohr (website), accessed August 27, 2021, https://www.taramohr.com/inspirational-poetry/you-shaped-hole-2/.

10   "Alpha-Gal Syndrome: The Epidemic You've Never Heard Of," AGI: Alpha-Gal Information, a Project of the Alpha-Gal Syndrome Awareness Campaign, accessed August 27, 2021, https://alphagalinformation.org/.

11   Paul Hope, "Tickproof Your Yard without Spraying Pesticides," *Consumer Reports*, June 5, 2021, https://www.consumerreports.org/pest-control /tickproof-your-yard-without-spraying/.

12   "Alpha-Gal Syndrome," Mayo Clinic, updated November 19, 2020, https:// www.mayoclinic.org/diseases-conditions/alpha-gal-syndrome/symptoms -causes/syc-20428608.

13   "An Emerging Epidemic," AGI: Alpha-Gal Information, accessed August 27, 2021, https://alphagalinformation.org/what-is-ags/#An%20 Emerging%20Epidemic.

14   W. Landon Jackson, "Mammalian Meat Allergy Following a Tick Bite: A Case Report," *Oxford Medical Case Reports* 2018, no. 2 (February 2018): omx098, https://doi.org/10.1093/omcr/omx098; Scott P. Commins et al., "Delayed Anaphylaxis, Angioedema, or Urticaria after Consumption of Red Meat in Patients with IgE Antibodies Specific for Galactose-alpha-1,3-galactose," *Journal of Allergy and Clinical Immunology* 123, no. 2 (February 2009): 426–33, https://doi.org/10.1016/j.jaci.2008.10.052.

15   J. S. Gray et al., "Effects of Climate Change on Ticks and Tick-Borne Diseases in Europe," *Interdisciplinary Perspectives on Infectious Diseases* 2009, no. 593232 (2009), https://doi.org/10.1155/2009/593232; Abdelghafar Alkishe, Ram K. Raghavan, and Andrew T. Peterson, "Likely Geographic Distributional Shifts among Medically Important Tick Species and Tick-Associated Diseases under Climate Change in North America: A Review," *Insects* 12, no. 3 (March 2021): 225, https://doi.org/10.3390 /insects12030225; "Ticks on Upsurge Again This Spring," *Detroit Free Press*, May 31, 2021, https://www.freep.com/story/news/local/michigan /2021/05/27/tick-population-exploding-climate-change/7438784002/.

16   Katelyn Newman, "Ticks and Lyme Disease Are a Threat for Cities, Too," *U.S. News and World Report*, May 15, 2019, https://www.usnews.com/news /healthiest-communities/articles/2019-05-15/lyme-disease-ticks-a-threat -for-cities-study-suggests.

17 "Every Year, 300,000 Tick Bites in Urban Areas," RIVM: National Institute for Public Health and the Environment, April 19, 2017, https://www.rivm .nl/en/news/every-year-300000-tick-bites-in-urban-areas.

18 Susanne Rust, "Ticks on a 'Quest' for Blood at California's Beaches. Is Lyme Disease a Rising Risk?," *Los Angeles Times*, June 6, 2021, https://www .latimes.com/california/story/2021-06-06/ticks-california-beaches-lyme -disease-unknown-carrier.

19 "Project Evaluation: EVOKE (Official Evaluation Commissioned by the World Bank, by Edmond Gaible and Amitabh Dabla)," World Bank, https://www.worldbank.org/en/topic/edutech/brief/evoke-an-online -alternate-reality-game-supporting-social-innovation-among-young-people -around-the-world; Robert Hawkins, "EVOKE Reflections: Results from the World Bank's On-Line Educational Game (Part 2)," World Bank Blogs, August 20, 2010, https://blogs.worldbank.org/edutech/evoke-reflections -results-from-world-bank-educational-game-part-ii.

Chapter Eleven

1 Avery Hurt, "A Glimpse Inside the Mind of Dreaming Animals," *Discover*, January 20, 2021, https://www.discovermagazine.com/mind/a-glimpse -inside-the-mind-of-dreaming-animals; Liz Langley, "Do Animals Dream?" *National Geographic*, September 5, 2015, https://www.nationalgeographic. com/culture/article/150905-animals-sleep-science-dreaming-cats-brains; Jason G. Goldman, "What Do Animals Dream About?," BBC News, April 24, 2014, https://www.bbc.com/future/article/20140425-what-do-animals -dream-about.

2 Erik Hoel, "The Overfitted Brain: Dreams Evolved to Assist Generalization," *Patterns* 2, no. 5 (May 2021): 100244; https://doi.org/10 .1016/j.patter.2021.100244.

3 Jim Dator, "Alternative Futures at the Manoa School," in *Jim Dator: A Noticer in Time* (Cham, Switzerland: Springer, 2019), 37–54.

Future Simulation #1

1 Bill McKibben, "Do We Actually Need More Gas Stations?," *New Yorker*, March 24, 2021, https://www.newyorker.com/news/annals-of-a-warming -planet/do-we-actually-need-more-gas-stations.

2 Silpa Kaza et al., *What a Waste 2.0: A Global Snapshot of Solid Waste Management to 2050* (Washington, DC: World Bank, 2018), https:// datatopics.worldbank.org/what-a-waste/.

3 Hannah Ritchie and Max Roser, "CO_2 and Greenhouse Gas Emissions by Sector," Our World in Data, May 2017, rev. August 2020, https:// ourworldindata.org/co2-and-other-greenhouse-gas-emissions.

4 M. Vrijheid, "Health Effects of Residence Near Hazardous Waste Landfill Sites: A Review of Epidemiologic Literature," *Environmental Health Perspectives*

108, suppl. 1 (March 2000): 101–12, https://doi.org/10.1289/ehp .00108s1101; Francis O. Adeola, "Endangered Community, Enduring People: Toxic Contamination, Health, and Adaptive Responses in a Local Context," *Environmental Behavior* 32, no. 2 (March 2000): 209–49, https://doi .org/10.1177/00139160021972504; Olga Bridges, Jim W. Bridges, and John F. Potter, "A Generic Comparison of the Airborne Risks to Human Health from Landfill and Incinerator Disposal of Municipal Solid Waste," *Environmentalist* 20, no. 4 (December 2000): 325–34, https://doi.org /10.1023/A:1006725932558; Jean D. Brender, Juliana A. Maantay, Jayajit Chakraborty, "Residential Proximity to Environmental Hazards and Adverse Health Outcomes," *American Journal of Public Health* 101, no. S1 (December 2011): S37–S52; https://doi.org/10.2105/AJPH.2011.300183.

5   "Facts and Figures on Marine Pollution," UNESCO, accessed August 27, 2020, http://www.unesco.org/new/en/natural-sciences/ioc-oceans /focus-areas/rio-20-ocean/blueprint-for-the-future-we-want/marine -pollution/facts-and-figures-on-marine-pollution/.

6   Marie Donahue, *Waste Incineration: A Dirty Secret in How States Define Renewable Energy* (Institute for Local Self-Reliance, December 2018), https://ilsr.org /wp-content/uploads/2018/12/ILSRIncinerationFInalDraft-6.pdf.

7   Silpa Kaza et al., *What a Waste 2.0*, https://datatopics.worldbank.org/what -a-waste/.

8   "National Overview: Facts and Figures on Materials, Wastes and Recycling," United States Environmental Protection Agency, last updated July 14, 2021, https://www.epa.gov/facts-and-figures-about-materials-waste-and-recycling /national-overview-facts-and-figures-materials.

9   Ann Koh and Anuradha Raghu, "The World's 2-Billion-Ton Trash Problem Just Got More Alarming," Bloomberg News, July 11, 2019, https://www .bloomberg.com/news/features/2019-07-11/how-the-world-can-solve-its -2-billion-ton-trash-problem; Renee Cho, "Recycling in the U.S. Is Broken. How Do We Fix It?," Columbia Climate School, March 13, 2020, https:// news.climate.columbia.edu/2020/03/13/fix-recycling-america/.

10   Douglas Broom, "South Korea Once Recycled 2% of Its Food Waste. Now It Recycles 95%," World Economic Forum, April 12, 2019, https://www .weforum.org/agenda/2019/04/south-korea-recycling-food-waste/; Hope Ngo, "How Getting Rid of Dustbins Helped Taiwan Clean Up Its Cities," BBC News, May 27, 2020, https://www.bbc.com/future/article/2020 0526-how-taipei-became-an-unusually-clean-city; Kristin Hunt, "This American State Is Using a New Pay-as-You-Throw Programme to Have a Big Impact on Waste," World Economic Forum, November 19, 2018, https://www.weforum.org/agenda/2018/11/new-hampshires-pay -as-you-throw-programs-are-reducing-waste-by-50-percent/; Germà Bel and Raymond Gradus, "Effects of Unit-Based Pricing on Household Waste Collection Demand: A Meta-Regression Analysis," *Resource and Energy Economics* 44 (May 2016): 169–82, https://doi.org/10.1016/j.reseneeco .2016.03.003.

11   "The Kamikatsu Zero Waste Campaign: How a Little Town Achieved a
     Top Recycling Rate," Nippon.com, July 13, 2018, https://www.nippon
     .com/en/guide-to-japan/gu900038/.

12   "Frequently Asked Questions," Buy Nothing, April 13, 2021, https://
     buynothingproject.org/about/faqs/.

13   Stephen Leahy, "How People Make Only a Jar of Trash a Year," *National
     Geographic*, May 18, 2018, https://www.nationalgeographic.com/science
     /article/zero-waste-families-plastic-culture; Peter O'Dowd, "This Jar
     Represents One Family's Waste for an Entire Year," WBUR, May 20, 2019,
     https://www.wbur.org/hereandnow/2019/05/20/zero-waste-family.

14   Emily Matchar, "The Rise of 'Zero-Waste' Grocery Stores," *Smithsonian
     Magazine*, February 15, 2019, https://www.smithsonianmag.com/innovation
     /rise-zero-waste-grocery-stores-180971495/.

15   Winston Choi-Schagrin, "Maine Will Make Companies Pay for Recycling.
     Here's How It Works," *New York Times*, July 22, 2021, https://www.nytimes
     .com/2021/07/21/climate/maine-recycling-law-EPR.html.

16   Mike Pomranz, "California Coffee Shops Test Reusable To-Go Cups
     Backed by Big Companies Like Starbucks," *Food and Wine*, February 20,
     2020, https://www.foodandwine.com/news/reusable-cup-trials-starbucks
     -mcdonalds-california; Mike Pomranz, "Burger King Tests Eco-Friendly
     Packaging Options," *Food and Wine*, May 4, 2021, https://www
     .foodandwine.com/news/burger-king-loop-new-sustainable-packaging.

17   "Renew," Eileen Fisher, accessed August 27, 2021, https://www.eileenfisher
     .com/renew.

18   Anna Ringstrom, "IKEA Opens Pilot Second-Hand Store in Sweden," World
     Economic Forum, October 30, 2020, https://www.weforum.org/agenda
     /2020/10/ikea-opens-pilot-second-hand-store-sweden-circular-economy/.

19   "Why Hyla?," Hyla Mobile, accessed August 27, 2021, https://www
     .hylamobile.com/why-hyla/.

20   Alex Thornton, "These 11 Companies Are Leading the Way to a Circular
     Economy," World Economic Forum, February 26, 2019, https://www
     .weforum.org/agenda/2019/02/companies-leading-way-to-circular
     -economy/.

21   "This Is Cyclon," On, accessed August 27, 2021, https://www.on-running.
     com/en-us/cyclon.

Future Simulation #2

1   Yaryna Serkez, "Every Country Has Its Own Climate Risks. What's
     Yours?," *New York Times*, January 28, 2021, https://www.nytimes.com
     /interactive/2021/01/28/opinion/climate-change-risks-by-country.html.

2   Cecilia Tacoli, "Crisis or Adaptation? Migration and Climate Change in a
     Context of High Mobility," *Environment and Urbanization* 21, no. 2 (October
     2009): 513–25, https://doi.org/10.1177/0956247809342182; Agence
     France-Presse, "Asia Is Home to 99 of World's 100 Most Vulnerable Cities,"

Guardian, May 13, 2021, https://www.theguardian.com/cities/2021/may /13/asia-is-home-to-99-of-worlds-100-most-vulnerable-cities.

3   Chi Xu et al., "Future of the Human Climate Niche," *Proceedings of the National Academy of Sciences* 117, no. 21 (May 2020): 11350–355, https://doi .org/10.1073/pnas.1910114117.

4   Camila Bustos et al., *Shelter from the Storm: Policy Options to Address Climate Induced Displacement from the Northern Triangle* (University Network, Harvard Immigration and Refugee Clinic, Harvard Law School Immigration Project, Yale Immigrant Justice Project, and Yale Environmental Law Association, April 2021), https://www.humanrightsnetwork.org/s/Shelter_Final.pdf.

5   Katrina M. Wyman, "Ethical Duties to Climate Migrants," in *Research Handbook on Climate Change, Migration and the Law*, eds. Benoît Mayer and François Crépeau (Cheltenham, UK: Edward Elgar Publishing, 2017), 347– 75; Joseph Nevins, "Migration as Reparations," in *Open Borders: In Defense of Free Movement*, ed. Reece Jones (Athens, Georgia: University of Georgia Press, 2019), 129–40; Aaron Saad, "Toward a Justice Framework for Understanding and Responding to Climate Migration and Displacement," *Environmental Justice* 10, no. 4 (August 2017): 98–101, https://doi.org/10 .1089/env.2016.0033; Jesse J. Holland, "Poll: Millennials More Open to Idea of Slavery Reparations," AP News, May 11, 2016, https://apnews .com/article/b183a022831d4748963fc8807c204b08; Alec Tyson, Brian Kennedy, and Cary Funk, "Gen Z, Millennials Stand Out for Climate Change Activism, Social Media Engagement with Issue," Pew Research Center, May 26, 2021, https://www.pewresearch.org/science/2021/05/26 /gen-z-millennials-stand-out-for-climate-change-activism-social-media -engagement-with-issue/.

6   Qi Zhao et al., "Global, Regional, and National Burden of Mortality Associated with Non-Optimal Ambient Temperatures from 2000 to 2019: A Three-Stage Modelling Study," *Lancet Planetary Health* 5, no. 7 (July 2021): e415–e425, https://doi.org/10.1016/S2542-5196(21)00081-4.

7   "Open Borders: The Case," Open Borders, accessed August 27, 2021, https://openborders.info/; Zoey Poll, "The Case for Open Borders." *New Yorker*, February 20, 2020, https://www.newyorker.com/culture/annals -of-inquiry/the-case-for-open-borders; Ben Ehrenreich, "Open Borders Must Be Part of Any Response to the Climate Crisis," *Nation*, June 6, 2019, https://www.thenation.com/article/archive/climate-change-refugees-open -borders/.

8   Adrian Raftery, "The Dip in the US Birthrate Isn't a Crisis, but the Fall in Immigration May Be," *Conversation*, June 21, 2021, https://theconversation .com/the-dip-in-the-us-birthrate-isnt-a-crisis-but-the-fall-in-immigration -may-be-161169; Damien Cave, Emma Bubola, and Choe Sang-Hun, "Long Slide Looms for World Population, with Sweeping Ramifications," *New York Times*, May 22, 2021, https://www.nytimes.com/2021/05/22 /world/global-population-shrinking.html.

9"Why 100 Million?," Century Initiative, accessed August 27, 2021, https://www.centuryinitiative.ca/why-100m.

10Matthew Yglesias, *One Billion Americans: The Case for Thinking Bigger* (New York: Portfolio, 2020); Sonia Shah, *The Next Great Migration: The Beauty and Terror of Life on the Move* (New York: Bloomsbury, 2020).

11Maanvi Singh, "In California's Interior, There's No Escape from the Desperate Heat: 'Why Are We Even Here?'," *Guardian,* July 10, 2021, https://www.theguardian.com/us-news/2021/jul/10/california-central-valley-extreme-heat-race.

12Abrahm Lustgarten, "Climate Change Will Force a New American Migration," ProPublica, September 15, 2020, https://www.propublica.org/article/climate-change-will-force-a-new-american-migration.

13Alex Steffen (@AlexSteffen), "Discontinuity breaks our mental models of how to act and what to expect. In the planetary crisis, relocation is not refuge and adaptation is not ruggedization. (More to say on this topic the newsletter after the next . . . part three in the WSGR series.)," Twitter, June 29, 2021, 6:32 p.m., https://twitter.com/AlexSteffen/status/1410003337978679299?s=20.

14Maurice Stierl, "How Migrants and Their Supporters Are Reviving the Ethos of the 19th-Century Underground Railroad," *Conversation,* December 19, 2019, https://theconversation.com/how-migrants-and-their-supporters-are-reviving-the-ethos-of-the-19th-century-underground-railroad-128445.

15Jude Joffe-Block, "Arizona Volunteers Form 'Underground' Network to House Migrants Released by ICE," *World,* March 26, 2019, https://www.pri.org/stories/2019-03-26/arizona-volunteers-form-underground-railroad-house-migrants-dumped-ice.

16Marina Gorbis, *The Nature of the Future: Dispatches from the Socialstructed World* (New York: Free Press, 2013), 17.

Future Simulation #3

1"From Wet Waste to Flight: Scientists Announce Fast-Track Solution for Net-Zero-Carbon Sustainable Aviation Fuel," National Renewable Energy Laboratory, March 15, 2021, https://www.nrel.gov/news/program/2021/from-wet-waste-to-flight-scientists-announce-fast-track-solution-for-net-zero-carbon-sustainable-aviation-fuel.html.

2Jack Williams, "The Epic Volcano Eruption That Led to the 'Year without a Summer,'" *Washington Post,* June 10, 2016, https://www.washingtonpost.com/news/capital-weather-gang/wp/2015/04/24/the-epic-volcano-eruption-that-led-to-the-year-without-a-summer/.

3"What Is Geoengineering?," Oxford Geoengineering Programme, accessed August 27, 2021, http://www.geoengineering.ox.ac.uk/www.geoengineering.ox.ac.uk/what-is-geoengineering/what-is-geoengineering/.

4   Based on a Google Scholar search for scientific papers published between
2016 and mid-2021 with the keywords "geoengineering" and "climate
change."

5   Daisy Dunne, "Explainer: Six Ideas to Limit Global Warming with Solar
Geoengineering," Carbon Brief, September 5, 2018, https://www
.carbonbrief.org/explainer-six-ideas-to-limit-global-warming-with-solar
-geoengineering; Aylin Woodward, "We're Altering the Climate So Severely
That We'll Soon Face Apocalyptic Consequences. Here Are 11 Last-Ditch
Ways We Could Hack the Planet to Reverse That Trend," Business Insider,
April 20, 2019, https://www.businessinsider.com/geoengineering-how-to
-reverse-climate-change-2019-4.

6   Jeff Tollefson, "US Urged to Invest in Sun-Dimming Studies as Climate
Warms," *Nature*, March 29, 2021, https://www.nature.com/articles
/d41586-021-00822-5.

7   Solar Radiation Management Governance Initiative, accessed August 27,
2021, https://www.srmgi.org/.

8   Dana Varinsky, "Silicon Valley's Largest Accelerator Is Looking for
Carbon-Sucking Technologies—Including One That Could Become 'the
Largest Infrastructure Project Ever,'" Business Insider, October 27, 2018,
https://www.businessinsider.com/silicon-valley-accelerator-y-combinator
-startups-remove-co2-2018-10.

9   David Fork and Ross Koningstein, "Engineers: You Can Disrupt Climate
Change," IEEE Spectrum, June 28, 2021, https://spectrum.ieee.org
/energy/renewables/engineers-you-can-disrupt-climate-change.

10 "Climate-Related Geoengineering and Biodiversity: Technical and
Regulatory Matters on Geoengineering in Relation to the CBD; COP
Decisions," Convention on Biological Diversity, March 23, 2017, https://
www.cbd.int/climate/geoengineering/.

11 Natalie L. Kahn and Simon J. Levien, "Indigenous Group Petitions Harvard
to Shut Down Controversial Geoengineering Project to Block Sun," *Harvard
Crimson*, June 27, 2021, https://www.thecrimson.com/article/2021/6/27
/saami-council-petition-shut-down-scopex/.

12 "What Is Stratospheric Aerosol injection and Why Do We Need to Govern
It?," Carnegie Climate Governance Initiative, accessed August 27, 2021,
https://www.c2g2.net/wp-content/uploads/governing-sai.pdf.

13 Andrew Freedman, "In Summer of Apocalyptic Weather, Concerns Emerge
over Climate Science Blind Spot," Axios, July 19, 2021, https://www.axios
.com/extreme-weather-heat-waves-floods-climate-science-dba85d8a-215b
-49a1-8a80-a6b7532bee83.html.

14 John Paulsen, "Attack the Climate Crisis with Exascale Supercomputing,"
Seagate Blog, July 19, 2020, https://blog.seagate.com/human/attack-the
-climate-crisis-with-exascale-supercomputing/.

15 Zeynep Tufekci, "Where Did the Coronavirus Come From? What We
Already Know Is Troubling," *New York Times*, June 25, 2021, https://www
.nytimes.com/2021/06/25/opinion/coronavirus-lab.html.

16 Michael Morrison and Stevienna de Saille, "CRISPR in Context: Towards a Socially Responsible Debate on Embryo Editing," *Palgrave Communications* 5, no. 110 (September 2019), https://doi.org/10.1057/s41599-019-0319-5.

17 Mark Buchanan, "Contacting Aliens Could End All Life on Earth. Let's Stop Trying," *Washington Post*, June 10, 2021, https://www.washingtonpost.com/outlook/ufo-report-aliens-seti/2021/06/09/1402f6a8-c899-11eb-81b1-34796c7393af_story.html; Steven Johnson, "Greetings, E.T. (Please Don't Murder Us.)," *New York Times*, June 28, 2017, https://www.nytimes.com/2017/06/28/magazine/greetings-et-please-dont-murder-us.html.

18 Simon Anholt, "If the Whole World Had Voted, Clinton Would Be President of the US," TED Ideas, May 11, 2017, https://ideas.ted.com/if-the-whole-world-had-voted-clinton-would-be-president-of-the-us/.

19 Alex Steffen, "When **it Gets Real. Part One: This Is Your Brain on Discontinuity," *Snap Forward*, June 28, 2021, https://alexsteffen.substack.com/p/when-it-gets-real.

20 Erik Hoel, "The Overfitted Brain: Dreams Evolved to Assist Generalization," *Patterns* 2, no. 5 (May 2021): 100244, https://doi.org/10.1016/j.patter.2021.100244.

ABOUT THE AUTHOR

Jane McGonigal, PhD, is a future forecaster and game designer who creates games to improve real lives and solve real problems. She is the author of two *New York Times* bestselling books, *Reality Is Broken* and *SuperBetter*, and her TED talks on how gaming can make a better world have more than 15 million views. She was named a Young Global Leader by the World Economic Forum; one of *Fast Company*'s Top 100 Creative People in Business; and one of the Top 35 Innovators Changing the World through Technology by *MIT Technology Review*. She is the Director of Games Research & Development at the Institute for the Future, a nonprofit research group in Palo Alto, California.